Hans Küng

Breaking Through

Hans Küng

Breaking Through

Hermann Häring

Continuum   New York

1998

The Continuum Publishing Company
370 Lexington Avenue
New York, NY 10017

Translated by John Bowden from the German
Hans Küng. Grenzen durchbrechen
© Matthias-Grünewald-Verlag 1998
Translation © John Bowden 1998

Printed and bound in Great Britain by
Biddles Ltd, Guildford and King's Lynn

Library of Congress Cataloging-in-Publication Data

Häring, Hermann, 1937-
    [Hans Küng. English]
    Hans Küng: breaking through/Hermann Häring.
        p.   cm
    Includes bibliographical references and index.
    ISBN 0-8264-1134-7 (pbk.)
    1. Kung, Hans. 1928– . 2. Theology. I. Title.
BX4705.K76H3713   1998
230'.2'092--dc21   98-27568
                                              CIP

This English translation of this book is dedicated by the translator
to Hans Küng for his seventieth birthday
with much admiration and affection,
in gratitude for his friendship
and for his deep commitment to the things that matter,
19 March 1998

Contents

Abbreviations

In the case of books translated into English, the date of publication of the German original is indicated in brackets if it differs.

AH   *Anwälte der Humanität*, 1989
AQM   *Art and the Question of Meaning* (1980), 1981
BoL   *Brother or Lord?* (1976), 1977
C   *The Church* (1967), 1968
CCR   *Christianity and Chinese Religions* (1988), 1989
Chr   *Christianity* (1994), 1995
CR   *The Council and Reunion* (1960), 1961
Cr   *Credo* (1992), 1993
CWR   *Christianity and the World Religions* (1984), 1987
DGE   *Does God Exist?* (1978), 1980
DisC   *Diskussion über Hans Küngs 'Christsein'*, 1976
DisK   *Diskussion um Hans Küng 'Die Kirche'*, 1971
EL   *Eternal Life?* (1982), 1984
F   *Fehlbar? Eine Bilanz*, 1973
FK   *Der Fall Küng*, 1980
GC   *Grundfragen der Christologie*, 1975
GCT   *Great Christian Thinkers*, 1994
GE   *A Global Ethic*, 1993
GEGP   *A Global Ethic for Global Politics and Economics*, 1997
GR   *Global Responsibility* (1990), 1991
HK   *Hans Küng. His Work and Way* (1978), 1979
I   *Infallible?* (1970), 1971
IG   *The Incarnation of God* (1970), 1987
J   *Justification* (1957), 1964
Ju   *Judaism* (1991), 1992
LR   *Literature and Religion* (1988), 1991
NHFT   *New Horizons of Faith and Thought*, 1993 (abbreviated translation of NHGD)
NHGD   *Neue Horizonte des Glaubens und Denkens*, 1993 (with bibliography)

NT	'Das Neue Testament als Kanon', 1972
OBC	*On Being a Christian* (1974), 1977
PU	*Zum Problem Unfehlbarkeit*, 1971
RCT	*Reforming the Church Today*, 1990
Ref	*Reform und Anerkennung kirchlicher Ämter*, 1973
SC	*Structures of the Church* (1962), 1965
T	*Truthfulness*, 1968
TTM	*Theology for the Third Millennium* (1987), 1991
UW	*Um nichts als die Wahrheit*, 1978
WP	*Why Priests?* (1971), 1972
YGE	*Yes to a Global Ethic*, 1995

Introduction

No Catholic theologian of recent decades has attracted more attention within his church (all over the world), provoked more opposition from the church authorities, and at the same time found broader assent both inside and outside the church than Hans Küng. Before the Second Vatican Council (1962–1965) he made a name for himself as a champion of the ecumenical cause. During the Council he became known as an ally of the progressive forces. To the present day, through both the spoken and the written word, he has done his utmost to show his church a viable form for the future. Since the 1980s his work has taken on a new and unexpected openness as a result of dialogue with the world religions. Most recently, during the 1990s he has been discussing global questions about the future of the world, the role the religions have to play, and the responsibility of men and women all over the world, of which they must once again be reminded.

Despite the vast range of his work, despite the many contacts with colleagues and personalities all over the world, despite the demands of the media and despite all the questions with which he has been bombarded in the meantime, on religion, society and world politics, Hans Küng has remained a Christian theologian. Christianity is the focus of his thought, lends power to his argument, and stands at the centre of his visions of the future. And that is what this book is about. After an introductory chapter which provides some general orientation, we shall be following the long and intensive development of a theology which is always backed up by substantive research while remaining related to the situation of church and society. The most difficult problem in writing the present book proved to be how to cope with the ever-new subject-matter and at the same time to avoid giving the impression that reading the book could replace coming to grips with Küng's works. As a result, most chapters have been given the following basic structure: after a brief introduction indicating the substance of the topic to be discussed and the material relevant to it, one or more problems are singled out, and the hermeneutical and methodological points which are decisive for the development of Küng's theology are discussed. Where it seems appropriate, the chapter ends with an indication of the implications of what has been discussed.

This book is not meant to be a personal biography; at most it is a theological biography. So apart from some scant information about Küng's youth and education there will be no mention of further aspects: personal contacts, academic honours and activities at other universities, collaboration in working parties, visiting professorships and lecture tours, life-style or personal interests. It is still too early for a biography. Even an investigation of reactions to Küng's work would be beyond the scope of this book. However, after long consideration, one exception has been made. It relates to Küng's conflicts with the church's magisterium, which culminated in December 1979 with the church's withdrawal of his *missio canonica*, his credentials as a Catholic teacher. This measure has never been reversed and is a heavy burden on his reputation as a Catholic theologian and a hindrance to the reception of his work within the Catholic Church. To have kept silent about this would have directly affected the judgment made on his theology. Therefore on this point I shall speak openly and from my own personal standpoint.

Readers should know that I owe my academic career to the theologian Hans Küng. I worked for ten years in his Institute in Tübingen and still maintain a close friendship with him. So I hope that this presentation of Küng's theological thought has not become too uncritical. Be this as it may, readers deserve an introduction which is marked by deep sympathy and – I hope – intimacy with the living source of Küng's theology. That theology has not yet come to an end, even if in spring 1998 we shall be wishing him God's blessing on his seventieth birthday and thanking him for all the hard work he has now been doing for fifty years (including his student days). And he is still working hard, for church, theology, the dialogue between the confessions and religions and the forces that work for peace in the world.

Nijmegen, 18 November 1997

A Consistent Way? Expectations and Questions

Spero unitatem ecclesiarum: I hope for the unity of the churches.
Spero pacem religionum: I hope for peace among the religions.
Spero communitatem nationum: I hope for community among the nations.
Where does the strength of my hope come from? For me personally, as for millions of religious people throughout the world, the basis of my hope is that utterly reasonable trust which is called faith: '*In Te, Domine, speravi; non confundar in aeternum.*' 'In you, Lord, I have hoped; I shall never be confounded' (TTM 173).

1. The beginning

Hans Küng is a significant theologian, although the theologians among his critics like to play this down; a Catholic theologian, although the church's permission to teach has been withdrawn from him by instructions from on high; a church theologian, although many deny that he can legitimately speak in the name of the church. His actions are still followed with great attention even now in the Tübingen theological scene, and up to the time of his retirement he filled the lecture halls, although in 1980 he had had to leave the Catholic theological faculty and in 1996 there was still resistance to his rehabilitation. Seen from the outside, his theological career has been marked by conflicts and interruptions, disappointments and repeated new beginnings, but looked at from within, it has preserved those very qualities which have marked his theological vitality and impact from the beginning.

(a) Hard-won

Against this background we may be amazed how he has kept falling on his feet, how his following has shifted and increased with each new conflict: from an audience which was strictly within the church to an audience with an open ecumenical orientation; from a markedly Christian readership to a following of questioning people. These have ranged from believers who have often been alienated and disappointed in their hopes for the Council to thinking people in the 'world', i.e. in business and politics. More than most, Hans Küng has managed to address people of almost every category. As he himself remarks in the preface to *On Being a Christian*, perhaps his best known book, he envisages his audience as 'all people who will not accept Christianity at a reduced price'. Today he would probably add: 'who are not seeking faith, religious authenticity or humanity on the cheap, but quite seriously'. He would also mention those who have never heard any serious talk about questions of faith, binding values or responsibility for the future and who suddenly – perhaps under bizarre circumstances – discover that a life 'just for fun' is perhaps not enough. He also has something to say to them.

Insiders have always been clear that Küng's significance is not limited to this increasing influence on the outside world. Time and again he has been and is asked by pastors for advice and sought out by doubters; political or church communities in other countries and continents seek his support. The list of church and political figures who have sought and still seek to make contact with him is considerable. He himself has never had any problems with meeting church leaders if the occasion demands, even if they have proved to be his fiercest opponents. But that is not the decisive criterion for his behaviour. Something else that he has heard often enough, and still hears, is much more important to him: he makes it possible for many of those who are no longer happy in the jungle of church doctrines and rules to hold on to a meaning in life, to believe in God or not to turn their backs on the church. For this reason both the successful and the disappointed keep trusting his words after the official proclamation of faith has lost all credit for them: what use are solemn and lofty doctrinal statements if they only serve to bolster up a stunted piety?

Hans Küng has criticized much and *written* endlessly, but he is more than a knowledgeable journalist critical of the papacy and an eloquent man of letters. Undeterred, he has researched, argued and revised his judgments. Even in a car or plane he is accompanied by the A5 spiral-bound notepad in which he writes down both his first ideas and developed texts. How hard he has planned and worked, the passion with which he drafts schemes, tries them out on collaborators, openly asks colleagues for advice, allows himself to be criticized, informed and inspired, can be read in the thanks often expressed – above all in the prefaces and postscripts of his books. The collaboration with his colleague and friend Walter Jens over many years is a good example of this. Küng thinks it important to keep pointing out that he has written every line himself (which some people think impossible), but at the same time he indicates that he tries out his ideas systematically in conversation with others, improves them, and subjects them to the test of a first reaction, whether spontaneous or considered. The more Küng becomes a public personality and moves on the international scene, the more intensively he can try out his ideas and arguments, allusions and comparisons, analogies and appeals in lectures and public appearances before they appear in print. Of course this presupposes theological knowledge and an in-depth knowledge of the world, everyday curiosity and a delight in getting to the bottom of things and events, while remaining specific and understandable for contemporaries.

Küng's fluent writing is hard-won, the transparency of his style often the result of many new versions and corrections. In the days when there were neither effective copiers nor PCs (for young people a mythical prehistory), we often counted the individual versions of difficult sections or chapters; sometimes there were more than ten of them. Over the years the style has become more fluent and the criteria have been sharpened accordingly. From the verbose periphrases of the initial period (a Swiss colleague once described the language of *The Church* as 'Lucerne baroque') has developed a slimmed-down, matter-of-fact but urgent language. The scholar's battle with jargon and the subject-matter of specialist disciplines, with complex cross-references and insiders' perspectives, still goes on. Küng tries hard to keep on the wavelength of his readers and to speak their language ('to look the people in the mouth', as Luther put it), while at the same time taking them further. As he says after any introductory account, 'But there is yet more to think about.' The art of presenting complicated matters in a transparent way has finally developed into a brisk style with often short, swift and pertinent statements, particularly where the topic turns to the secular field of politics and economics.

Walter Jens has described Küng's style in a matter-of-fact way: 'main clause after main clause, a prose structure which is convincing but only rarely makes the pulse beat faster. He prefers to leave the art of moving the audience, a genuine example of the orator's craft, to the poets, whose showmanship he admires – but only in moderation. Histrionic writers need to make their metaphors flash out; fundamental theologians can dispense with this. Their prose gives splendour by its precision – artistically varied and never becoming a formula' (DHK 58). But I prefer this in a scholar. One piece of information follows another, one argument replaces another. It is vital to keep up with the dialectical approach which takes the discussion to a new level. Contrasting definitions are used to narrow down and evaluate concepts. Consequently the Orthodox, Catholic and Protestant churches can rapidly degenerate into traditionalism, authoritarianism and biblicism. Moreover Küng uses a polemical vocabulary in support of church reforms. Can the reader keep up? Of course, since Küng has a keen sense of readability and inner plausibility. Imprecision and false profundity remain taboo. Furthermore, at a very early stage the question of translation also arises in corrections: 'How does that sound in English?' One can also see from Küng's language how in the last decade the international forum has gained influence. So it is not surprising that he has won himself a wide readership in German and that the international response to almost all his books – of course taking account of national differences – can often match that in the German-speaking world.

(b) Education in Rome

Hans Küng's work is not yet completed, but the lines of his development can be traced. So it is also possible to read all his work so far in the light of a unity and continuity which virtually forces itself upon the reader. It is work which keeps breaking through new frontiers, inside and outside the church.

Hans Küng's theology is a theology of repeated and consistent crossings of frontiers (Baumann, NHGD 27–62). Of course, from the beginning, personal events and temperament influenced the thought of the budding Swiss theologian, born in 1928. He grew up in the quiet, peaceful town of Sursee, a place which forms solid character, between the mighty Mount Pilatus and the Sempacher See. On the other side of the lake, on 9 July 1386 the heroic Winkelried drew down upon himself the arrows of the Austrian army in order to save all the confederates. Such memories leave a mark. Küng has five sisters with whom he still keeps in touch; sadly, a brother died prematurely. Küng is forthright and self-confident, a born leader of Catholic youth groups, gifted with natural authority, someone to set high standards. From a very early age he has had a lively interest in political issues, and a keen sense of justice. Once he has recognized that something is right he can be unyielding.

His school was the canton gymnasium in Lucerne, which he left in 1948; immediately after that he went to the famous Germanicum in

Rome to study philosophy (1948–1951) and theology (1951–1955) at the Gregorian Papal University. The very name 'Collegium Germanicum et Hungaricum' is an indication of the old tradition from a time when there was still a Roman Empire of the German Nation, and when Hungary and Austria were still united under the Habsburg crown. Founded in 1552 by Ignatius Loyola (Küng was there to experience the celebrations for the quatercentenary), and over the centuries run by Jesuits, it claimed to educate the elite for the Catholic Church of Germany. The career of a professor, a bishop or prominent church leader was certain for many of its pupils. At an early stage they were given the necessary self-confidence, and also the necessary self-discipline and sense of responsibility. An ambitious group gathered there, who prepared themselves with great intensity for their tasks.

Küng knew where he was. He studied with keen eyes and learned to look behind the scenes, to the real action. In the Holy Year of 1950 he saw the crowds on pilgrimage to Rome. In a flowing red soutane the young Swiss took his fellow countrymen and -women through the Holy City and at the same time witnessed the discussion of the significance and problems of a unique drama: on 1 November Pius XII declared the assumption of Mary into heaven a dogma. Within the Germanicum Küng became involved in conflicts; it was not that he was overbold and overtaxed by discipline, but he did ask critical questions. Finally, with the guidance of a good spiritual director, to whom Küng was to dedicate a book on the centenary of his birth in 1990, he raised fundamental questions about the significance of obedience to the church. This basic attitude, with a readiness for criticism, developed early and lasted. Küng was later fond of speaking of 'loyal opposition' or 'critical loyalty', notions which for him were profound and worthy of a theologian.

(c) Ecumenism with Karl Barth

As I have remarked, the school of independence began with domestic questions in the Germanicum. Küng fought for the social interests of the employees and learned to interpret church rules loyally, but critically. This independence continued in his choice of topic for his licentiate in philosophy, in which he grappled with the atheism of Sartre and thus already indicated that he was interested in the burning questions of the present. He therefore thought that he could see philosophy and theology as a unity. Finally, his independence became evident in his decision also to devote his theological work for the licentiate to a subject which was topical at the time. This was Karl Barth's doctrine of justification and its ecumenical significance: again Küng was not interested in minor issues, so he was not content with second-rank people or secondary themes. Nor did he limit his topic to a partial Catholic perspective which would have guaranteed an innocent result. After the theological licentiate a first rumble of thunder could be heard at the Gregoriana. Formally his work was immaculate. But didn't the young pupil go too far in his claim and his conclusions? Küng continued the work at the Institut Catholique in Paris and developed it into a dissertation, which was published in German as early as 1957 by a publishing house founded by Hans Urs von Balthasar. The result was felt to be a fundamental ecumenical breakthrough. For the first time a Catholic theologian was saying openly, supported by arguments, what others were perhaps already thinking: the doctrine of justification can no longer be an issue which separates the churches. In this way a new frontier for traditional Catholic thought had been crossed.

2. Exciting times

This shifting of the frontiers in one direction was followed ten years later – of course, after preliminary studies which need not concern us here – by a shifting of the frontiers in another. And the topic which Küng now took up was no less bold and demanding.

(a) Reform of the church

It was the time of the Second Vatican Council, when it became clear to many Catholics that an extremely interesting period lay ahead. Moreover Hans Küng was called to Rome to work – first as a companion to his bishop, the Bishop of Rottenburg, and then as a *peritus*, an expert nominated by the pope. However, he was soon forced to ask himself whether the majority of bishops were capable or willing to grasp fundamentally and consistently enough the questions of the Counter-Reformation which had been pending for 400 years. Küng outlined his own picture of the church, which was biblical and at the same time had an ecumenical orientation. At its heart were fundamental questions about the nature and central criteria of the church.

His book *The Church* appeared in 1967, eighteen months after the end of the Council. And again questions of principle were raised. For the first time the exegetical questions were worked out systematically from the Catholic side, and specifically Catholic views – the sacramentality and authority of the priesthood, the status and rights of the episcopate, the position of the papacy – were tackled critically in the light of scripture. Now the foundations were laid for a whole catalogue of questions which were to be discussed in theology down to the present day, and by which Rome has felt itself threatened now for thirty years. Here scripture was consistently regarded as the ultimate norm for today's church. This phase ended with one of the shortest of Küng's books, but the one that was most fateful for his career, *Infallible?*, in which he simply makes an enquiry. Rome responded with a ban on the question, which was accepted by the German Conference of Bishops, anxious and wanting a quiet time, and supported by a phalanx of evidently faint-hearted theologians led by Karl Rahner.

(b) Questions about Jesus

Meanwhile the period of assimilating the legacy of the Council (in ecclesiastical jargon known as the 'post-conciliar period') had begun. Some things had to be done. Many questions remained open, so rear-guard actions over an understanding of the church which was scriptural and at the same time Catholic flared up fiercely. A whole range of problems came under discussion, and their number increased over the years. The specialists set to work intensively – of course including Küng, who was challenged to defend his Catholicity, to answer many questions and to develop his arguments; at the same time he also championed the many concerns of Christians. After his meteoric start, Küng could now have been caught in the jungle of routine theological activity; he could have styled himself a specialist on Catholic or ecumenical questions or made a name for himself in a church secretariat by working out broad compromise formulae. As we know, Rome would have valued his work highly; peace could have been made with the Curia – of course at the price of a few, albeit far-reaching, concessions.

However, Küng turned to another fundamental question, and a second breakthrough in the same direction was in the making. He addressed what is technically known as the question of the 'historical Jesus' and a 'christology from below'. Would it have been meaningful, he asked, to remain entangled in the jungle of church problems when it was still unclear whose message the church was to proclaim and whose life it was to follow? Küng's new question is not a private one, nor is it plucked out of thin air; it had been prepared over a longer period than is usually assumed, and had a long prehistory in Protestant theology.

His reflection began with a large-scale monograph on Hegel entitled *The Incarnation of God*. A fundamental decision was already being made here, which ultimately affects the question of Christ and the Christian image of God; for the new concern with the Jesus of history (the 'historical Jesus') at the same time amounts to a new approach to God. At this point Küng shifted perhaps the most decisive frontier in his theological development: this represents a departure both from the traditional philosophy and a theology bound up with metaphysics. However, the public perceived another aspect, as the completely unexpected success of *On Being a Christian* in autumn 1974 showed: it is possible to advocate the cause of Jesus openly and in a new way, independently and without attachment to traditional formulae, and to reflect critically on one's own faith (thus Gomez Caffrena in NHGD). *On Being a Christian* and *Does God Exist?* form a unity, and with their humane impulse stemming from Jesus' life and his own faith caused a theological earthquake. It is understandable that many structures threatened to collapse and that anxious rescue parties were quickly on the scene. The only question is whether these structures did not need inspection even without Küng; we shall have to discuss this in detail later.

Now it is well known that success is not in itself a direct theological criterion. However, a success which does not spare readers the effort of reading, which makes demands on their understanding and challenges them to make their own decisions, is another matter. Here of course Küng not only broke through a frontier but also reached a new theological readership. He reached a public which had long ceased to concern itself with theological questions because it had lost touch with questions of faith and with the churches. And that in turn had an effect on his thinking, which now more than ever could not stand still.

(c) The religious situation in the world

We move on a decade. The year 1980 was perhaps the most important turning point in the whole of Küng's theological life. Rome withdrew his licence to teach, but he was still allowed to call himself a theologian. In retrospect, that history of a refusal to understand, of rejection and humiliation, can be read as a history of success and helpful clarifications. However, given the adjustment needed, that was easier said than done. Küng now had to ask himself some sober and pragmatic questions. Why in this inflexible situation should he devote himself to explosive questions within the church, the discussion of which only hardened attitudes? Why continue to steer a collision course with the church, when other important and extremely interesting topics could be worked on? Küng turned to the world religions. In the 1980s he laid the basis for a theology which made it possible to look at the religions without distortion. All over the world they are the context of the most varied experience of God and the most intense encounter with God. All over the world there is a need to overcome the Christian claim to superiority, both generally and in many details, and to begin a dialogue in partnership. Certainly for Küng the question and the programme were not new, but now he gave this dialogue a comprehensive and unmistakable form, related to our time. A dialogue would develop which was theological through and through.

Küng's goal quickly became clear: the dialogue did not aim at a casual acquaintance but at a substantive conversation; its subject-matter was not exotic information about the religions but the common future of humankind. This has to be made clear. The tone of the discussion is set by the slogan that world peace is impossible without peace between the religions, and all men and women are asked to collaborate in this as much as possible. 'Global ethic' is the most recent watchword in Küng's theology. For the theologian, however, a critical limit is reached here. Now the issue is no longer 'the critical location of the Christian in the world' (Kuschel, DHK 10), but the world as a comprehensive horizon for humankind. So here is a Christianity which relates itself dialogically and without reservations to the whole of humankind. It is as if no further lines could now be drawn. But the conclusion is deceptive. Certainly Küng has reached geographical limits, but in so doing he simply demonstrates how 'limited' theology had been so far. When it comes to subject-matter, countless further areas could be explored. Nevertheless, now his scholarly activity is set against a universal background. What did this mean for his theological career?

3. Against a universal background

It will subsequently prove that from the beginning Küng had subscribed to a theology which was attentive to the demands of the present. In 1957 the issue was the ecumenical situation, and ten years later the radical reform of the church. After 1970 he took up the question of the origin of Christianity and the meaning of faith, which was by then widespread, and in the 1980s he widened his horizons once again. Here Küng has always kept listening to what interests people, what their problems are, and what a theologian has to say to them. This basic dynamic gives him extraordinary curiosity and flexibility.

Küng's theology is rarely just a summing up. The big books are detective works, often shaped by unexpected discoveries. But that is only a superficial observation. Is Küng curious by nature, or can theological reasons also be identified? How is the dynamic of Küng's thought to be classified in terms of its in-depth structure, if there is such a thing? I shall attempt to give three answers which indicate such a depth, but are not a direct description. I have headed them extension, radicalization and humanization.

(a) Extension

This basic tension does not represent a revolution for twentieth-century Catholic theology, but was initiated in France in the 1940s by the representatives of the *nouvelle théologie*. Their theology did not seek salvation simply in the church, but in this world. It began in the France of the 1940s, at that time already a highly secularized Catholic country, where the churches were becoming emptier and emptier and the message of salvation was gradually disappearing from peoples' minds. Therefore it was important to discover salvation anew in the 'world', for it and from it, and to demonstrate that Christ's salvation is intended not just for members of the Catholic Church and on its conditions, but for the whole world. This approach was consistently adopted by Küng, and in the course of his theology he developed an unexpected dynamic, though he was initially interested (only) in questions within the church and between the churches – in 'domestic policy', as he would later put it. But from the beginning, being a Christian and being human went together as closely as 'church' and 'world' (both still used in the 1940s in the singular as constructs which were superelevated by theology), or belief in God and commitment to one's neighbour. Later this dialectic expands. Christian religion comes to stand over against the world religions, and the Christian duty to love one's neighbour finds a place in the worldwide responsibility of human beings for their survival and for shaping the world in the direction of a viable future.

In addition to this extension of the subject-matter of Küng's theology there were two qualitative extensions which led to an earthquake in the Catholic sphere. Programmatically, Küng – backed up by Vatican II – introduced scripture as an independent source of God's revelation and subsequently – quite contrary to the Protestant tendency – entered into an intense discussion with modern philosophical thought and later trends in modern criticism. In the 1980s he went one step further by encouraging an intensive engagement with other cultures. In the preface to a 1994 book, *Christianity*, he wrote: 'This book has been written in a German university, but by a "world citizen" and as far as possible *against a universal horizon*' (Chr xxv). This statement is both a claim and a qualification. The horizon of an appropriate theology is to know no bounds; to put it simply, it must grow beyond its limitations and become worldly. However, Küng knows that this universality will never be achieved completely. What are its actual limits? They are set by the problems of translating a theology which at the same time cannot and will not give up its particular religious tradition. Küng is a Western theologian, and for all his solidarity with colleagues from other continents, he does not think that it makes sense to ignore this origin, to hide behind other theologies as an excuse for home-made problems, and to act as if with the jargon of liberation theology or the like Catholic theology could rise to a new global universality. Nevertheless, a European, too, can be a citizen of the world, and therefore a theology rooted in Europe can indicate from its own standpoint what can be done for the world.

It is understandable that this worldly theology of Küng's is often accused of being too worldly. He is said not to take the tradition of the church seriously; to be advocating a theology which betrays the church and even Christianity; to have left the sphere of theology far behind long ago, in order to play around with current affairs. But in fact Küng is only following a line which all Christians today must follow if they do not want to turn their backs on what is happening in the world. They do not have the right to ignore the world's questions, problems and cries of despair. Biblical thought always had this concern. Certainly it is focussed on the mystery of God (and with good reason Küng has reflected intensively on that), but it always reckons that God is to be sought and found in his significance for this world. The parables of Jesus do not tell us anything about God, but they do tell us in a much more worldly way about God's kingdom. Scripture is not interested in the eternal vision of God, but creates visions of a life together in peace and justice. 'To seek God in all things' is later the Ignatian, thoroughly modern, slogan by which Küng's theology too is to be measured. This is to be maintained against any pressure of opinion which wants to measure the quality of Christian theology by an unmediated nearness to God which has no context.

This tension between explicit faith and concern for the world, between secularity and religion, therefore has to be maintained. So we shall have to examine Küng's work to see how he resolves it in each particular instance, in what areas he finds ways and how he deals with the growing secularity of his fields of research. For beyond any doubt, while he increasingly detaches himself from the narrow limits of specific questions, first about the church and then about Christianity, and leaves the problems of a particular tradition of faith behind him, deliberately and on the basis of a decision for which he continually gives reasons he remains a Christian. He practises a Christian theology, and discusses the world religions and the religious situation of his time from a clearly Christian standpoint, not without opposition from prominent North American colleagues. But what does being a Christian mean against a world-wide background and in the world as it is? These are questions to which, I hope, theological answers may be expected.

(b) Radicalization

Alongside the processes of extension, at the same time processes of radicalization can be observed in Küng's theology; otherwise the whole enterprise would get out of balance. However, in saying this I do not mean that Küng has turned into an extremist. Labels like 'bourgeois', 'liberal', 'fundamentally conservative' will always be attached to him, but they are basically uninteresting. Rather, it can be observed how at each phase of his development Küng again looks for the roots and lays them bare, yet – and this is the surprising thing – does not at some point come upon the root of all roots. Rather, he keeps encountering comprehensive networks of roots ('rhizomes', as Deleuze and Guattari call them). Alongside the memory of Jesus there is the Jewish tradition; alongside the original Christian faith there is the contemporary horizon; alongside the experience of God in the religions there is the world-wide question of survival. Not one but three criteria keep guard over a Christian theology of religion: reflection on one's own Christian belief, the authenticity of the other religions, and the commandment to show humanity, which binds everything together.

This list already makes it clear that here the progress is not down any one-way streets; networks of tunnels have been developed which lead into the depths. Just as theology has to be done against a universal horizon if it is to understand all human beings and their situation, so ways into the depths, to what is truly divine, must be found, ways which are common and accessible to us all. Here Küng adopts a clear position: all theology, in so far as it also understands itself as the science of faith (and thus presupposes the contents and decisions of faith), must correspond to the universal conditions of understanding; even Christian theology knows no special rules. All thinking people must therefore be able to understand theological statements and assertions, and these statements have to be examined by universal standards.

Küng is by no means sparing with words. He can find them, and is never stuck for an example, a reminiscence or an illuminating metaphor. But the real reason for the proverbial bulk of his books lies in his effort to hold his readers' attention – which tends to get blocked by associations and recollections, emotions or laziness. God can be reached only by a variety of approaches, and only a firm grasp on the ultimate question will provide the energies for constantly renewed searching. For Küng there is an evident need to clarify historical developments, the state of debates, the discussions which are being carried on. He passionately homes in on the main point despite all the limits of language. He delights in illustrating concepts and great theories, and also in translating theology for secular contexts. Because of his theological concern, he insists on the possibility of communication.

Küng assumes that his theology will be understood even by those without specialist theological training. Is that possible? Does such an expectation enhance or diminish the theological quality of a text? Doesn't his approach do the often complicated material an injustice, as it often needs a complicated response? Of course Küng does not extend his expectation to specialist historical, philosophical or palaeographical problems. He is thinking of the central statements of the Christian faith, of central directives for action and their exegesis. He believes that the Christian faith must be understandable if it is to become human. The real depth does not lie in the incomprehensible, but where Christian faith addresses men and women in many ways which can illuminate their existence. Anyone who wants to understand Küng's language and arguments, the way in which his text is arranged, must begin from a basic hermeneutical principle: what is difficult to understand need not be wrong, but probably insufficient effort has been made in expounding it. It must be possible to express central human concerns, Christian faith and religious practice, in other words the deepest structures of humanity and reality, in a comprehensible way, even if they can never be reduced to a formula. Multiplicity does not exclude radicality, but is the basis for it. Is that Küng's principle? This too will be a question to his specific theology.

One could say that this basic concern to be understandable is in many ways fundamentally Catholic and has also been emphasized in much-criticized (neo-)scholastic theology. With it Küng also offers an answer to Karl Barth, who accords the word of God a unique authority and thinks that we can know nothing and say nothing about God with the aid of the human mind. Against this Küng argues that human reason is competent in matters of truth, thus assuming that all men and women – regardless of whether they are Christian or even religious – are capable of believing in God, of discovering a way to God. Therefore theological thought has to be open not only to 'worldly' questions but also to dialogue with the secular world.

(c) Humanization

(i) The humanity of God

Küng grapples intensely with the core of Christian faith, and we have to ask how in this specific process of interpretation he means to remain true to his principle of being understandable. One of his epistemologically most exciting publications is his discussion of Hegel's christology, since it does not end with major agreement, but with clear criticism (see Chapter 5 below). The basis of this criticism lies in the question who Jesus Christ is for Christian faith. According to Küng, in the first place Jesus Christ is accessible to us and tangible for us as a human person. So the central question of Christian faith is: Who was Jesus of Nazareth, and how have Christians understood him at the beginning and in the course of their history? Küng's answer, which we shall be discussing in detail later, is that in Jesus of Nazareth we see an image of God and of the future of human beings which today is still topical, binding on Christians and of the utmost significance for the world situation: God accepts us human beings and the whole of humankind unconditionally at every moment of our life and death. Therefore any commitment to a better future is worth the effort.

With such a principle, God and our faith in God are unreservedly brought within human dimensions. So Küng's conclusion is that the goal, criterion and possibility of Christian faith is true humanity in the comprehensive sense of the word. Not only are Christians in salvation, but *de iure* (thus Karl Barth) in Jesus Christ the *whole* of creation is redeemed. Here too Küng takes up the traditional principles of Christian theology, but here too we shall have to see how and with what consequences he carries them through.

It goes without saying that this principle needs constant interpretation. It is not simply the answer to a question, but opens up a discussion. And of course precisely for that reason it provokes many questions, because – at any rate apparently – it leads away from faith, from an orientation on God and his will, from the inner themes of religion. Here we have reached a core position of Küng's theology. Therefore we shall have to ask whether he relaxes this centrifugal dynamic at any stage of his theological development. Nor can the principle let him rest until the questions of origin and goal, failure and future, anxiety and hope, the boundary cases of human experience and human behaviour, have been discussed. So it is only consistent if after his grappling with being a Christian and the question of God, Küng tackles the question of religions and the world. What transformations the poles of redemption and the world then undergo remains an exciting question.

(ii) Human well-being

The bias in Küng's theology is towards human beings and the world. That is honourable, one might say, but was it needed for true humanity and a humane future for theology? Küng often raises this question, but in the answers that he gives, God and human beings, belief in God and humanity, do not become mutual rivals. All his life Küng has maintained the irrevocable theological principle that God's salvation and God's word are prior to all human action and speech. He has maintained this down to his most recent publications. This does not necessarily lead to criticism of the church, but it does lead to the possibility of criticizing the claims and concrete action of the church in the light of its origin; we shall be discussing that at length later. Küng has developed an extraordinary sensitivity to all attempts to domesticate this criterion of all Christian faith, to bring it down to human or church needs or to apply it to current questions. Sometimes his starting point has been called vintage Protestant. The question will be whether Küng can transform it into a vintage Catholic requirement and reforge it so that it becomes the Archimedean point of his proposals for Rome. To give God the glory, as Küng keeps saying, is what he believes to be important. So what will be the consequences for a global future?

Küng gives a paradoxical interpretation of the priority of God's will. Christians do not believe that God is given a human form only in Jesus of Nazareth. They also believe that God's will is now unconditionally the well-being of humankind. Again Küng is not alone in making such a statement, but he draws his conclusions from it with emphatic consistency. He does not like domesticated interpretations, as if in life we had to seek a balance between God and human beings, between commandments which are unfriendly to human beings and a humanity which is remote from God. His attention to secular questions is the consequence of this theological principle. If God's will is the salvation of human beings, then dedication to the future of humankind is unreservedly worth while – regardless of whether its religious behaviour is good or not.

Thus right up to *Global Responsibility* and its programme Küng increasingly champions human well-being. His current involvement on various continents, with religious and political leaders and world organizations, with business leaders and the media, is simply a legitimate consequence of this for him. 'Would we have expected anything else?', ask those involved in the wider world. 'Won't this discovery of the world make him lose sight of the original Christian impulse?', worry the pious. 'In his quest for a new world paradigm isn't he cherishing the illusory expectation that the world will once more be made whole?', doubt the sceptics. Küng has gone his theological way over a good 12,000 pages of publications. So we may eagerly wait to see the result of this test.

4. Secular theology?

Küng began with 'domestic' questions within the church and moved consistently to the comprehensive questions of the world situation. Would it be still possible for him to break through further frontiers? The answer depends on the perspective; I shall return to it later. In fact his comprehensive approach is always specific. He seeks a final resolution of ecumenical problems, the renewal of the church as a whole. He wants to know what being a Christian and believing in God actually mean, how the religions are to be brought into dialogue with one another. As with apocalyptic questioning in Judaism at the time of Jesus, and entirely within the framework of a universal belief in creation, the issue now is the destiny and future of all creation.

Here Küng is not activating any eschatological fantasies; rather, under the heading of global politics he is concerned with the action of people who (as individuals or together) make a claim about the world as a whole and refer to the conduct of humankind as a whole. At the same time he writes about the global economy, i.e. about the totality of economic activity within a global network, which – and this is the critical point – threatens to evade the overall demands of politics and its ethical standards. Action which is responsible and – if things go well – explicitly committed comes up against action which constantly threatens to go beyond its partial sector. There is a threat that economics will determine politics. Surely this is an exciting issue, and one which will decide our future. As I hope to show in Chapter 10, it is the theme of a secular theology, i.e. secular talk of God's will and kingdom.

(a) Listening to the time

The term 'secular theology' is not being introduced here as an epistemological novelty, as a signal for unprecedented innovations. Those who know Küng know that he makes no claim to be an innovator, a guru or a prophet. He points out where something should have been said, done or initiated long ago. Often he does not even claim to have discovered a question himself. The secret of his dynamic and flexibility lies elsewhere. Certain he always knows what he wants; he cannot quickly be dissuaded once he has made up his mind. But he never develops his theology as a monologue. Examples of this are not just his communication with colleagues in his Institute, regular conversation with professional colleagues, and dialogue with specialists in religion (Chapter 8), but also the intensive collaboration with his colleague Walter Jens, who is not a theologian (see 25f. below).

(i) Collaboration

In Küng's scheme, theology and other disciplines, faith and world-view, trust in God and humanity, are not to be brought into a predetermined relationship, whether this is the traditional scheme of 'nature' or 'grace', the pedagogical rhythm of question and answer, or even the mediaeval pattern of mistress and maid. I cannot ask, 'Where do the questions of literary criticism, biography or sheer humanity stop and the theological questions begin?' The perspectives overlap, as long as secular scholars also have answers to offer and theologians are oppressed by ultimate questions. Religious and theological reflections only cease to seem like officious instruction when they remain deeply rooted in the everyday life of men and women and accept the pressures of a recalcitrant reality. This modesty and capacity for dialogue with the world gradually emerges in Küng's theology and reaches its climax in the 1990s. There he tackles the difficult questions of the future of the world on the basis of a religious ethic.

So the removal of frontiers in Küng's theology, which has been prompted in many ways since the 1980s, is important. General Studies in the University of Tübingen came to provide a wide-ranging and stimulating forum. Together with two other colleagues, in 1995 Jens and Küng wrote a very thought-provoking book on voluntary eutha-nasia, *A Dignified Dying*. Küng has written about Mozart and Wagner, the natural sciences and the Swiss situation, about artists and writers. The question whether all these writings, books or articles are theo-logical is of little interest here: perhaps it distracts attention from a really fruitful theology. Where should this theology begin and where does it end? Theological aspects and visions are also involved; questions of meaning and limits, questions of a last hope, a last trust, ultimate binding values, are touched on and worked out here.

(ii) Self-limitation

Much more interesting is the observation that all his life Küng has made choices. Think of all that could be discussed here! Thus this opening up of his horizons has not simply meant extension but – on closer inspec-tion – repeated limitation, selection, the pressure of choices and priorities. Küng occasionally describes (most recently in his farewell lecture of February 1996, DHK 71–111) a memorable audience with Paul VI, who indicated to him that a church career was not unthinkable. However, one had to behave in a certain way in the church: his writing so far gave rise to critical questions. It would have been better, accord-ing to Paul VI, for him to have written nothing ('niente!'). In 1965 it was probably not difficult for Küng to make his choice, though even then it had to be made; freedom in Tübingen was the decisive factor. But it was not this kind of choice which became increasingly important, and some-times also more difficult and burdensome. It was the daily limitations. The topics and the areas of research were the problem. They became increasingly broad and posed increasingly radical questions. The rapid developments in the church and society – from criticism within the church to liberation theology, from social erosion to unexpected new revival movements, from open resistance against the nomination of bishops to an increasing decentralization, from the progression of secularization to the new awakening of religious needs – all these developments pulled a theology seeking to be contemporary into a maelstrom of disappointments and expectations, controversies and new approaches; they tempted flight into comprehensive theories or specialized detailed research. However, neither attack nor flight, but steadfastness and resistance, was called for. That was the lesson which Küng later drew from the history of Erasmus of Rotterdam, from the fiasco of the polarizations of the Reformation.

How did he react? Certainly, his development can be understood as a consistent course, and that is also how it is described in this book. But the substantive (not the psychological) other side should not be forgotten. The wealth – sometimes the excessive wealth – of the material which he has used can also be interpreted as an attempt to bring as many questions as possible into the discussion. His urgent style also indicates the impatience of someone who almost despairs at the stubbornness of the traditionalists and the immovability of the church government. And his constant choice of the more central and at the same time more comprehensive theme also seems like a cry of distress which ultimately expects a hearing for these questions.

Shouldn't his advance into the question of justification have been enough for a start, and couldn't it have been taken more seriously? Why did the Council only half sort out its domestic affairs in the matter of the 'church', without any real consistency, so that now an individual had to follow it up and bring in the scriptural evidence? Shouldn't the key questions 'Who is a Christian?' and 'Who believes in God?' in the 1970s have acted as giant fishing nets, gathering up almost any problem floating around in the sea of modern culture? Probably only those in the know will be aware of the further possible questions, philosophical positions and cultural developments which Küng had to cut short or simply ignore. But even now it is clear from the books that he wrote then that in that decade he felt himself to be a mixture of Sisyphus and Laocoon. Again he faced a situation which he felt to be a dramatic emergency and which he could master only with extreme concentration. Of course part of the problem remains that the opposing parties often saw him in a different light: as someone who became the focus of attention, involved himself in every problem, and thought that he alone had the solution. Obscurantist regulations about language and hierarchies within the church, theological sensibilities and the domestication of self-criticism – in fact most of this was of little interest to Küng. But that does not mean that he did not show colleagues and fellow Christians due respect.

The turn towards the world religions in the 1980s benefited from Küng's curiosity and interest in other religions and cultures, but again he was driven by a disturbing discovery which is already recorded in the introductions to his books on the theology of the religions: the Christian churches (at any rate in our cultural circle) can be helped only if they stop contemplating their navels and recognize the religious character of the world. Certainly, others too were occupied with this theme, and certainly Küng did not get too close to any of his colleagues, but again he sensed the urgency of the situation perhaps more strongly than others. Surveys had to be made, wider contexts analysed, focussed, summed up, taken account of. Again selection was necessary. This new burden will be understood only by those who know how many meetings and trips, airports and climatic zones, codes of behaviour and courtesies have to be coped with, and how much energy it takes to programme meetings successfully. Again selection was necessary.

At the latest this was the case when a question was raised by Küng's theology of religion. What are religion and religions good for? How do religion and culture hang together? What do they mean for a world and a human race whose survival is threatened? Anyone who hears the question precisely can already judge why it engages the mind with an ultimate passion. This is even more the case when at the same time it leads to a discovery of how criminally economics and politics have ignored, despised and neglected the religious dimension (the dimension of convictions and values, of respect and partnership, of truthfulness and an unconditional humanity, responsibility for one's fellow human beings and the future) in their shaping of the world. Again a note of alarm can be heard in Küng's publications which is enormously difficult to follow with the same energy.

The dynamic (the emergency and the sure aim) in Küng's theology can perhaps best be understood in the light of John XXIII's watchword for the Council, *aggiornamento*. This is not simply to be translated 'adaptation' but 'contemporary action', 'orientation on the present', 'listening to the time'. Since John XXIII, this *aggiornamento* has become the programme for many Catholic Christians throughout the world. All attempt in their way to give a biblically responsible and deliberately contemporary language, praxis and form to their way of being a Christian, and one which convinces them. They attempt to do so in their specifically national and social contexts, but without recourse to particular theories of society, political options and official church programmes which are conservative. With John XXIII they criticize an antiquated church structure which is stamped by hierarchical and centralistic thought. It is this common driving force that is part of the explanation for Küng's great reputation among Catholics over several decades.

(b) Responsibility for a worthwhile future

The driving force, to put it in a still more pointed way, is responsibility. Anyone who knows Küng knows his directness and consistency: he gets on with what he thinks has to be done. And if belief in God as it is made concrete in discipleship of Jesus is meaningful and true, this must also prove to be the case in dialogue with the 'world'. Küng is continuously carrying on conversations, and conversation with him is continuously sought. So if Christians and theologians have a responsibility for the situation in the world, that must also be perceived. Küng's maxim is increasingly clearly that theologians of whatever shade are responsible not only for Christianianity and for faith, for religion and religious feeling, but also – without flight and escapism – for the situation in the world. They have to make their contribution; they have to get involved in inter-religious and global dialogue. Both forums, the forum of the religions and the forum of the world, belong together; for the religions are still the strongest force in their cultures and will remain so. Despite all talk of secularization, postmodernism and loss of faith, Küng finds his views increasingly clearly confirmed here.

So there is a substantive reason why Küng's last major book bears the demanding title *A Global Ethic for Global Politics and Economics*, and why he allows this topic to find a way into his research into the basis of the world religions: only those who – as far as possible – grasp not only details but also the overall context can have a good understanding of the world, religions and faith. At the same time there is also a practical principle: only those who join in the dialogue, who get involved and leave the ghetto of their studies, their research programmes and a highly institutionalized church, will understand this in detail and in context. Only those who actively subscribe to this commitment will experience the freedom of the Christian today. How can this vision issue in the reality of the life of a Christian and a theologian? We may eagerly await Küng's answer.

(c) Art and literature as an example

Küng, as I said, practises listening. He is in communication, he carries on conversations. We also asked whether with his worldwide dismantling of frontiers Küng had not come up against an absolute frontier. Could yet other themes captivate him? In answer to this, one need only think of what has happened in recent years at Küng's university Institute. What, we could ask, apart from a personal friendship, brings him so close to Walter Jens, the orator and distinguished literary critic? Why is there such intensive work on literary questions in Küng's Institute?

Küng does not see this opening up to the 'world' in absolute terms.

First, he relates political and economic action to the ethic of the world religions, which manifestly cannot be reduced to politics, economics or other partial spheres of human culture. He does not adopt the stance of the economic or political theorist. Secondly, he carries on a theological discussion with wider sectors of culture, perhaps more out of curiosity and interest than with a programmatic plan, but certainly also in the expectation that here he can come closer to the questions of our culture and what moves human beings. Here I shall be referring to publications which cannot be pursued further in later chapters.

In September 1979 Küng gave a lecture on the occasion of the annual exhibition of the German Association of Artists in Stuttgart under the title 'Art and the Question of Meaning' (AQM). What has art to do with meaning, even with meaning that can be discussed theologically?

> 'Don't worry. I have no intention of administering publicly the last sacraments to the supposedly dying patient [= art]. Nor should you expect any miracles from the theologian or – I hope – any prophetical clairvoyance about the remaining possibilities and future prospects of the visual arts . . . What you can expect from a theologian is a contribution to sober diagnosis, and to understanding, and perhaps also a little hope. So let it be said from the very beginning that I am not abandoning the patient. I believe in his recovery' (AQM 11f.)

Küng's mode of procedure – I shall not summarize here a small book which is well worth reading – is characteristic. Here is the voice of someone who knows the relevant literature and to some degree is up in the arts, who clearly knows how to deal with stylistic trends, with the testimonies of artists and their way of thinking today. At the same time it is the voice of someone who – a year after the appearance of *Does God Exist?* – evidently has at his disposal a scheme of interpretation within which a dialogue between theology and art is possible, since each in its own way depicts or deciphers the spirit of the time. Küng is concerned to distinguish the competences: art is not religion. But he is even more concerned with the way in which they supplement each other: he attributes to art the capacity to depict meaninglessness (and meaning), to hold up a mirror to an age, or to anticipate an experience of meaning. In its own, autonomous way, art too deals with the great questions of humankind: where we come from, who we are and where we are going.

I shall break off here, but not without indicating the basic point. Küng himself does not fence off either religion or faith from art. He seeks their correlation (as Tillich put it) with the questions mentioned, sees how many artists are grappling with spiritual foundations which are tottering and have perhaps been shattered, and gives art the right (and the duty) in principle to address in its own way the dimensions of meaning, future, humanity and an ultimate trust. Here Küng abandons the pose of a theology which judges and supervises everything, which criticizes everything and thinks that it knows better. At the latest from this point on, he has announced a dialogue between faith and the 'world', thus unconditionally acknowledging that the world and culture can make their own distinctive contribution.

Küng's attitude becomes even clearer in his repeated preoccupation with prominent figures of European literature, on whom he keeps reflecting in dialogue with Walter Jens. In 1984 there was a first series of dialogues. Paradoxically Küng is now open not only to the particular forum of the theological faculty, but also to the really universal dimension of the university as a whole. *Literature and Religion* is the programmatic title of the book which appeared later. Küng discusses the significance for intellectual history of eight literary figures, representatives of modern periods of culture. Küng always explicitly does theology against the background of modernity and above all its end.

Each of these authors represents an epoch-making situation. Pascal stands for the disputed beginning of modern rationality. Gryphius grips us with his Reformation struggle between the perception of a painful crisis and an ultimate trust in God. Lessing inculcates the new standards of true tolerance, respect and human dignity, leading to the question whether a church and a theology whose doctrine and principles were alien to Jesus of Nazareth would not still have the theological Enlightenment ahead. The problematical Hölderlin, who returned to Tübingen only as a failure, strives for a reconciliation between antiquity and Christianity which never comes about. Novalis, known to many merely as a Romantic dreamer, is discovered to be a clear-sighted critic not only of a modern rationality which has ultimately forgotten God but also of both Catholicism and Protestantism. After that the analyses get even closer to us. Kierkegaard, for whom an accusation of Christianity for Christ's sake became a way of life and a destiny, calls for an existential Christianity. Küng infers from reading him 'a reintroduction of Christianity into Christendom from the bottom up' (LR 202). In *The Brothers Karamazov*, Dostoievsky works through the problem of suffering in the face of a world which has become absurd and discovers a solution only in an active love. Finally, the collapse of modernity is mirrored in the work of Kafka. The lesson which Küng draws from a promenade through this gallery of the great writers is clear to him. Had the better alternatives propounded by each of these figures been taken seriously in the Reformation and the Enlightenment, in the nineteenth and twentieth centuries, we would have been spared a history of catastrophes which ended up with Auschwitz (LR 276). It is evidently literature which makes it possible for theologians, too, to discuss the problem of modernity.

Küng does not stop with this journey through earlier positions:

'For me as a believing Christian, however, Auschwitz is for precisely this reason not the last word in world history. On the contrary, forty years after, Auschwitz demands the alternative vision of a renewed religion in a renewed society. The eclipse of God, the subsequent twilight of the gods, the downfall of the modern pseudo-gods, can be followed by a new morning in a paradigm of "postmodernity" (a name for something which is still unknown)' (LR 276f.).

The basic perspectives which Küng developed in the 1980s, and subsequently formulated with increasing precision, become as clear in these analyses as in his second dialogue volume with Walter Jens (*Anwälte der Humanität* [Advocates of Humanity], 1989), about some great writers of our century, Thomas Mann, Hermann Hesse and Heinrich Böll. Again these authors become witnesses to their age and the vehicles for penetrating diagnoses of the time. They raise questions about religion and its force in our culture, the challenge to Western culture by the world religions, and finally the state of a church structure which has become the victim of its own encrusted institutions. With a passionate interest in developments, Küng wants to know what has happened and is happening in Europe, how this continent could have lost religion and faith, how careers took concrete shape in this field of conflict, and what is to be learned from them today. His profound curiosity leads him to ask questions with the equipment that he has developed in his theology. But in the face of the specific lives, the poetic worlds and the urgent narrative, imaginative and challenging language of these figures, he constantly allows himself to be torn away from schemes of theological thought. On every side the task of theological reflection in the service of men and women again becomes clear: to stimulate thought and then to relativize itself; to recall the discrepancy between everyday fulfilment and the experiences of limits, and then to listen to specific recollections, to bring into play the discernment of the spirits, and yet to add the criteria of humanity, to champion the cause of faith, and to read ways forward from human biographies, suffering and hopes.

5. Touchstones

However, in this chapter we shall not anticipate further the content of Küng's theology. Perhaps it makes sense here to formulate 'touchstones' by which readers can measure Küng's theology. I shall not be returning to them again. But I presume that they may make it easier to arrange and evaluate the wealth of material that I shall be presenting in this book. They are also meant to make it possible to depersonalize the Küng phenomenon. Of course Küng's influence, capacity for spiritual leadership and enormous achievement are beyond dispute, but nothing would be more alien to him than to become an unattainable hero. So I shall mention five formal aspects which arise out of Küng's orientation on the present (in his sense). These are: intensity, concentration, criticism of ideology, keeping to the point and continuity. They will be discussed at most indirectly in subsequent chapters, but can serve as the most important background variables for a deeper understanding of the processes of theological communication. In what follows the shorthand term 'contemporary' is to be understood in the sense of *aggiornamento* indicated above.

(a) Intensity

Given the intensity and speed of present-day social and cultural change, listening to the present must lead to an extraordinarily intensive and committed theology. The danger of such a theology could be the impatience of those who want 'all or nothing'. Küng's theology shares this impatience; it is stamped by intensity and a high degree of commitment. Therefore we shall have to note whether topics are not only taken up, outlined brilliantly or sketched in essay form, but are worked out and shaped from the foundations. Küng meets this requirement. Against this background he keeps formulating answers, highlighting arguments and attempting to define praxis. This includes public statements and support for effective actions, the organization of scholarly symposia and regular conversations with his colleagues. But it is clear that not everything can ever happen simultaneously. That always remains a problem for a contemporary theology.

(b) Concentration

In view of the tremendous variety of questions, problems of orientation and debates on values, all of which are still unresolved, theological solutions can only be achieved by the utmost effective concentration. We must learn to discover what the issue is. A danger here is the claim of those who think that they have the true overall view. Therefore we shall have to see whether Küng is intent on such effective concentration, without falling into the one-sidedness of the know-all. In fact he practises a systematically comprehensive and integrating theology. For him that means a theology which not only seeks and defends valid statements, but is also aware of possible justifications and refutations, anticipates opposition, mediates between real and apparent oppositions. Therefore his theology seeks always to be related both to the subject matter and to norms, in keeping both with the present time and with Christ, and to be both pastoral and incorruptible. As a result, Küng seeks reasons and justifications, criteria and interconnections, consistent conclusions and intellectual imagination. These include strategies which go beyond disciplines, a language which seeks consensus, and a hermeneutic, sometimes a conceptual apparatus, which has a dialectical orientation and makes use of paradoxes. This includes an effort to reflect and also a criticism of critics who are not disposed to engage in a discussion aimed at consensus. Clarity requires great theological concentration.

(c) Criticism of ideology

In view of the increasing obscurity of social processes, part of the task of contemporary theology is to show up illusions, appeasement, individual and institutional laziness, the legitimation of power. A contemporary theology must be critical of ideology. It is therefore threatened by a moralizing tendency marked by mistrust, which can only be compensated for by intensive reflection. So we shall have to see how Küng addresses this potential to be critical of ideology and whether such criticism does not become an end in itself. From the beginning Küng in fact reacts sensitively to structural untruthfulness, falsification and concealment. He pays attention to the legitimation of power and to the connections between theory and self-interest, but at the same time he understands his work for the churches as critical and constructive commitment. According to Küng, a church theology has to fulfil a task of its own, and if need be warn or accuse. What scholarship has to contribute to society generally, theology has to contribute to the church and religion: independent, incorruptible, and if need be critical, thought. That is the reason for a tension in Küng's theology which irritates some readers and which others find it interesting to think through.

(d) Keeping to the point

Theology is expected to counterbalance the growing influence of technology and the humanities on present-day society. For all its methodological reflection it is expected to be related to issues and strong on content, neither evasive nor manipulative, keeping close to reality, to which it listens and which it expresses. The danger is that such a theology could fear any theoretical reflection and take all 'facts' at their face value. Now it is striking how deeply interested Küng is in working out and developing direct statements. He wants to clarify without distortion, to draw distinctions and to define. For this purpose he coins terms and repeats core statements until they have been illuminated from many sides and related to other contexts. This usually makes his message to the reader concentrated and direct. At the same time – as we shall see – he cultivates an expressly hermeneutical consciousness which interprets, seeks to understand from within, and takes note of the depth structures of human phenomena. How are these two aspects brought into balance?

Küng has always also reflected on methodological questions. However, his view is that one should not (or may not) burden the interested non-theologian with them. Thus there are no reflections on method or conversations with other disciplines; in his writings these are usually summed up concisely in the text, gathered into footnotes or presented in specialist articles. So the well-informed reader could never get the impression that Küng's approach is streamlined or journalistic. He delves not only through great areas of epistemology and theological or philosophical theory, but also through mountains of individual methodological problems, even if he does not often present them. In his first theological phase the significance of tradition plays a major role; in the second phase the normative nature of scripture; and later the validity of historically confirmed statements and their translation into new cultural contexts. Since the 1970s, questions of contemporaneity and translation from religious to secular contexts have been at the centre of his interest. In the 1980s Thomas Kuhn's paradigm theory became his key to an appropriate investigation of the great religions and their cultural contexts.

(e) Continuity

Connected with this is the fact that today a broad and continuous, trust-worthy and well-tried theology is being asked for. Perhaps continuity will be preferred to an appropriate interpretation. The danger of such a way of thinking is its fundamentalism and its inability to take account of new knowledge, changes of direction and even breaks. Küng is certainly aware that he has 'continually been changing' (HK 127), but in the eyes of many people he is engaged in a strikingly continuous theology which is based on intensive research and well-thought-out conclusions. Certainly he speaks of 'abrupt conversion' and is aware of being 'obsessed by a boundless intellectual curiosity' (ibid.), but in more than forty years, for all the changes, from the question of justification to the global ethic, a stable structure has come into being, tested by attacks and disputes. The interweaving of continuity and change, tran-sition and rejection, stability and sensitivity is also clearly an element in the art of a contemporary theology. This flexible continuity in change will have to be examined in the coming chapters.

In short, a contemporary theology increasingly robbed of its classical standards is an endangered theology. Intensity and passion then turn into proverbial impatience and theological fury. Behind the concentra-tion lurk a systematic narrowness and the terror of the concept; behind the criticism of ideology, mistrust and the impression of knowing better. Concentration of content is threatened by density in reflection, and continuity is in conflict with the constantly new challenge. The more clearly theology engages in *aggiornamento*, the more it will find that its sphere of work is like a stormy sea. In that case involvement, not rest, is the prime duty of the theologian, who is unprotected and risks failure. We shall have to investigate whether and how Küng has exposed himself to this risk.

To sum up, Küng presents to contemporaries in his cultural sphere a theology with many levels. Anyone who begins to read his *oeuvre* will face a long journey through thoughts and moods, appeals and argu-ments. None of his books is really out of date and none has failed to find an international response. But none is so completely written that readers do not need to comment on it. Küng was and is a theologian who draws one in: very Western, yet with friends all over the world; very demanding in what he says, yet using comprehensible language; emotional and impatient, yet extremely warm to those who put requests to him. He does not hide behind his works but often emerges in single combat, yet all his projects – both the topics and the way in which they are worked out – are rooted in networks and teams, groups of friends and theological circles. What he has stirred up and continues to stir up in the church will only become evident in future years. The attempt to put him in intellectual quarantine has proved a failure. That Küng is still a Catholic and understands himself to be a theologian distinguishes him from some of his contemporaries. Against this background it will be interesting to see what keeps his theology, his readership and his influence on the church and the global dialogue together. The following chapters should serve to answer this question. I hope that reading them will prove an exciting engagement with the works to which they set out to be an introduction.

2

Justification – A Question Pointing to the Future: Relying on God

It was a time of restoration and also of inner upheaval; the pontificate of Pius XII had passed its peak. The authority of the pope had been undermined by the experiences of the Second World War. No discussion of his political behaviour at that time had yet flared up, but the creation of the dogma of the Assumption of Mary into heaven (1950), the encyclical *Humani generis* (1950), resulting in the deposition of well-known theologians, the suppression of the worker priests (1953), and a generally harder line undermined the myth of the papacy. In the German-speaking world the Catholic milieu had consolidated itself again for the first time, but there was no escaping the wave of new thinking. It could not be hidden even in Rome, certainly not in the Germanicum and in the Gregoriana, where Küng lived and studied.

1. No more than a beginning?

Küng's work for a licentiate in theology was ambitious. It compared Karl Barth's doctrine of justification with the Catholic tradition. Without further reservations Küng came to the conclusion that the doctrine of justification could not be a reason for a continuing separation of the Catholic Church from the churches of the Reformation. So if what was continually said was true, namely that the doctrine of justification was at the heart of the Western split and the real reason for it, this conclusion had to have far-reaching consequences. Thus the investigation was worth pursuing even further; above all the result had to be consolidated in the light of Catholic tradition. In no more than eighteen months at the Institut Catholique in Paris, under Louis Bouyer, Küng developed his work into a dissertation which appeared in 1957 under the title *Justification. The Doctrine of Karl Barth and a Catholic Reflection*. He formulated a 'Catholic response, which can be no more than a beginning' (J 262). No more than a beginning? At least it was a strong, impressive beginning. *Justification* was to influence Küng's way of working, thought and aims, and also the boldness and later impact of his theology.

(a) The topic: justification

The content of the work can be summed up briefly. By general consent, at the Reformation it was the doctrine of justification which led to the separation of the Protestant churches from the 'old' church. Luther regarded the new understanding of justification as his decisive discovery, and the other Reformers followed him. We human beings do not find grace and salvation on the basis of our own efforts, and there is no way in which we can make a claim upon God. But God declares us righteous, as scripture already explains with the help of this legal metaphor. In this way, God grants us real righteousness. In other words, God unconditionally shows us his goodness, so we are freed from guilt and wickedness through him. In 'declaring us righteous' God makes us righteous; so guilt is not only covered but really obliterated. Paul impresses this on the readers of his letter, in opposition to Judaism. For him, a concentration on the Torah threatens to become a way of thinking in terms of achievement and claim, as if we could earn our salvation before God. God's salvation reaches human beings 'through faith alone, independently of works' (Rom. 3.28). Even those who think that one need not use the classic word 'alone' in translating this passage cannot deny that 'works' (the claim to merits of one's own) are irrelevant here. We need not go more deeply into why for Luther, with his discontent over sacramentalism, the trade in indulgences and a high esteem for asceticism, a comparable explosive confrontation had developed.

However, that is not all that the New Testament has to say on the matter. 'What does it profit if someone says that he has faith but has not works? Can faith save him?' (James 2.14). Luther would not have understood this remark, and we have to concede that James introduces a very narrow concept of faith here, as if faith did not primarily mean unconditional trust but something that one can achieve, instead of allowing oneself to fall into God's hands. But a problem is evident here. As the Catholic reaction is generally understood, while faith in the goodness of God cannot be denied, one's own action must be added to this faith. How could God call someone who showed no kind of commitment? Küng suggests a historical understanding here – nowadays we would call it an understanding based on a conscious hermeneutic: 'To avoid dealing unfairly with whole periods in the history of theology, we must remember that it is not necessary to be equally conscious of all the truths of faith in every age' (J 206). The different reactions of Paul and James are an example for him here. But the differences between the Reformation and the early church emerge in an opposition which the centuries could not bridge. Clearly Luther's concern made it necessary to speak a new language.

As early as 1957 it was evident to interested theologians that the answers had to be much more complex. Luther, in the heat of the conflict, did not deal with all the nuances of the question, nor did the Council of Trent simply say no in its decisive reply to Luther's solution. Could there not be a truth 'in the middle', on which both Catholics and Protestant agreed? Could one not get at least a little closer to the truth? Küng was not content to make just one more contribution to the discussion; he wanted to hit the nail on the head. Nor did he limit himself to a purely exegetical or historical work, in which the study of scripture or church history might have had their uses. He was concerned with current problems.

(b) The dialogue partner: Karl Barth

So how does Küng proceed and what conclusions does he draw? First of all he makes the texts and the vast topic manageable. This is a problem involving the Reformation and Catholicism, so he compares a representative Protestant position with a representative Catholic one. The choice of the Protestant representative may have surprised some people at the time. Küng does not turn, say, to Luther's doctrine of justification or to that of a Lutheran theologian, but to the Reformed theologian Karl Barth. As will prove later, this has enormous advantages.

First, at that time there was no Protestant theologian with greater authority; Karl Barth had earned it in the battle against National Socialism. Secondly, by far the greater part of the *Church Dogmatics* had appeared. In it, Karl Barth did not present an isolated doctrine of justification (faithful to history, biblical or specifically Lutheran), but an overall theological conception which had been developed from the notion of justification for his time and (above all!) was through-composed. Barth worked out the connection between christology and anthropology and radicalized it so that it became an image of God which was to be immune from all modern falsifications. It cannot be denied that this choice was also influenced by Hans Urs von Balthasar's brilliant monograph (von Balthasar 1951). Nor can it be overlooked that there was a deep affinity between Karl Barth's style of thought and – to put it briefly – that of the Gregoriana: an encyclopaedic character, a delight in logical stringency and consistency, responsibility to the history of theological thought, confrontation with the present. It was later to prove how deeply this great master of contemporary theology in his turn shaped Küng's theological style.

But with what or with whom was this position now to be compared? This question was (and is) much more difficult to resolve, since already at that time the picture offered by one Catholic theology proved – especially from a historical perspective – to be a fiction. Scripture, to be expounded and interpreted by the later tradition, was still the undisputed norm of Catholic theology. And dogmatic statements were no longer regarded as final doctrinal results, but rather as propositions which had to be explained further, indeed developed. Küng made use of this newly awakened historical consciousness in Catholic theology. Consequently he resorts to scripture, mentions decisive emphases in the theological tradition and draws the lines as far as contemporary proof texts (J 115). As a decisive key text – for the purpose of testing and self-criticism – he uses the decree on justification from the Council of Trent, the best product of this council, which was approved in 1547 and still stands out even after 450 years for its balance and careful theology. Küng can show that this text – like the earlier Catholic tradition – argues in a far more sophisticated way than later textbooks and a black-and-white polemic would have it (J 103ff.). Here too justification by faith is accorded unconditional priority, even if systematic theology time and again refers to inappropriate categories, which have no ontological relations and are often apersonal. At the same time Küng – whose interpretation has a critical element – shows that Barth's understanding of justification is far less one-sided than might appear at first sight. Therefore what is also decisive for Küng even over against Trent is the independent reference to scripture and to those witnesses of the Catholic tradition who are close to the concern of the Reformation. There in fact he finds more than a statement which maintains the Reformation 'through faith alone'.

But can Barth's position really be brought into the framework of problems which are binding for Catholic theology? This question indicates a decisive problem. Here for Küng comparison does not mean an unhistorically logical procedure, nor even the attempt to pin Karl Barth down to individual statements, to look for defects or catch him in the network of Catholic convictions. 'Comparison' is a misleading word and does not appear in Küng's monograph. Küng does not compare, but discovers perspectives and intentions and keeps showing how and why contrary statements are not comparable.

Already at that time Küng was doing hermeneutics in the best sense of the word: 'The implicit truth-content of any formula, in so far as it is divine truth, always exceeds its implicit formulation, and therein lies its character as mystery' (J 198). In his view, theological or even dogmatic formulae are not an end but a beginning: 'We must therefore continually strive to move away from the formulation – not in order to give it up, but rather to understand it "according to the Spirit"' (J 112). So he does not tie his investigation to statements about justification but investigates the contexts in which justification arises: the doctrines of creation and of sin, and christology (J 179). He attempts to decipher censure of basic attitudes in censure of individual doctrines (ibid.) and understands the message of justification among other things as a statement about human freedom (J 176). In questions about the doctrine of sin and christology he can show that the great Catholic-Protestant controversy over the human need for redemption merely represents the continuation of earlier controversies within Catholicism over Augustinianism, Thomism or later Scotism. Moreover he does not come to the conclusion, say, that Karl Barth advocates a Catholic doctrine of justification, but remarks: 'In regard to the foundations of the theology of justification, Barth, considered as a whole, stands on the same ground as we Catholics do' (J 185). And later: 'It is undeniable that there is a fundamental agreement between Karl Barth's position and that of the Catholic Church in regard to the theology of justification seen in its totality. Within the scope of the questions treated, Barth has no genuine argument for separation from the ancient church' (J 264).

Such statements create an understanding and at the same time space for further discussion. Therefore in connection with the topic of grace Küng goes intensively into its original significance in scripture. He attempts to express the different perspectives in formulae which prompt further reflection: '. . . Protestants speak of a declaration of justice which includes a making just; and Catholics of a making just which pre-supposes a declaring just. Is it not time to stop arguing about imaginary differences?' (J 211). Or he refers to a (terminological) misunder-standing on the part of Karl Barth: 'As it turned out, the "objective" event of salvation on the cross, to which Barth applies the scriptural term "justification", is generally designated by Catholics "redemption" (an equally scriptural term) to distinguish it from "justification" as a "subjective" saving event.' Thus he is 'unconsciously comparing his ("objective") justification with the Catholic ("a subjective") justification' (J 222). In order to avoid a fixation on formulae and individual doctrinal statements, he finally mentions three further criteria which must govern any theology. Every theology has its own particular bias (with strengths, weaknesses and tendencies); every theology has its polemical limitations; every theology 'is life and life is theology' (J 265–8). Nowadays we would speak of historical conditioning, of knowledge and self-interest, and the question how a theology legitimates the praxis of a community.

In this way Küng paraphrases a term which can overcome this polemic, these poles and divisions, and which will thus remain central and decisive for his whole theology. Justifying faith is described as trust and recognition that 'God himself achieves the justification of the sinner – not human beings through some work of their own (the work of faith, for instance)' (J 246). In conclusion Küng is no longer thinking about human beings or redemption through Christ but about the only decisive question, whether in all this reflection and in the praxis of the church God alone receives the glory (*Soli Deo gloria*)' (J 251–61). With this formula he finally mentions the one great concern in which he sees Christian faith of whatever shade united.

Now if Barth is representative of Protestant thought (which is Küng's presupposition), and if Küng's assessment of Catholic theology is accepted (thus Barth's condition in his preface to the book), the conclusion can only be that the main reason for the separation between the Catholic Church and the churches of the Reformation has been removed. The two sides have come nearer to each other. Barth requires the sovereign act of God in the doctrine of justification to be taken seriously. According to Küng that has not always happened as clearly as might be desired in the Catholic tradition, but it is accepted in principle. On the other hand, the Catholic side requires Barth to take justification seriously as justification of the human being. This too cannot be denied.

(c) The consequence: an understanding

What is to be said about this conclusion? In retrospect, two conflicting points need to be made. The first relates to the validity of Küng's conclusion: what a good forty years ago still caused a stir and led to discussions and official statements, is now largely accepted in both Catholic and Protestant theology. The immediate reaction to the book was one of amazement, but generally positive (Hempel 8–20). It resulted in intensive research (Brosseder, NHFT 138–51), and Küng could feel that his views had been confirmed at the latest by O.H.

Pesch's pioneering investigations of Thomas Aquinas and Martin Luther. The fact that finally ecumenical agreements followed also gave Küng's thesis a significance which went beyond the churches, as Brosseder shows. The question of justification, for centuries the great stumbling block between the confessions, no longer offers any reason for a split between the churches. Of course there are still different interpretations, historical statements, linguistic rules and emphases, but now the fronts run straight across the confessions.

The second relates to the consequences of Küng's conclusion for church action. His own church did not draw any conclusions worth mentioning from the new position in the discussion. The problems relating to justification do not feature in the Second Vatican Council's Decree on Ecumenism. Certainly this decree celebrates the new ecumenical spirit, and ecumenical contacts were considerably intensified – there were and are plenty of dialogue groups – but new reasons kept being mentioned or invented in order to delay a recognition of the churches of the Reformation, their ministry or their worship. Why? The dialogue within Catholicism 'with the biblical, historical and dogmatic experts', which Barth still called for (J xviii), had finally led to a positive result. So after a good forty years the amazed question remains how the doctrine of justification worked out afresh by Küng could still be refuted by the life of the Catholic Church. Or did the burden of proof still lie with those who wanted mutual recognition?

Now Küng was also already sufficiently sober and matter-of-fact to take seriously the concrete difficulties of the process of recognition: church governments would have to be convinced of the cause and be spurred on to use their imagination. Habits would have to be broken, and many Catholics would perhaps feel that their identity was threatened. Küng has always seen and understood that. His problem emerged later, more at the juncture of knowledge and self-interest. Obviously some theologians of all camps make their statements dependent on interests that are unexpressed, suppressed or even denied. That a long-term conflict was in the making with the publication of this book at the time of an ecumenical standstill is all too obvious in retrospect, in so far as Küng respected his own statements and expectations.

The Küng of the first years occupied himself with classical topics of theology, with questions of the past, with questions internal to the Christian churches. Later these questions automatically became outdated. Does that mean that they were settled as far as Küng was concerned? We should not be as simplistic as that in our interpretation. Rather, with this ecumenical project there begins a thought of amazing continuity. Here Küng sees himself as a church theologian through and through. Precisely for that reason he takes up church questions and seeks to resolve them within church limits; he tackles them with the tools of Catholic theology. Where now is the continuity? Let us attempt to deepen the picture of Küng's theological style. We have to show why this first work was more than just a beginning.

2. Theology in the footsteps of Karl Barth: four pillars

Küng understood the question of justification not as an individual question but as a basic form which shaped Christian faith. It can be regarded as a stroke of luck that he not only followed Barth in this basic conviction but also took up basic characteristics of Barth's theological work. This laid the foundation stone for his own consistent and indefatigable theology. That can be shown from four basic pillars which support his theology.

(a) Connections as a theme of theology

One might think that the question of justification is a limited topic, which can be defined in the same way as, for example, the question of angels, sin, or the miracles of Jesus. But already for the Letter to the Romans and even more for the Reformation it was of such central significance that the question whether a person has understood or failed to understand the core of Christian faith could be read off the doctrine of justification. Is someone able, particularly in critical times, to draw the appropriate conclusions from his or her faith, as Paul did in the transition to Gentile Christianity and the Reformation did in the transition to modern times? The same goes for Barth. One of his great pieces of anti-Catholic polemic was directed against the Council of Trent's doctrine of justification. Well though it had been worked out, this decree later became the writing on the wall for a church which did not understand the Reformation approach, perhaps did not want to understand it, and thus essentially falsified the Christian message.

Of course there is a psychological explanation of this. Luther's great experience of a breakthrough now crystallized in the doctrine of justification. Thus as a mark of the Reformation it developed its own dynamic, and the repudiation of it became the hallmark of a separated Catholic Church. Furthermore, since the time of Luther and Calvin the concentration on the problem of justification has led to a distinctive language, because the Aristotelian categories came under pressure. This problem also applies to the discussion between a Catholic theologian of the 1950s and Karl Barth. 'The vocabulary and the whole system of categories, the choice of words and the pattern of thinking are strange. Whereas the Catholic theologian generally thinks and speaks along Aristotelian and scholastic lines, Barth's thought and language take their shape from German Idealism. Barth has assimilated, especially through the theology of Schleiermacher, the whole development from Kant through Fichte and Schelling to Hegel. He has also drawn upon later Protestant theology' (J 7).

Furthermore, the doctrine of justification has taken on different significance in the Protestant and the Catholic spheres. Küng mentions it under two headings, 'central problem' and 'individual problem'. For Luther it was beyond doubt a central problem, perhaps the fundamental and central dogma of Christianity. For Barth that is already no longer the case. Certainly the doctrine of justification is very important for him, and for him too everything is corrupted if the doctrine of justification is corrupted. Nevertheless, he sees that the doctrine of justification formulates 'only one special aspect of the Christian message of reconciliation. For the fundamental issue is the Christian message of reconciliation' (J 11). At the heart of the message stands the confession of Jesus Christ. Küng has discovered that and refers to it expressly at the beginning of his monograph.

Thus in clarifying the overall problem Küng sees himself compelled to take detours, though these ultimately prove to be the most direct route. He is interested not only in the whole of Barth's *Dogmatics*, i.e. in the connections in salvation history (God's gracious choice, the relationship between creation, the breach in the covenant and reconciliation), but in the whole process of justification. That is the way of Jesus Christ, human sin, the role of faith, love and 'works'. Küng then follows the same detours in Catholic tradition, with an amazing result:

'No human works, not even the best works, are responsible for justification. Human beings are justified by God on the basis of faith alone. In faith the sinner submits himself to divine justification which has occurred for all men and women in the crucifixion and resurrection of Jesus Christ. This is where justification gets its "subjective" character. Thus justifying faith, proceeding from a trust which includes repentance and penance, involves both acknowledgment and realization of God's declaration of justification which has happened once and for all in Jesus Christ. God himself achieves the justification of sinners – not human beings through some work of their own (the work of faith, for instance). They simply acknowledge the work of God' (J 246).

Let us analyse this statement briefly. First of all there is a formulation of the classical negation, i.e. the target of the doctrine of justification. 'Works' is the great anti-concept which needs explanation today. Against this background the formula becomes more complex, 'justified by faith alone'. Then Küng mentions which process is to be protected by the doctrine of justification. Now the most different entities are activated which come together here: the sinner, God and Jesus Christ. Then, and only then, is the matter summed up quite simply. God is active who recognizes human beings.

Thus from the time of his conversation with Karl Barth it is clear to Küng that doctrine and a good theology of faith do not know any isolated individual statements, any detached themes which can be discussed objectivistically 'in themselves'. Statements of faith are related to one another and work as an overall system; concepts, terminologies and questions interact and always lead to mutual development, expansion or correction. So the nearer a question gets to foundations and principles, the less it can be objectified, marked off and treated as a fact or a statement that can be isolated logically.

This hermeneutical insight is not new, but often leads to a more convenient approach. A truth must always be understood as an overall conception, so to speak intuitively, as what Ebeling calls a 'pre-judgment', in the light of its pre-understanding. So it must not get caught up in a network of individual statements. Where this is forgotten, theology no longer has its feet on the ground. In conversation with Karl Barth (and as a consequence of a solid Roman training), Küng develops another approach, without taking the easy way out and with great attention to detail. Only thus does the overall conception take on concrete form. With Barth he goes through all the individual stages, illuminates the key data and the critical points, puts everything in its historical context, and with great intensity investigates the biblical basis. Had he had a fixation on concepts and precise definitions, he would have overlooked the background, both in Barth and in the Catholic tradition.

Thus it is possible to argue in retrospect which topic was the most important in this book: the question of Jesus Christ, of God or human faith. In the 'Catholic Reflection' (the second part of the book), Küng once again goes through all the stages: the significance and activity of

Jesus Christ, creation, sin and death, grace, and only then the specific controversial questions of the doctrine of justification. He once again refers back to scripture and tradition before coming to his own conclusions.

Since this book Küng has always thought out and explained his topics in an overall context, and his orientation is taken from the Bible, the history of theology, and increasingly from contemporary history and world history. Theology requires not only intuition but also the most detailed information. Only then are overall verdicts, simplification, criticism and polemic allowed. Even later Küng never has the ambition to engage in other individual disciplines (exegesis, church history, philosophy or religious anthropology). But it is important for him to know their results and he always argues at a high academic level.

The Church, On Being a Christian and *Does God Exist?* are examples of this style of working, but so too are *Eternal Life?, Judaism* and *Christianity*. Take *The Church*, for example. Küng – with the sobering experience of the Council behind him – certainly advocates quite definite concerns and a particular vision of the church. Precisely for that reason the book offers a wealth of information about the Bible, the history of the church and theology, and strategic arguments which have been worked out on both the Protestant and the Catholic sides. The bibliographies are complete; the system of Catholic church teaching is comprehensive. This book of more than 500 pages is still, after thirty years, an unsurpassed treasure trove of facts, references and possible interpretations. The same is true of *On Being a Christian* and *Does God Exist?*. Had Küng wanted to write best-sellers, he certainly would not have written books 720 and 840 pages long. Here too he is supported by the conviction that the truth only arises out of the whole, that a brilliant notion is no substitute for theology, and that the hard work of the scholar benefits a solid theology which leads on further. Nor has Küng given up this comprehensive way of working in later years. His two most recent major works on the religious situation of our time (*Judaism* and *Christianity*) are 750 and 950 pages long respectively: quarries of information, case studies and reflection. Here too the wealth of detail and the clarity of the aims are related. The more therefore Küng emerges as one who can tame recalcitrant masses of material, the more clearly his techniques of concentration are perfected. The two works mentioned above are almost systematically full of summaries, theses and 'questions for the future'.

For Küng, theology begins with the discovery and organization of connections. A theology without theological, philosophical, even exegetical knowledge is doomed to failure. Only when the work has been done well can viable results be hoped for. This is not because of a particularly diligent type of academic theology but because the task is very topical. As a critical companion to faith, theology has to do more than produce pious suggestions; it is not just about ecclesiastical piety and religion. As a critical companion and elucidation of faith it embraces the whole complicated structure of the reality of human beings and the world and in its reference to God comes up against the limits of human language. This last feature does not lead to a negative theology which can only keep silent, any more than it does in Karl Barth, but to a service to human beings which does not end until their questions (hopefully) are silenced.

(b) Faith as reasonable trust

The basic question of Luther's quest for justification is well known: how do I get a gracious God? It was the question of faith in the face of personal guilt and inability to overcome this by one's own strength. For the Küng of the 1950s the question of justification played an important role for ecumenical reasons, since the fundamental difference between the confessions had become attached to it. But at the same time here Küng touches on a key point of faith and Christian theology. By not isolating the problem of justification but following Karl Barth in treating it as a comprehensive problem, he discloses the overall connection between God, faith and human beings. Today this tricky knot is not tied in the same way as it was by Luther or even Paul. For Barth, *the* theologian of the twentieth century, the question of God has assumed a more dramatic form. Today the identity, meaning and future of human beings are more radically at stake than they were 500 years ago.

However, Luther and Paul cannot be put to flight too quickly, since undoubtedly already at that time faith was a central, fundamental act which for religions was virtually beyond time. This elementary perspective then opens up the question of justification in a simple way: 'Human beings simply recognize the work of God.' That is an unmistakable principle which later proves to be a basic motif, a cornerstone, of Küng's theological thought. It keeps making progress in the later books. According to the index of *The Church*, 'faith' is the most-used term in the book after 'Bible'. Its central role explains why the church is always the church that is *believed*. Beyond doubt, in Küng's understanding of the church, too, faith in God has become the central topic which provides criticism and direction for all further considerations. This priority of faith as a critical criterion unmistakably comes into play later in the debate on infallibility.

Already at that time it could have been clear to any critic of Küng how untenable the charge was that he was disloyal to the church:

'So for the Christian the church is primarily there not to be admired nor to be criticized but to be believed. Neither admiration of the church nor criticism of the church really matters. What matters is the faith of the church . . . Arising out of faith, an "admiration" of the church is possible for the Christian in some circumstances, but it will always be a surprised admiration which sees the church's "un-nature" and yet trusts in its good nature in spite of it . . . Neither admiration nor criticism is absolute, but is essentially fragmentary, "dissolved", positively and negatively' (C32).

But at the same time it becomes clear that faith in God always remains the core and criterion of being a Christian. In faith in God this church which is believed in is at the same time relativized; it is a relativization of a fundamental nature:

'Faith is never, in the final analysis, a matter of adherence to objects, rules or dogmas, but is the sacrifice and self-giving of one person to another . . . But radical personal self-giving, something that in each and every case will be unconditional and irrevocable, can only be made to God; only God can be believed, in the fullest and most radical sense of the word. To believe in a human being in this absolute and completely unconditional sense would be to make him into an idol; it would be a blasphemy against God, who alone is worthy of totally unconditional self-surrender; it would mean enslavement for the person who made himself an unconditional follower of another mortal and sinful being. The Christian believes, in this sense of the word, only in God and in him whom God has sent' (C 31).

The early central theme of 'faith' recurs in *Does God Exist?*, to some degree in a new key; one could understand this book as a resumption of the problems of justification. In it Küng sketches out the specifically modern context of this problem rather than its classic context of the church. The question of faith forms the scarlet thread of the book and determines its whole dynamic. The very first part is a discussion of the alternatives 'Reason or Faith?'. Descartes and Pascal, those pioneering figures, stand at the centre (DGE 3–92). The question is then made more pointed in the third and fourth parts with a view to modernity; the alternatives are now no longer justification by works or quietism, but atheism and nihilism (DGE 189–424).

The discussion with Friedrich Nietzsche (DGE 343–424) is one of the most exciting chapters in Küng's work, since there for the first time he accepts the modern threat to faith in all its force, and he goes a long way. Now reality itself appears as a questionable entity threatened by meaninglessness, of which neither the meaning nor the truth can be demonstrated. Alongside a 'fundamental trust' a 'fundamental mistrust' enters the believer's horizon. I can say a fundamental no to this questionable reality, the world and myself without showing myself to be unreasonable, foolish or malicious in the process. Only in this way does the 'Yes' to God return to the sphere of human freedom, since the opposite is also possible: 'Fundamental trust means that a person, in principle, says Yes to the uncertain reality of himself and the world, making himself open to reality and able to maintain this attitude consistently in practice' (DGE 445).

Thus qualitatively Küng goes one step further than the current theology of faith. He does not just speak in an abstract way about belief in God, i.e. about a trust in the origin and goal of all reality, but confronts this model of trust in Christian faith with a battle which is being fought every day, and reflected on by scholars, a battle between mistrust and trust towards a threatened world, unpredictable fellow human beings and an impenetrable self. At the same time Küng makes it clear that the whole of our existence is woven into this dramatic reference of faith to God. The whole of existence, the whole truth of the world, stands in this faith, and our capacity to criticize all other powers which want to bind us under their spell is also involved here.

In his analyses of mistrust and trust, Küng shows that precisely at this sensitive point human beings are not only subject to a total demand, because only they can decide for themselves, but also keep and are given all freedom because they can really decide. Therefore he has added to the understanding of faith two perspectives of faith which are essential for modernity. The first perspective, directed outwards, acts as a qualification: indeed faith in God is utterly rooted in a 'fundamental trust' in reality, but this fundamental trust is not yet to be identified with faith in God. This follows from the experience of a secularized world; atheists too are in the end human beings and can live by an unbroken trust in reality, in their fellow human beings and the world. However, the question remains whether this tension between trust and unbelief can be sustained without a break, and where and how this break is to be located, if it escapes the grasp of morality and rational thought.

The second perspective, directed inwards, is an answer to this; it serves as a radicalization of the question of faith. Trust and faith cannot be shown to be rationally compelling decisions, but fundamental trust 'manifests (!) its essential reasonableness in its realization (!)' (DGE 447). Nor can atheism be refuted or demonstrated; we can accept God only in a trust (!) which is at the same time offered. Therefore for Küng the conflict over belief and unbelief does not end in a symmetrical stalemate which neutralizes the question of freedom. For in his view, those who affirm God know in the act of faith, and only in that way, why they can trust in reality (DGE 574).

Küng speaks of the 'intrinsic rationality' of faith. By that he means a reason which cannot be made independent, objectified, instrumentalized or misused for discrimination. It is a reason which in its action remains wholly bound up with communication and the credibility of the situation, and perceives its significance from within. There is no doubt that such an image of reason is more at home in a hermeneutic of critical perception, of the understanding of meaning, than in what Wils calls the discourse of powerful arguments. It alone guarantees that freedom for understanding without which we can hardly cope with the present in a dignified way. It alone also brings 'God' back into a sphere of perception with which we had parted company in the modern clash between the proof of God and contempt for God. Here it can gently be conceded that Küng has posed as many questions to theological reflection on faith as he has given answers. Thus there is still something for fundamental theology and theological hermeneutics to do.

The short book *Credo* (1993) then presents in more open language ('explained for today') what faith means for Küng – thirty-five years later – after embarking on a great journey through the world religions and engaging in an investigation of the religious situation of the world. First of all he takes up what he has already said: no one is compelled intellectually or philosophically to accept the existence of God; faith is an act of 'reasonable trust', an understanding in the realization, inner rationality. Faith means a trust which includes thinking, questioning and doubting, but in which human beings can completely and comprehensively rely on God (because God is *with* this questioning and doubting). Here the issue is once again summed up. At the same time this summary of what had been a very intensive and differentiated intellectual journey sounds amazingly restrained. Why?

I suppose that after a phase of abstract discussion (to which we shall be returning later) the whole weight of a concrete faith stamped by the religious tradition has now emerged. Just as formerly the concept of justification fluctuated between the 'central problem' and the 'individual problem', so now does the concept of faith. In the 1970s Küng analysed it in detail and selected it as a separate problem (in the language of traditional scholastic theology, he analysed faith in terms of fundamental theology). Now that he has brought out its central significance, explained its role in the philosophical tradition and clarified the way in which it is rooted in human life, he is again convinced of its comprehensive, all-embracing meaning, that it is a matter of course. Not only the pages of *Credo* mentioned above (Cr 10–12) but the whole book is about faith, this 'primal word' (Cr 11). Thus in the last resort all accounts and analyses of the world religions serve only this one aim: to show the content of faith and what it means for the world.

But with so much summarizing, two aspects must not be domesticated or even forgotten: they are too important for Küng. The first is a polemical (and typically 'prophetic') demarcation from everything that could replace a faith exclusively directed to God in a Christian way of life. Christians believe neither in the Bible nor in tradition, neither in the church nor in the text of the 'creed' itself, far less in any world-views, theologies or convictions to which people like to attach the label 'Christian'. Christians believe only and exclusively in the one whom the Bible attests, whom the tradition hands down, whom the church proclaims, and whom the creed has as its the theme. The main problem for believers is not that no pre-eminence is accorded to faith, but that it is constantly misunderstood, narrowed and misused. Faith must insist on its identity, which cannot be alienated.

The second aspect is solidarity with everything that humankind and the world rightly expect from faith. The issue here is the constantly disputed relevance of faith in our time. A faith which was simply fixated on its identity would inevitably become rigid and ultimately insignificant. That is now stated on the last pages of *Credo*, as it was twenty years previously in *On Being a Christian* (OBC 602). It is the traditional first question of the Catechism, 'Why are we on earth?' (cf. *Concilium* 108, 1978). Küng's answer then as now is: faith becomes concrete as discipleship and is related to the 'world of today'. It is about the discipleship of Jesus Christ, and Küng continues: 'The Apostles' Creed ultimately focusses on a new meaning of life and a new praxis, on a way which lives by hope, which rests on faith and finds its fulfilment in love. Faith, hope, love – in that way one can express the meaning of life for Christians, "but the greatest of these is love" (I Cor. 13.13)' (Cr 190).

(c) Human being and being fully human

This is the third abiding characteristic of Küng's theology. It too has its origin in the dialogue with Karl Barth. Barth's anthropology has many levels and is often misunderstood – as is the anthropology of the Catholic tradition. Barth is discussed under the label of an authoritarian understanding of God and human beings. The Catholic tradition is associated with an authoritarian understanding of the church and salvation. Both see human beings as unworthy sinners, who can be helped to a life which has some degree of human dignity only by God's gifts. These are caricatures, quite certainly grounded in many disappointing and often humiliating experiences, provoked by those who in their actions assumed the authority of a Barth or – worse still – of a church, and continue to do so. All his life Küng has campaigned against an authoritarian, inhuman abuse of faith and religion. His opposition, his polemic and his pen, which if need be is a sharp one, could not and cannot be challenged more than by contempt for human beings, the scorn of reason and freedom, contempt for human beings in the name of religion. He reacts and promptly comes forward when this sort of thing happens in his own church. It is not surprising that it is often objected that he is a modern man, bourgeois through and through, and that his championing of freedom and humanity are not fed by the sources of Christian faith but by contemporary ideas of freedom. However, the critics are wrong.

Now we are not concerned here with biographical or psychological analyses but with theological terms of reference and the basic decisions which continually govern Küng's thought. Let's begin once again with Karl Barth. It is striking (and here I keep to Küng's interpretation) that Barth's picture of human beings is essentially more balanced than that of the Lutheran tradition. Barth does not follow Luther's polemic about the enslaved will; he emphatically holds fast to the honorific title of Christian freedom. But it is even more important that, contrary to a traditionally Catholic picture of Protestant theology, Barth is not concerned with the mass of human corruption; he does not go into this question (J 51). In 'misery' and in grace Barth is concerned with the *whole* person. So Barth can also give 'sanctification' – what human beings can and do achieve themselves – more its due than is customary in his tradition. Trained in existentialist thought, Barth can therefore hold opposites together: 'Thus, precisely in its negative emptiness and passivity, justifying faith is found in most positive abundance and activity' (J 75). The righteousness that is given can have an effect as its own creative action. In love human beings can do real good.

Thus in his answer to Barth, Küng similarly arrives at a dialectical reaction. On the one hand he argues that the Catholic Church takes God's priority in all action more seriously than usual. On the other hand, he supports Barth by saying that the human dimensions are taken seriously even in faith. It is precisely his 'Catholic' answer which leads him to emphasize the value of the human being as an independent entity. Küng's summary on Barth is this:

> 'The question of Catholics was: Does Karl Barth take justification seriously as the justification of *human beings*? Having investigated the corresponding Catholic teaching we must acknowledge that Barth does in fact take the justification of human beings seriously. In Jesus Christ God has from eternity been gracious to human beings as autonomous creatures. In him, human beings and the whole creation were created good. In him the covenant remains in effect even in opposition to human sin, so human beings remain human even in sin. In Christ, however, human existence confronts anew the free grace of God because in him God makes the sinner inwardly righteous, though men and women – as new creatures in faith who through love want to be active in works – have to actualize it' (J 261; references to previous chapters omitted).

Now the monograph on justification was written with an ecumenical purpose, However, along the way questions about the Christian image of human beings had accumulated. What is only provisionally indicated in the text quoted above (and this was to be made even clearer in a christological context) would later take on sharp contours. As soon as there is mention of God, human beings are in question. Precisely because Küng abandons the superficial metaphor of 'collaboration' between God and human beings, he has to speak of both at the same time and relate them to each other: Jesus Christ is true God, precisely in becoming human (J 38). But human beings are highly active precisely in their passive receptiveness. God wants to be a partner to human beings, even where he is the active one. So it is not a matter of 'joining in' but of engaging in his own highly personal action. Because justification is to be understood as an effective word of God, it functions as a 'sanctification' in which human beings really come into their own. 'As faith must be operative in love, so justification must be operative in sanctification' – "You shall therefore be . . . holy, for I am holy" ' (Lev. 11.33; cf. 19.2; 20.7f.)' (J 256).

What is said here seems – now, after forty years – as outdated as the language of Canaan; of course it needs to be translated. But this connection is important for Küng's development: the question how God redeems us human beings, a central theme of theology, prompts the question of human freedom and activity, the partnership of human beings and God – which is quite modern and yet has a Christian basis. This question arises so clearly because in the definition of relationships any superficial model of co-operation is to be avoided:

> 'Is not the creature annihilated in all this? On the contrary, it is within the theonomy and divine rule of this gracious primal choice that the autonomy, individuality and independence of the creature is fully realized. This, too, is firmly based on the eternal and gracious election of God' (J 18f.).

Later Küng deals with this question consistently. He debates the idealistic solutions in his investigation of Hegel's christology (IG): can we think of divine and human action together in the categories of history, and if so how? What is the relationship between divine will and human freedom? In his extremely detailed monograph on Hegel's christology (Kuschel, NH 171–97), first intended as a Habilitation thesis and then completed in 1970 along with other projects, Küng follows up the possibilities offered there of thinking of God and human beings together. He reconstructs Hegel's farewell to theology and his move to philosophy; he analyses his reflections on the death of God and the problem of pantheism, and an image of God which is exhausted in categories of knowledge. Going beyond Hegel, he wants a God who is alive in a new way:

> 'The dialectic of love creates fresh space for God's divinity, freedom and love and for all those factors which are one-sidedly commandeered by a stunted dialectic of knowledge. Against any modernistic appeal to the God of the (modern) philosophers it would thus be possible to express God in the world, transcendence in immanence, the beyond in the here-and-now in a new way' (IG 237).

Later he continues the idea:

> 'Through the dialectic of love, space would be created *within* the one reality not only for God to be himself but also for human beings to be themselves, indeed for all those things to which Hegel's dialectic

easily fails to do justice: the importance of human willing, the power of human freedom to decide, the reality of sacrifice, provided that human beings do not culpably fail. It could be made clear what love means in relation to God. This is a love which, like all love, can be genuinely perceived by those who themselves love; a love which cannot simply be known, but which wants to be dared; a love which presupposes trust. And a quite different trust is expected in one who is not seen, who is not tangibly present or immediately accessible in the world, from the trust that is placed in one who is seen . . . I can only love God when I rely on him, trust him, *believe* in him. The *pistis* of God is matched by the *pistis* of human beings: only those who trust God become certain of the faithfulness of God. To this extent love presupposes faith . . . Hence ultimate unity with God can never simply be a question of pure knowledge, of reason, of knowing, of a branch of study which absorbs all else the whole. Human beings in their unreduced totality are here challenged in their freedom – which is the primordial human risk – to let themselves be given everything that is not simply at their disposal' (IG 239).

As is well known, Küng did not follow Hegel's christology, and it is not surprising that the reasons for his restraint – though in 1970 still enciphered in christological terms – are connected with the freedom of a personal encounter which can only be grasped and realized in the relationship of love. Much as Küng praises his teacher Hegel for breaking through the static nature of the traditional image of God and taking seriously God's 'career' (his changing nature, his suffering, indeed the fearful talk of the death of God), ultimately he refuses to follow Hegel because Hegel's speculative answer to questions got in the way of a relationship between God and human beings shaped in freedom. Already in the Hegel monograph, for Küng it is in Jesus' proclamation, conduct and fate that the truly human message of Christian faith is unveiled. Jesus preaches a 'kingdom of peace, righteousness and fullness and of reconciliation between God and humankind' (IG 499).

Jesus' conduct always relates to the 'quite specific person, the neighbour who is often so remote, on whom God's will is constantly focussed, working through the law and yet beyond its letter. But he is wholly committed to God, God's rule and human well being, manifestly even beyond God's holy law and God's instructions where the specific human being is concerned.' According to Küng, this becomes clear from 'the indisputable fact that he sided with the impious and the lawless, who were neither able nor willing to keep the law, to the great annoyance of the pious who were faithful to the law. He had fellowship, shared meals, with the despised, the outcasts and the oppressed, indeed even with the religiously degraded and depraved, so that he was regarded as a friend of notorious sinners, heretical Samaritans, tax-gatherers (with their questionable business ethics), collaborators and prostitutes. All this represented an utmost intensification of God's demand, along with a most prodigious augmentation of his grace' (IG 500f.). Thus Jesus' fate makes it clear that here 'a friend of God's enemies' was at work who stood 'for the love of God and human freedom'; a man 'in whom for those who had entered into a personal relationship with him, God's very Word, will and love had themselves taken personal form, and in whom God's kingdom of reconciliation, peace, liberty and love seemed already to have arrived. And this was the man who was liquidated before the public gaze' (IG 502). Thus Küng was finally concerned with the incarnation of God, which has taken place 'for the incarnation of human being' (IG 508).

Thus the decisive bridge had been built in Küng's theology which explains his later commitment to a humane and humanizing theology for theological motives, the direct confrontation of God and human beings. Then in *On Being a Christian* we find the formula under which Küng develops the programme of the 'incarnation of God' broadly and intensively. Jesus' message is understood as God's cause, and his will is none other than 'the human cause' (OBC 249f.)

'From the first to the last page of the Bible, it is clear that God's will aims at human well-being at all levels, definitive and comprehensive good: in biblical terms, at the salvation of all men and women. God's will is a helpful, healing, liberating, saving will. God wills life, joy, freedom, peace, salvation, a final, great human happiness, both of the individual and of all humankind. This is the meaning of God's absolute future, his victory, his kingdom, which Jesus proclaims: the comprehensive liberation, salvation, satisfaction, bliss of humankind. And this radical identification of God's will and human well-being, which Jesus took up from the standpoint of God's closeness, makes it clear that there is no question of putting a new patch on to old clothing or of pouring young wine into old wineskins. Here we are actually faced with something new, and it is going to be dangerous to the old' (OBC 250)

Thus love of God and love of neighbour cannot be separated, and love of neighbour is heightened so that it becomes love of the enemy and partisan support for the disadvantaged. And finally the span – now more concrete and vivid – reaches back to the starting point of Küng's theology: God's will is not the punishment of evil but the justification of the sinner: 'It is God who forgives' (OBC 277).

Thus a formula is arrived at which is open on two sides. Consequently – depending on the situation and the question – it has to be interpreted in two directions. The first is: the distinctive Christian element is none other than Jesus Christ himself. I shall be returning to this. The other is more clearly than ever that the criterion of Christian faith is its humanity. This is the formula which Küng then later extends and understands as a criterion of all religion and religious feeling: the good of human beings and humankind. This formula will serve him as a bridge to dialogue with all religions and – together with other religions – about the world situation and a common ethic, which will further a shared future in questions of peace (GR), economics and politics (GEGP).

Thus it emerges that the commitment to inter-religious dialogue, to the Global Ethic project and the Declaration of the Parliament of the World's Religions are all consequences of the one central line which has constantly moved Küng's theology forward. If today the world is in agony (GE 13), what better work is there for a Christian theologian to do than to join others in seeking ways to help? But why this bias towards the world religions, towards global questions? Certainly there is no question of constructing ideologies here. Küng could also have adopted a different approach. But we must note a final perspective which provides a theological explanation for his universalism. It too was laid down forty years ago. Perhaps he has simply taken it more seriously than others who shared it with him at the time.

(d) A God of all human beings

It has already became clear that Küng has constantly and consistently developed his field of theological interests. Here too the biographical and psychological reasons for this development are only of limited interest. Here too, what is striking is a theological, perhaps even typically Catholic, constant. This is a trend towards universality, grounded in the image of a universal God who always acts as the God of all men and women.

Let us return once more to the question of justification. As we saw, Barth does not treat it in isolation, but grounds it in the whole saving event, i.e. in redemption through Jesus Christ. For Barth, justification is grounded in the 'eternal election by the grace of God in Jesus Christ'. In Christ all humankind is elected; God makes his covenant with it, and this in turn is grounded in creation. Thus not only the covenant of God with human beings, but also the mercy of Jesus Christ which is confirmed in an almost cosmic way in his resurrection, has a 'universal character' (J 23). Barth overcomes any Christian provincialism. Finally he sees the justification of human beings as God's justification of himself; so it is more than just an anthropological question. Everything that happens to each individual is at the same time the concern of all.

This statement is significant for Küng, for one of the problems of the Catholic doctrine of justification was its anthropological narrowness. So in the second part of *Justification* Küng resolutely seeks a christocentric and thus a universal way: 'In christology – and with it in the doctrines of creation and sin – the decisive questions of the doctrine of justification are answered. So these foundations of the doctrine of justification must first be discussed' (J 120). But just as Jesus Christ in his pre-existence stands before the Father 'together with the whole of humankind', so too does the church.

In this connection Küng quotes at length the exegete H. Schlier, who presents the church as 'mystery of Christ'. According to Schlier's exegesis of Ephesians it represents 'essentially a will which antedates everything in the history of this world of ours, transcending even creation. It has fixed the ages in advance to Christ and his salvation . . . And it implies something else besides. The church is *a priori* focussed on the whole of humanity and the human world. It is governed by the mystery of a will of God which embraces and is concerned with heaven and earth' (J 125). Thus the mystery of the church is hidden in creation, which is created in Christ and therefore orientated on salvation. But because the whole creation is to be seen in the light of Christ and with a view to him, salvation is possible for all human beings. Küng would probably no longer follow Schlier's picture of the church today, but as is also evident from *The Church*, he never gave up the notion of this universal determination (or better, universal task) of the church. The topic finally expanded for Küng. That is evident above all from the first excursus in the book, which deals with 'The Redeemer in God's Eternity' (J 272–88). Jesus Christ, born before all time, is the culmination of this momentous work, the content of which Küng would view just as critically today, though he would still maintain its universal perspective. I shall not go in more detail here into the further speculations, the exegetical, patristic and mediaeval patterns of thought. They are not important, and today Küng would probably no longer feel very close to them. The one thing that is clear is that God's action has a universal, almost cosmic, breadth for him.

Creation and redemption are to be distinguished, but in fact all creation has been redeemed. Everything that theology can say about creation and its realization is to be referred to the whole of humankind. Provincialism is ruled out, and world-wide thinking is announced. Thus during the Second Vatican Council Küng saw that precisely here there was an opportunity for the church to become aware of its world-wide dimensions, its ecumenical breadth and its relationship with the world religions. He could not have assented with fewer reservations to any solution other than the solution of *aggiornamento* (i.e. orientation on the present) and the question what task this church has 'in today's world'.

That God is a God of all human beings is given a new range of interpretation in *On Being a Christian* in the light of the cause of Jesus. Now the accent no longer lies on cosmological models which are open to misunderstanding but more (as in *The Church*) on the expectation of God's kingdom and (as we shall see) the fact that in principle Jesus was on the side of the poor. It is from this that *Does God Exist?* derives its broad impact, for here it is now finally clear that God is not just there for Christians, believers or religious men and women, and does not show himself only through revelation and special care. No, because God is a 'God of *all* human beings', it is also possible for all human beings to have access to him, provided that – as will emerge – they seek a last ground of their reality.

This universality is then once again put to the test in the discussion with the world religions. For now it has to be shown that these very different images and symbols of God can be brought into dialogue with one another. We shall be going into that more intensively. This universality not only enriches, but also sometimes imposes a painful yet fruitful restraint on the discussion. Still, it is possible to come to a concrete understanding about the 'God' of all human beings – even with Buddhists. Certainly (against an Indian background) they reject this concept or name unreservedly, but they know a tremendous amount about it, as they approach the unnamed and unnameable (nothingness/Nirvana, the void/Shunyata, the body of teaching/Dharmakaya, the primal Buddha/Adi Buddha) (GE 63). This is done in a language which does not describe that which is to be named in the light of a logical definition, but in the light of human conduct and hope, the universal sphere and a shared responsibility:

'As religious and spiritual persons we base our lives on an Ultimate Reality, and draw spiritual power and hope therefrom, in trust, in prayer or meditation, in word or silence. We have a special responsibility for the welfare of all humanity and care for the planet earth. We do not consider ourselves better than other women and men, but we trust that the ancient wisdom of our religions can point the way for the future' (GE 19).

With the success of this common formulation at the Parliament of the World's Religions (1993), the 'God of *all* human beings', as Küng understands him, has been given a contemporary endorsement. It is as if Küng's biblical vision of this universal God has been confirmed there. So it makes theological sense to him to promote it in international bodies and with the world-wide influence of his books. In UNESCO and the Parliament of the World's Religions, in the religious centres of the world, he successfully finds a hearing for his cause.

Just as at the beginning of his career there is a reference to the creation of the world 'in Jesus Christ' in the language of insiders and specialists, so today Küng is aware of his responsibility for the world as a Christian theologian in the language of our time. What once sounded partly mythical and partly speculative is now transformed into analyses and models for action. At the end of his most recent book, he writes:

'I hope that I have succeeded, as promised, in taking the global ethic project further and demonstrating a realistic vision, pointing towards the future in a global perspective which makes clearer the outlines of a more peaceful, just and human world . . . Both in the sphere of politics and in that of economics we need a new sense of responsibility' (GEGP 277).

The hope expressed here – in the language of Christian tradition – is a consequence of the conviction that this world is not only created in Christ but also reconciled in him. The one important thing is not always to look at the identity of one's own faith but at its responsibility for a better future.

3. What is ecumenical theology?

The concept of ecumenical theology is still a controversial one, and the dispute cannot be resolved here. Küng has always understood ecumenical theology in terms of its task, namely a systematic purging of the theological differences between the Christian churches. That is a task of theology generally, so that ecumenical theology cannot claim a special status. Thus Küng is strictly concerned that solid systematic work should be done, in his case according to the rules and norms of Catholic theology. That applies even after the extension of the term 'ecumene' to its original significance: the whole inhabited world. Now Küng speaks of a theology 'in an ecumenical spirit' (Kuschel 1978, vi). It sees Christian theology all over the world 'confronted with shared questions which it can answer convincingly only together' (ibid). So the content is not laid down in advance and could change. What remains for Küng, apart from the basic rules of Christian theology, is evidently a particular style, an attitude which is governed by the goal of ecumenical theology. *Justification* indicates this. All his life Küng will remain loyal to certain basic ecumenical rules which he adopted in the period of transition between learning theology and becoming a theological teacher. If my view is correct, for Küng an ecumenical theology has three indispensable characteristics.

(a) Theology capable of dialogue

An ecumenical theology is ready for and capable of dialogue. Ecumenical theology is not for individualists but for those who think together. For Küng it does not move in an abstract sphere, so to speak in the contact between the book and its learned reader, but between persons who represent and put forward views and ground them in a particular practice of thought or life. So for Küng theology was and is always a theology which is lived out. Emotions, passions and the art of disputation – which is to be carried out in a disciplined way – find a place in it. Therefore he has always sought dialogue with experts and those in positions of responsibility, and has engaged in it with interested parties. His training provided a good basis for this, since after the Second World War Rome proved to be an extraordinary vital forum for questions, movements and manifold experiments.

This atmosphere returns in *Justification* and in later books. Here is Küng in conversation and argument! From the beginning he insists that he is speaking (only) about essentials, but that he is really speaking about them. He wants 'to prevent a discussion being sought where dispute is unnecessary'. But he also insists on the right to put his question to Barth about Barth's inability even to begin to understand the concern of Catholic theology. Küng will also pursue this principle of focus and directness later. So one can ask of his books: with whom is he in dialogue, what is his concern and what does he want to change?

In a theology of intensive dialogue it is indispensable to ground theological statements and reactions: in the tendency of a theology, in emphases and imbalances in the posing of a problem, and in the life of the community concerned. Some years later Küng would have had more modern categories at his disposal. As we have already seen, he was concerned with no less than a hermeneutical approach: understanding is always a fluctuating process or, as he himself says within the framework of the infallibility debate, statements contain no truth which can be objectively assured. Statements fall short of reality, can be misinterpreted, can be translated only to a limited degree, are prone to ideology and always on the move: 'My language is not mine alone. Language takes place in communication. Language takes place as dialogue' (I 129–32: 131). He was censured for this over the definition of infallibility.

More important, however are the theoretical reflections which Küng presents from *Does God Exist?* onwards, and works out intensively in the 1980s. I mean the adoption of Kuhn's paradigm theory, to which further perspectives are added (TTM 123–226). On Küng's initiative a congress was devoted to the question in 1983. Here Küng is careful not to enter more deeply into the theoretical debate; he is interested in the degree to which the perspectives can be used. In *Christianity* and *Judaism* the paradigm theory then becomes a central model of analysis. It makes it possible to distinguish stages of development within the religions and thus – possibly – to compare them.

But even such considerations remain too abstract for Küng, since he does not rest until he has got clear answers to controversial questions. Let us return to the problems connected with justification. Küng connects two different positions. Certainly, he criticizes Barth loudly and clearly. But another perspective is more important. Though he cannot forecast how a discussion should or indeed may turn out, Küng resolutely adopts a self-critical attitude. He is ready to correct himself. The important thing, as he said at that time, is self-appraisal. I see this readiness for self-appraisal (or self-criticism) as a basic attitude in Küng's thought. It can still best be studied in *Justification*, since it is clearly explained and openly formulated there. Küng is not just a curious theologian, but also one who is eager to learn:

'We had him [Karl Barth] speak, where possible in his own words. We had him review for us his doctrine of justification in its breadth

and depth. We sought to follow him with understanding, to understand him as he understands himself. If we have interrupted him with
some brief questions, it was only to hear and understand him better.
In this way we hope to have arrived at one thing, that is, to have
understood what his questions to Catholic teaching are. Even this is
not altogether easy.' Then follow the important statements: 'It is easy
to understand these questions as reproaches but it is difficult to
understand them as questions. Reproaches invite counter-attack.
Questions invite self-appraisal. We have by now sufficient material
for self-appraisal . . .' (J 89)

Examined closely, in Küng each new approach, each new book, leads to
the programme of this self-appraisal and to a self-criticism which others
have read all too easily as criticism. Here, as we know, Küng is not
afraid of complications. With good reason his own ranks often feel
insecure, rather than the others. Perhaps that is because for Küng this
'self-appraisal' has become far too much second nature. Perhaps, too,
self-criticism asks too much of some people. It is part of the tragedy of
Küng's development that this programme has not been understood.
Küng has explicitly used the principle of 'enquiry' in matters of infallibility. As forecast in *Justification*, the enquiry was understood as an
attack. The response was not self-appraisal but counter-attack.

(b) Theology intent on change

For Küng, an ecumenical theory takes the possibility of changes
seriously. From the beginning he thinks of goals, effects, visions. He sees
his work as a service to the church, to his fellow men and women and
to the future of humankind, and develops a sense of what can be done.
Thus at a very early stage he became a theologian who asked concrete
questions and offered viable solutions. His reflections on justification do
not express an abstract interest but concrete commitment. He wants
nothing less than for the ecumene to take a step forward. This concrete
interest will persist later: in questions of church structure and abuses in
the church, in the discussion of infallibility and papal centralism. Küng
has specific aims when he reflects on the message and fate of Jesus or
analyses the question of God. He wants to help to change positions and
revise standpoints.

So Küng has never been content with abstract answers. The church
must reform itself, and in a new time Jesus must be talked about in a
new way and faith in God thought about in a new way. Attention must

be paid to the world religions, and responsibility to the world must be discovered in concrete terms. As I have said, Küng's theology is a theology which breaks through boundaries. First these were the boundaries between the confessions, soon the boundaries between believers and non-believers, and finally the boundaries between the religions, who are asked once again to speak in harmony on questions of a global ethic.

Küng developed a method for this in *Justification* which later has often been misunderstood. In my view this is the main reason for many later tensions, partisan moves and misunderstandings in discussions with German-language academic theology. Already in his student years in Rome he studied the fusion of power and conviction and at a very early stage developed a feeling for the ideological misuse of theology, for the sometimes corrupting power of influence within the church (and where could that be analysed better than at the centre of a great organization active all over the world?). So nothing could make him more impatient than the suspicion that here interests were being supported, arguments of expediency devised, coalitions forged, and free dialogues steered or prevented. We shall have to go on to discuss how he came to experience this in his own person.

Nevertheless, aims and visions remain the constant motive force behind Küng's theology. He wants to convey them, hence his constant struggle to develop an understandable language. At a very early stage publications appeared like the programmatic *The Council and Reunion*, or letters to young people, *That the World May Believe*. Küng founded the series Theologische Meditationen, to which he made by far the most contributions. The big books *On Being a Christian* and *Does God Exist?* attempt to make the most complicated matters transparent. *Eternal Life?* is an example of a theology which can go into very personal human questions and answer them. Later, short books like *Credo* and *Global Responsibility* became models of a comprehensible theology.

But this comprehensibility is always at the service of particular visions and goals. There is no question that Küng wants to introduce change, or more precisely wants to show from theological perspectives what can be changed, in what direction and for what reasons. Thus he has always kept to his aim of overcoming the split between the churches. He maintains his belief that a fundamental reform of the church can finally bring the period of the Counter-Reformation to an end. He is buoyed up by the vision of a free society of Christian men and women in a reconciled church and still inspired by the vision of a growing understanding between the religions and a new ethical awareness among the religions in the face of the threatening global situation.

(c) Theology responsible for reconciliation

Finally, an ecumenical theology takes responsibility for universal peace and universal reconciliation. We should remember that peace and reconciliation are already striven for in *Justification*. The later intensive concern with questions of the church serves the same purpose. Here Küng always remains a passionate champion of the basic form and basic idea of the Catholic Church. It has preserved the form of a world-wide organization and even today – despite serious problems – can function as the forum of a world dialogue. Therefore Küng has never expressed any doubts even about the idea of the papacy, far less called for its abolition.

But that is not enough. In all the great topics which he discusses, he emphasizes the universal tasks which really fall to the church. That happens in *Justification* where, following Barth, he emphasizes the universality of redemption through Jesus Christ:

'Jesus Christ, in his pre-existence, does not stand alone in the Father's sight. According to the words of Sacred Scripture, he stands before the Father together with the church and, indeed, together with humankind. In God's eternity we human beings, too, were chosen with and in Jesus Christ' (J 124).

The same is also true of God's will to offer his salvation to all humankind:

'This eternal decree has to do with *all* men and women, indeed with the whole world ("heaven and earth"). God accomplishes it, however, . . . in the *church*' (J 125).

Certainly one can also read the last statement – as often happens – in a restrictive way: the church then becomes mistress of the world, as the world becomes dependent on it. Küng's bias develops in the opposite direction. In *The Church*, he shows quite clearly that the church is in the service of the salvation of the world and not vice versa: the church has come into being out of the experience that God's kingdom is now beginning. But it is not itself the kingdom of God.

'Thus the meaning of the church does not reside in itself, in what it is, but in what it is moving towards. It is the reign of God which the church hopes for, bears witness to, proclaims. The church is not the bringer or the bearer of the reign of God which is to come and is at the same time already present, but its voice, its announcer, its herald.

God alone can bring his reign; the church is devoted entirely to its service' (C 96).

Under the heading 'In the service of the reign of God', there then follows a section of several pages which works out this aspect. Jesus' own message must not be forgotten behind the message about Jesus. Thus five 'ecclesiological imperatives' arise out of Jesus' preaching for the church:

1. The church must not become an end in itself in the present;
2. It must not build on its own achievements;
3. It must not understand itself as a religious-political theocracy, but rather as a spiritual diakonia;
4. The church is not there for the pious and just but for the godless and sinners;
5. The church has to do God's will:

'It must not shut itself off from the world in a spirit of asceticism, but live in the everyday world, inspired by the radical obedience of love towards God's will; it must not try to escape from the world, but work in the world' (C 101).

Only in radical obedience can it be truly free, 'free for discipleship in Christ's service to the world' (C 102). With this vision Küng not only hopes that the churches will come closer together but sees that the ways of reconciliation lead through the question of the situation in the world.

Some years of theological upheaval were to follow before Küng extended the concept of ecumenism. In 1967 it was still a matter of clearing up theological differences. In 1978 it was a matter of 'practical clearing up'. Only against this background does the second change, which has already been discussed, become significant. Thus Küng, very much in keeping with ecumenical theology, prepared a breakthrough for himself which was fully worked out three years later. Now the world religions became the main theme of theology. The plan was disclosed with a great gesture in the summer semester of 1981: Küng grounded the new project in the publication of a series of dialogue lectures on Islam, Hinduism and Buddhism. Only around a third of the world population are Christians, and this must be of significance 'on the way to a global ecumenical consciousness':

'Despite all the obvious obstacles and difficulties, we seem to be witnessing for the first time in world history the slow awakening of a global ecumenical consciousness and the beginning of a serious religious dialogue between both leading experts and broad-based representatives. This is possibly one of the most important phenomena of the twentieth century' (CWR xvf.).

That is how those who want to be aware of their own situation must begin dialogue with the religions.

Again the decisive contours of his understanding of theology appear:

'Reciprocal information, reciprocal discussion, and reciprocal transformation. Thus we can slowly arrive not at an uncritical mishmash but at a mutual critical enlightenment, stimulation, penetration, and enrichment of the various religious traditions. This has already been seen in theory and practice, for some time now, between the various confessional traditions in Christianity itself' (CWR xx).

And again the dialectic of religion and the world, the question of the situation in the world, the common future of humankind, returns. The 'global ethic project' makes itself felt:

'No survival without a world ethic. No world peace without peace between the religions. No peace between the religions without dialogue between the religions' (GR xv).

The stages towards this ethic are an analysis of the times, the accumulation of knowledge to provide an anchor which will hold in a time of growing floods of information, and finally a more careful look at the challenges which the religions face today.

Can the religions give answers? Of course Küng cannot presuppose that in theory, nor does he want to do so; first, detailed proof must be given. But his trust in the binding message of the religions generally is as characteristic as his fundamental trust in the Christian message. Küng has subscribed to the vision and realization of an ever more comprehensive reconciliation. He commits himself to the religions reacting in the present situation in a basic and saving way, to the possibility of their reconciliation. Thus ecumenical theology has reached its goal – certainly as far as drawing global boundaries is concerned. Küng is also aware that the programme far transcends the possibility of carrying it out. His ecumenical hope is that it can unleash unsuspected forces.

3

Between Church and Kingdom of God

'Perhaps the reader of these various pieces will be able to sense how strange it felt for me to reread everything that I had written on the subject of church reform over the last two decades. On the one hand I could not quite repress a feeling of melancholy . . .On the other hand I am overjoyed by the realization that my own work for church reform in the light of the present, hopelessly backward-looking course is perhaps better understood now than in earlier years' (RCT 1f.).

These lines come from the preface of a 1990 book with the programmatic title *Reforming the Church Today. Keeping Hope Alive* (RCT). It is a defiant comment, marked by many disappointments. The individual articles, written in different years and for different occasions, show the same resistance to a conservative church regime, the same fighting spirit which seeks to shape a church with a future, the same enthusiasm for the cause of Jesus which should still be the cause of the church, and also the same resoluteness to be ecumenically open and at the same time to stand up for the Catholic Church. A documentation at the end reproduces four declarations from four decades which are concerned with problems arising in crises internal to the Catholic Church. The first two were drafted by Küng. They show that Küng, who works so hard at his desk, keeps standing up for the reform of the church in public – and that he has paid for it. But Küng's reaction to church disciplining after ten years characterizes his whole attitude: 'This book was put together in the tenth anniversary year of the revocation of my permission to teach as a representative of the Catholic church. I feel that this is a particularly important sign. The attempt to silence a critical voice has failed. On the contrary, this book shows my determination – in season, out of season – to continue my way for this church in hope' (RCT 4). Such persistent yet always creative resistance can hardly be explained from a sense of being in the right or even from stubbornness. This chapter will show that – as Küng himself claims – a radical, constant and coherent Christian view of the church underlies his position (RCT 3). For him the church is the 'advocate of the cause of Jesus Christ', no more and no less (RCT 11). That keeps him in the church and also strengthens him in his still loyal opposition. So how has he survived as a theologian now for all of thirty years? To answer that question we must go back forty years.

1. In expectation of the Council

In 1959 John XXIII announced the summoning of an ecumenical council in the Vatican. This 'Second Vatican Council' lasted from 1962 to 1965 and was to be the decisive event of this century for the Catholic Church. The mere announcement of it was a sensation, yet it was as though this was what people had most ardently expected. There was a rapid dissociation from the standstill of the final period of Pius XII, who died in 1958. Plenty of topics for discussion were proposed north of the Alps: reforms within the church (questions of the 'people' and the hierarchy), relations with other Christian churches and other religions (an ecumenical religion and a theology of religions), a new definition of the relationship with the present-day world (its cultural, political and social situation), and finally the great concern that this Council should not emerge as a dogmatizing body, but as a college of pastors, who would enter into the concerns of ordinary people with some understanding: it was to be a 'pastoral council'. Obviously memories of the periods of anti-modernism, of the condemnation of *nouvelle théologie* and of the repeated sanctions against exegetes intensified both the pressure of problems and the expectations. It should, however, be remarked in passing that despite the mood of a new start both inside and outside the church, the 1960s were still a very Eurocentric decade: the questions of other cultures, continents and religions hardly affected awareness of the problems.

Küng seemed very well prepared indeed for this council. His ecumenical thrust was manifestly gaining ground and also attracting attention in other countries. Although he had been intensively engaged in studies of Hegel, he seized the opportunity offered by the Council. After a year as assistant in Münster, in 1960 he was called to Tübingen. *The Council and Reunion* appeared in 1961, and *Structures of the Church* in 1962; *The Living Church* appeared a year after that. The verve and the attitude of expectation in those years can hardly be overestimated. Suddenly much seemed possible; expectations and visions could now become reality. So total commitment was worth while – and for a young man like Küng that was no problem. Of course his first years in Tübingen expanded his horizons still further and increased his pleasure in what was now a hopeful theology. The Barthian E. Diem and Bultmann's pupil Ernst Käsemann became a challenge for him, and colleagues like Jürgen Moltmann and Eberhard Jüngel, and finally Josef Ratzinger, whom Küng so wanted to come to Tübingen, became rivals and discussion partners. For Küng, a theologian intent on making connections (he was first Professor of Fundamental Theology and from 1964 Professor of Dogmatics), this situation meant decisions and choices. He now decided to concentrate his energies on questions of ecumenical theology and ecclesiology. The Institute for Ecumenical Research was founded in the winter semester of 1963/64, and was to be the basis for all Küng's work until his retirement in March 1996.

Ecumenical theology and church reform are very closely connected. Küng joined in the ecumenical dialogue critically and self-critically, in order to advance it in a critical spirit. He first took his bearings from Yves Congar, whom he got to know in Rome and later in Paris, but then went beyond him. More strongly than Congar and other Catholic predecessors, on the eve of the Council – taking advantage of the moment – he introduced self-critical elements. Ecumenical progress first of all called for 'domestic' reform. In the Catholic-Protestant dialogue, that led to the question whether and to what extent the Catholic Church could respond to the questions of the Reformation. Alongside justification and the sacraments, these were primarily questions of church structure. Because the Council was now beginning, impetus and an experience of community could be expected from this event and could prove helpful. The Council began. Küng was there first as an advisor to his local bishop, and then as a *peritus* appointed by the pope.

However, Küng's thought and reactions were more basic and decisive than his colleagues expected. Certainly, he backed the interests of the Council unreservedly, and during the sessions he gave lectures to the Conferences of Bishops in many states. He composed important Council speeches; he advised, did publicity work, and promoted the Council and its vision. Together with Yves Congar, Karl Rahner and Edward Schillebeeckx, he was the founder of the international theological journal *Concilium* which had been proposed by the Dutch publisher Paul Brand. As he says, he has never doubted the significance of this council.

'The reform of the liturgy, the introduction of the vernacular, the new attitude towards the other churches both in theology and in practice, the new relationship with the Jews and the other major religions of the world, and in this context too, in diametrical opposition to previous papal doctrinal statements, the affirmation of freedom of religion and of conscience and, bound up with all this, a new attitude on the part of the church to the world's needs and hopes up to and including atheism, as well as numerous internal church reforms: all this was what made Vatican II an epoch-making turning-point in the history of the church. There can be no going back on it' (HK 167).

However, Paul VI made a few unacceptable decisions after the death of his predecessor in June 1963. Discussion of birth control and celibacy was forbidden; council documents were corrected on 'higher' authority; without reference to the Council he appointed a council of bishops which had no rights of its own. Küng could not bring himself to collaborate in the preparatory commission for the Constitution on the Church, since the first stages did not give any hope of a break-through. Despite general displeasure the chairman was and remained the arch-conservative and unyielding Curia Cardinal Ottaviani, who gained notoriety as President of the 'Holy Office' (formerly the 'Most Holy Inquisition' and today the 'Congregation for the Doctrine of Faith').

Küng did not break solidarity with the Council. But he resolved, so to speak in competition with the planned conciliar document, to write his own book on the church. This decision testifies to his self-confidence, but also to his resolve to go the whole way theologically. He wanted to present a scheme which corresponded to the discussion on exegesis, the history of the church and its dogma, and ecumenism. The title of the book is a brief one, to which nothing needs to be added, but from which nothing can be removed: *The Church*. In it Küng makes a comprehensive statement about his understanding of the church and of ecumenism (which is Catholic and at the same time ecumenical), and of how Christian faith is to be lived out. Again some basic features which govern his later theology become clear.

2. *The Church:* what is it about?

What is this 600-page book about? Like *Justification*, *The Church* is systematically comprehensive and is meant to be complete. As in *Justification*, Küng goes further than the topic at first seems to require. In a first part (C 3–39) ideal and reality are compared, now under the categories of historicity and brokenness. Here again the aim is to provide room for critical and self-critical reflection. It is important to overcome static notions of the church and to take account of the twofold experience which still stamps Christians in the church and under which they sometimes suffer: admiration and criticism; sober analysis and a core worth believing in.

The second part (C 43–104) indicates the main perspectives in which this confrontation is to be interpreted. The problem is not (primarily) one of moral failure or achievement, but a fundamental tension which arises out of the history of the church's origin. Instead of a clear myth about when and how Jesus founded the church, theology has to learn to understand how the church developed out of the proclamation and the fate of Jesus. He laid the foundations (preached and brought people together), but only after Easter is there a church which is to be understood completely as a 'divine institution'. Thus in its origin the church is not simply grounded in the purpose and command of Jesus (the pre-Easter Jesus, as he tended to be called), but

> 'in the whole Christ event: that is, in the entire action of God in Jesus Christ, from Jesus' birth, his ministry and the calling of the disciples, to his death and resurrection and the gift of the Spirit to the witnesses of his resurrection. It was not just the words and instructions of Jesus before Easter, but God's will in raising the crucified Christ and giving the Spirit in the end time that turned the group of those who believed communally in the risen Jesus into a community which, in contrast to the unbelieving ancient people of God, could claim to be the new eschatological people of God . . . It was not any particular words of Jesus, nor ultimately his teachings, but his person as the hidden Messiah and as the risen Christ, which historically speaking constitutes the roots of the church' (C 76).

This gets over the church's usual static view of itself, since now it enters completely into the dynamic of the original event, which is not focussed on the church but on the kingdom of God. The church is neither from nor for itself, as the ecclesiological imperatives described above illustrate (see above, 61f.). It is a church which understands itself as discipleship of Christ. The notion of justification has stamped this picture of the church. However, the christocentric tone has fundamentally changed. Whereas *Justification* spoke of the pre-existent Christ, we now hear of the 'pre-Easter and post-Easter Jesus'. We shall be discussing this in Chapter 5. Thus beyond question Küng has critical reservations about talk of the church, which will be developed later.

Only now, after more than 100 pages of preliminaries, does ecclesiology in the classic theological sense begin. It follows a classical scheme. The 'Fundamental Structure of the Church' is discussed (Part 3, C 107–260). The key terms here are 'people of God', 'creation of the Spirit' and 'body of Christ'. The classical marks of the church are also discussed (Part 4, 263–359), here interpreted as its 'dimensions': the one, catholic, holy and apostolic church. Only after all these elementary, decisive and fundamental statements have been made, i.e. after almost 400 pages, does Küng come to speak of the 'services' of the church (Part 5, 363–480). Here first of all the priesthood of all believers is discussed (C 363–387), and then the church's service of leadership (C 388–443); only then in last place do we have just under forty pages on 'The Petrine power and the Petrine ministry' (C 444–480). Is this a climax or a relativization? Küng senses that readers may be irritated: 'Readers who begin reading at this point are making a mistake' (C 444). We must not misunderstand the author of this Catholic book on the church. He is not concerned with trivial relativization. It is not as if the papacy is unimportant to him, as if it comes last and is a negligible factor. Rather, if one is to be systematic, everything else has to be discussed before this profound structural question, which is complex enough in itself and becomes even more so in ecumenical dialogue. How else can fixations and over-hasty solutions to the one problematical issue for ecumenism be avoided?

So far Küng has been described as a theologian who does not rush things, who is not concerned with revolutionary innovations but with connections. So the structure of the book is important. Some readers think that the second part, about the preaching of Jesus and the kingdom of God, is superfluous, an entertaining prelude. They have not understood much. This is the part which provides the continuity and the background, the new presuppositions and perspectives which put all ecclesiology on new foundations, in a new context of understanding. So this is the most important and most necessary part.

The Church is thirty years old. In the meantime a tremendous amount has been written about the church, directly and indirectly, with a theoretical and practical intent, motivated by enthusiasm and disappointment, sympathy and an aversion to the ecumenical movement. Ecclesiology has proved to be the most complex and most misused theme of everyday theology. Amazingly – for all the flood of literature – there have been only a few attempts to depict the church not only in depth but as an overall topic, using knowledge and understanding. That is now more necessary than ever. So Küng's book is still significant, not only in its approach but also in its execution. In my opinion there is no other book which includes so much material, assembles and analyses so many historical facts, discusses and weighs up so many arguments against one another. Some historical surveys, systematic development of problems and use of exegetical material are still models in an area which often overflows, becomes fluid on the periphery and is treated emotionally.

Nor do I know any book on the question of the church in which so many cross-connections are taken up and worked out, individual topics are put in context and material for discussion is prepared: whether this is the historical and systematic question of the Jews, the 'enthusiasts' or the 'heretics', or contemporary basic questions about the local community, charisma or sacrament, lay preaching, the depictions of the pope in history or concepts of ecumenical union. The need for salvation and inner renewal of the church are discussed, along with its apostolicity, discipleship and ministry.

Of course today the book needs to be revised where scholarship has moved on, where the discussion has become more complex and where Küng himself has developed positions. This would also be important because – alongside the developments brought by contextual and emancipatory theologies – the Second Vatican Council still serves as the great point of reference for developments within the church. Only a Third Vatican Council could extend this point with comparable authority. But to the present day, Küng's ecclesiology has remained a great success as an ecclesiology which is emancipatory, aware of freedom, critical, ecumenically open and – above all – biblically inspired. I shall bring this out in more detail in discussing individual topics.

3. The great themes

It would be difficult to present the whole content of Küng's ecclesiology, nor is that my task. As in the previous chapter, a few key points must suffice. They are: discipleship of Jesus, a community of free men and women, ecumenical openness and a relativizing of ministries.

(a) Discipleship of Jesus

Probably no theologian will dispute that the community of believers called 'church' in the Christian tradition is grounded in the gift and the praxis of discipleship of Jesus. The debate is as to whether this is the first or only, a sufficient, or merely a secondary definition of what discipleship of Jesus means. Let us begin with the last point: Küng will later describe discipleship as accepting the message and practice of Jesus, as relying on Jesus as the normative one in whom God's will becomes manifest to us. At the same time he is ultimately not dependent on such definitions, because this discipleship is described in detail, figuratively, concretely and in many shades in the Gospels. The Gospels describe the way which women and men take in company with Jesus. They have to endure dangers and overcome misunderstandings. Finally they are led into situations in which the question arises what their life is worth – in respect of Jesus' cause. The church as a community of discipleship leads to a very dynamic and historical picture of the church.

Reality, historicity and brokenness are therefore the great key words under which Küng introduces the theme. The analysis of essence or ideal structure, constitution beyond time or divine presence, does not go far enough. At the same time Küng makes it clear from the beginning that all analysis, admiration or criticism will always remain embedded in a dialectic of success and failure. There will always be an abiding precious nucleus (which obviously can only be narrated) and a complex, manifold reality which cannot be summed up.

However, another point is decisive for Küng, which has still to be discussed at a methodological level. Here there is a repetition of the structure of *Justification*. The church is not a self-sufficient entity related to itself, an end in itself, a system which rests in itself and is even autonomous. Its origin, its purpose for existing and its goal are always present. Therefore there is no sense in working out a self-contained theory of the church as its own fulfilment, even a closed system of the kingdom of God. If one wants to understand what the church has to be about it is enough to understand what Jesus proclaimed, did and suffered. This approach could be said to be essentially Protestant. But Küng would rightly object, since he regards discipleship in the church as unconditionally possible and necessary. He does not feel that this way of talking leads him into a self-righteous way of thinking in terms of achievement. The church is more than a 'creature of the word', i.e. fully sacramental, with sacramentality legitimated in its ministry. Moreover, as we saw, Barth's christocentricity has already offered him a way of reconciling the traditional oppositions.

Now this mediation is extended in a surprising way, which finally brings liberation from the problematical arguments about the classic doctrine of justification. Of course the Christian way of life remains fully related to Jesus Christ and made possible by him. However, the mediation no longer takes place in an abstract sphere, in a timeless action of the pre-existent Christ, but in discipleship of Jesus of Nazareth. With the notion of discipleship Küng now ties the church to the preaching and practice of Jesus. The church must make Jesus present; that is what it is to be measured by. This idea is of fundamental significance for Küng's picture of the church, since in the light of it he can shed critical light on the reality of the church, without falling into a bottomless pit.

Therefore for Küng the right and future of the church are not in question and never were, because for him the idea of discipleship is always a realistic, practical idea which points forward to the future. Above all the recollection of Jesus of Nazareth is an impregnable bastion for him, from which he can openly criticize the structure and function of the church's ministries. In the light of the notion of discipleship he can find a foundation for the apostolicity of the bishops in the apostolicity of the church – and relativize it. Discipleship becomes specific for all individuals, depending on their task and the ministry that they perform inside or outside the church, in the service of others and in the service of the community. For Küng, that clearly follows from Paul's doctrine of charismas. Therefore for him successful discipleship of Jesus is always also discipleship in the Spirit.

What applies to the church as a whole, to all those who hold office in it and to all its actions, also applies without qualification to each individual, including the pope. Discipleship is a democratic and democratizing idea, and in the face of the constrictions of church law also a liberating idea:

'The decisive thing is succession in the Spirit: in the Petrine mission and task, in the Petrine witness and ministry. So if someone could prove conclusively that his predecessor and the predecessor of his predecessor and so on backwards were ultimately successors of the one Peter, indeed even if he could prove that the predecessor of all his predecessors had been "appointed" Peter's successor by Peter himself with all rights and duties, yet completely failed to fulfil this Petrine mission, if he did not carry out the task entrusted to him, if he did not give witness or perform his ministry, what use would the whole "apostolic succession" be to him and the church? Conversely, if there were someone whose succession, at least in the earliest years, were difficult to establish, whose "appointment" two thousand years ago was not even documented, but who fulfilled the Petrine mission as described in scripture and performed this ministry for the church, would it not be a secondary, albeit important, question whether the genealogy of this real servant of the church was regular? He might not perhaps have a call through the laying-on of hands, but he would have the charism, the charism of governing, and basically that would be enough' (C 463).

The exegetical arguments open up an amazingly large scope for this Petrine ministry, and of course the pre-understanding and expectation of a theologian are directly involved in its interpretation. For Küng, its ecumenical task is of central importance. So he gets to the decisive question. This indicates no superficial criticism of the pope but zeal for an ecumenically renewed church:

'It is an absurd situation that the Petrine ministry, which is intended, as Catholics in particular see it, to be a rock-like, a pastoral ministry, preserving and strengthening the unity of the church, should have become a gigantic, apparently immovable, insuperable and impassable barrier of rock blocking the way to mutual understanding between the Christian churches. Those who are convinced of the value of a Petrine ministry should be particularly taxed by this situation' (C 465).

What is important here is not the criticism of the pope; it would be nonsense to reduce all this to a 'feeling of hostility against Rome'. It is important to recognize that the notion of discipleship also offers a concrete criterion for this sensitive case in ecumenical ecclesiology. It makes possible a direction, criticism, and the shaping of a vision which in the biblical tradition is called 'kingdom of God'. The church as a community of discipleship is a theme which will always accompany Küng. 'Discipleship' not only emerges as the great theoretical battle cry and formula for life but also appears in Küng's constant reference to the picture of Jesus, as a matter of course and without thinking about it. Küng asks whether Jesus would have done this or that, what he would have done here or there. We know from literature how important this question is for the Grand Inquisitors.

(b) A community of free men and women

In many respects the structure of Küng's ecclesiology can be called conservative; in fact the biblical origins are discussed time and again. But his perspective is completely modern. The emphasis on the freedom of

Christians is striking. Küng opens the chapter on the church as the 'creation of the spirit' (C II) with Nietzsche.

'They would have to sing better songs to make me believe in their Redeemer; his disciples would have to look more redeemed! . . .Truly their Redeemers themselves did not come from freedom and the seventh heaven of freedom' (C 150).

Küng uses this expectation of freedom as a criterion for his reflections. For him, freedom is primarily a Pauline concept with a theological background. It has to be deciphered dialectically, because it is not exhausted in political, social or intellectual freedom. Küng is anxious that middle-class respectability should not over-hastily commandeer the concept. Following Paul, it is freedom from inner threat and the law of sin; it is freedom proved in life, suffering and dying (C 161); put positively, it is the freedom to rely completely on the one ground which only freedom can give and ensure. But:

'Love is the core of this freedom. In the love in which faith becomes effective (Gal. 5.6), in which the differences between circumcision and uncircumcision are removed, the master becomes a slave and the slave a master, independence becomes obligation and obligation independence. To be open to others, to exist for others, to live in self-less love, is the way to realize freedom: "For you were called to freedom, brothers and sisters; only do not use your freedom as an opportunity for the flesh, but serve one another through *love*" ' (C 156).

This quotation from Paul reminds us that not all questions are settled with such solemn freedom, neither those of the patriarchate nor those relating to the body. But Küng commits himself to his vision and he will work on it all his life. Yves Congar rightly understands Küng's books as a 'sensational return of Paulinism into Catholic thought' (DisK 161).

But we do not end prematurely in solemn statements. The next section – apparently – embarks on another theme. It is now about the 'church of the Spirit' (C 162–79). 'Where there is the Spirit of the Lord, there is freedom' (II Cor. 3.17). Now if the church is understood at the same time as a 'structure of the Spirit', it will have to be measured by its experience of freedom. Küng promises the church a 'continuing charismatic structure' (C 179–91). As Congar has rightly seen, that means a basic shift of accent. Discipleship is not our achievement; rather, everything it comprises, everything that happens in the community and for its well-being, is God's gift. Paul calls it 'charisma'. Küng draws his conclusions with a reference to him.

'Charisms are everyday rather than primarily exceptional phenomena; they are various rather than uniform, and they are found throughout the church rather than being restricted to a particular group of people. These conclusions lead to others: that charisms are phenomena not exclusive to that time (possible and real in the early church), but very much present and relevant; and not just peripheral, but central and essential. In this sense one can speak of a charismatic structure of the church, which includes the hierarchical structure of the church but goes far beyond it. The theological and practical implications of this are evident' (C 188).

So this Spirit is omnipresent. The Spirit ensures that neither human beings nor events can be controlled, just as the Spirit itself remains outside our control. Just as according to Küng's view all the structures and dimensions discussed interpenetrate one another and lead to a complex totality, so this charismatic structure (i.e. this enabling of freedom and this appeal to freedom) is omnipresent. The charisma becomes a signature of Christian life-style, Christian creativity and inner multiplicity. It is obvious that such a comprehensive vision of freedom cannot stop here if it is applied to a community and the regulation of its structures. Küng himself will work to make sure that this history of freedom and its problems is yet further realized and radicalized in the present. The structure of the church, too, will never come to its end.

Küng has interpreted the 'church of the Spirit' in the light of the idea of Christian humanity. For him the 'community of free men and women' later means a community in which human well-being comes about and which is itself a whole community. This notion too will be continued later in other words.

(c) Multiplicity within, reconciliation with outsiders

As is known to those who took part in it, the Council did not open its Constitution on the Church – after long and thorough discussion – with a chapter on the hierarchy but with a chapter on the people of God. Küng would not have been a defender of this council had he not arranged his book in comparable way. The church is a people of Jews and Gentiles (C 120); the whole community is elect, priestly and holy.

Thus war is declared on any clericalization, and any privatization of Christianity which hypostatizes and idealizes the community of God is excluded. Nevertheless it is striking that in a departure from the tradition and in complete contrast to neo-scholastic ecclesiology, the chapter on 'The Church as the Body of Christ' (C III) is put after the chapter on spirit and freedom that we have discussed.

Again the arrangement is a programme, for only now, after a reflection on the challenge of discipleship, a discussion of our origin from Jews and Gentiles, and a defence of the vision of freedom, is our unity in Christ mentioned. All are baptized in the name of Christ, so all are identified before him and – publicly – put under an obligation: 'There is neither Jew nor Greek, there is neither slave nor free, there is neither man nor woman; for you are all one [!] in Christ Jesus' (Gal. 3.28). Only against this background can we assess why union in a shared meal draws on such a crude symbolism of flesh and blood, why it expresses the boundless extent of Christian and church unity precisely in this way.

Küng discusses the question of the eucharist, not without explicitly defending its central position in the Catholic understanding of the church. But he also shows the problems of the mediaeval Catholic interpretation. There is no mistaking his reservations about any sacramentalistic and monistic view. The beginnings of what we hear later in the theory of a pluralistic and decentralized church are presented here. Baptism stands in a conditional relationship to faith and its public proclamation (C 207–9). Thus 'faith, as an act of radical human self-offering and trusting acceptance of grace, is a *condition* of baptism'. So magical objectivism is excluded. According to the Letter to the Hebrews the sacrifice on the cross has been made once and for all and therefore cannot be repeated (C 215); thus an important piece of the fabric of the traditional Catholic understanding of the mass is removed. Finally, in the sacramental presence of Christ – in accordance with a Reformation concern – the aspect of the spiritual and the personal presence must not be overlooked (C 221).

Thus the symbol of the 'body of Christ' must not be exhausted in a sacramental-magical notion. Basing himself on the New Testament, Küng makes use of personal categories of decision, faith, memory, community and hope. Here too the notion of the risen Christ has an effect. Christians recall him in worship and in the practice of discipleship. Therefore in the eucharist the dimensions of time interlock: the past (memory), the present (community) and the future (messianic time). It is important that Jesus is present here and now in the spirit of discipleship, and it is important to see that without this spirit the question of Christ's presence becomes superfluous. Against this background, 'It is in the body of Christ, the church, that the area is indicated in which the blessing and the dominion of this death is and remains efficacious' (C 226).

We should not fail to notice that the sacramental aspects of Küng's scheme are still fluid. He introduces personal categories and thus puts the crude language of the tradition in question. This process is already well advanced in the analysis of baptism (C 206f.), but the crude symbols of body and blood still bear a weight which Küng today – in view of his knowledge of the religions – would probably explain in much more detail and put in an anthropological setting. Küng's strength lies in the sociological treatment of metaphor: 'body of Christ' also means the community in its unity, in its dialectic of individual community and community association, of a unity and multiplicity of views, of the inclusion of the united members of the community and the exclusion of those others who do not (yet) belong to the community celebrating the meal. Küng indicates clear emphases here. Three perspectives may be singled out.

The first is that the body of the Christ is not (just) the church as a whole but every local community. That is where the metaphor begins: when Paul speaks of the body of Christ he means unity within it (I Cor. 12; Rom.12). Küng pleads for the matter-of-fact and realistic look not to be lost:

> 'The community is included in the destiny and the way of Christ, just as tribe and people were included in the destiny and the way of the tribal ancestor. The connection between Christ and the church as his body is not a physical and substantial one, as in Gnosticism, nor a symbolic and metaphorical relationship, as the Stoics would have understood it, but an actual historical relationship in the Old Testament sense' (C 230).

Thus the use of this symbolism must be rethought. A monolithic exegesis is not backed up by the New Testament; even in Colossians and Ephesians the aspects shift, and 'the doctrine of justification, eschatology and anthropology, seem to be neglected' (C 230). This notion of the rights of the local community, also accepted by the Council but not expressed clearly, which is here backed up by exegesis, has meanwhile come to be widely accepted, though it is regarded with mistrust by Rome. According to Küng, the church of Christ is 'not a centralized egalitarian or totalitarian monolith' (C 275). He calls for multiplicity in worship, multiplicity in theology, multiplicity in church order. He cannot see anything wrong with the multiplicity of churches in itself, since unity presupposes multiplicity, 'a common life shared by all the local churches' (C 274). Such a programme is often discussed today under the watchwords of a decentralized or polycentric church. Küng is not exactly fond of neologisms, but he has always supported the concerns of contextual theologies, whether in Latin America, Africa or Asia. Just as important to him remains the concern that the churches of the different cultures, continents, countries and localities should preserve their due freedom, including the right for women to make their due and imaginative contribution in and from the local community without being discriminated against.

The second perspective, which is illuminated in a section of twenty pages, is on 'the church and heresy' (241–60). Küng argues that the fixation on doctrine, the addiction to a simplicity that can be controlled, and impatience with those who think against the grain or dissent, must finally be altered. What he says made many readers at that time prick up their ears: 'Only great men have produced heresies' (C 245). The elements of truth in heresy must be noted, as must the elements of error in truth, and love must also be given its due in questions of faith. In view of the tragedies involving heretics from Priscillian to the present system of denunciation (this too is vividly summed up by Küng, long before Deschner's *Criminal History,* and to the disapproval of some bishops), Küng here is simply pleading for a humane and friendly, understanding way of dealing with one another. What is important is hearing and understanding, a capacity for communication and differentiation. One does not have to be a theologian to do this, but there are theological reasons for it.

A third perspective which follows here is ecumenical friendship. It is clear that the union of the churches is Küng's great concern and the great demand of the hour. The whole of *The Church* is written with a view to the reunion of the churches. That becomes clear in the question of ministry and the sacraments, the universal priesthood and the significance of scripture, the apostolic succession and the marks of the church. Everywhere omissions are mentioned, obstacles removed and one-sided positions corrected: time and again scripture is examined and reference is made to the one origin in Jesus Christ and the Spirit. One can read the whole book as a great plea for the reunion of the church, i.e. as an attempt to remove the stumbling blocks which the churches have themselves erected. 'The question of God is more important than the question of the church; but the latter often stands in the way of the former. This ought not to be the case' (C xiii).

Finally, Küng has presented his own position under the heading 'Reunion of the churches' (C 276–96). He argues historically in order to work through the mistakes of the past. He argues biblically, in order to find incorruptible criteria for a new unity. Lastly, he mentions principles which determine future action. Over wide areas today these principles seem like a confirmation of the ecumenical reconciliation that has meanwhile come about. Over wide areas they have a sad ring, because the horizon of Küng's own church has hardly expanded – especially in questions of ministry and the papacy. Küng's fourth principle is: 'Truth must not be sacrificed, but rediscovered' (C 289). In his view, this happens in discussion with one another and in the awareness that the guise of faith can sometimes change (C 290). If only the Catholic Church could struggle through to such a relaxed and ecumenically friendly attitude!

(d) Ministry as service

What appears here as the last perspective is usually understood to be the first and only point in Küng's reform programme. That is a pity, because it conceals his theological motivation and gets the question of ministry bogged down in the question of power and being in the right. We must be quite clear about this. Küng makes no secret of the fact that the problem of ministries is bound up with questions of power, and he is realistic enough also to understand functions of church leadership as the exercise of power. But it is his resolute concern to break up this thinking about belief in God and discipleship of Jesus in terms of power. Here he is motivated by the biblical message and the experience of history, and also by the requirements of humanity. Despite the complex situation, Küng has arrived at a simple and plausible standpoint which can easily be reached. So it can be summed up quickly.

The starting point, which is virtually a formal principle of Küng's thought, is the unconditional priority of God's action – the fact that it is impossible to keep up with this action, in other words its mystery and greatness. Hence the unconditional priority of what Jesus means to those who follow him. This priority shows itself not only in faith as unconditional trust in God but also in the experience of human freedom, over which none of us has control, but which can be given to all of us. *All* members of the community enjoy the favour of the Spirit; they are endowed with the Spirit (in an elementary and primary sense) and 'priestly', and they all stand in continuity with the Christian message of the apostles, and are therefore (in an elementary and primary sense) 'apostolic'. What is meant here is the ministry of leading the community at a local, regional or universal level, regardless of whether the structure of the community is presbyteral or episcopal or cannot be defined further. Here, for reasons of church unity, Küng argues for the preservation of the episcopal-catholic, i.e. also sacramentally grounded, structure – right up to the Petrine ministry, which is rooted in the Bible. So if – in whatever sense – endowment with the Spirit, priestly authority and apostolic tasks are a mark of leadership of the community, the result is a twofold determination of those who hold office in the church.

First, as those who in the church community believe in God and follow Jesus Christ along with others, church leaders have no advantage over others. They merely perform functions of which in principle all men and women are capable (just as every Christian can, for example, baptize); with permission from the community they can preside at the eucharist, forgive sins in the name of God and speak for the community.

Secondly, as those who have been given a task of leadership by their community, they must and may carry out this task on their own responsibility and at the same time in the name of the charge that they have been given. At all events the priority of the community must be made clear, the proclamation of the word of God must be possible, and there must be agreement with the original message, so that there can be dialogue with the church. The most important criterion is the ministry which is in fact performed:

'Just as the church is a fellowship of gifts of the spirit, so it is also a fellowship of different ministries. Charisma and diakonia are correlative concepts. Diakonia is rooted in charisma, since every diakonia in the church presupposes the call of God' (C 393f.)

I need not go into particular ministries in this context. The same conditions hold for the papacy as for pastors or bishops. Küng has never emerged as an iconoclast. He pleads for a strong but clearly controlled papacy. Privileges which limit the church's freedom and right to speak within the framework mentioned are neither legitimate nor supported by the New Testament. This also applies to the qualities bestowed by priestly ordination or episcopal consecration. The only relevant question here is whether – to use Karl Barth's words – people hear from the mouth of the person in office 'the voice of the Good Shepherd'. It is already amazing that what one might have thought to be a balanced, ecumenically acceptable and unspectacular conception should have come up against so much resistance.

4. Catholic theology?

The Church appeared shortly after the Council, in a phase of great openness and reorientation in Catholic theology. Neo-scholasticism was thought finally to have been overcome. People studied the Council documents, discovered the history of their own theology and – we should not forget – learned from Protestant theology. There was an abundance of material; what was sought was an orientation. Great shifts took place in Protestantism: from Karl Barth through existentialist interpretation to a theology of social responsibility. Küng took note of the new developments, but consistently pursued his programme of a new ecumenical theology. How could the renewal of the Catholic Church be encouraged and what would be the shape of a new, ecumenical, useful theology (i.e. one extending beyond the limits of one's own church)? The question of (the further development of) Küng's theological method is therefore also extremely interesting.

If I am right, *The Church* represents an important deepening of this method for three reasons. In it Küng develops a theology which is inspired by the Bible, instructed by history and related to the present. Inspiration through scripture, instruction by history and responsibility to the present are three aspects which any theology that recognizes its responsibility to hermeneutics and to its context has to respect. However, at that time these terms were not yet in vogue, and even later Küng did not simply adopt them. Still, let us approach the issue by means of the three perspectives.

(a) Inspiration through scripture

Küng learned this once for all from Karl Barth: Christian theology can only come forward with a claim and authority if it relates itself to scripture. Here it is well known (but often forgotten) that the ways by which this relationship is established differ. So the question is: precisely what does Küng do with scripture?

In *Justification*, Küng adopts an elementary approach, given to him by Barth and many other colleagues, which is also not unknown to Catholic theology. Statements from scripture are taken up, interpreted and compared with others. Acceptable and convincing interpretations arise out of the overall context. Here historical criticism is not necessarily brought into play, but a kind of biblical theology which arises out of the synthesis of biblical statements. They are appropriated within later tradition in trust that the results will be convincing, understandable and explicable then and now. At all events, it is decisive that a hermeneutical relationship comes into being between here and now which does not impose on any statements and does not degrade scripture into a quarry for proof texts, but makes it possible to discover and appropriate meaning. In *Justification* Küng assumed responsibility for this task, which was not always taken for granted in Catholic theology. In *The Church* the method has changed. Küng writes:

> 'I have tried to allow the original Christian message to dictate the themes, perspectives and balance of the book, so that the original church may light the way once more for the church of today. Taking this starting-point has certain consequences, the justification for which can only be found in the origins of the church. Those who have doubts about this method may care to recall that it is the one which is expected of post-conciliar theology: "Dogmatic theology should be so constructed that the biblical themes are presented first; from this starting-point it should then pass through historical research to a systematic penetration of the mysteries of salvation" (Decree on Priestly Formation 16)' (C xiii).

But what makes this general programme possible? Is it already the basis for methodological decisions? Fatefully, there was hardly any reflection on this in Catholic theology. I can see three ways in which Küng approaches scripture.

(i) Results of historical-critical exegesis

First, Küng takes over the results of historical-critical exegesis. He investigates scripture in terms of what happened, what scripture bears witness to and what it recalls – working through interpretations, conjectures and errors. This exegesis becomes clear in *The Church* above all in two groups of themes. The first is the preaching and activity of Jesus, the second the origin and significance of the church.

Thus Küng first of all presents an in-depth picture of Jesus of Nazareth, the content of his preaching, and its consequences in his death and resurrection. It is important for systematic theologians not to intervene at this point, or at any rate not to get down to interpretation over-hastily, but to let the texts speak through scholarly exegesis of them. Systematic theologians must take historical criticism seriously, describe it, and only then attempt to draw their conclusions.

The same thing happens in the second group of themes. Küng sums up current exegetical literature, emphasizes particular points, and draws conclusions. Of course in both cases his evidence is second-hand, but he can compare different results, discover agreements and judge the academic competence of his colleagues. Here disciplined exegesis, matter-of-fact historical work and a critical eye for systematic speculation pay dividends, and the consequences for discipleship and ecclesiology have the firmest possible foundations. If I am right, this method, which is so comprehensive and applied with such consistency, was new in the sphere of Catholic theology: one wishes that some of the great speculative theologians had used it. It leads back to the beginning of Christian faith, to which it owes its own inalienable authority – not because the beginning must be better than the consequences, but because no one can go back behind the beginning. In the specific case of a church interpreted as discipleship it leads back to the recollection of the one whom the church claims to follow.

Küng has remained faithful to scripture (interpreted in a scholarly way) as the great inspiration of his theological creativity. A knowledge of the state of the discipline was always important for him and has remained so: in this respect *The Church* was as unassailable as *On Being a Christian* (1967), *Christianity* (1994) and other later works, down to *Credo* (1993) and the discussion with other religions (1984, 1988). In his discussion of Judaism (J 1991) he extended this study systematically to the Hebrew Bible.

Thus Küng (alongside Edward Schilllebeeckx) counts among the systematic theologians of his generation best versed in exegesis. His capacity to sum up the often complex results of scholarship and relate them to systematic questions is the decisive reason why he can hardly be attacked from the exegetical side – and this is also true of his later works. Certainly questions have always remained, and scholarly work progresses. But even that has hardly refuted Küng so far, but rather has endorsed him on central points (e.g. Chr 83–105). Küng's theological work shows what pioneering results historical criticism can produce if it is listened to, taken seriously and thought out (in support or in criticism of dogma) by systematic theologians. In the long term, Christian theology will find that fear of historical criticism does not pay. Had Catholic theology only learned that from Küng, it could look to the future with confidence.

(ii) Conclusions from exegesis

Secondly, Küng draws conclusions for systematic theology from exegesis. In his own field he argues on the basis of scholarly exegetical insights. On closer inspection, this is a normal type of theological argument; the results of exegesis become contextual: they serve an aim, support or weaken an assertion. Usually they do so implicitly. In that case it is the duty of exegetes to intervene and to see that their work is applied legitimately (which happens all too rarely). But sometimes the argument must and should be explicit. Küng gives good examples of this in *The Church*; one might take the various structures of ministry (from charismatic structures to the monarchical episcopate) or the concept of apostolicity.

In these cases the New Testament does not give clear but multiple answers, by showing the development of several possibilities. Is multiplicity an argument? In that case, which conception is to be followed? The first? The last? Or do we have to go our own way? To arrive at answers which relate both to the subject-matter and the situation of our time, here Küng works above all along the lines of present-day liberalism: where scripture offers conflicting answers, it simply cannot be forced to give an answer – assuming that the arguments remain the same. Arguments about misuse or about what actually happened do not get us any further. Though, for example, freedom within the church has continually led to chaos, that does not mean that it must be suppressed, just as a monolithic structure may have remained the same only because so far it has been victorious (C 423–6). Therefore for Küng: 'This ministry, as far as one can see from the New Testament, was exercised in many different forms' (C 428). This plurality now compels us to rethink, to argue and to relativize all regulations.

Of course we must then reflect on the difference between then and now, the original phase and the following period:

'The church saw itself, contrary to its expectations, obliged to reckon with a long period of existence and saw the gap which separated it in time from its origins, from the historical Jesus Christ, its crucified and risen Lord, continually growing. True, the Lord remained with it as the exalted one in the Spirit. But in order to remain with him, the church was directed towards the original witness of those who guaranteed it, the apostles. There came a time when one after the other these original witnesses died; the original testimony could no longer be directly heard.'

Thus holding fast to the original apostolic testimony became tremen-dously important, and this included 'the special commissioning of ministries intended to preserve the original apostolic testimony' (C 425).

This new situation, the insight into the limits of biblicistic references to the past, leads Küng to one of the most complex arguments in the book. It produces an understanding of ministry which has been able to hold its own in the forums of professional exegetes and historians and of ecumenical dialogue to the present day, which is precisely what Küng critically and self-critically wanted. 'The church of the present must face up to the history of its origins in the matter of church constitution as well. In order to ensure continuity it must take note of the gulf which separates it from its origins, without fuss but perhaps a little ashamed' (C 417). Thus recourse to scripture shows not only what the criteria but also what the freedoms and possibilities are. Other examples could be added.

This kind of argumentation seems to me to be even stronger in *On Being a Christian*, which must be regarded as the result of long and extensive exegetical studies. Küng was not naive in writing this book – after grappling with questions of ministry, the papacy and infallibility. He knew that central statements of Christianity were at stake, zealously guarded not only by the Catholic magisterium but also by other churches and by many Christians of all confessions: divine Son-ship, the pre-existence and divinity of Jesus, Mariology, questions of the Trinity. These are not subjects for intelligent conjectures, but require careful, responsible thought which has made thorough checks.

In *On Being a Christian* Küng introduces readers to the problems: to the nature and character of the New Testament witnesses to the faith, which are 'engaged and engaging'. He asks what kind of certainty history can give. He judges the Jesus tradition to be 'relatively reliable':

'The transformations, developments and oppositions in the New Testament tradition prohibit the convenient assumption that Jesus himself or the Holy Spirit made provision for an exact retention and transmission of his words and deeds. We must always allow for changes of perspective and shifts of emphasis, growth and regression, disclosures and concealments, within these traditions' (OBC 157; 145–65).

He points out that theology (even a biblical theology) cannot replace faith. Only then does the most intensive exegetical work begin, and in part it is hard labour. In it, Jesus' message, fate and life-style are worked out in relation to theological questions (OBC 175–342). And because in this way the transition from report to believing interpretation and to the confession of faith in our days, from the message of the resurrection to the dogma of Christ, has not yet been achieved, the exegetical work will be taken up yet again. But this will now no longer aim to give a responsible report but to answer the question 'How can we speak appropriately about Jesus Christ today in an understandable and responsible way, but in the light of scripture?' (OBC 343–463). Here too the complexity of the results is striking. Nor are they rejected by exegetes as false, senseless or irresponsible.

This method is then brought to bear once again in the question of the Christian God (in *Does God Exist?*). But here it is even more exciting, because now the argument must be not only exegetical but also philosophical (see below, 181f.). Methods overlap, and the important thing is not to confuse them.

(iii) The role of scripture

However, *The Church* shows yet a third trend which was perhaps even more important in 1967. As we saw, Küng wrote this book as an alternative to the texts of the Council, of which he later says, 'The German critical school of exegesis was not in fact represented at the Council' (HK 168). For Küng it soon became clear that in matters of the church the argument at the Council was extremely traditional, i.e. it used postulates from tradition, dogmatic assertions and theologically abstract discourses. By contrast – and this is the most surprising thing for many readers – over wide stretches of *The Church* an unparalleled immersion not only in the subject-matter but also in the arguments, images and contexts of scripture is evident. Much of the book is marked by a concentrated scriptural directness, in which there is hardly any distinction between quotation and application, between image and reality, between reference and Küng's own thought. Of course he would have said that 'people of God', 'body of Christ' or 'creation of the spirit' were metaphors had anyone asked him. But in fact they work as realities which are immediately present.

There are many passages in the book in which scripture directly provides the world of ideas, the linguistic gestures, the sphere of thought. It becomes natural to follow it, in hermeneutical texts making what Ebeling calls a 'pre-judgment', which spontaneously directs thought and judgment. Sometimes this has led Küng to be accused of biblicism. That would only be fair had he skipped the first two stages and shied away from the effort of argument in critical moments.

Never again has this phenomenon been repeated in Küng with such concentration. Perhaps it was necessary as a stage of development; for probably only this intense recourse to scripture allowed him to break through the bonds of traditional argument once and for all, and to reorientate his thought and language. He uses images, symbols and situations from the New Testament which are evidently more elementary and fundamental for the church than the neoscholastic, monocratic and doctrinally rigid ecclesiology of the time. He adopts priorities which played a role in the first decades after Jesus' resurrection and now – in a secularized world – are probably regaining their significance. To use Wittgenstein's terms, he takes over the language games and world of the first communities, and sets them against our time. For the first time the cause of the church is no longer stated in neo-scholastic concepts or in the concepts of Protestant orthodoxy; the great images of people of God, body of Christ or temple of the Spirit are now snatched away from the rationalization of them by the magisterium. This represents an enormous gain in language which could only follow from this deep familiarity with scripture.

Was and is this procedure legitimate? Didn't it, doesn't it, verge on an unconsidered biblicism? Doesn't it ignore and skip fruitful interim periods? Mustn't the translation of a biblical 'then' into our present also be safeguarded? Those are questions which Küng certainly did not answer at that time, in principle or in his methodological reflections. At the same time, however, it can be shown that Küng is not repristinating a church of the very first period. He is much too realistic for that, and devotes himself much too directly to the problems of the present-day church. But this approach is forced upon him for three important reasons.

First, as I have already been indicated, there was the rivalry with the Second Vatican Council. Now was not the time for elaborations and detailed studies, for solving riddles, but for new 'paradigms', as Küng would put it later. A Catholic ecclesiology which still persisted in justifying itself was finally to be opposed by another concept which relied completely on scripture, on the basis of which it could argue. Precisely for this reason, at this point Küng had no need to become an exegete himself. Abundant material was available; Protestant exegesis had done all the preliminary work. Now it was time for systematic theology with an ecumenical bent to rely on it – in season and out of season.

Secondly, it is clear that there are unresolved controversies in the New Testament. For example, the application of metaphors and symbols is partly spontaneous, partly well-established, but nowhere is it closed or systematized: the talk of the people of God is still polyvalent and undefined. The talk of spirit and charisma, of ministers and prophets, Jews and Gentiles, baptism and the local community, all shows an originality which is as yet unresolved. It is this openness and elemental nature, not the romantic ideal of an unfalsified primitive church; the disputed issue of unity, not the illusion of a peaceful idyll; the exciting question of the messianic end, not a sophisticated eschatology (in other words an effort to understand, not a naive and even fundamentalist acceptance) which makes grappling with the New Testament evidence so interesting for Küng.

Thirdly – and this was probably most important – there is the vitality and creativity of narrative and report. The narrative power of truth (outside and inside Christian religion) was discovered only later. Extensive use is made of it in *The Church*. In this book, there is an account of the preaching of Jesus, the activity of the early communities, the conflicts between Jewish and Gentile Christians and the various community orders. It is and always was the strength of historical criticism that it proved constructive: one could relate what happened and what did not happen, what was real, what was probable and what was erroneous. For a long time historical criticism has been seen only as the great destroyer of unconditional truth. Thus historical investigation, especially when it has a conscious hermeneutic, has come to be seen as relativistic, not least in the controversy with Küng. This perception is extremely one-sided, because it overlooks the distinctive value and the force of truth in historical accounts. Certainly these accounts develop a moral impulse, but they are not moralistic. Certainly they present model situations, but they do not commit anyone to repeating them. They call for a mimesis which is achieved by one's own creativity, and translation into one's own time and situation.

Thus one simple question to the church follows from Küng's approach. Is the church ready and able once again, in a very critical period, to reflect on its own origins and to understand its own questions anew in the light of these elementary contexts and situations? It might be mentioned in passing that all this has to do with discipleship.

(iv) Historical accounts and discipleship

This fourth point does not relate to a differentiation of method but to an orientation of content. The notion of discipleship leads once again to a comprehensive theological project. If the church is to be understood as discipleship of Jesus Christ, then so too is being a Christian. But if being a Christian means discipleship of Jesus Christ, it presupposes an account of and knowledge of Jesus of Nazareth. I have already referred to Küng's concern for exegesis and exegetical argument. Isn't that enough? Isn't it enough for a systematic theologian to build further on exegetical knowledge and otherwise to follow his speculative business?

I shall not answer this theoretical question here. The fact is that Küng's theology is increasingly inspired by a picture of Jesus of Nazareth which in fact penetrates all argument and thought structures, particulary those in which the discussion is about the world and a threatened future, politics and economics, ethics and humanity, freedom and true liberality in church, religions and society. This seems to me – given Küng's creative power, eloquence and an effective secretariat – to be the secret of his marked public impact as a theologian. The Christian Küng knows his sources. He has identified with them not only cognitively, but also emotionally.

'No "hymns to the church" should be sung here. But it should be pointed out what faith in the crucified Christ, preached by the church, can accomplish. For this does not all fall from heaven . . . It is made possible time and again when a pastor preaches this Jesus, when a catechist teaches in a Christian way, when an individual, a family, or a community prays from the heart without empty words. It is brought about when baptism binds a person to Christ, when the eucharist is celebrated with implications for the community in its everyday life, when a guilty person is incomprehensibly promised forgiveness by the power of God. It is made possible when God is worshipped and human beings are served; where the gospel is truly preached and lived through instruction and involvement, dialogue and pastoral care; in short, wherever Jesus is followed and his cause taken seriously' (RCT 12).

That is talk inspired by discipleship of Jesus. Here questions of method coincide seamlessly with the content to be covered. Over the course of the years, what is still aimed at in *The Church* and worked out broadly in *On Being a Christian* becomes an intellectually justified but personal inspiration, which is made possible by the visionary power of what is meant in the Christian tradition by lived out, responsible and attractive discipleship.

(b) Instruction from history

It cannot be claimed that Catholic theology has forgotten the history of its church. There has been intensive preoccupation with it and, at the latest in the twentieth century, to the history of the church has been added the history of its thought. At the same time the normative significance of church history has been recognized and hermeneutics has readily confirmed that faith and culture are always also part of its historical conditions. That means thinking historically and escaping the illusion that we could construct our future in or as a sphere free of history. We cannot either bracket out or skip areas of history. Since the 1960s Catholic theology has been fond of adopting such arguments to support itself and its church. In faithful discipleship of Gadamer, history becomes the place of its truth, and only those who are loyal to this history discover its identity.

For Küng's method, after *The Church* the context becomes more complex. He treats history first of all as the past, or more precisely as a history which can be and has to be told. Independently of criticism and self-criticism, there are events on which scholars are agreed. They agree that these events happened and how to interpret them. And a faith community can also reach agreement over them. Theologians can and must grapple critically with history. Küng's criticism in *The Church* (which is certainly indirect) is that traditional theology has perceived the history of the church and theology in an extremely selective way and often ideologically.

Against this background, Küng's strategy and challenge become clear. He gives his readers examples of how to deal with the history of the church, of thought, and of faith. He consistently illustrate the topic he discusses historically, usually in general surveys. *The Church* has instructive histories of concepts (C 218f., 225f., 239f., 243f., 320f., 335f., 389f.) or unedifying histories of power (C 249–52, 449–55, 468); histories of achievement or guilt (C 132–40); background analyses of long-term developments (C 193–7, 277–81, 313f., 333–4, 394–505); the presentation and analysis of historical texts (C 147f., 193–7, 277–81, 285f., 287, 289, 418–20). There are indications of problems (C 305, 311, 315–18, 333–4, 337–9) and hermeneutical reflections (C 442–4), and recollections to serve as both models (C 470–2, 477–8) and deterrents. History and histories are introduced here to instruct, to warn, but also to encourage, and as an exercise in healthy realism. Above all Küng attempts to break through the selective perception of history as self-legitimation. Guilt need not be suppressed, since it can be accepted. Realism need not lead to opportunism, since one can talk about principles and the possibility of living up to them.

Of course Küng is no innocent. His criticisms and appeals are blunt. But he forces himself – here too following scholarship – to be objective in the best sense of the word, i.e. to accept the discipline of making responsible statements. He too accepts the obligation to discuss positive possibilities and – as a member of this church – to regard them as achievable. For him the recollection of history is simply a means by which the principle of justification can be transformed into a way of thinking which is self-critical and critical of ideology. At a very early stage Cardinal Döpfner accused him of drawing a line from the 'centuries-old antisemitism' of the Christian church to National Socialist antisemitism (Küng, NH 522). Küng was thought to be disobedient, guilty of washing dirty linen in public, and deeply disloyal.

He manifestly takes a different view, and it can be seen from his works that he does so for fundamentally theological reasons. We need not accept all his judgments, but the way in which he presents facts and interpretations has so far stood up in the scholarly forum. However, today we also know better than in 1967 that repression does not heal, but hardens.

Küng will also trace the history of every new topic in later publications. Moreover, in the course of years it becomes increasingly important to him to investigate history. This never becomes an end in itself; he is far too interested in the present. However, it serves as a remembrance, a warning and a reservoir of knowledge. In *The Church* the span between scripture and the present sometimes threatens to suppress the two thousand years which lie between. Küng also draws clear lessons from historical case studies (for example the Council of Constance). The controversy over the question of God in modern times (*Does God Exist?*) is a high point of recollection, detection and learning. It becomes an intimate grappling with the question of God in our own theological, philosophical and everyday culture. In figures like Nietzsche, historical research comes to life. Stages of thought in the past serve as building-blocks for Küng's own argument. It is part of his heuristics that he makes the great thinkers of European history incessantly formulate the truths on which a contemporary theology must be based.

Küng has never thought much of over-hasty criticism and ideological classifications. Therefore he has dismissed the message of all those who have been praised by the church or put on the index, and discussed as an example of true faith or reprehensible unbelief. Here it will not prove surprising that Küng listens most closely to the critics of faith and the church in order to learn from them: Descartes and Pascal; Carnap, Popper and Wittgenstein; Kant and of course Hegel, with their forerunners and successors; Feuerbach and Marx; Freud and Nietzsche; the

Frankfurt School and many others whom I shall not name here. He learns lessons from all of them, and gains clarity and far-sightedness by standing on their shoulders. Anyone who has read *Does God Exist?* will have become familiar with modern intellectual history and a good deal of cultural history as well.

One feature of the way in which Küng deals with history cannot go unmentioned here. Just as in the sphere of biblical knowledge he loves reports and narratives (the history of Jesus and the primitive community, the conflict between Peter and Paul, the settlement of the Israelites, the downfall of Israel and the career of the prophets, the rise of the new state of Israel and Luther's 'return to the gospel' all appear to him to be simply exciting stories), so too he sees philosophies and scientific theories, the great moves towards new theological and cultural paradigms, as biographical events. Descartes and Feuerbach, Hegel and Marx are interesting as people who grew up, learned, coped with their disappointments, loved, felt grasped by God or humiliated by the church, expressed religious feeling or despaired of the world. Only in this way do backgrounds and hidden motives, the complexity and challenge of patterns of thought, become clear. This gives rise to ever new portraits, of Paul and Origen, Augustine and Thomas Aquinas, Luther, Schleiermacher and Karl Barth (GCT), not to mention the literary figures who have already been referred to (see above, 23–7).

In this way, too, little biographical gems have kept appearing, particularly where faith and doubt encounter each other under the surface. I might mention Freud (DGE 262–339), Nietzsche (DGE 343–415) and Pascal (DGE 42–92), not to mention the attraction of the Jens–Küng dialogue. These deviations from the everyday business of theology in particular show the reason for Küng's concern with history. He wants to show people and their reality, conflicts and their results; alongside the God and faith of the churches he quite simply wants to know the God and the doubt of our world. Here, in the world of our history, there develops the reality which a theologian has to know if something is to be detectable of the divine drama, the divine mystery and liberation. Anyone who wanted to bracket off this side of Küng's theology would not have understood much about him and about what Catholic theology means for him, which here too is to be translated 'all-embracing'.

(c) Responsibility to the present

So far we have discussed inspiration through scripture and instruction through history. The third aspect for Küng is the one on which he reflected least in 1967, but which he was already practising intensively. However, for him then 'the present' was still the church's present with all its perhaps uncontemporaneous problems. For all its extensive knowledge, for all the historical instruction and biblical inspiration, *The Church* is related through and through to the present problems of this church. It is a book which grapples with the situation of the Catholic Church so to speak on every page. This church is the church of the 1960s, a church in ecumenical dialogue and in inner turmoil. It is a church which was able to experience itself and speak about itself in the Council, a church with a high presence, at a favourable hour when it was concerned with reform, when it had a creative theology and great pastoral commitment.

This church had just rediscovered 'the world', even if the categories sound clumsy and as yet no one saw the consequences. At that moment (let us take the years 1963–66) it was still very preoccupied with itself. Even Küng's epilogue on the church in the world (C 481–9) seems abstract and remarkably pale. But he does everything he can to make sure that this preoccupation of the church with itself does not degenerate into narcissism. It is a happy time of transition, full of promise, but also full of anxieties about the change of course which Küng and others are urging. So where he gets a grip on the world, he hangs on to it.

If we read *The Church* at a distance, taught by what are now thirty years of discussions, we are struck by the lack of bitterness in the book. On the contrary, we are amazed at most by the directness and matter-of-fact way in which already at that time Küng offers another way of dealing with Jews and non-Catholic Christians and models for other structures of the church and an ecumenically responsible papacy. Once again, the topicality which is woven into all the themes of the book, the cross-fire of current questions, is manifest; nowhere is it better attested than in the amazingly rich reactions which this book provoked. His method has not yet been formalized. Perhaps that is also a good thing, since directness and detached reflection only seldom coincide.

The coming chapters will show how Küng's gaze increasingly clearly extends to the present day. This begins with the churches, extends to his own culture, encompasses the world religions and finally discovers a comprehensive, globalized world. Already in Chapter 1 I indicated that for all his universalization Küng remains a theologian. Thus, conversely, the present in its most comprehensive sense explicitly becomes the horizon of a theology with an ever wider span.

4

Specifics: Reform of the Church

In 1957 Küng still enjoyed the opportunities of the newcomer; in 1967 people knew whom they had to deal with. By then, he had written what many people at the time thought was a brilliant and inspiring book, overflowing with knowledge and expertise. However, in the course of time it would already be relativized, put in the context of the ongoing discussion and finally be domesticated. Moreover in any case it was very biblical and Protestant. People underestimated how serious Küng was when he said, 'The time is ripe for a systematic clearing up of the theological differences between the Christian churches' (Kuschel 1978, v). He was intent on establishing positions once he had recognized that they were correct. A picture of the church renewed from the Bible must result in a church renewed from the Bible. While the later reform writings must not be separated from his great works on *Justification*, *The Church* and *On Being a Christian*, these major works cannot be understood without the reform writings. Küng never drops this claim; at the same time it will determine his development. Here I shall indicate the way from theory to praxis, from the presentation of the theory through the more popular accounts to the specific demand for reform. I shall begin with two case studies, then mention some reform writings, discuss Küng's communication with the public, and end with the problem of infallibility, the decisive test case for him.

1. Two case studies

(a) The Bible: unreconstructed catholicity

I begin with an article which goes back to Küng's inaugural lecture in Tübingen (in 1962) and which argues with his Protestant colleague Ernst Käsemann. The article is about 'early Catholicism' and the question how the New Testament canon of scripture is to be dealt with. It is entitled 'Early Catholicism in the New Testament as a Problem of Controversial Theology' (NT 175–204). Is there a 'canon in the canon', or is the canon of scriptures even responsible for the separation of the churches?

According to the Catholic perspective of that time, Protestant theology had been caused problems by exegetical research. With Luther it still defined the centre of Christian faith in terms of the doctrine of justification; here it referred to the New Testament in which the writings normative for faith are collected. Now the New Testament had proved to be increasingly 'catholic'; it recognized works and merit; it held the sacraments in high esteem; in Acts and the Pastoral Epistles it had an amazingly high view of the church, its apostolic ministry and its vital structures. None of this fitted into the picture of pure justification by faith. Historically the phenomenon had already been recognized by Harnack; it was called 'early Catholicism'. This posed questions for the New Testament canon. Can it be binding as a whole on faith and the church? Are some writings, e.g. the Letter of James or even the Pastoral Epistles, to be excluded? Or is there a 'canon within the canon', i.e. are there some writings in terms of which the others are to be judged binding and are to be interpreted? And if that is the case, by what criteria is a distinction made between the normative and the 'catholic' writings?

Of course soon afterwards a large part of the discussion at that time settled itself, as Küng writes in a 1970 postscript:

'Since 1962, before Vatican II, much water has flowed not only down the Tiber but also down the Neckar. The Catholic polemic of that time against Protestant one-sidednesses, constraints and exclusivities – similarly determined by polemic – was necessary. Much would need to be said differently today, and some things have been settled, on both sides' (NT 204).

This new situation included the fact that the Council rediscovered scripture as a source of experience and a norm for faith and church, showed that it valued the churches of the Reformation, and relaxed the harshness of oppositions in doctrine by the formula of the 'hierarchy of truths'.

In 1962, the battle was still being carried on vigorously. Certainly Küng was immune from the suspicion of being a Catholic *éminence grise*, but for him too something fundamental was at stake with this question. On the one hand he had discovered justification and saved its Catholic honour; but on the other hand he also had to arrive at an honourable interpretation of the 'Catholic' elements of the New Testament. That led him to a question which is important in both method and content, namely his attitude as a Catholic to the problem of the canon as posed in Reformation terms. Would he too introduce a

gradation within scripture, or would he say of every line without distinction, 'The canon is the canon'?

Granted, today the discussion has gone several stages further.
Hermeneutical, linguistic or contextual considerations have put further
categories at our disposal for coping with the problem. Nor can we any
longer bracket off the Jewish Bible (which we call the 'Old Testament').
But that is not the issue, since Küng's argument is about fundamentals.
The attempt to make a new selection within the New Testament canon
is not an option for him. If the canonical writings – accepted as such by
all the confessions – are the sole 'un-normed norm' of faith, on what
criterion outside the canon could one fall back? Nor can the multiplicity
of confessions be legitimated or derived from the multiplicity of New
Testament writings, as it is by Käsemann, for according to Küng the
church precedes the New Testament: 'The church as the New Testament
people of God has handed down to us the New Testament, changeable
through the history of its canon may be; and it has handed down to us
the New Testament as a whole. Without the church there would be no
New Testament' (NT 205). However, confessions came into being –
contrary to the original intention – as a result of selections from the
already existing canon.

'Catholicity' (i.e. comprehensive multiplicity) thus became *haieresis*
(reductive selection, heresy):

> 'So on close inspection one has to say that in its lack of unity the New
> Testament canon is a presupposition, an occasion for the multiplicity
> of confessions, but not the ground, the cause in the strict sense. The
> combustible material, the framework of the house that supports it,
> can be the presupposition, the occasion, for the burning of the house;
> but the reason for, the cause of, the fire is the arsonist who sets fire
> to the wood. The real cause of the multiplicity of the confessions is
> not the New Testament canon which, understood in its unity as
> "catholic" (*kath'olou*), is the presupposition for the unity of the
> church, but the *hairersis* which dissolves the unity of the ekklesia'
> (NT 189).

Thus Küng does not retreat to an authoritarian argument. But he
makes it clear that anyone who looks for a canon in the canon is want-
ing to be 'more biblical than the Bible, more New Testament than the
New Testament, more evangelical than the gospel and even more
Pauline than Paul' ((NT 193). Against this attempt, in the name of
Catholic thought Küng calls for 'openness in principle to all the direc-

tions which the New Testament opens up, excluding no New Testament line in principle or in fact' (NT 198).

However, he does not see the catholicity which he sketches as a happy possession of the Catholic Church; rather, it is a task which has to be rediscovered from the multiplicity of the New Testament writings. So, after criticizing Protestant exclusiveness, he now turns to criticism of the 'atmosphere of anxiety, the totalitarian-type supervision and the hypocrisy and cowardice to which it leads'. Here an important presupposition of good exegesis gets lost, namely 'an atmosphere of freedom, sober theological honesty, undeterred matter-of-factness, and precisely in this way loyalty to the church' (NT 200f.). It is in fact appropriate here to demonstrate the significance of the multiplicity of the New Testament in all freedom, and to grasp that any testimony of the New Testament is an element in the history of proclamation (NT 201).

Here Küng has clarified in principle the methodological presupposition of his biblical argument. Certainly he still concedes gradations in the authority of the New Testament documents, but they move within this framework: 'Here we must take into account three different kinds of originality, distinguishing them and yet combining them: those of chronology (I Corinthians is earlier than Ephesians), authenticity (I Corinthians is genuinely Pauline, Titus probably not) and relevance (I Corinthians is nearer in content to the gospel of Jesus himself than James)' (C 19). Here with the last criterion he does not fall back again on the problem of the canon, since he seeks to cast the last anchor not in any kind of interpretation but in the message of Jesus himself.

What are we to learn from this? The matter-of-factness with which Küng allows discussion about a closeness to the heart of the matter and the 'centre of scripture' but protects the framework of the canon is interesting and hermeneutically justified. We shall have to discuss the further development of the problems again in Chapter 5 (see below, 156f.). The acknowledgment of the multiplicity of the New Testament makes it possible for him to deal positively with the Catholic understanding of ministry. But this acknowledgment also becomes a weapon for him against any claim to absoluteness within the church. His criticism becomes decisive where a structure of ministry presents itself exclusively as the only possible form of the church. Therefore this criticism is never concentrated on particular conceptions of church structure but always on claims to exclusiveness which suggests that only one structure, only one authority, only one form of ministry is possible. Misunderstandings arise, a biblicistic or fundamentalistic thought-form creeps in, as soon as one confuses the level of actual forms with that of exclusive forms. For only where an exclusive claim is defined must there be unqualified contradiction – in the name of the New Testament and in the name of Catholic thought. So *de facto* Küng develops a concept of Catholicity which is in principle open. Consequently it is not surprising that some years later his basic conflict with Rome flared up specifically over the question of infallibility.

(b) The papacy: historical mistakes

For Catholic theologians, the years between the announcement of the Council and its beginning were a hectic time, and full of work. Research was done, results were collected and conceptions developed. Küng was sufficiently matter-of-fact and historically knowledgeable to foresee the Council, not as an event of idyllic peace but as a place of hard work, discussions and vigorous controversies. The resolution of conflict is announced at councils, and that is a good thing. For Küng, for example, it was clear that 'ecumenism', as the topic was called in Rome, had to become central. But he also knew that this topic could be tackled credibly only on one presupposition: the Catholic Church must be ready for painful internal reforms.

In what direction were they to be implemented? At a very early stage it was also clear to him that the reforms must take account of scripture and of the justified concerns of the Reformation. At the same time, as the theologian trained in Rome immediately recognized, a beginning had to be made with reforms of church structure; anything else would get bogged down. In 1962 *Structures of the Church* appeared. For Küng, this, alongside his programmatic writing *The Council and Reunion,* was a programme for the self-understanding and action of an ecumenically inclined council with a scholarly (i.e. biblical, systematic and above all historical) foundation.

(i) The Council as the representation of the whole church

Right at the beginning of the work he finds the decisive compelling tone: *ekklesia,* in its original meaning synonymous with 'council', is the whole church, the assembly from all the peoples convened by God. A 'council' is an assembly from all the peoples, though it has been convened by human beings. One can certainly speak of the church without thinking of the council, but not *vice versa*. Connections and reciprocal references are obvious. If a council represents the whole church, then this representation can and must be investigated critically. The Council must 'represent the church in some degree by personifying it' (SC 19); Küng understands this as 'gift and task' (SC 27).

Here Küng has opened up an argument with which the understandings of the church and the Council can reflect each other. Because the Council is meeting soon, there is an urgent need to focus this strategy on the question whether the Council will represent the church credibly. Küng's test question is developed in three ways:

1. The Council must not stop at being an external manifestation of unity, but like all councils must contribute to inner harmony.

2. If the Council is to be Catholic, 'all the individual churches with their specific histories and their traditions, with their problems and needs, their objections and concerns, their wishes and demands', will find expression in it (SC 36); at that time the people of Asia and Africa and the multiplicity of Orthodox and Protestant Christians are already mentioned (SC 38f.).

3. The interpretation of a church which is holy in a credible way is interesting; for Küng the all-important thing is that the Council should want to hear only the voice of the Spirit and to interpret scripture. It was precisely this nearness to scripture that helped the first four councils to gain high ecumenical authority.

Küng has thus found a course of argument which even a traditional Catholic theology can hardly escape. Above all he gives a firework display of historical information on all topics and all arguments, as for example on the participation of the laity in the Council. They were always represented under different titles and in different functions. Since Luther again brought the 'universal priesthood' of all believers into the centre, there has also been a really theological argument for their participation, independent of all social, political or social structures. Küng sees no tenable argument to the contrary which would exclude their participation and right to vote, nor would he be a Catholic theologian did he not relate the Catholic understanding of office to this position which is friendly to the laity.

Now at the latest a second strategy in Küng's argument becomes clear. The topics and the historical development of them give him the opportunity continually to introduce the interventions of Martin Luther, the strongest opponent in this matter. Thus Luther's programmatic writings are quoted at length, his understanding of laity and ministry is depicted in a differentiated way, and above all it is shown how important Luther thought a council to be and for how long he backed one. However, these times are past, and according to Küng the understanding of ministry in Protestantism has not developed in a satis-factory way. Thus he gives the Catholic Church and the family of Protestant churches two tasks which supplement each other in mirror fashion: 'The specific [ecumenical] task of the member churches of the World Council of Churches concerns the function of office and thus the unity of the church' (SC 198). 'The specific ecumenical task of the Catholic Church, above all, is concerned with the function of the indi-vidual community and hence the multiplicity of the church' (SC 199).

So far Küng has produced a work which invites, relativizes and differentiates. He has always tried to maintain a conciliatory tone, presented failure as a difficult problem, and the invitation to act as a great possibility. That also remains the case in the following, decisive chapter. What position does the pope have over against the Council?

Again the criticism voiced by the Reformation is introduced, and the First Vatican Council is discussed with restraint. Here too the recollection of the history of the councils leads to cautious positions. But in the case of a conflict between the pope and the church the questions become more pointed, and Küng advises looking 'at the facts of church history soberly, without embellishments of any kind' (SC 224). Processes were instituted against popes, and even now there is a conviction that the pope could lose his office for five reasons: through death, resignation, mental illness, heresy and schism. Thus the possi-bility of heresy and schism is reckoned with. As a rule a council will have to note this controversial legal title. But can a council put itself above the pope?

(ii) Does a council stand above the pope?

For Küng, answering this question means relating the history of the Council of Constance (1414–1418), the only council which succeeded in abolishing a schism in the church (SC 242). Even more exciting is the fact that at a highly critical hour this council declared its rights over against the pope, that it immediately deposed three popes, elected Martin V as a new pope and only appointed him to office when he had recognized its decrees and its conviction that a council stands above the pope. Once the council had ended, however, there was a reversal: the papacy and the Curia consistently established their own claims and rejected the conciliar claims to superiority. At the following council, the Fifth Lateran Council (1512–1517), the wind finally changed. Now the superiority of the pope over the council was declared, and Rome firmly took in hand the matter of this assembly of the church. Moreover the council became a fiasco: Luther published his theses six months after it ended.

To return to the Council of Constance: according to Küng's historical argument there is a problem which – strictly speaking – has not been solved even today. After Martin V had established himself in office, he dismissed the council's claim to its rights, by virtue of which he had had himself elected pope in 1417. Why then did he accept papal authority at the hands of the council? That is at least a problem of credibility which burdens the papacy even today. Granted, no strict conciliar parliamentarianism was 'defined' in Constance, and the term 'conciliarism' was used in extremely varied ways; but there was an insistence on 'a distinct kind of "superiority" . . . according to which an ecumenical council has the function of a kind of "control authority" over the pope, not only for the emergency of that time but also for the future, on the premise that a pope might again lapse into heresy, schism or the like. All the participants at the Council, even the moderate Council Fathers and the pope, were in favour of the necessity of a certain control over the pope by an ecumenical council, viewed as the representation of the universal church' (SC 255).

According to Küng, the church would have been spared much misfortune (including the Reformation) had the intentions of this council been maintained. Küng draws decisive consequences for the council that is awaited.

> 'However, with respect to the reunion of separated Christians it is a cause for rejoicing to see that the Constitution of the Catholic Church in no way closes all doors from the outset, but gives a great deal of scope for a serious ecumenical encounter. But we should entertain no illusions because of this. The way to reunion is long and arduous, not only in theology. The way to reunion requires patience, penance, a genuine renunciation on the part of all participants, who indeed are not all without guilt, a renunciation – and Constance can be a lesson for us here – even of the Petrine office, as a service of love for the sake of the unity of Christendom' (SC 304).

According to Küng's judgment at that time the history of the church is time and again played out between the problems of Vatican I (the primacy and infallibility of the pope) and the problems of Constance (the controlling rights of the whole church represented in the Council). For Küng it is important 'to maintain and to resolve the fruitful tension between Peter and the community of the apostles, between Peter and the church, the centre and the "periphery"' (SC 280). This description corresponds to the situation at the time, but also shows how much Küng still kept to perspectives within Catholicism. He speaks in a mediating and eirenic way of balance, openness and (as in scripture?) the repudiation of a selective heresy. However, for all insiders who could read, Küng's message to Rome was abundantly clear: please do not continue the power politics of a Roman centralism! Do not keep attempting to suppress the voice of the church and do not repeat the fiasco of a centralist council! At last take the questions of the Reformation seriously, be concerned for inner freedom and world-wide plurality, and listen to the message of the gospel!

People did not yet suspect how serious Küng was with these demands. He recalls and warns, cautiously before the Council and then increasingly clearly, already at that time with a critical eye and incomprehension of a theology for which the way from theory to a praxis in accord with the gospel was not yet a theme. Conversely, Küng underestimated how very much the confirmation of Roman centralist praxis had become second nature to Catholic theology. However, neither at that time or later was his theology limited to theoretical discussion; his thought was directed by specific questions. Precisely for this reason he did not stop at intuitions, and increasingly distanced himself from a language which, while friendly, tended to be obscurantist. The suspicion hardened that people did not want to understand his warnings. The recollection of irrefutable historical reality became all the more precious to him.

2. Reform writings

One genre of Küng's theological works could be described as research in the interest of church reform. The interconnection of theoretical conception, structural form and appropriate action in the church can be studied particularly well in them. Küng is concerned to encourage and to warn, to deter and to confirm, with indirect language, deciphering the message in past histories. Whoever has ears to hear, let him hear! Some reform writings go one step further. In them criticism and hope, assent and a desire for reform are expressed directly and without beating about the bush. The dramatic course of the decade between 1959 (the announcement of the Council) and 1968 (the encyclical *Humanae vitae*), which was decisive for the church, can be read off them.

(a) Theological boldness

Küng's understanding of himself as a theologian was clear at that time. He saw himself in the service of his church, but he understood this formula in concrete terms. His concerns were counsel and criticism, involvement and intervention; mediation between the church government and the people, between church practice and scholarship. Therefore he also called for an appropriate freedom for theologians: courage, truthfulness and a sense of the current situation are among its virtues. The reform writings of this period are models of the reciprocal relationship between current events and thought. First of all this was the period of the refreshing, almost open, beginning. Now historical disillusionments were mentioned and discussed, new programmes formulated, visions presented for discussion. It was no coincidence that at that time Küng was occupied with Luther's great programmatic writings (1521), as is evident from *Structures of the Church*. For Küng, too, freedom became a central concept. Accord with scripture, truthfulness and Catholic multiplicity were others. The moral appeals were clear. But no person was attacked and no one needed to feel violated. The call to independence or to resistance was still to come.

Only gradually and imperceptibly did the tone change. The experience of lost opportunities soon became stronger, and the pressure of demands intensified. Küng, whose youth was noted at first, gradually became a player, involved in the course of history. His intensive involvement in the events of the Council gave him a new self-confidence. In those years people listened to him and his colleagues. Of course personal experiences came into play, countless meetings, some good and some unsuccessful, personal disappointments and the disappointments of those involved. They will not be discussed here. That they cannot be reconstructed from Küng's writings speaks not only for the confidentiality of many interventions and the *ésprit de corps* which developed among the masters in Rome, but also for his concern for matter-of-fact and responsible argument. We shall begin with his first programmatic work.

(b) The Council and Reunion

In January 1959 John XXIII announced the convening of the Council; in June written confirmation followed in an encyclical: 'The Council will certainly be a marvellous scene of truth, unity and love, a scene the sight of which, we firmly trust, will be a gentle invitation to those who are separated from this Apostolic See to seek and find that unity for which Jesus Christ so ardently prayed from the heavenly Father.' Küng knew how to distinguish between curial language and the sober description of a programme, but he took such statements at face value. In spring 1960 he presented his programme in *The Council and Reunion*, hesitantly, and legitimated as far as possible with official church statements or papal statements. The preface by the Archbishop of Vienna, Cardinal König, was protection for him. Above all he referred to Yves Congar, whose reform work had fallen on deaf ears in Rome in 1950 (Congar). Here reunion and reform within the church belong together, and a beginning must be made with the latter: '*Ecclesia semper reformanda* – the church always needs to be reformed.'

So the renewal of the church is a permanent necessity, since the church consists of sinful men and women: it is set in the dimensions of space and time and is never perfect on this earth. Its particular historical form – one might think of its Jewish, Greek, Roman, Germanic inculturation – is at the same time both a formation and a deformation. Even now it stands between the dangers of unqualified surrender to the world and ecclesiasticization: 'How little does it often have to say, spiritually, in that central arena of modern life where the questions essential to present and future are decided?' (CR 33). Thus to talk of the church as a community of sinners is nothing new. Unlike Congar, and with some effort to justify himself, Küng (like Rahner) also spoke of a 'sinful church'. The trained ear pricked up then, and the message was clear: Küng was bidding farewell to an idealistic picture of a church in love with itself. The church itself is 'burdened, wounded, deformed'.

What can we do about this? Küng's first answer may seem surprising: 'We can suffer' (CR 53–7). What he means by this is: 'We are not obliged to act before the world as though everything were for the best with us. We can display our poverty, our wretchedness, our shame. We can allow our suffering really to pierce to the heart, our suffering over the church as it is, unrenewed, unreformed' (CR 54). Today we would speak of the 'capacity to mourn' and of courage to note the abuses.

The second answer is: we may pray (not against one another but for one another, for God's will to be done). The third answer rightly deals with criticism. There has always been criticism in the church, and Küng (as ever well-versed in history) can mention a cloud of witnesses, not least Pius XII, who in 1964 emphatically asserted the necessity for a critical public opinion in the church (CR 66).

Finally (fourth answer), we can act. The framework for this action is love, a concern for fellowship, patient resolution and a return to tradition. But the criterion for such action can only be 'Jesus Christ, the Lord of the church, who speaks to the church of every century in his gospel, making his demands on it' (CR 79). Only then is there a mention of the Ignatian 'feeling in the church' in which the freedom of the Christian must be shown.

The longest chapter in the book then offers a survey of church reform attempts and reforms. This chapter concentrates on the question why the Catholic Church rejected the Protestant Reformation and later increasingly entrenched itself in self-defence. The text becomes more exciting, the closer it gets to the developments in the nineteenth and twentieth centuries. Critical description and an understanding of the reactions go hand in hand, until a whole package of demands for reform has been tied up, including an understanding of the religious concerns of the Reformation, a revaluation of scripture, a renewal of the liturgy, a theoretical and practical significance for the universal priesthood and a demolition of Europeanism and Latinism, a depoliticization of the papacy, reform of the Curia, revision of Canon Law, respect for tolerance and the individual conscience, the abolition of celibacy, and the interiorization of popular piety (CR 149–61).

Then much attention is paid to the question of doctrine – how could it be otherwise? This is presented at the most advanced level of awareness of that time: the development of dogma, its polemical content, its reference to scripture and the distinction between theological pedantry and church teaching. Here, too, the aim is at least to provide some negative clarification of the conditions for a reunion:

'In order to have the right to live in separate churches, we should have to be certain (to put it in broad general terms) that we were unmistakeably disunited about the truth, and not merely be slightly uncertain whether we were really entirely at one, or just exactly what the other side really meant, or whether we were quite sure that we had rightly understood it. This principle follows (it seems to me) on the one hand from our Christian duty to be united in one church, and on the other from the essential impossibility of reaching absolute certainty about our ultimate interior identity of conviction. Such absolute certainty would presuppose an absolute certainty of the rightness of our own inmost belief in the sight of God, which seems to me as impossible and un-Catholic a thing as absolute certainty about our own righteousness in his sight' (CR 176).

This question of the presumption of innocence and the burden of proof is among Küng's fundamental starting points. But of course they cannot also overcome the hardest core of all the obstacles which arise out of the concrete structure of the church's organization. Once again Küng discusses Luther's criticism of the pope and the papacy, and finally formulates his own criticism quite clearly, even if in so doing for the most part he uses the voices of others: criticism of the 'absolutist, centralist, indeed in some respect totalitarian features in the papal church' (Dombois, CR 196); Rome's centuries-old technique 'which in fact actually hinders the growth of the one Catholic body *in Christo*' (Lackmann, CR 198); the independence of individual communities or dioceses and the lack of understanding in Rome of what Christian freedom means (Asmussen, Klompé, Karrer, CR 201–4); and the inability of the popes to give themselves spiritual legitimation as 'representatives of Christ' (Barth, CR 204). We Catholics, Küng then supposes, can deal with this claim, but in the case of a reunion we must 'get to know and try to understand' (CR 206) the doubts of Protestants, and see to it that non-Catholics too hear the 'gentle invitation' of the pope. John XXIII is then presented as the example of a winning pope.

What is the Council to do? Küng exercises restraint. Given the role of the bishops, it is not the task of theologians to make renewal plans for the Council. But they can point to possibilities. He makes a selection from the countless ones. He mentions the revaluation of the office of bishop and contributes extended arguments here about the independent function of the bishops and their churches. On this basis Küng sees rich possibilities of conciliar frameworks for new orders differentiated according to states, within the framework of a new decentralized legal and administrative structure, for example relating to the celebration or the eucharist and the praying of the breviary, the administration of the sacraments and the compulsory celibacy of priests and deacons, the reform of the marriage law and the abolition of the Index. Here positive work could be done towards a revaluation of the word of God and a fundamental declaration on the significance of the laity. Finally Küng expects from the Council a word of penitence especially to separated Christians, with a request for forgiveness and a word of faith: 'a joyful and courageous confession of faith in the living God, who is as near to us as ever in this age of artificial satellites and space-travel, who has not forgotten us in the sufferings of two World Wars and the menace of atomic death . . .' (CR 273).

How will reunion then take place? It must not become the immediate aim of the Council. Rather, it is important to make our own church more credible by reform. Reunion cannot be enforced. It is important for it to grow, since the aim is not uniformity but 'unity in the sense of the living *koinonia* of the Scriptures, which is unity in diversity, unity in a variety of rites, languages, customs, modes of thought and action and prayer. Such unity is more perfect than uniformity' (CR 279).

Here Küng has extended his proposals. It was more important to him to describe the situation, to list the many things needed and to indicate that the gospel of Christ has to precede all self-satisfaction than to make concrete proposals. On all points he has argued biblically and historically and with an eye to the churches of the Reformation. Some central points become clear from the book: 1. The Council must enter again into the questions of the world; these include openness to science and culture and to the riches of a varied world. 2. The Council has to pay its dues to the churches of the Reformation, above all to Luther's concerns; this includes the significance of God's Word, the position of the 'laity' and the shaping of the liturgy over against a self-righteous church. 3. The Council must come clean about itself and its own history. Here the main problems are an exaggerated centralism and the undervaluation of the office of bishop, in so far as it guarantees the inner multiplicity of the church. 4. Above all it must not be overlooked how important the appearance and action of the pope himself are for closer ecumenical relations. To a great degree it will depend on him whether the voice of the Good Shepherd is to be heard from Rome.

Interested circles at that time welcomed Küng's book. Rome did not intervene, although the authorities had give him a control number as early as 1957. Battle was not yet joined. It could not yet be foreseen that a conflict would develop in the coming years. Meanwhile Küng worked at his desk, in the lecture room – and in Rome. With a view to these dramatic years he developed his programmatic positions in some shorter writings. Here freedom became a central concept for him. He developed his understanding of Christian freedom by means of Thomas More, who remained increasingly important for him and gave him a direction (*Freedom in the World*). He made it clear that the church must become the sphere of freedom for its own sake (*The Church in Freedom*). Finally, he called for a freedom for theologians which would make it possible for them to offer an appropriate service for the well-being of the church (*The Theologian and the Church*). All three meditations appeared in 1964 and partly go back to lectures given on a memorable visit to the USA in 1963 (Modras, NHFT 348–57).

Küng had an active experience of the dramatic years of the Council, with the death of John XXIII and with Paul VI as a very cautious and hesitant successor, with the growing polarizations into a conservative and a progressive wing of the Council, and finally with the results of the Council, the compromise character of which resulted in an era of interpretations and counter-claims. In 1968, that significant year, Küng again intervened in the discussions with a book which made yet more precise the programme of the post-conciliar period. *Truthfulness. The Future of the Church* was its title and central theme.

(c) Truthfulness

This is no edifying book, but a book on repentance. Two points determine Küng's description of the situation in the first years after the Council. On the one hand much has been achieved, or at least set in motion:

> 'the biblical renewal, the liturgical renewal, the movement for greater lay responsibility, finally too the theological and ecumenical renewal . . . a positive, new orientation in regard to the other Christian churches, in regard to the Jews and the great world religions, in regard to the whole secular world, and thus in every respect a new orientation of the Catholic Church in regard to what had hitherto been its own traditional structure' (T 10).

That is tremendous; therefore it is understandable that this church is still in transition and has got itself into a paradoxical situation. The new interest is met with doubts; the pressure for change with resistance to anything new; openness to the outside world with a striking 'inability of the official church to engage in positive acts of reform'.

This leads to the second point. Küng sees the real basis for these difficulties in a crisis of leadership caused by the many compromises in conciliar texts, a half-hearted implementation of reforms decided on, and the inability of Rome to deal creatively with the difficulties which have arisen; the Curia is immovable.

> 'And thus most of the Roman institutions are still in fact dominated by pre-conciliar forces, which frequently indulge in an equivocal conciliar verbalism and in their concrete measures provide little evidence of being filled with the original gospel of Jesus Christ, with the conciliar spirit, and with the relevant technical and general knowledge. Many, particularly the best orientated and most lively, still regarded Rome as a centre, not of conciliar renewal but of pre-conciliar resistance. The unintelligent intervention of a hopelessly backward

Roman theology against the Catechism approved by the whole Dutch episcopate, the rejection of the North American episcopate's request for permission for liturgical experiments, the negative reaction to post-conciliar or theological solutions in Europe and to attempts at a thorough renewal, particularly of orders of women in the USA – these and many other factors have strengthened this impression' (T 14).

In addition to the situation in Rome, some conferences of bishops were dogged with uncertainty, passivity, fear of Rome and its insistence on long outdated positions and privileges. In addition there was an arbitrary practice in retiring aged bishops. The contact with theologians had been broken off; at most convenient advisers were still tolerated. Küng could refer to his *The Church*: the theology developed there is now made concrete and applied to the difficult situation after the Council.

Küng's offensive begins from the keyword 'truthfulness'. He finds a quest for truthfulness in art, science, culture, the young people of his time. This is natural, because the Catholic Church has difficulties with precisely this attitude. The truth has been understood too objectivistically, has been reified and understood intellectualistically; thought has been unhistorical, and in a siege mentality people have believed that the church must be defended by every means. ' "He is an absolutely honest man," said a journalist about an archbishop. "He would never lie except for the good of the church"' (T 99f.). By contrast the message of Jesus must be understood as a call to truthfulness and authenticity. But a truthful and thus authentic church means a provisional church which makes no claims, which serves, which is aware of its guilt and is obedient. 'The eye is the lamp of the body. So, if your eye is sound, your whole body will be full of light; but if your eye is not sound, your whole body will be full of darkness' (Matt. 6.22f.). Such an inward and outward truth which is deeply binding on Christians is called for in all dimensions of church action, in preaching and theology, in ecumenism and the church press, in church government, in relations between the church and the world.

There is no mistaking the fact that in 1968 the tone changes. The tremendous opportunity of the Council is possibly being wasted; hopes are beginning to wane. Individual cases – the encyclical on birth control had just appeared – come to symbolize the incompetence of the reform. Once again, and now with greater emphasis, Küng sees the hour of the theologians with which the church government must collaborate; for it is their calling to analyse situations, examine them critically and loosen up rigidities.

But what precisely is meant by truthfulness? Küng thinks that truthfulness means honesty, authenticity, dissociation from mistrust and concealed chumminess; at all events putting one's cards on the table. This includes argument, honest resolution of conflicts and open decisions. In those years Küng's thought was related to the many latent and open controversies with Rome. Basically, behind these virtuous-sounding words Küng is expressing a serious doubt and a far-reaching reproach, the scope of which he develops in many ways. It is interesting that those were the years in which Habermas was developing his argumentative model of truth, correctness and truthfulness, which shows that authenticity of expression essentially shapes the social process of truth (Habermas I, 44f.). This also makes it clear that Küng is not criticizing persons, but a system which socially is extremely powerful. His purpose is not to put the integrity of persons in doubt but to show up the falsifying dynamic of structures, anxieties and claims to exclusiveness. This is doubt in ultimate honesty, the suspicion of motivations with apparently focussed zeal which are alien to the issue. It is a criticism of the old siege mentality, which does not allow an open, let alone a self-critical, comment.

Results are emphasized, the value of the old is conjured up: in modern terms, what Küng is practising is ideological criticism. He complains about the mixture of knowledge and interests, a way of talking which may not be lying but which creates illusions and fundamentally conceals the truth. People say 'Christian truth' and mean 'Catholic Church'. It is not as if the Catholic Church were simply falsifying the gospel, but accents are shifted, perspectives narrowed and problems suppressed; complexity is reduced opportunistically. In Luther's language, the 'gospel' is degraded so that it becomes 'law'. So failure must constantly be swept aside and false decisions must still somehow be defended. Thus the supposition arises among outsiders that not all the cards may be put on the table. Politicians still call this syndrome 'loss of credibility' or, as a witty bishop wrote down on a scrap of paper during bitter debates at the Council: 'The senate does not make mistakes, and if it should, it does not correct them, in order not to appear to have made them.' Such a subtle manipulation of the truth is analysed by means of a repeated clash with the church's claim that it alone brings salvation (T 187–203).

Therefore the church must begin by conceding its mistakes, reforming the shape of its offices, and conceding the failure of its institutions; in respect of Nazism, Fascism, the Jews, the race question and the war (T 139). Only in such truthfulness will it once again become capable of change. There has never been a real recognition that *Truthfulness* is a book in bitter earnest: 'Anyone who wants the church to die out, to become the grave of God, must want it to remain as it is. Anyone who wants it to live, as God's living community, must want it to change' (T 141).

Against this background Küng now develops his post-conciliar reform programme, which is partly a continuation of what has been achieved, and partly an implementation of what has been prevented.

1. He again calls first for the introduction of an ecumenical age: complicity in the split in the church is recognized, and other Christian communities are accepted as churches. Now an ecumenical attitude and collaboration at all levels of the church are to be achieved.

2. Again he recalls the concern of the Reformers: high esteem for the Bible, renewal of worship, revaluation of the laity, decentralization of the church and reform of popular religion.

3. The demand to take the truth of the religions seriously is new; here the relationship with the Jews plays a special role.

4. A positive relation to the 'secular world' is called for: solidarity with humankind, self-criticism in the face of atheism, intercession for the weak, repudiation of war, affirmation of religious freedom.

5. Finally, emphasis is put on various points of church reform: the overcoming of triumphalism, the practice of episcopal collegiality, reform of the Curia, concern for a renewed training of priests, and new reflection on the practice of mission, all this in the spirit of a more historical way of thinking which at the same time recognizes the concern of non-Christian churches.

Of course here again the question of doctrine proves difficult; Küng devotes a separate chapter to it, in which in part he anticipates the results of his *Infallibility?*.

Thus the future of the church opens up endless perspectives; for why should one keep silent about the long-term demands in addition to the well-known short-term ones: co-determination, election of the church government at all levels, an examination of the traditional priestly form of life, other reforms including the revaluation of the position of women: 'Admission of deaconesses and serious examination of the concrete conditions for ordaining women against which no biblical or dogmatic arguments can be raised' (T 230; see 113 below).

This book is extremely important for understanding Küng's development. Without being fully aware of it, he is formulating for the first time and in embryo an ideological critical theory which will accompany him over the coming decades in a number of forms – as a question of norm and horizon, the problems of the time, life-style and humanity (Tracy NHFT 81–92). But simultaneously, for the first time he reformulates his demands for reform in a new and decisive way in the face of the situation after the Council and a dilatory authoritarian papacy. He is not interested in soft words and playing for time. 'Truthfulness' does not allow this either. The book is not sparing with criticism, but it argues instead of blusters and marks out its own theologically responsible positions. However, as is clear in retrospect, this book also sufficiently clarifies the fronts. Here it should not be forgotten that Küng is not (or no longer) appearing in single combat, but in the name of countless fellow Christians. Granted, in 1964 procedures were set in motion against *Structures of the Church*. At Christmas 1967 it was decreed that his book *The Church* might not be translated into other languages. Küng took no notice. *Truthfulness,* this 'passionately objective book' (back cover), showed why he could not do so if he took his own demands seriously.

3. Communication with the public

Twentieth-century theology has become considerably more complex, not only because of a differentiated scholarship but because alongside theology and church government many levels of public have come into being, both within the church and outside it, with which theology is involved in exchanges. Public opinion within the church was already discovered in the nineteenth century by the rising conservative forces: since then, church leaders have loved to appeal to the faithful. Public opinion outside has taken an interest in theology and the church in this century. The Second Vatican Council was a stroke of luck for making contact with the public in the initial days of a television culture. Interest in these events was enormous: bishops and theologians were suddenly sought as dialogue partners. Some – for the moment they were men – grew imperceptibly into a role which they had not sought but which they gradually learned to treasure.

That was certainly the case with Küng. He made contact not only with bishops but also with journalists from all over the world. With the founding of *Concilium* (1964; Brand in NHGD), a centre of communication for theologians developed which was to endure. Now at the latest, Catholic theology discovered that – as at the time of public disputations – it could assume a political function in the church. The group around *Concilium* began to exercise influence through their journal, which appeared internationally. It was concerned to communicate theological knowledge to pastors, teachers of religion and interested parties (for the moment still male, as can be inferred from the first presentation). Two years after the conclusion of the Council, discontent with the course being taken by Rome increased dramatically. Papal encyclicals again emphasized obligatory celibacy (1967) and a prohibition of artificial birth control, regarding infringements as grave sins. Towards the end of this year Küng drafted a public statement 'For the Freedom of Theology' which was eventually signed by 1360 Catholic theologians, men and women. It argued for an expert and international representation of theologians with a wide range of disciplines on advisory and examining Roman commissions. This was to be stipulated in procedural rules and in regulations in canon law (RCT 177–80). Further appeals, statements and articles followed.

In 1969 the professors of the Tübingen Catholic Faculty of Theology published a statement (initially J.Ratzinger was also among the signatories) which called for time limitations to the election of bishops. A 1972 declaration 'Against Resignation' was initiated by Küng. The urgent text analyses the situation of crisis and gives five directives: not to be silent, to take personal action, to proceed jointly, to strive for interim solutions, not to give up. It was signed by thirty-three theologians with world-wide reputations. Many further declarations followed, some of which Küng initiated, helped to formulate, or simply signed (Greinacher, NHFT 43–64). It was the aim of all these declarations to create or to seize space to guarantee the freedom of theological or pastoral action. They also include programmatic personal statements, like an article on shared decision-making by the laity in church government and at church elections (1969); an invitation to self-help on the occasion of the papal decree on mixed-marriages (1979); and 'Theses on the Place of Women in Church and Society' (1976), in which, as already in 1968, there is a reference to the ordination of women (see T); interventions on the election of bishops; and finally, in summer 1978, on the occasion of the imminent papal election, a declaration by ten theologians on 'The Pope that we need'. Many contributions were written at the request of newspapers; Küng did not avoid making statements on radio and television if it seemed important to him. There were also major and striking newspaper articles on Küng's own situation and the situation of colleagues. Three of the most important and fundamental statements are included in the documentation of his book *Reforming the Church Today*. For him, none of these are polemic or angry calls for resistance, but 'documents of Catholic theology's self-respect' (RCT 2).

These activities were and are important for Küng. He sees them not only as possibilities of influencing the development of the Catholic Church but also as a service to those who are dependent on expert help. This costs him and his colleagues time and energy; a Roman dignitary once marvelled at his 'effective secretariat'. But the benefit for him is great. In critical times he maintained (and maintains) lively contact not only with colleagues but – and this is just as important to him – with Christians attempting to cope with their everyday life in faith. Groups like the 'Church from Below' and 'Kirchentage from Below', the readers of the journal *Publik Forum*, activities for the group Christian Rights in the Church over a church plebiscite and comparable movements abroad continue to be important for him. Perhaps these contacts and a constant commitment to them is the secret of a theology which constantly discovers new questions, ways and visions.

In the 1970s, collaboration in the Ecumenical University Institutes Group (Bochum, Heidelberg, Munich [Catholic and Protestant], Münster and Tübingen) were particularly important for Küng. A memorandum on 'The Reform and Recognition of Church Ministries' (1973) was the result of many years of collaboration. The aim was to work out a conception of the ministry of leadership in the church which could serve as a basis for an ecumenical agreement. Here Küng could check this understanding of ministry by other positions, extend it, and test the degree to which it was capable of achieving a consensus. The collaboration of Professors E. Schlick, H. Fries and W. Pannenberg were important for him. The core of the approach of *The Church* was confirmed. The task of proclaiming the gospel lies primarily with the community. The apostles, who were themselves members of their communities, had four special tasks: founding and leading communities, concern for internal and mutual unity, and concern for authentic preaching. From the beginning this ministry was surrounded with manifold other ministries. The task of church 'ministry' today is public perception of the common cause. The key words here are leadership, stimulation, co-ordination, integration and representation both inside and outside. Ordination is recognized as authorization of the public perception of the mission of Christ, but it cannot be reduced to a reified event. The discussion which followed was full of reservations and restraint on the official Catholic side. It was felt that ordination and the office of bishop were being surrendered to mere 'functional thought'. In short, what was expected was more a theology inspired by the sacraments.

In this connection a brief publication is significant for Küng. Even now it is not out of date, though it may be thought to need expansion. It raises the question *Why Priests?* (1971), and once again spells out an understanding of ministry which for Küng follows from the New Testament (WP 25–36) and the historical development (WP 37–51). Again Küng begins with the picture of a community responsible to the gospel, and then compares this with the modern awareness. The key words are democratization, community, freedom, equality and fraternity (WP 15–24). These great utopias of our present are accepted in principle, but thought through in the light of the message of the New Testament. A democracy is sought which finds its laws in the New Testament and takes over the aims of the New Testament; a community which does not allow any states or ranks; a freedom in the spirit which flows from an advocacy for the world; an equality which overcomes the differences of class, race and caste.

In this little book Küng develops a very sober picture which resists the later developments towards the sacralizing and sacramentalizing of the ministry. Here he takes several steps. Instead of office he proposes the term ministry, since it is backed up by the New Testament and emphasizes the functional dimension, and because the functionary can be imprisoned in the praxis of the ministry. Küng then speaks of the ministry of administration (WP 54, 74–8) instead of priesthood, and here too allows himself to be guided by the New Testament witnesses. Again he makes it clear that the community as a whole is apostolic discipleship, since it knows that it is supported by abiding agreement with the apostolic testimony. Only in this framework and the framework of manifold functions can one speak of the 'special' apostolic discipleship of the ministries of leadership which lead the churches, ground them and guard their roots in the gospel. After this foundation has been laid, Küng traces the development in church history and finally arrives at some concrete characteristics of the church's ministry which today could lead to some relaxation: the ministry of church leadership must not be completely full-time, life-long, bestowing rank, academic, celibate and exclusively masculine (WP 54–60). It is to be understood as a permanent ministry to a Christian community in the sense of spiritual leadership, co-ordination, inspiration and representation (WP 60–4). Depending on the requirements, it is to be shaped flexibly and examined in the light of the community in the sprit of Jesus. Here ordination assumes an important function; not, however, in the sense of a sacrament but as a sign which protects the tasks of those who are called and makes an ecumenical understanding possible (65–70).

Küng never resumed this work, which is incorporated into the memorandum mentioned above in a different form. That is regrettable. So he stopped before working out a doctrine of the sacraments, which never appeared because of the pressure of circumstances. The general development indicated a different way for him.

4. Infallible?

Küng wrote his *Infallible? An Enquiry* on the centenary of Vatican I; it was prepared for in two ways. On the one hand, in Küng's books and proposals for reform one question had always proved to be the most difficult: what about the truth of dogma, i.e. for the Catholic Church the Christian truth which has been laid down infallibly? This question appears constantly as the last and most complicated in Küng's series of enquiries, reform proposals or new formulations. That is true of *The Council and Reunion* (CR 216f.), *Structures of the Church* (SC 305–51), *The Church* (C 343, 447–9) and *Truthfulness* (T 176–86). The Council made no contribution to a new reflection, but rather brought confusion. So it was natural that this question should be discussed again thoroughly – precisely because of its central and at the same time symbolic significance for the papal claim to power. On the other hand, the critical analyses of the church's truthfulness at least raise the question whether such a claim to authenticity can really be intrinsically compatible with the claim to infallible teaching. Again a problem of church structure and a question of the conditions of Christian truth supplement one another. The catalyst is the argumentation of the encyclical on birth control (*Humanae vitae*), which – at any rate implicitly – insists on the immutability of this doctrine. Küng had already referred incessantly to this in *Truthfulness* (T 175ff.).

(a) Ecumenical irritation

What was, what is the problem? Let's recapitulate: Küng's theological concern is the reform of the Catholic Church, against both a biblical and an ecumenical horizon. This undermines the stability and immutability of doctrinal statements and puts in question the function of infallibly true doctrinal statements as guarantees of truth – especially when they are obligated to Vatican I's rationalistic and legalistic concept of faith. To a Platonically timeless ideal of truth are added, as we saw, dynamic elements: the recollection of Jesus of Nazareth, the influence of cultural (Greek, Roman, Germanic and finally modern) contexts, the interplay of new attempts and polemical demarcation, the tragedy of a repudiated Reformation, dialogue with other churches and dialogue with a profoundly changed world. It seems that true statements never remain the same, and if they remain the same, they constantly change their significance and interpretation without our action. Word for word in *Structures* and *The Church* Küng has repeatedly and indeed incessantly referred to this: 'Every statement can be true *and* false – in accordance with its aim, structure and its intent. Its meaning is more difficult to discover than its form' (SC 351; C 343).

In short, we have a hermeneutical problem; 'historical interpretation' alone satisfies the demands of a radical theological truthfulness (T 195), as Küng already states in 1962:

'The faith can be the same, the formulations different, indeed contradictory. Behind the different and opposing formulations of faith stand different ideas and mental images, concepts, judgments and conclusions, and different forms of perception, feeling, thinking, volition, speaking, describing, acting, different forms of consciousness of existence and of the objective world, different physiological, psychological, aesthetic, linguistic, logical, ethnological, historical, ideological, philosophical, and religious presuppositions, different individual and collective experiences, languages, world views, environmental structures, conceptions of human nature, and the different traditions of individual peoples, of theological schools, of universities, and of orders. Is it any wonder that the Christians of one faith often do not understand one another, that they were separated when they could have been united?' (SC 345f.).

Küng's problem can only be solved hermeneutically, as part of the process of understanding, and no longer with Aristotelian logic. Now processes of understanding first of all run pre-consciously, spontaneously, in the depth of immediate perception, guided by individual and collective factors, and constantly caught up in the circle of pre-understanding and interpretation. They remain hidden from us as long as understanding functions unproblematically in communication, linguistic argument and mutual understanding. They become a problem as soon as communication goes wrong and understanding is blocked. Far-reaching blocks to understanding within the church and a defective elementary understanding about the basic interpretations of faith are the real reason for Küng's intervention. It is intended to overcome barriers, instead of allowing them to grow up without any control. For

Küng the discussion about infallibility is a discussion about the way in which truth is dealt with inside the church that is hermeneutical and at the same time related to church practice; it is not a discussion about the capacity of the Catholic Church for truth. That it was understood in the latter way by Küng's opponents, who are the guardians of an idealistic hermeneutic, is conceptually their problem, but a catastrophe for the discussion and further developments in the Catholic Church (Pesch, NHFT, 13–16, 24–7).

Therefore it must be clear what Küng is not concerned with:

1. He is not concerned with the question whether the Christian faith has or may have a claim to truth. On the contrary, the claim to truth is the starting point of his problem.

2. Nor is he concerned with the question whether in particular situations the community of believers, called church (whether this is understood to be Catholic or ecumenical may be left aside here), has the right or the duty to mould particular aspects (fundamental, threatened, particularly open to misunderstanding) into binding statements which are agreed in the community and protected by it. In no way does he put in question the ecumenically binding doctrinal structure of the Christian tradition. Here one should read his exposition of the creed (Cr), of classical christology (OBC 273–7) or the doctrine of the Trinity (OBC 343–462). That colleagues or members of the hierarchy do not agree with details of this exposition is another matter, part of the everyday course of theological disputes.

3. Küng repeatedly and in different arguments justifies and defends his conviction that the church remains 'maintained in truth' by the power of the Spirit (e.g. in *Justification, The Council and Reunion, Structures of the Church, The Church, Truthfulness, Infallible?, The Church Maintained in Truth*). However, he insists that the mode of this being maintained in truth must be discussed.

4. Küng presents his (quite critical) interpretation of the papal claim to infallibility not as definitive but as 'an enquiry', comparable in status and aim to a parliamentary question or intervention. Here he is not proclaiming any monological theses but introducing important perspectives into the debate. Anyone who knows the development of Küng's theology can confirm that the form of an enquiry is no trick, but a status appropriate for a theological thesis. He cannot present the interpretation differently if he does not want to fall victim to the mistake of which he accuses the official doctrine of infallibility. In formal terms, he is not looking for dialogue about the positions themselves but for backgrounds, aims and arguments.

5. Küng expected a vigorous reaction and in a sense was being provocative; this was to serve to open up a problem which had already been addressed in terms of ideological criticism in his *Truthfulness*. However, as yet no comprehensive analysis had been made of its theological basis. Yet if Küng's enquiry were to be recognized as indicating a problem, then the main theological barrier to all wider reforms, the *point d'honneur*, the aura surrounding what was called the 'Roman' system, would be overcome.

6. Küng's intervention is concerned with theory, with pragmatics (in the sense of speech-acts), with hermeneutics, but these always have a practical purpose. He is looking for dialogue about the most suppressed complex of motivation for Rome's action, but one which is central and at work everywhere; it manifestly lies in the wrong interpretation of an understanding of faith. However, it is this complex which legitimates Roman centralism, the Roman claim to exclusiveness and its historical way of thinking, and surrounds it with an aura of unalterability. There is no question that those who are caught up in it and draw their identity from it react emotionally instead of arguing. There is also no question that it will be denied that those who act in an overheated way have good reasons, pure motives and loyalty to the church. The rest is quickly and simply told.

As I have already said, the starting point of the argument is the controversial decision on birth control in which Paul VI does not follow the moral theological arguments of substance but the formal argument of the Roman theory of infallibility. In the minority opinion of the commission concerned it runs like this:

'If contraception were declared not intrinsically evil, in honesty it would have to be acknowledged that the Holy Spirit in 1930 (*Casti Connubii*), in 1951 (address of Pius XII to midwives) and 1958 (address to the Society of Haematologists in the year of Pius XII's death), supported the Protestant churches, and for half a century did not protect Pius XI, Pius XII and a large part of the Catholic hierarchy against a very grave error, one most pernicious to souls; for it would have suggested that they condemned most imprudently, on pain of eternal punishment, thousands upon thousands of human acts which were now approved. Indeed, it can be neither denied nor ignored that these acts would be approved for the same fundamental reasons which Protestants alleged and which they (popes and bishops) condemned or at least did not approve' (quoted from I 46).

(b) A shocking intervention

This argument, with its latently anti-ecumenical spirit and its doubtful identification of the Holy Spirit with the Catholic hierarchy, is based on the theory of the 'ordinary' infallible magisterium which comes into force when the individual bishops 'preserving amongst themselves and with Peter's successor the bond of communion, in their authoritative teaching concerning faith and morals, are in agreement that a particular teaching is to be held definitely and absolutely'(Vatican II Constitution on the Church, no. 25).

So according to this theory the prohibition against birth control – like the prohibition against the ordination of women! – belongs to the universal infallible Catholic deposit of faith. Moreover this argument agrees with the traditional neo-scholastic textbook approach which Vatican II adopted in its own partly obscurantist argument – obscurantist because, to put it in technical terms, with a bad theological hermeneutic it does not apply the distinction between the 'norming norm' of scripture, the 'normed norm' of tradition, and the current church magisterium (I 56–64).

In a further step Küng refers to the exegetical studies in *The Church*. Since from a biblical perspective first of all the church as a whole stands in the apostolic succession, the hierarchical monopolistic claim of church teaching can hardly hold. The language of faith cannot be binding without a consensus stated by the church as a whole. It can also be demonstrated on what specific grounds the one-sided definition of papal infallibility came about in 1870, how entangled this definition is in legal categories, and why in view of the exaggerated veneration of the pope at that time the final formulation with its provisos was understood as a restrictive definition. Pius IX's deep commitment to his own cause, the lack of freedom at the Council and the way in which the pope discriminated against a strong minority must not be concealed. In a later historical investigation of the Council, A.M. Hasler was to deny outright that there was freedom of speech and action (Hasler 1977 and 1979).

These are the main elements of Küng's enquiry. There are

  1. serious problems with the biblical basis;

  2. objections in principle from the tradition of the whole church;

  3. massive questions about the representative character, course and freedom of the Council which made the decision; and

  4. criticism of the legalistic, centralistic and rationalistic narrowing of the concepts of faith, doctrine and infallibility. In addition there is

5. the question whether faith depends at all on infallible statements or on infallibly true propositions.

What solution to the problem does Küng himself propose? Hermeneutically he points out that statements could never be true or false in an absolute way. Statements fall short of reality, are open to misinterpretation, can be translated only to a limited degree, move on, and tend to become ideologies. These limitations of propositional speech also attach to church definitions. Hence such assertions as that statements defined in this way could be infallibly true; that the one who makes them could not err over their definition; that the statements themselves therefore cannot be revised – such assertions, which in turn present themselves as infallible, get nowhere. For this reason and for the reasons mentioned above, Küng holds that errors are possible in principle – unless there are new insights. He does not claim that any statement is erroneous. But he regards it as impossible to make a claim to infallibility *a priori*, i.e. prior to all definitions of content, intention and situation. In accordance with biblical tradition he holds to the conviction that the church is maintained in truth – a truth in the comprehensive sense. Küng prefers to speak of indefectibility. His proposal is: 'The church will remain in the truth in spite of all the errors which are always possible' (I 144). This formulation maintains the biblical conviction, can hope for ecumenical assent, does not undermine the certainty of faith, and shows the church to be a community capable of truth and endowed with the truth, but a society on the way to the truth, and not yet at its goal. The dispute over infallibility is thus not a self-contained one, but has a representative function for the understanding of faith, truth and the church.

With good reason Küng quotes Hebrews and I Corinthians at this point. Both begin from a picture of the church which corresponds to the present situation of upheaval:

'Thus the Epistle to the Hebrews sees the church as a pilgrim community of the faithful, exposed in all its members to temptation, error and upheaval, its only truth being the great promise revealed in Christ. The admonition is plain, and no one in the church is exempted, not even the leaders, whose faith is held up as an example (13.7): "So hold up your limp arms and steady your trembling knees and smooth out the path you tread; then the injured limb will not be wrenched, it will grow strong again. Always be wanting peace with all people, and the holiness without which no one can ever see the Lord. Be careful that no one is deprived of the grace of God and that no root of bitterness should begin to grow and make trouble; this can poison a whole community. And be careful that there is no immorality, or that any of you does not degrade religion like Esau, who sold his birthright for one single meal" (12.12–16)' (I 148).

Or as Paul says: 'Our knowledge is imperfect and our prophesying is imperfect; but once perfection comes, all imperfect things will disappear' (I Cor.13.9) (ibid.).

(c) An alarming reaction

Küng had touched a sensitive nerve. That was shown by the excessive reactions from the church authorities and theologians, but also from many Catholics and other Christians. Unfortunately he could feel that the official church indirectly confirmed his view. His intentions had not been understood and his intervention had in fact been seen as a general attack on the Catholic Church (on what the professionals call its 'formal principle'). The reactions confirmed this suspicion: the authorities were incapable of open communication and an exchange of arguments. At this level communication seemed to be no longer possible, and Küng's position in church politics reached a dangerous point. The theological reaction was overwhelming, given profile by no less a figure than Karl Rahner, who with others organized and edited a collected volume – deliberately without involving Küng (PU). Küng had expected a technical theological discussion (including him, not without him) and theological mediation. He found allies in the fight who later joined forces in another extensive composite volume (F), but soon a broad front of influential colleagues was drawn up against him.

Why, with a few exceptions, did they sweepingly reject Küng's intervention? Why were the first reactions so emotional, and why in his disappointment did Küng also react so emotionally? A first element in the answer is the subject of the discussion. Manifestly the question 'Infallible or not?' did not allow any qualifications, and manifestly the public within the church associated with it the question 'Catholic or not?' A second element is the state of the church. Those involved knew or sensed that the future form of the church was under debate. And finally, Küng's question spread theological terror, as though the Catholic Church was harbouring a mystery which had been made taboo and now had been violated. So soon nerves became raw and the discussion took on a dangerous life of its own, until finally it died down out of frustration.

On closer inspection, speechlessness spread. Hardly any detailed arguments were advanced. Neither exegetes nor church historians, neither the interpreters of Vatican I nor Protestant theologians, rejected Küng's arguments. The arguments from linguistic philosophy to the effect that Küng had confused infallible speech with irreformable propositions did not help, given the praxis of infallibility. Detailed exegeses of the 1870 definition did not meet Küng's questions. Here a tendency made itself felt to see Küng simply as a bad mediator and a muddled thinker, an inconsequential critic. Küng, it was asserted, had interpreted Vatican I in a maximalist way so as then to be able to refute it. However, the softer interpretations proposed did not stand up to the Roman view. One could think that in this small book Küng had not argued comprehensively enough, but no one really helped this argument on one side or another. There were no more than argumentative skirmishes. Even in retrospect the observer still remains helpless.

After what is now twenty-six years and a recent re-reading, I still find Rahner's reaction as incomprehensible as it is amazing. I cannot understand why it is so sweeping. He finds 'the whole style arrogant', of course successful 'among people who are *a priori* aggressive and allergic to Rome, the bishops and traditional theology'. He can speak with Küng only 'as with a liberal Protestant', for whom even scripture is no longer the *norma normans*. Even later he was unaware of the latent arrogance shown in this statement both towards Protestants and towards Küng. Rahner is so excited that he asks the reader in the case of his own answer 'not to make too strict logical demands on the train of thought as such'. Why not, if in effect he is pressing for Küng to be excluded from the church? Didn't Küng deserve a precise refutation based on exegesis, church history and theology, rather than such severe charges, which would justify excommunication? What point was there in the accusation of that Küng was making a scene, when he had already approached the problem repeatedly, sometimes with extensive material? In commenting that he still 'thinks that within the church as it is one can fight with what in its own self-understanding is binding teaching against depravations in the church' (PU 47), Rahner should not have acted as if Küng thought otherwise. Shouldn't he have noted that Küng is not concerned with the binding faith of the church but with infallibility as the dogma of dogmas?

Thus he emphasizes positions which Küng never disputes, and imputes alternatives where Küng differentiates. The 'operative union' offered mentions conditions the introduction of which betrays a deep ignorance of Küng's theology and the presuppositions of which insult

Küng as a Catholic colleague. No, Rahner's zeal for the truth may be to his credit, but he does not really take in Küng's approach, any more than his fellow-fighters do. Instead of this, he denies Küng the right to a home in his church and thus makes an open discussion of the problem impossible. What alternative is there than for Küng to defend himself with all his strength? Manifestly transcendental theology cannot accept ideological criticism any more than it can accept the correlation of praxis and theory. There seems never to have been a intensive dialogue with Protestant theology. I do not mention this to take up a theological dispute again, but because even now many people believe that the Roman sanctions against Küng can be defended by Rahner's intervention at that time.

The conflict with Rahner makes one problem clear which Küng had consciously or unconsciously kept raising in the preceding years. At a very early stage it struck him that it was possible to speak relatively openly and critically about the reforms in the church – except on questions of doctrine and doctrinal development, on conciliar and papal doctrinal authority. In these questions the argument had to be careful and cautious, indirect rather than direct, with the help of a quotation rather than in one's own words. Küng described this problem increasingly clearly, and most clearly in *Truthfulness*. The critical category of truthfulness also came closest to the matter. There seemed to be an insistence on the truth, on not conceding errors and – in good rationalistic fashion – on avoiding the supposedly slippery slope of constantly proving the truth. On this presupposition the claim to infallibility then issues in the paradox that a formally legal bond to definitions of truth represents the greatest danger for authentic truth. The *bon mot* about a senate free of error (quoted above, 110) shows the inner, so to speak existential, danger of a love of truth which does not face up to the realism of the provisional everyday.

Put in epistemological terms, the main problem of understanding rests on a fundamental misapprehension, which still cannot be discussed officially in the church. It is the difference between a hermeneutical idealism (one thinks of Heidegger) and a hermeneutic which is critical of dialogue (as we know it from the Frankfurt School). Hermeneutical idealism interprets texts for its own understanding, in a splendid and certainly fruitful naivety. It projects its protective covering on itself: for Gadamer this is the horizon of history; for Heidegger language as the house of being; for theologians the living tradition. Such metaphors ignore the storms, and people think that they know how the texts were meant 'in themselves' and how they have to be interpreted, i.e. understood today. Then everything that is historically conditioned is filtered out and made excusable. This is to overlook how deeply the facts shape us and to give them irrational confirmation – they are said to be unfathomable and to save us. Küng is convinced that such an approach leaves out praxis and also any appeal of Jesus orientated on praxis.

By contrast, a hermeneutic which is critical of ideology has discovered – in good biblical fashion – this praxis as a significant element and critic. Texts do not disclose themselves in a purpose-free reflection, but where they govern the everyday, resist it or yield to it. The church, too, is not the construct of a protective cloak, but living praxis, and no word is said in it which is not related to that. Therefore, sobering though this is, a hermeneutic which is critical of ideology relates texts to their often trivial, blind context, governed by power. It shows what they really confirm, disclose, or also veil and legitimate. In one case – one thinks of the drama of Constance – the praxis is that of the winners, the successful Roman system. So if an authority has not only the competence in interpretation but – as in the highest court of appeal – an overall competence which is beyond the reach of any appeal, then clearly what applies is not the interpretation devised by hermeneutics but the one for which Rome decides. In that case, what is being debated is not the quality of a particular idealistic interpretation but Rome's claim to interpret even the definition of infallibility in a binding way and to impose it at will. Küng is simply asking whether and how this development can be justified theologically. Whether we have good or questionable popes is irrelevant here. For Küng the simple question is whether this monopoly corresponds to the intentions of the gospel.

Küng – like his critics – does not regard the prohibition of artificial birth control as infallible. Of course not! But he shows that the minority of that commission and the pope regarded the prohibition as infallible on the basis of their criteria. That false decision had the advantage enjoyed by the *agent provocateur:* a mistake came to light. Instead of this, many saw Küng as the *agent provocateur* – and were surprised when in November 1995, twenty-five years later, the prohibition against the ordination of women was presented as infallible doctrine.

For Küng and his theology a dangerous point had been reached. In the present circumstances only fixation and hardening were possible. The Cassandra effect hit him. Küng recognized that, and therefore in essentials concluded his ecclesiological project. He no longer addressed the context, but the content of Christian faith.

5. What picture of the church?

The debate on infallibility not only stirred up the dust but also formulated tasks and brought clarifications. These cannot be gone into here (see *Fehlbar?*). Unfortunately a critical theological assimilation of what took place still lies ahead. The discussion of Küng's position has still not been freed from the fatal pincer movement represented by the question 'Catholic or not?'. Only when it has been recognized that his approach corresponds to a Catholic form of thinking (Riplinger, NHGD 211–33) – or at least is related to it – can and must the critical theological discussion of it begin.

Küng's concern with the Catholic Church has not ceased, but the basic work had been done by 1970. The questions of church reform got stuck in the interplay between the Roman line and local reaction. Although the Roman attitude developed in a difficult and disappointing way in coming years, the development took an interesting form, open to the future, on various continents, in the communities, and among mature and not just young Christians (Hebblethwaite, NHFT 65–78). Meanwhile an ecumenical approach has developed a dynamic of its own which cannot be stopped. Many communities take it for granted that they should be responsible for themselves. Küng can feel that his proposals for reform, visions and points of criticism have found confirmation. But in his view, what has been said once need not be developed a second time.

Twice Küng has composed programmatic works. In 1980, the year when the church's permission to teach was finally withdrawn from him, he wrote in the Preface to *Wegzeichen in die Zukunft*: 'The order of the day remains: do not lose sight of the goal, act calmly and firmly, and keep hope alive' (14). More important and more topical is the volume which appeared ten years later under the title *Reforming the Church Today. Keeping Hope Alive* (RCT). Anyone who wants to form a picture of the 'present' Küng, the state of his thought and his abiding resolve, should read this book. However, it should not be forgotten that behind these programmatic writings, these objections and pleas, visions and objections stand the results of intensive research which has been developed over decades. Increasingly, three characteristics of a contemporary church have emerged here.

1. Küng increasingly clearly paints the picture of a church which is ecumenically open and reconciled. Ecumenism between the churches is not only possible but called for by the situation and expectations of

many people. The Catholic Church would do well at last to take the great questions of the Reformation seriously.

2. Küng increasingly expects a church which discovers and takes up the questions of the time. These are not just the values and norms of the present, which even the church can no longer avoid: freedom and participation, respect for one another and concrete solidarity. Our time also brings with it a church's capacity to criticize false developments and dangers. However, Küng insists that we children of Western culture should stand by our own demands and not seek salvation in other continents.

3. With increasing intensity it becomes clear to Küng that the memory of Jesus of Nazareth does not exclude confrontation with the present. Discipleship makes possible a vital and creative immediacy to our time. The model of discipleship is proved to be right.

Küng can be a polemical author and an impatient critic, perhaps also a visionary who simplifies. But that has not caused him his difficulties. Whether he wanted it or not, for the Catholic Church he assumed the function of the troublesome Cassandra. With the problems of infallibility he instinctively touched on the heart of the problem. If this question is resolved along the lines of the New Testament and ecumenical understanding, the other visions of a church with a future can be developed.

The discussion on infallibility was carried on with grandiose words. It is not clear to some of Küng's readers precisely what his own proposed solution is. What does it mean to be preserved in the truth *despite* all possible errors? I think that this became clearer to me when I came upon the last sentences of *Structures of the Church*:

'The ecumenical task of theology on both sides is seriously to consider the truth in the error of the other and the possible error in one's own truth. In this way an encounter in shared truth takes place by turning away from alleged error. In this way the church increasingly clarifies its position as a pillar and bulwark of truth' (SC 351).

Küng contrasts a static concept of truth with a dialogical process of truth. We are never held in truth by the Spirit in an abstract way, but by concretely working through supposed and real error, real and supposed truth. So what Küng wants of the magisterium is quite simple: he calls for a spirit of partnership and brotherhood, in which it guides the process of mutual deliberation and assessment, and at least then arrives at a binding nature which is worked out dialogically and maintained dialogically. The discussion could have been so simple, if only it had been carried on in an appropriate way.

Küng himself sums up his picture of the church in four perspectives. We need a church which is not in love with the past, but which is related to its origin and the present; which is not patriarchal but characterized by partnership; which is not confessionalistically narrow but ecumenically open. And finally, it is not Eurocentrism that brings us salvation but respect for the ever greater truth, a high regard for the other religions and the sense of a multicultural plurality. Since none of this is new, Küng is convinced that 'this global future of the church has already begun' (RCT 156–62).

5

Being a Christian as Discipleship of Jesus

'This book is written for all those who, for any reason at all, honestly and sincerely want to know what Christianity, what being a Christian, really means . . . It is an attempt, in the midst of an epoch-making upheaval of the church's doctrine, morality and discipline, to discover what is permanent: what is different from other world religions and modern humanisms; and at the same time what is common to the separated Christian churches. The reader will rightly expect an account of what is decisive and distinctive about the programme of Christian practice, both historically exact and up to date, in the light of the most recent scholarship and easy to understand' (OBC 19f.).

Küng's programme of ecclesiological reform had been rejected by the church government and had provoked a divided response from his German-speaking colleagues. Many of those who also supported the central points of reform still hoped for pragmatic solutions. But it was also clear to Küng that he could not force reforms; the price of polarizations or even a split within the church would have been too high for him.

1. The new question

But about theological criteria? Weren't there simple principles which a church that appealed to Jesus Christ had to follow? On the one hand Küng insisted from the beginning on the difference between the message of the gospel and its (legitimate and necessary) interpretation by the church, whether this was justification of the sinner or discipleship of Christ. On the other hand he was aware that the gospel and faith in Jesus Christ were to be had only in a form mediated by the church; and this form continually had to be renewed. Therefore his first conclusion was that church structures needed to be reformed. The more fundamental the crisis, the more the church as a whole had to be activated. So his next conclusion was that there was a need for a reform of church proclamation. The more monopolized and irreformable the church's claim to truth, the more the powers of self-healing were blocked: 'self-appraisal', i.e. self-criticism, criticism of ideology and structure could not come into play. Obviously it was difficult to convince people who had the responsibility of everyday leadership of the need for changes. Had he not pointed out that the canon of scriptures had itself been instituted by the church? So in the last resort was not the church the ultimate authority of binding faith in God?

Precisely this problem now led Küng to the central question. What is the Christian message? How is the relationship between the binding gospel and the church's interpretation to be interpreted? Is it not possible to indicate an inner structure which – in accordance with a general Christian intuition – makes clear the priority of the gospel over the church, without detracting from the task of interpretation posed to present-day Christianity? Of course this development did not run in a straight line chronologically. Küng did not first begin to reflect now, disappointed by the response to *Infallibility?*. The question of the 'historical Jesus' was already being discussed intensively in the 1960s, but in September 1970 events began to pile up in a dramatic way. On 11 September Karl Lehmann wrote a very critical article on *Infallibility?* in the Catholic weekly *Publik*. At the same time Karl Rahner began to put into writing his heartfelt annoyance about the book. And in Brussels, at the first international *Concilium* congress, Küng presented a twenty-minute text on the Jesus of history; this was the basic scheme for *On Being a Christian*.

So Küng could begin the discussion on infallibility in the awareness that he had not yet spoken his last word. His concern was not once again to expound the great formulae of early christology, perhaps more critically than others; he was on the track of deeper foundations. First of all he related who Jesus was, what he preached, did, suffered and what the disciples experienced at Easter. It had to be worth taking the trouble to work out such a christology 'from below' and to see how far it led. At all events it promised clarification and illumination, and ventured a step back into a time when there was still no church. That Küng is specifically appealing to this time already became clear in *The Church*. Here a theological dimension is announced which has not yet been fathomed. And certainly it is important, since it is no longer enough simply to paraphrase faith as obedience or as 'feeling with the church'.

Küng wanted to illuminate the content and practice of faith from deeper roots: discipleship of Jesus, the proclamation of his mighty acts and his fate, and remembrance of him. Therefore it was important to relate Jesus' life, his fate and God's action in him after the event – of course in a historically responsible way – and to follow it up (a course which is different from imitation). The preaching, teaching and action of all those who refer to him can be measured by this.

As Küng soon discovered, this approach has yet another advantage: the message of Jesus can again be presented to outsiders in such a way that it presupposes a sympathetic audience, but as yet no Christian faith. The message itself then sees to the rest. The structure and the model of faith in the Gospels again come alive: people gather round Jesus of Nazareth, experience him, and go with him – half not knowing, have having made a decision. 'Faith' is not the consequence of an abstract decision (of which theologians are so fond of dreaming) but a quite practical programme, trust which succeeds and fails: one has only to read the Gospels. It is embedded in streams of experience and in attempts to understand them before God, before an ultimate reality. Faith is this vital and living dynamic, not an abstract assent to propositional systems or charismatic exclamations.

The rediscovery of this model 'behind' the later models (one thinks of Paul's belief in Christ or the incarnation christology of the early church) is certainly connected with a new cultural situation in Western Europe. For many of our contemporaries the traditional material of faith, whether Protestant or Catholic, has dissolved; at any rate it has forfeited its claim to be taken for granted. So they begin the way literally from the start. They have the opportunity to encounter companions in faith anew in elementary and quite worldly situations. Küng's new approach derives its real theological force from this contemporary situation.

So strictly speaking Küng is not concerned with a theoretical question which is perhaps of historical interest, namely 'Who *was* Jesus of Nazareth?' This question could have been put and answered only against the background of the history of faith hitherto. Küng's opponents would have been quite right in making this objection to him here. The question is a much more elementary one, 'Who *is* Jesus of Nazareth? What can he be (for me) if I rely on him? What form does the life of a disciple of his take, and what does this have to do with God?' In keeping with the shift in our culture which has already been mentioned, the question is no longer secondary and ontological, but primary and 'historic', as Bultmann understood it. Of course the question who Jesus of Nazareth was had often been put already. There were novels about Jesus and committed scholarly investigations by exegetes. Küng wanted to know what Jesus means for Christian faith. So he got down to his new project. Assimilating historical research, presenting it and interpreting it for the present day, was to take him at least three years of the most intensive work.

It is one the truisms of historical research that significant answers presuppose significant questions, i.e. a comprehensive awareness of the problem. Therefore in *On Being a Christian* Küng paces out the horizon of his questions. He formulates the key issues. What is to be made of the present-day world, which has become so autonomous and is seeking a future (OBC 25–56)? How can the question about God be formulated appropriately and in terms of the present day (OBC 57–88)? How do the Christian churches respond to the challenge of the world religions (OBC 89–116)? That this description of the horizon is already shaped by Christian perspectives need not be a problem. Küng's questions and perspectives must take up the hopes, anxieties and possibilities of humankind in an elementary way. He must also explain why Jesus is not a myth but a historically guaranteed, historically documented figure into whom a critical investigation can be made. The specific experience of Christian memory is that in a particular time and at a particular place there lived a human being of flesh and blood. According to all the criteria at our disposal he was endowed by the spirit of God, a Jew, to some degree a rebel, who ended on the cross (OBC 333). The chapter in which Küng explains this utterly human peculiarity of Christian faith is entitled 'The Decision' (OBC 117–174).

2. A history of provocations

'If we reflect on all that has been said here about changed awareness, the will of God and the revolutionary relativizing of the most sacred traditions and institutions, we shall understand how essential – in the tradition of the Old Testament prophets – the combative element is to the make-up of Jesus. Jesus cannot by any means be understood merely as a soft, gentle, unresisting, good-natured and humbly acquiescent figure. Even the Jesus image of Francis of Assisi has its limits, and still more does the pietistic and to some degree also the hierarchistic Jesus image of the nineteenth and twentieth centuries. Nietzsche, a pastor's son, rightly rebelled against this feeble Jesus image of his youth, which he could not associate with the Gospel statements about Jesus as the pugnacious critic of the hierarchs and theologians' (OBC 254).

(a) In the Jewish context

Küng reconstructs the figure of Jesus of Nazareth as far as historical criticism allows. But no fragile object appears at the end, like an ancient, weathered vase, cracked all over, which can only survive behind glass. The figure prompts urgent questions. Küng seeks the surprise, the provocation, the contrast to later projections.

'Jesus has often seemed to be "domesticated" in the churches, turned almost into the representative of the religio-political system, justifying everything in its dogma, worship and canon law: the invisible head of a very clearly visible ecclesiastical machinery, the guarantor of whatever has come into existence by way of belief, mores and discipline. What an enormous amount he has been made to authorize and sanction in church and society in the course of Christendom's two thousand years! How Christian rulers and princes of the church, Christian parties, classes, races have invoked him! For what odd ideas, laws, traditions, customs, measures he has had to take the blame! Against all the varied attempts to domesticate him, therefore, it must be made clear: *Jesus did not belong to the ecclesiastical and social establishment*' (OBC 177).

Therefore in good historical-critical tradition it must always remain clear who Jesus was not: he was neither a priest nor a theologian; neither a party-politician nor a revolutionary nor a monk; neither a priest nor a member of a religious order. One has to pay a price for seeing him out of his time. Nevertheless, Jesus was clearly a radical: he cannot be commandeered by any social grouping. Küng shows this by means of four key words: 1. establishment, 2. revolution, 3. emigration, 4. compromise; these refer to the Sadducees and the Zealots, the Essene ascetics and the Pharisees (OBC 177–213; cf. also twenty years later the cross of co-ordinates on the option within Judaism and on the world religions, Chr 33–6).

1. Jesus did not belong to the establishment; he was buoyed up far too much by an intense expectation of the end, though he was wrong about its chronology.

2. Despite all his concern for change Jesus distanced himself from a Zealot ideology which was ready for violence and did not avoid contact with collaborators and the outcast. Instead of violence he wrote something else into his social-political programme: love of enemies, forgiveness and a beatitude on the peace-makers.

3. Unlike John the Baptist or his friends from Qumran, Jesus did not withdraw ascetically from the world and society in an elitist way, either in expectation of disaster or in hope of a supernatural renewal of a community threatened by politics, society and culture. He wanted to remain accessible to all. And finally,

4. Jesus did not want to make the current compromises being developed in the Pharisaic movement, which was philanthropic, close to the people, highly respected and politically important. In it people were too ready to replace a readiness to do God's will with casuistry, and sometimes to avoid the unqualified well-being of men and women by slippery tricks, in order to get round regulations in the Torah. All the criticism of the Law which later found its way into the tradition is connected with this controversy.

These four demarcations mark out the social framework of a fateful career. At the same time Jesus pursues his course down to the last entanglements in Jewish thought and in Jewish traditions. There is nothing in Jesus that is not Jewish, that does not go back to Moses and the prophets, the wisdom literature and the psalms. Therefore Küng can also show without contortions how Jesus was solely concerned with God's cause (OBC 214–248), and how he was concerned solely with the human cause (OBC 249–77), which again had Jewish dimensions (OBC 278–342). This involved him in a fatal conflict.

(b) God's cause

'God's cause', too, is an abstract term, which is treated in a concrete way in the Jesus narrative. In Jesus' intensive world of narrative and imagery it is called 'kingdom of God', and in apocalyptic notions it is bound up with the end time. Jesus and many others expected God's kingdom in the imminent future; they were disappointed here, and demythologization is unavoidable. But that does not affect the core of Jesus' conclusions, since for him it is the message of 'God's infinite goodness and unconditional grace, particularly for the abandoned and destitute' (OBC 215). It is a kingdom to be created through God's free action, as is shown in the 'Our Father'. God's absolute future is discussed there. What Jesus means to say is this: at the end (of human life, of human history, of the world) there is not nothing, but God: 'There is an ultimate meaning . . . which is freely offered to human beings . . .' (OBC 223).

Certainly God's kingdom cannot be had for nothing: 'The time of relativizing God's will is past.' Here, as the Sermon on the Mount shows,

God's will is contrasted with the Law and external rules with the utmost degree of radicalization:

> 'Not only are adultery, perjury, murder contrary to God's will, but also those things which simply cannot be brought under the Law: even an adulterous disposition, untruthful thinking and talking, a hostile attitude. To use the word "only" in any sense in interpreting the Sermon on the Mount means curtailing and weakening the unconditional will of God. There is no question of "only" a better fulfilment of the law, "only" a new disposition, "only" an examination of sin in the light of Jesus who alone is righteous, "only" for those who are called to perfection, "only" for that time, "only" for a short period' (OBC 247).

However, because Jesus sets the signs of the kingdom already here and now, the kingdom can already begin here and now. If the blind see and the lame walk, if the good news is preached to the poor, then Jesus is establishing signs: no practitioner of salvation or miracle-working doctor (the miracle stories must be treated cautiously and interpreted critically) nor any over-spiritual pastor and confessor, but someone animated by God's spirit is acting here in a way at which people can only marvel. One of the many small, concentrated and very precise gems of the book is the section on the Sermon on the Mount (OBC 244–8), which has been understood so differently and which Küng explains in such an illuminating way (for his time!).

For Küng, the Sermon on the Mount knows only one common denominator, 'Let God's will be done', without any relativization. As the examples from Matthew 5 show (left cheek, two miles, shirt as well as cloak . . .), God's demand is not aimed at a formal obedience but appeals to human 'magnanimity'; it is always a demand for more. God demands 'not something, but myself – and myself wholly and entirely' (OBC 246). Precisely for that reason, for Jesus the problem does not begin with adultery, perjury and murder but with an adulterous disposition, untruthful thought and a hostile attitude. The early church already began to blunt these demands, but they have continually asserted themselves.

(c) The human cause

At the same time the human cause? The connection is only apparently paradoxical and complicated, and is far more than a dialectical game.

Certainly Jesus expected a total (mental and practical) focus of human beings on God; that is what is meant by the key term *metanoia*, 'a change of mind' (formerly a favourite translation was 'penance') in the direction of gratitude, trust and joy. But what God wants is human well-being and – if this is thought through to the end – the fulfilment of individual commandments, social and cultic duties simply for the sake of fellow human beings. This is what Jesus argues for: the sources make it clear to Küng '. . .how much Jesus combined unselfishness and self-assurance, humility and severity, gentleness and aggressiveness . . . Whenever Jesus had to assert God's will in face of the resistance of the powerful – persons, institutions, traditions, hierarchies – he did so aggressively, with no holds barred. He spoke in this way for the sake of people on whom no unnecessarily heavy burdens were to be imposed' (OBC 254).

That is what is meant by the formula that love of God and love of neighbour coincide. Küng speaks (in all historical seriousness) of 'an unparalleled reduction and concentration of all the commandments into this dual commandment', which 'combines love of God and love of man in an indissoluble unity' (OBC 255). That means a departure from egotism, a concern for self-surrender, the encounter of God in one's fellow human being and in accordance with the parable of the Good Samaritan. I cannot choose my neighbour; my neighbour is the one who needs me, perhaps even my enemy. Since *all* human beings are cared for by God, Jesus does not recognize the 'frontier and estrangement between those of one's own group and those outside it' (OBC 259).

Küng describes the radical quality of this love under the key terms forgiveness, service and renunciation and then extends this traditional perspective under the key word 'solidarity'. It is not just that law and temple are relativized; that would again tie the breakthrough to religious questions. The centre is occupied by Jesus, who was himself biassed in favour of the poor, who was himself poor and announced happiness for the poor: not as a general rule but as a promise; as a promise which is fulfilled for those who do not just listen in a neutral way but appropriate it in trust. Trust in God can already lead to a new life, to unlimited readiness to help, to a well-considered lack of care, to undemanding contentment. But the foundations of religion are also shaken, for he accepts traitors and presents foreigners and heretics as models. One must forgive the guilty endlessly.

'Evidently an opportunity is offered to everyone, independently of social, ethnic, political or religious divisions. And the sinner is accepted even before he repents. First comes grace, then the achievement!' The feast is prepared for all, including beggars and cripples out on the streets. Jesus gives the feast, and it includes people who continue to be excluded from respectable tables (OBC 274).

By comparison with a common christology it is interesting to see how late and in what form the question about Jesus himself is now put.

First come action and experience: what Jesus said and did. First come his dealings with men and women, his behaviour, the hopes that he had and communicated, and his relationship with God, which had an effect and arose in the circles around him; his social position and the challenges which he put to fellow men and women and society. Had this all been a matter of course, one could now go on to the order of the day. But clearly a conflict arose. This conflict first forms the background to the question of his identity, here introduced as a specific question: 'Who really was this Jesus?' Thus there comes into being not a theoretical, even metaphysical christology, but a narrative, a relational, i.e. a narrated christology. Because this christology can be told as a deadly and at the same time healing history between human beings, contrary to frequent criticism it does not remain in the sphere of the visible and external event but penetrates into an open sphere of perception and understanding.

In my view the parable of the sower expresses this precisely: I know that we can also formulate what is said in a different way, with other examples, and fit it into other contexts. The impression never arises of an unalterable truth, formulated timelessly and finally. The accounts are unexpectedly interesting, gripping, even dangerous; revealing in terms of present-day situations (personal or social), binding, true. So already while reading the book, readers of *On Being a Christian* can note that the need for ontological reflection does not arise, or it is needed only as a helpful addition. There is no objection to this.

As always in life, human identity is questioned only when there is an occasion for the question. We want to classify people, understand them, and also express their action in words. The question is often put in psychological terms, as a question of conduct, motives or emotions, of predictable decisions. It is often put sociologically, as a question of our role in community or society. Friends, relatives, lovers ask more comprehensively – and probably right across these questions with an academic structure. Religious questioning is like this comprehensive questioning. Küng raises the question against the background of what he has reported so far. Only now does he sum up.

Of course one could say that that is a matter of organizing the material and presenting it dramatically. However, for theological reasons, Küng is concerned with more than that here. He takes up a dynamic which arises from the Gospels. It is not that here a prophet appeared with high claims for himself ('Now I'm coming!') and as a result provoked conflicts. No, Jesus provoked conflicts by what he actually did and the cause to which he committed himself. Unless all appearances are deceptive, it was offence at this which first raised the question who he was. The question of Jesus' identity is manifestly connected with the fact that by his behaviour he compelled decisions for or against himself, and Küng's very deep discontent with classical christology probably derives from a lack of this elementary demand. This 'compulsion' to a decision was evidently connected with the fact that Jesus was utterly consistent in standing behind his preaching and action, authentically and credibly. At the same time the result of this was that he gathered a group (or groups) of people around him who were for him and in whom the plan of his life was realized.

Therefore the question 'Who are you?' is given answers which were directly provoked, were rooted in encounter and experience, before abstract answers, the result of philosophical reflection, even ontological answers, followed from it. To think that these latter answers could stand without their roots in life is one of the misunderstandings of a later period. This hierarchy of answers can be noted in later discussions of Küng's scheme. If I am right, his christological achievement is that he discovers this connection with others and reconstructs it more intensely than most.

(d) The conflict

The structure of the most important part of the whole book ('The Conflict', OBC 278–342) follows from this. It is clear that decisions have to be made in Jesus' life; they are made in specific relationships. There are the people who listen to him, wonder at him, praise him. The question is how long they will stand by him. There are his supporters, men and women (not unusual in Jewish circumstances), who go with him through thick and thin. The strongly schematized call narratives make it clear how here a shared life and destiny is beginning in which God himself is at stake. Here the Gospels are already reporting about the church, but Jesus did not intend to found a community of salvation distinct from Israel. There is finally the question how Jesus saw himself. The answer is a sobering one: Jesus was evidently not interested in this question. He did not apply religious honorific titles to himself (perhaps with the exception of the mysterious apocalyptic title Son of man), and that was good. So initially all that is left is a historically plausible answer. Jesus identifies himself with God's cause and the human cause in such a way that he 'is wholly devoted to this cause and thus, without any claim to title or authority, becomes the supremely personal, public advocate of God and man' (OBC 293). In concrete terms (and perhaps against Jesus' will) that means that at the end of his life the great question about his person arises: is he a false teacher, a lying prophet, a blasphemer, one who leads the people astray (OBC 291)? When Küng later – to the displeasure of his critics – speaks of a 'functional' christology, he has this concrete role (or 'function') towards God and human beings in view. Perhaps he could also have spoken of a relational, a dynamic or a narrative christology, which shows – more plausibly than some theories of redemption – why Jesus really had to die. At all events, in this life-and-death context it is absurd to speak of an external functionalism.

In fact it is clear that, examined closely, the dispute over Jesus' identity cannot be seen as a question about Jesus. It is a 'dispute over God' (OBC 304–17). This is no new God ('Jesus' originality must not be exaggerated', OBC 310), but the God of Israel. However, through Jesus, in a unique way God now becomes a God who is close to us ('Abba'), a God with a human face (embodied in Jesus), the father of the lost, the God of the godless. The account of Jesus' passion then becomes breathtaking. The paradox is that here someone is executed on no specific charge, but for very understandable reasons: his general direction did not suit the politicians and hierocrats (and probably would not have suited us either). When he then died with a loud inarticulate cry (if he could cry at all by then), abandoned by human beings and God, the decision could not be postponed. Here, in this shocking event, which upsets all illusions of a religion which functions well and in a peaceful way, the question of who Jesus is is now decided. It is brought to a head. The answer arises out of the Easter experience, the witnesses to which now speak of God's action.

(e) The answer

A question is put; a decision is called for. The situation of extreme absurdity serves as a touchstone, and in practice all answers have to match it. So Küng can describe the Easter experiences as a new beginning (OBC 343–80). He takes great trouble to clarify the preliminary exegetical questions, the philosophical background and the accumulated misunderstandings. Only then is a simple answer allowed: 'God intervenes where from a human perspective everything is at an end'; that, and not the breaking of natural laws, is the true miracle. The legends of the empty tomb vividly illustrate what in Paul proves to be a call experience. All titles given to Jesus within the framework of Jewish traditions – Son of man, Messiah, Lord, Son of God, Logos, to mention just a few – are then to be understood in the light of this basic experience. In short, Jesus is experienced by the disciples as the normative figure (OBC 381–95), in whom a last distinctive characteristic has become historical reality: the cross. This is not replaced by the resurrection; rather, its significance is confirmed. 'The Crucified lives for ever with God, as obligation and hope for us' (OBC 356).

It is not surprising that in Küng's book, at these concluding and summary passages, a heading again appears which has accompanied him from the beginning: 'By faith alone' (OBC 402). It is not surprising that Nietzsche, for whom the only Christian died on the cross, could fail to understand Paul's cry as a concentration on this Christian. For Küng, too, this message is 'Back to Jesus':

'At the heart of Paul's thinking we do not find human beings (anthropology), the church (ecclesiology), or even salvation history in general, but the crucified and risen Christ (christology understood as soteriology). This is a christocentricity working out to human advantage, based on and culminating in a theocentricity: "God through Jesus Christ" – "through Jesus Christ to God" ' (OBC 403).

A large-scale defence of Paul (OBC 402–10) finally leads Küng to make three succinct identifications. These are not theoretical, but must be implemented in the practice of discipleship, and they give Christianity its unmistakable identity over against world religions and humanisms.

- The distinctive feature of Christianity is this Christ himself;
- The distinctive feature of Christianity is the Christ who is identical with the real, historical Jesus of Nazareth; to be specific, this Christ Jesus;
- The distinctive feature of Christianity is, to use Paul's language, Jesus Christ and him crucified.

Küng was the first Catholic theologian (though almost contemporaneously with Edward Schillebeeckx, 1974 [English translation only 1979]) to present this 'christology from below', i.e. an exegetically and historically reliable, systematically coherent account which is related to the discipleship of Christ, in a dramatic style. This made his book a great success. But church leaders were suspicious. Ostensibly he was gaining readers for the cause of Jesus. But anyone who followed his train of thought would also no longer have difficulties with his criticism of later christology, which essentially arose in the Hellenistic sphere, under the conditions of a growing empire and with the help of the categories of Greek philosophy. This christology contains statements about the incarnation of God and the divinity of Jesus, pre-existence and virgin birth, the privileges of Mary and finally the doctrine of the Trinity, formulated completely in antiquity and made increasingly precise (OBC 411–62, 472–7).

For Küng it is clear that the account of Jesus' life, death and resurrection contains all that is decisive and that it always says more than later interpretations, which reconcile Jesus' provocation with a new way of thinking. He readily adopts the metaphor of incarnation, but he sees it as an interpretation of Jesus' action:

'It was in Jesus' whole life, in his whole proclamation, behaviour and fate, that God's word and will took on a human form. In his whole speech, action and suffering, in his whole person, Jesus proclaimed, manifested, revealed God's word and will. Indeed, it can be said that the one in whom word and deed, teaching and life, being and action, completely coincide, is the embodiment of God's word and will: God's word and will in human form' (OBC 443).

If readers on the threshold of the twenty-first century understand this, they can hardly go on accepting the claim of church authorities that Jesus is fully divine. Evidently the epoch-making significance of a theological revolution born of a concern for church and public has not been understood. Here is no useful metaphor; rather, Küng is convinced that it is a new understanding which fulfils the following conditions.

1. It takes up the great concerns of classical christology: in Jesus, God was and is unreservedly present, i.e. definitively present in word, action and being. What more can one really ask of Christian faith?

2. It puts this concern back in its original sphere of understanding and perception, the original relationship between Jesus and those around him, friend and enemy, events and consequences included. In this way a new and elementary appropriation of Christian faith becomes possible.

3. New christology?

(a) God's word – in human form

The wealth of individual themes treated will not be discussed here. Far more important is the question of what has changed in terms of method. Has Küng adopted new methods? In a strict and objectifiable sense the answer is no. It is striking that here too in principle Küng keeps to matter-of-fact work and treatment of the sources. Scripture is quoted (but the biblical references are banished to the footnotes); exegetical results are adopted on a broad front; questions of fundamental theology (what are miracles and natural laws, how do we deal with Jesus' mistake about the future, and with ideas about the end of the world?) are taken up and developed in the light of historical information. As a matter of course new categories and arguments arise which leave behind the classical framework of dogmatic theology: these categories keep to the point in the most basic way possible, so that the reader forgets the considerable degree of reflection which has gone before. This scholarship makes its apparatus superfluous.

God in human form, i.e. God no longer above but *in* this world: ontological categories are replaced by dynamic categories of action ('God acts in Jesus'). The question who God is is answered in terms of relationships and human conflicts, the drama of social catastrophes, the abandonment of this one just man. The dangerous talk of the uniqueness of Jesus, increasingly open to misunderstanding, is replaced by the concept of singularity – not to relativize Jesus' uniqueness but to clarify what it means: a distinction which is experienced and can be experienced in history, which is also open to everyday comparison. And above all, the church no longer appears as the guardian of a well-defined 'truth', but convincingly and vitally as the body which – to use a phrase of Ernst Käsemann's – has never separated itself from the dynamite of this dangerous memory. How good it is that the church has always lived from the dramatic tension between action and gift. It almost goes without saying that proven experiences are preserved in formulae – once the fixations have been left behind.

And finally, here Paul's and the Reformers' central concern of justification is formulated in quite a new way. Initially Küng gave it a christocentric twist in order to open up the dialogue between the Protestant and the Catholic churches. Now the christocentricity is continued in the direction of Jesus, in order to give the Catholic Church a wider horizon in a critical situation. In the last part of *On Being a*

Christian the consequences for human action are formulated against this background. Certainly Christians must adopt a standpoint on all social questions (OBC 568), but what is decisive is the possibility of enduring, fighting and coping with suffering (OBC 576–80; cf. also the mediation 'God and Suffering') and thus finding an indestructible freedom. What is the real issue? An unconditional trust in God which is given and exercised in the discipleship of *Jesus.*

'That there are those who, healthy or sick, able or unable to work, stronger or weaker achievers, accustomed to success or passed over by success, guilty or innocent, who cling unswervingly and unshakeably, not only at the end but throughout their whole lives, to that trust which with the whole of the New Testament we call faith, then when they address their "Te Deum" to the one true God and not to the many false gods, they can also venture to refer the end of this hymn in any situation as a promise to themselves: *In te Domine speravi, non confundar in aeternum,* "In you, Lord, I have hoped; I shall never be brought to shame"' (OBC 589f.).

So the book ends with two very simple yet far-reaching formulae. One is that what is distinctively Christian is none other than this Jesus Christ himself. This is not to be misunderstood as a constant, since the concentration does not rule out any wider horizons. It applies only if Christians seek what is specific to them, their special identity, in other words what makes them Christians. Moreover – in keeping with the approach of the book – this identification is not ontological but historical. The point is made even more clearly in 'Twenty Theses on On Being a Christian': being a Christian cannot be fixed to a doctrine, a particular ethic or cultic obligation: 'A Christian is not simply someone who attempts to live in a humane, socially responsible or even religious way. Rather, a Christian is one who attempts to live in a human, socially responsible and religious way *in the light of Christ*' (Th 1). Therefore discipleship, too, which is the final issue, is more comprehensive than ethical imitation. Discipleship means going along with Christ, working out one's own identity in debate with him, being enriched and inspired by him. Convictions, actions, attitudes and ritual practices can follow from this. However, in a time of reorientation it can be a good thing to concentrate on the core.

The second basic formula is humanity, to the point of love of enemy, in trust in God. This formula and this obligation are so central for Küng that he hardly expands them further. He does not think of developing a distinctive and specific morality from them. I shall be returning later to this criterion of Christian action, humanity. It will mean that in the long run Küng cannot limit himself to questions of the church and Christianity.

(b) A hermeneutical shift (The Incarnation of God)

It is difficult, if not impossible, to indicate new methods in this methodologically precise book. It is Küng's intention to submit himself consistently to the standards of well-tried (historical, exegetical and philosophical) methods in order to be really convincing, both inside the church and outside it. But there has been another very fundamental change in him. This is in the overall hermeneutical perspective from which he gathers, assimilates and co-ordinates information.

1. Here we have the rediscovery of history as a place in which God's action has become possible and real. Such a discovery does not divert us to the quest for at any rate a 'higher', 'deeper', 'other' or 'timeless' truth 'behind' our reality.

2. Küng's disappointing experiences with a church government have confirmed his new discovery, since on the traditional dogmatic approach the church government cannot be made responsible, as it acts by virtue of 'higher' authority.

3. Finally, there is the question, more implicit than precisely reflected on: in what model of truth are knowledge and action, truth and truthfulness, reality and experience effectively related, and how do we express the reciprocal relationship between knowledge and interest?

Thus a hermeneutical shift has taken place in Küng which had long since come about outside theology.

But a further perspective has to be added. As early as 1970, Küng's monograph on Hegel's christology appeared under the title *The Incarnation of God*. Küng started this work after his doctorate, then turned to other tasks, took it up again, had to drop it once again during the Council and while writing *The Church*, and finally finished it in 1970. Here we find a last reason for the hermeneutical shift which embraces the others. Already since his discussion with Karl Barth, Küng had been occupied with the question of a new, historical image of God.

After an analysis and a comprehensive survey of the origins of Hegel's christology, which reflects the general outline of his philosophical thought, Küng goes on to speak of the late Hegel. According to Küng, in his old age Hegel rediscovered a starting point of his youth. He rediscovered history and found a new interest in religion, in talk of God (IG

312–24). That also means a new interest in a history of the divine, in the historicity of God. God does not stand above history, to determine it, but takes part in it.

Of course Hegel knows that he is in good company in classical christology, even if here there is much to reflect on, order and transform. He claims that Christ is not just a chance phenomenon; rather, Christ must be able to occupy his precisely definable role in the whole of this history. But it can be the history of God only if it is explained against the background of the threefold God. This principle mediates between God and the world. According to Hegel,

'This new principle is the axis about which world history revolves. World history proceeds from and moves to this point. In this religion all riddles are solved and all mysteries have become manifest. Christians know what God is inasmuch as they know that God is triune. The first way to know this is by faith; and the second is by thought, which knows the truth and thus is reason. Between these two ways there is the mind, which holds fast to the differences' (quoted from IG 327f.).

This quotation already shows how deeply the notion of the Trinity has embedded itself in idealistic thought and offered itself as a solution to the most fundamental problems. Trinity means reconciliation between faith and knowledge, God and history, between perception of the everyday and speculation. So Hegel's influence can also intimate what significance systematic theologians down to the present attach to a speculative theology of the Trinity. In the incarnation everything is at risk. Now, at the turn of the ages, as God becomes man, there takes place in the dialectically spiritual course of the world a 'reconciliation between Judaism and the Roman world; between the Eastern and the Western principle; between belief in infinity and faith in finitude; between abstract subjectivity . . . and abstract objectivity' (IG 328). The same is true of Hegel's philosophy of art and of religion and of his history of philosophy.

'Hegel intended his entire thought to be historical thought, his historical thought to be religious thought, and his religious thought to be interpreted in the light of the incarnation of God – albeit philosophically conceived. What he intended to achieve was not a timelessly static metaphysic of Ideas, but a comprehensive and dynamic Christian philosophy of history. Hegel's ontotheologic manifested itself as a powerful theodicy, which, along its whole course and in all its strata, aimed to be at the same time a comprehensive justification of history' (IG 383).

Küng develops a deep sense of this achievement. 'Hegel's God is not a Spirit beyond the stars, who operates on the world from the outside, but rather the Spirit who is at work in the spirits, in the depths of human subjectivity.' Hegel did not practise a conceptual mathematics remote from reality. World history is not channelled into a narrow salvation history which simply devalues non-Christian religions and trivializes sin and suffering: 'Might this not be a middle way between the shallow reasoning of the Enlightenment and the pious irrationalism of feeling, both of which are simply not competent in a technical sense? Ought faith to have anything to fear in all of this, if it is conceived in rational terms?' (IG 385). Küng's deep respect for the way in which Hegel thinks of God and history together in christological terms was echoed years later, when Küng had long since decided for another approach (DGE 127–88). As Kern has pointed out, there is hardly a more comprehensive and more eloquent monograph in the theological literature of our century than Küng's. Even if later he criticizes Hegel, he does not speak as a blind man, but as one who sees.

It is a pity that Küng's great monograph on Hegel, which appeared in the year of the great dispute over infallibility, was soon overshadowed by conflicts with the church and did not meet with an appropriate reception. So there was hardly any awareness of the significance of the reorientation on the history of philosophy and theology which *On Being a Christian* introduces. Perhaps Küng followed up his admiration of Hegel too quickly with his criticism of Hegel. Perhaps the composition of the decisive, large-scale chapter on 'Jesus Christ in History' (IG 312–412) too much gives the impression that the praise is simply meant as an impressive preparation for criticism. In reality, Küng wrote the criticism only after his return from the Council and only after he had recognized that the shift was necessary.

Küng's critique of Hegel, which is formulated under the title 'God of the Future?' (IG 382–412), stands on its own feet and can be summed up in the statement that Hegel did not arrive at an unambiguous conception of the historicity of God. In fact 'he was obliged to concede that . . . empirical history in its sheer facticity, contingency and gloom cannot be fully subsumed in this process of Spirit' (IG 388). G. Bauer, Dilthey and Marcuse are summoned as witnesses. So Hegel does not arrive at any really eschatological approach either, since history ends in the present.

(c) 'Metadogmatic theology'

But what was hidden behind the rumblings of thunder was first to be expressed fully in the 'Prolegomena to a Future Christology' (IG 413–508). This programmatic text once again takes up the topic under discussion as reflected in the further history of theology. It is about the historicity of God: Hegel's doctrine of a God of history had to fail on at least two questions: on God's impassibility and on God's unchangeableness. And at the latest Hegel's pupil D.F. Strauss makes it clear that if christology is to be really scriptural, it can no longer be orientated on high ontological theses about incarnation and divinity. If God is a God of history, christology can no longer be a theology of the incarnation, with Jesus' suffering and death as an appendix. 'The decisive element in christology is that it is a reflection on this history of suffering and death which constitutes the central event of salvation' (IG 448).

Now finally I return to the topic of this chapter, since the same can be said of talk of a historical Jesus which cannot tolerate a fixation on the doctrine of two natures (IG 467f.). It becomes clear that in *On Being a Christian* Küng is simply drawing conclusions from a long accumulation of problems. The whole exciting history of the interpretation of the 'historical' Jesus, extending from D.F. Strauss to Bultmann and Barth, in which Catholic theology unfortunately played no part until the 1970s, bears witness to the seriousness and resistance of this problem. The last pages of the monograph then offer a summary in embryo of what appears at greater length in *On Being a Christian*. Traditional dogmatic thought is not simply to be shaken off but to be integrated into a more comprehensive historical framework, as described above. It has to be sublated and transferred to a 'metadogmatic' way of thinking:

> 'Metadogmatic theology in this constructive sense therefore involves building, notwithstanding all demolition, and a shifting of the centre of gravity, notwithstanding all reduction. Thus a metadogmatic way of thinking can express the originally decisive core of faith in Christ more concentratedly, richly and beautifully than a dogmatic school theology, which only holds firm for someone who, for whatever reasons, has long got used to swaying in time with its rocking foundations' (IG 498).

The success of *On Being a Christian*, this unexpectedly bulky and, from a publisher's perspective, far too comprehensive book (Küng wanted to write 200 pages at most and kept the question of God for another book), exceeded all expectations. For the moment it dominated the best-seller list in *Der Spiegel*, where it stayed for a long time. Probably readers did not reflect on the historicity of God, but they were interested and found answers to questions which had often been suppressed. Their number went far beyond the bounds of those who were still integrated into the church. For the first time in Germany it became clear that there was an interested readership which had long been disappointed by the literature accepted, and perhaps also domesticated, in the church. There were also indications that conflicts with the church authorities heightened the credibility of an author.

What is the secret of this success? It cannot simply be a bite-sized presentation; the knowledge required and the argumentation are too demanding for that. Nor can it simply be an exciting and always clear language, although Küng worked on that with the utmost intensity. Quite evidently it was the programme of a christology which began to narrate the cause of Jesus (and thus of God) 'from the front'. The complicated and highly theoretical questions about God's historicity and Trinity apparently draw life from a deep level in which contemporaries are very interested. They are not looking for a fundamental trinitarian theory but for an answer to the question what Jesus really has to do with God. *On Being a Christian* is full of answers to these questions. That makes all the more astonishing the opposition which soon formed from the hierarchy and theologians.

4. The opposition

(a) 'Modest remarks'

Küng was aware of his new approach and also made this clear; so he could not be surprised at vigorous reactions, though he was surprised at the nature of some of the argumentation. The arguments over *Infallible?* were still in progress. Küng hoped that he could open them up, illuminate the background. and completely remove the suspicion that he was dealing with questions of faith in a frivolous way. But church people and a group of German-speaking theologians devised a new attack. They took hardly any notice of methodological considerations, the weight of biblical arguments, the discussion from Hegel to the present which has been described, and above all the interpretations and formulations which were proposed. Fundamentally they raised just one question: is the divinity of Jesus preserved?

Thus the discussion began to take an unfortunate turn. Individual statements were detached from their background; sweeping judgments on the style of Küng's writing and scholarship, on his loyalty to the church and to his piety, became widespread. The more a wide public showed enthusiasm, the more resolutely the fronts formed or rather were formed – almost unnoticed by Küng at first. Rome was active behind the scenes; again – without Küng's knowledge and possible participation – a composite 'discussion' volume was organized (DisC 1976), prompted by the Faith Commission of the German Conference of Bishops and presented to Rome as a counter-measure against Küng (UW 173). It should not be forgotten that some critics reacted fairly, but as far as Küng was concerned the church-political situation was once again coming to a head.

Karl Rahner was again involved. Again with his customary under-statement ('a few modest remarks') he asked a few modest questions which Küng had already answered in 1967. In general one gets the impression from Rahner that *On Being a Christian* is a loosely formu-lated novice work, written for journalistic purposes, out of superficial resentment, and without a deeper awareness of the problem, as though more than 2,700 pages of preparatory, enquiring, challenging, but con-stantly argumentative theology had not preceded it. None of the critics went into the overall scheme of *On Being a Christian*; no one conceded that such attempts had to be ventured if progress was to be made. At most Joseph Ratzinger and (in a later article) Walter Kasper noted the new approach. But in Küng's case Ratzinger saw church faith 'given over to corruption'; the historical Jesus had always 'proved a surrogate which survived none of its inventors'. So Küng's book only 'sympto-matically demonstrated an emergency in theology' which down to the present day Ratzinger has made a determined attempt to fight (DisC 17).

By contrast, for all his delight in argument Walter Kasper applied a strange emergency brake. It was as if there had been no christological discussion since Hegel. So Kasper asks an amazingly simple question: 'Who is Jesus Christ? Is he a human person in whom God reveals him-self in speech and action, or is he the eternal son of God who becomes man in history?' (GfC 182). He, too, does not go into the basic questions. He either does not understand Küng or refuses to engage in theological dialogue with him.

At no point does he reflect on what questions arise from Küng's approach, but insists on his own questions and believes that the church is on his side. But why should Küng answer the question which Kasper puts? According to Kasper, the church and its tradition of faith are 'transcendental conditions' for the possibility of theology. Furthermore, according to another comment, one has to take the hermeneutical discussion of recent decades seriously, i.e. 'the heuristic interests and the sociological plausibility structures of any human knowledge' (GfC 179). In my view, in the first comment Kasper exaggerates a connection which is rather simpler. Theology can be simple and easy because there is a faith on which it reflects. It is hard to see what could be transcendental about this condition for its possibility. But Kasper's remark shows that in the current awareness of German theologians the term 'transcendental' does not help in making a sharp distinction between the levels of being and knowledge, as it does with Kant. It is precisely the transcendental character of this theology which must ensure that not a single categorical statement goes unquestioned. Here Kant is simply being misused. That applies even more clearly to the lead held by prejudgment and social plausibility, which can never be completely caught up with. Kasper pursues an explicitly idealistic, if not conservative, hermeneutic, which misuses the existence of history in order to beatify it. A hermeneutic which is critical of ideology and society, which is critical of the church, will be an occasion for this approach to intensify its questions. It is not that now Küng is once for all writing a new christology. The important thing is that Küng's christological approach needs constantly to be repeated. And that is what makes it always exciting. So the problem with Kasper is that where Küng is concerned he has not done his homework on the nature of the church and hermeneutics.

Kasper's question and comment are not naive, since he forges them into a weapon which is sharp because in the long term it is dangerous and fatal to Catholic ears. Rahner does the same thing. Only those who take the church seriously as the sphere of faith can claim to be Catholic theologians. Kasper simply cannot see 'how individual doctrinal views represented in this book, for example the interpretation of the divine sonship of Jesus Christ, are compatible with the traditional faith of the church' (DisC 19). It might be replied that that is really Kasper's problem, but he adds a further cliché, which had an impact on the bishops and the pope: the teaching office of the bishops is being replaced by that of the professors of theology. Once again he comments on the problem of infallibility (ironically with a reference to Luther), with the absurd suspicion that Küng is not taking the church's binding tradition seriously and is blurring the creed (DisC 30). Kasper does not give any reasons for this view, but at the latest in 1980 the tone was to have its effect. Again dialogue was nipped in the bud, since instead of putting critical theological questions to their colleague, others told him that he was not a good Catholic.

(b) A thought-provoking colloquium

Küng's reactions were vigorous for three reasons. First, discussions were again being organized against and about him which excluded his own person: that offended against all academic rules and against a minimum of collegial fairness. Secondly, the content of the discussion was a rule so much a matter of principle and so sweeping that he was compelled to make sweeping defences. There was no discussion of his proposed interpretations. He had to defend his Catholic civil rights. Finally, already after *Infallible?* he had come to see how so powerful an authority as the Catholic Church can influence and organize public opinion within its ranks all over the world. So he was the one who was being attacked and according to the official church strategy had to be attacked, although the magisterium always claimed to be the weak, the subordinate and violated partner.

The general charge was that he scorned the dogmatic foundations of the Catholic doctrine of Jesus Christ. This was heresy-hunting; such a charge was a crude one. There were also mediators. On 22 January 1977 – after intensive preliminary discussions about the nature and scope of the event – there was a high-level 'colloquium' between representatives of the German Conference of Bishops, Hans Küng and some expert theologians. The record was published later (UW 227–340) and is worth reading. It shows the somewhat helpless position of those taking part. They were more or less fixated on particular dogmatic statements and the absence of them from *On Being a Christian*. They could not indicate what in *On Being a Christian* contradicts official teaching; no heresies could be made out, but the formulae which would make the book impregnable could not be pointed out either. Cardinal Volk, who took part in the dialogue, declared at the start that 'theological truth has a certain totality. Theologically, a half-truth can be a total error' (UW 239). The meaning of this statement is not completely clear, but its consequences are: if there is no christology from above, no doctrine of incarnation, no prologue of the Gospel of John, no pre-existence in the book, the book is wrong. The pastoral aspects emphasized by Küng, the indications of method, the reference to the reception of the book by an interested public, were irrelevant here. Küng compared this attitude to the integralistic past.

Cardinal Höffner, Chairman of the German Conference of Bishops, had read the book and could not find the relevant statements. Why was Höffner not content even after an eighteen-page extract? Certainly p. 432 [ET 441] suddenly comes into the picture. Höffner could at least say: 'One passage is there in the 680 pages! So you must understand that I have read the book as a bishop and on page after page have looked for what it says there. And then I came to this point; and I am not satisfied even now' (UW 261). What does the passage say? Here Küng sums up the Christian doctrine of redemption in the sentence: 'God himself in his Son and Logos enters into the world and assumes a human nature.' He calls that at any rate 'a sublime Greek theology of redemption' and acknowledges a 'comprehensive Christianizing of the Hellenistic . . . conception of *paideia*'. But he adds that this Hellenization is purchased with 'too many negative features'. So the problem is clear. It is not enough for Küng to allow this conception its significance. At this point it is not a matter of interpreting, of relativizing hermeneutically, but of confessing. Is he God's Son or not? The Catholic magisterium does not allow any discussion at this point; by contrast, Küng speaks in a detached way only of a scheme, that of ontology with a Hellenistic stamp. And Küng, who is oppressed on all sides, must again defend himself as if he is denying a truth, simply because while he does not deny another formulation, the only one privileged by others, he does not use it either.

This is just an example of the tone and level, no more. The dialogue consists of generalized criticism on one side and a defence of individual passages on the other. The magisterium really cannot indicate what it does not like. That brings it to the introduction to the book and thus to Küng's alleged claim that he is giving a comprehensive description of the truth of faith. It is objected that he is presenting the book with the claim that it is a *summa*. Küng robs his accusation of its force by giving a precise analysis of the sentence in the introduction. This too does not get him any further. No basis on which a dialogue could take place is arrived at. So time and again general anxieties and suspicions arise, above all the bishops' anxiety about the wider dissemination of the book, which they want to prevent: one edition is appearing after another 'each with the same content as before'.

'You keep repeating that. What are we to do? This is simply not a proclamation of clear doctrine. You don't change anything. Then you say that for at least a couple of years you have noted how vulnerable the unity of the church is. We can't put up with just anything in the church. Different people react in different ways. We sense that things are beginning to collapse. The bishops cannot keep silent here. So the question now is – and we are gradually coming to the conclusion – what do we do now? How can we help the church here? That would be my question – how do we continue?' (UW 276).

That is the decisive point: the success of the book. This anxiety leads to exaggeration and projection. 'It is not just us,' says Höffner, 'but the college of bishops throughout the world. We cannot stop the proclamation of belief in the pre-existence of Jesus Christ, the fruit of salvation and the binding character of the councils until such a study group comes up with a result' (UW 304). Küng refers to the exaggerated view of his book, as though preaching could not continue, as though the reservations about it were not known. To this Volk retorts: 'That means that the book will continue to appear unchanged.' Küng, impatiently: 'Yes, why not? So far 160,000 copies have been printed. For the moment no new edition is planned. But what sense would it make for me to add anything to it?' (UW 305). Thus any intervention, any attempt at an agreement, got nowhere, because the dissent, its content and judgment, the aim of the Conference of Bishops and the analysis of the problem were fundamentally unclear.

The colloquium remained shrouded in a veil of obscurity. The real objections were not formulated; no one took up the book theologically. So a vague anxiety (which ultimately theologians talked themselves into) remained about further developments, along with the irrational fear that Küng's book was having a devastating effect. Against this stood Küng's remark that his book was helping many people. Of course other aspects came into play: now that the Conference of Bishops had joined in the debate, it had to save face. And of course there was Rome, whose clear expectations were known. So in the end it was disappointing and almost banal when Höffner pressed for a conclusion. He argued that between forty and sixty bishops were waiting in Cologne to congratulate him on his seventieth birthday. Surely that was the sign of a magisterium which was functioning well!

But Küng, too, showed himself in a light which for many people was perhaps unexpected. Certainly he was well aware what he wanted to communicate, what developments in the dialogue he wanted to avoid and what demands he would not accept. But he was not provocative in any way. Of course he showed emotion and pointed out the unacceptable behaviour of colleagues. He repeatedly pointed out how all over the world he was being forced into a corner, and how powerless he was against defamatory statements. But he also indicated that theologically he was still constantly searching, and wanted to reflect further and investigate questions together with colleagues. Of course he knew how far his new book on the question of God had already progressed. In it, he hoped, he would be able to explain some points relating to christology and the Trinity even more clearly. Was that a helpful excuse?

5. A theology responsible to history

We have already come a long way in this chapter. It began with an introduction to the problem and then a summary of Küng's account of Jesus. We considered the theological background to Küng's drastic change and the subsequent discussion and its hermeneutical dimension. We are now concerned with some methodological results. To introduce this section, we need once again to ask: what is the core of the problem, and what does it look like in retrospect? I shall sum up the methodological aspects under five headings:

(a) The centre of interpretation

Küng's drastic change from a propositional theology (i.e. one which argued in dogmatic or speculative terms) to a 'meta-dogmatic theology', i.e. one which is responsible to history, calls for a precise methodological analysis. Is there a break in method? It would be inaccurate to say that.

Certainly, Küng does not use any new methods now: exegesis, the history of theology, attention to binding linguistic rules, location in the current context, and argument which carries scholarly conviction remain in force. In a sense they come into play even better than in a strictly dogmatic scheme, which prescribes the course of interpretation strictly and makes any argument to the contrary very difficult. It is certainly part of Küng's methodological attractiveness that sub-disciplines – independently of the theological aim – do not feel forced into a corner or misused, but feel that they are being taken seriously. Anyone who knows the rising expectations and compulsions of systematization will realize that only consistent reference to these disciplines helps. With good reason, since the 1970s Küng has developed intensive contacts with representatives of other disciplines.

But Küng revises his method (by which I mean the sequence and interrelationship of the methods and the results which are worked out methodically). The approach pioneered in *The Church* is now established more confidently and worked out in the question of Jesus Christ. Here the status of the individual methods shifts. The focal point and critical centre of the exegetical constant have moved. We need to note two changes.

1. The focal point of theological work now no longer lies in later formulae of faith (which in fact have a Hellenistic or mediaeval stamp) – this in particular provokes the displeasure of bishops and some theologians – but in the New Testament message, which is investigated by means of intensive exegesis for the benefit of systematic theology.

2. The focal point does not lie in one document or another (e.g. the letters of Paul or the Gospel of John) or in one statement or another (e.g. the incarnation of the Logos or the doctrine of justification), but in the original event to which the New Testament bears witness or – as Schillebeeckx puts it more precisely, in a way comparable to Küng's intentions – in the original experiences of the disciples with Jesus. At any rate this applies to the topic discussed by *On Being a Christian*. It, rather than, say, a preference for the Synoptic Gospels, defines Küng's focus.

Finally, the hermeneutic shift which has already been discussed is to be distinguished from methods and methodology. Hermeneutics also has two aspects. First, this term denotes a reflection on all factors which govern a process of understanding (we might call this material hermeneutics). There were further comments above about hermeneutics in this sense. Really this goes without saying, since of course for example the far-reaching change in the understanding of God and history described above alters the perspectives, the aims and evaluations of theological statements. Here is a discovery of (new) questions, connections, perspectives. Results cannot be proved, but only inferred in a new approach to reality, in a totality of convictions (e.g. a paradigm denotes such a hermeneutical totality). Precisely because processes of understanding in fact take their course in contexts which govern them, it is important to know about this. The problem with Küng's 'opposition party' in the controversy described above is – from Küng's perspective – that it regards its own actual hermeneutic as the only one possible one, so no 'hermeneutical awareness' is developed in its argument.

Secondly, hermeneutic denotes the discovery that the concrete, holistic understanding of events, situations and text cannot be reduced to definitions or logical lines of argument, nor can it often be reduced to thesis-like statements or alternative assertions. Texts always say more than we can read out of them and one can ask of any dogmatic definition: 'How is it meant?' 'Can it be understood?' Or, 'Why is it notoriously misunderstood?' The question is one of hermeneutical sensitivity. Thus for Küng, dogmatic formulations are not to be replaced by new ones, but are to be investigated anew – in the light of scripture and the present. Kasper's alternative (human person or eternal Son of God?) already shows that he has misunderstood, and at the same time ensures that Küng will not answer: to do so would encourage an unhermeneutical understanding. Küng's hermeneutical concern can be clarified by means of many individual examples. It is incomprehensible and really scandalous that this has not been noted.

(b) The report as the core of Christian theology

However, one question has not yet been discussed. If a contemporary theology is looking for the origin of faith, it cannot stop at timeless statements. The original character of the core must itself be expressed. Therefore at the core of Küng's scheme there is no analysis or argument, but a report, i.e. the narrative of events – which has always already been interpreted. It is a report with laws of its own, which are not comparable to the logical analysis of modern theology. Küng does not aim to make his breakthrough by means of a fundamentalist reference to scripture but by bringing the narrative core of the Gospels itself into play. It is the basic structure of the Gospels which already has its home in the church before scholastic and even idealistic logic. Neither the Christian creed nor its necessity is put in doubt by giving the Gospels priority. But by remembrance and report the creed is always stimulated anew, protected from hardening and maintained in the flux of constantly new interpretations. Therefore the creed can never replace the Gospels. Christian understanding lives not (only) by penetrating intellect and spiritual meditation, but before that by a narration which points to the praxis of discipleship.

The amazing reactions to Küng's book are revealing from this perspective: the chains of permanent misunderstandings, the unhistorical demand for clear statements, the helpless charge of disloyalty to the church and the call for a powerful condemnation. They merely show that a sense of this wholly other quality of the communication of the truth and hermeneutical sensitivity to it has to grow again.

(c) The centre of the canon?

What is not discussed much in Küng's books and in their reception is a shift of accent in the canon of the New Testament writings themselves; it is of far-reaching significance and still did not play a role in the 1960s.

The New Testament takes on an unexpected depth and sharpness through remembrance and report. The Gospels come into the centre; their literary form becomes the initial, perhaps even the basic, form of a specifically Christian message. No canon in the canon is being constructed here, because remembrance cannot be played off against confession. However, the writings are to be distinguished clearly and related to one another. For example, Küng interprets Paul with full approval, but against the background of the memory of Jesus; for him even the doctrine of justification and belief in Jesus Christ remain the nuclei of Christian existence (OBC 402–10).

However, the questions of church authority and the authority of scripture can be judged in a new light, for the narratives about Jesus of Nazareth point to a memory and to experiences which were there before scripture itself with its reports, interpretations, perspectives and stylizations, and the narratives which were handed down. From a hermeneutical standpoint it is the task of historical criticism to trace these back, to clarify contexts, and through this to gain information, clear up misunderstandings, ensure that necessary differentiations are made, in other words put the reports in context better and translate them into the present. Here it is amazing that historical criticism has not dissolved or destroyed the memory of Jesus (this against the incomprehensible sweeping argument of Josef Ratzinger). Rather, a very clear and sharp picture has been extracted which has a theological dimension and is a challenge for our time. This does not relieve historical criticism and exegesis of the task of self-criticism any more than does the supposition that in a new generation the remembrance must be opened up to other questions. However, the suspicion that criticism undermines faith in Jesus Christ is untenable and quite ridiculous. On the contrary, it keeps it alive and responsible.

That puts the question of the canon in a new light. The danger of the vicious circle of a 'canon in the canon' is essentially blunted, if not completely done away with, since the remembrance of Jesus of Nazareth serves as a 'canon before the canon', as the living starting-point for all scripture. From this perspective it becomes clear that at the same time Küng's conception has brought the Catholic-Protestant problem of scripture closer to a new solution.

(d) Harmonious or critical interpretation?

Küng himself gives preference to a critical interpretation. What is meant by that? An article about Edward Schillebeeckx's *Jesus* makes it clear. It can only be regarded as a happy coincidence that Schillebeeckx worked out a christology 'from below' at the same time as Küng, with the same resolve and with the same concern to assimilate the current state of scholarship. It is only because the translations appeared at different times that their champions in different countries think that each deserves the prize of being first. But the similarity of approaches is striking. Küng now formulates the consensus as it appears to him. For Küng it is a question of the norm and the horizon of Christian theology.

Küng gives a classic description of the norm of Christian theology: 'The first "source", the first pole, the norm of Christian theology, is God's revelatory speaking in the history of Israel and the history of Jesus' (TTM 108). Here Küng directly assents to the hermeneutical essentials of any interpretation: revelation and experience are not opposites; rather, God's revelation can be perceived only by human experience, and this experience is given only through human interpretation. Only then follows the discovery that is decisive for both: 'The source, norm and criterion for Christian faith is the living Jesus of history. Through historical-critical research into Jesus, Christian faith is historically justified in the face of the current awareness of the problems facing it and protected against misinterpretations' (TTM 111). It is over against this pole that Küng now comes to speak of experience: 'The "second source", second pole or horizon of Christian theology, is none other than our own human world of experience' (TTM 116). Here too Küng sees further parallels. The experiences are not elitist, but normal, everyday and ambivalent. However, theology has to make 'a critical correlation' between the Christian tradition of experience and these present-day experiences.

But a difference now emerges. Küng formulates some questions about Schillebeeckx's idea of critical correlation which are significant for his own position. Küng clearly calls the first pole a 'norm' which has a particular effect on the second pole. By contrast, Schillebeeckx correlates origin and present more strongly on the same level. Küng reacts to this. He asks Schillebeeckx whether he does not think that he knows too much about the present-day world of experience and whether it is possible to sum up the present-day world of experience so generally and comprehensively. He asks whether Schillebeeckx does not render biblical statements in modern categories (e.g., in a theological, christological, ecclesiological and eschatological constant) all too quickly. The third question is: does not Schillebeeckx see the critical correlation between experiences then and today too harmoniously, too uncritically, over against our time? Must not the ambivalence of present-day experiences and criticism of them be taken much more seriously?

This is not the place to go more closely into these questions, especially as the background to them is a deep assent to Schillebeeckx. But what underlies this criticism? What really leads Küng to ask such questions? Now Schillebeeckx is concerned to relate scripture and the present, memory and present-day experience closely, and to engage them in open discussion. He wants to show that past and present are fused together in a new way in a process of understanding and how this happens; that there is no nucleus which each time takes on a new temporal shell. Küng, if I understand him rightly, has no reason to oppose this model, but he goes one stage further. His concern is that the critical and normative force of the message of Jesus must also remain in contemporary translations. Certainly Küng, too, does not distinguish between kernel and shell, essence and garb. But the original source retains the priority, and even now the memory of Jesus contains a force which is critical of ideology.

Thus Schillebeeckx replies at the level of the hermeneutical process of understanding, which is determined by many factors (see above, 155f.). In describing it, to distinguish between norm and normed makes no sense. I see *in fact* in the present statement how I can appropriate the past today. Küng answers on the level of hermeneutical sensitivity, the discovery that the memory of Jesus can never be completely reduced to our present, can never be wholly taken up in it. For there are always shifts, narrowings or domestications which I can very easily trace and to which in some cases I must react. Schillebeeckx experiences dealing with scripture and Jesus of Nazareth more as a liberating process which gives us modern men and women back our rights. Küng experiences it more as a critical process, one intended to bring about renewal.

This interpretation is confirmed by Küng's reaction to Kasper. According to Küng, Kasper takes scripture and history seriously, but treats them eirenically. He interprets this eirenicism as a lack of consistency.

'If Kasper were also to maintain without hermeneutical compromise the historical-critical method which he affirms consistently at the ("infallible") doctrinal points where the magisterium is burdensome, like Jesus' expectation of an imminent end and the virgin birth, he would come to similar conclusions to mine on those points. That would of course necessitate an evaluation of the post-biblical church tradition (including the doctrine of the two natures, the later doctrine of the Trinity and Anselm's theory of satisfaction) which was more critical, though by no means negative; important shifts of biblical perspectives could not accepted so easily, nor could clear breaks in the post-biblical tradition be jumped over. The continuity in the communication of the Christian message would have to be seen against the background of a discontinuity which keeps breaking through: everything at the service of an authentic systematic synthesis or harmonization of the contradictions' (GfC 174).

So Küng does not presuppose contradictions in principle, but as soon as they appear and prove recalcitrant, the requirement of truthfulness demands critical action. Truthfulness, that principle which is so essential for Küng, proves to be courage for discontinuity, i.e. courage for those discoveries which – as in the case of the problem of infallibility – test one's basic experience of church continuity.

(e) Christology from below

The last of the five key terms sums up the question of a historically responsible theology in connection with the question of Jesus the Christ. It would be hermeneutically naive to want to change the method and hermeneutical approach of a theology and to hope for unaltered results. The key phrase 'christology from below' stands for such a change. But is the divine dimension of the Son of God really being given up now? Is this really the announcement of an anthropological levelling down, a humanistic superficiality, a social-critical ideologizing or even a theology which gets by without God as either a concept or a reality? It cannot be denied that the critics of such a christology are fond of using such associations to give their warnings more weight.

Küng has never left any doubt about the challenge of his approach (and here he is not alone). But there are many levels to the slogan of a 'christology from below', to which Küng subscribes, and this slogan is more suitable for general definitions of positions than for scholarly precision. Küng knows that, so in an answer to Kasper (GfC 170–9) he gives a precise and at the same time vivid description of his scheme. What is decisive for him is not any aspect of the subject-matter but a methodological aspect. For him it lies in what has been described here as methodology (see 154 above). Methodologically, I cannot proceed in two ways at the same time. Therefore for Küng it makes an irreconcilable difference, 'whether in the interpretation of the New Testament evidence one thinks deductively about the man Jesus of Nazareth in the light of God, on the presupposition of doctrines of the Trinity and the Incarnation (= "from above"), as in traditional christology from the patristic period to Barth; or whether (like Kasper and many others), adopting modern exegetical questioning, I think from the human being Jesus towards God (= 'from below'), as it were ever anew from the perspective of the first disciples of Jesus, inductively and inter-pretatively. If the terms are defined exactly, one cannot think with methodological consistency "from above" and "from below" at the same time; methodologically speaking, this is a real alternative' (GfC 171).

We must note that for Küng 'from below' means 'from the perspective of the first disciples of Jesus, from the human being Jesus to God (= "from below"), inductively and interpretatively'. For Küng there are several reasons why the way has to lead from below. We have already discussed Hegel's doctrine of God and the problem of the historical Jesus (see above, 144f.). Only now do the perspectives governed by the subject-matter appear. For Küng an important reason is the epoch-making revolution in the cultural context: he appeals strongly to pastoral reasons. Here the unity between Jesus and the Father does not disappear. But it is understood in a 'personal, relational, functional' way (GfC 176). Kasper fundamentally rejects this conception if he insists on an ontological answer to the question of Jesus.

A way out of this impasse had already been shown. Therefore, for Küng, his discovery in those years of Thomas Kuhn's theory of para-digm change and his intensive preoccupation with it was a help in coming to an understanding of the problem. This discovery would be brought to bear later.

6. Held by God

To conclude, I want to attempt once again to clarify the differences and the background to this dispute over method and to relate it to substan-tive results. Here the formula with which Küng concludes *On Being a Christian* and which had already been developed at an early stage of work of this book plays an important role.

(a) The right of Christian criticism

The dispute over methods and subject-matter contains components which are critical of theology, faith, the church and society. Here each time Küng rejects conclusions deriving from the way 'from above', which he no longer follows. Sometimes the criticism becomes so clear because, as we saw, Küng originally followed the way 'from above'.

Küng first of all begins from the components which are critical of theology. A christology 'from above' is one which starts from a developed christology of divine sonship, pre-existence, the divinity of Jesus. Here there are some remarkable coincidences.

1. From the perspective of symbolics, such christologies work with titles and qualifications which are derived from the vocabulary of rule, the victors, and nearness to an exalted God. Such a christology is characterized by its sacrality. The so-called titles of majesty are an example of this.

2. From the perspective of the subject-matter, such christologies (*de facto* or in ontological reflection) presuppose a descent from above and treat the situations above as the ideal situation or the situation that is aimed at. The beyond appears as a continuation of present-day life. Küng opposes this conception.

3. From a formal perspective, such christologies – at any rate in their mature form – are preferred and defined by highly institutionalized bodies, for example the imperial councils of antiquity, the mediaeval hierarchy and the modern papacy.

4. From an anthropological perspective the binding quality of a christology 'from above' tends to be legitimated by the argument that faith requires obedience to revealed truth, and thus also an attitude of believing subjection.

From here the substance and message of the term 'christology from below' as Küng understands it can be reconstructed more comprehensively. Küng's theological intention is that appropriate talk of Jesus Christ should begin with the memory of the words, actions and fate of a human being. The subject-matter evoked here relates to humility, poverty, sin, remoteness from God, i.e. the opposite of the ideal components of a christology 'from above'. They are not projected on to the words of Jesus but arise from his surroundings, his conduct and his fate. That does not exclude ways upwards. The message of the resurrection and later christology are indisputable. While this christology 'from above' interprets the 'lowly' material, it does not replace it.

An approach which is critical of faith goes hand in hand with this approach which is critical of theology. It runs like this. Faith does not begin as obedient assent to 'revealed' statements but as an option and a praxis, as courage for community and a readiness to be committed to the man Jesus, regardless of how his relationship to God is to be defined. Christology from below is a christology from the perspective of the discipleship of Jesus. Thus the key metaphor is not obedience, but voluntary and resolute following.

From this stems that component which is critical of the church. I used it to clarify Küng's development towards a theological breakthrough. A community of faith understands itself as a 'church from below' when it does not define itself in terms of church officials but directly in terms of its common discipleship, a shared action. It is here that Küng's criticism begins: a church government which does not listen to the questions and problems of 'church people' because it insists on claims to exclusiveness does not do justice to the seriousness of the hour. That is discussed at length.

The approach which is critical of society hardly plays a role in the immediate discussion, but should not be forgotten – for example in the case of Ratzinger, Küng and some of his allies in the struggle. Certainly Ratzinger sees connections between more recent tendencies in the church and social positions which run counter to his conservative picture of the world. That can be demonstrated everywhere in his publications. For Küng the situation is more complicated. His remarks in *The Church* that the church is neither of itself or for itself are not (just) meant as a moral appeal, an appropriate task, but also as a description of the situation. Already in 1974, i.e. before the victorious course of liberation theology in the northern zones, Küng describes the Christian God as 'God of the godless' and 'Father of the abandoned' (OBC 312f.). Thanks to his intensive communication with many people also outside 'church' circles, Küng increasingly perceives a disturbing fact: the question of Jesus, of faith, of an unconditional trust in God is being put as intensively outside the church as inside it. Furthermore, the boundary between 'inside' and 'outside' is fluid. Even people who are committed to the church, and by all standards are to be termed 'believing', often no longer know whether they believe and how they should believe.

Therefore Küng adds another very pragmatic argument to his biblical, ecclesiological and christological arguments: since the tradition of a high christology is no longer known by many people and – even more difficult – is no longer understood because of a cultural shift, there remains only one way, which is elementary and moreover is suggested by the Bible: to report on and to follow Jesus of Nazareth and then – if things go well – the experience that in him God's word and will are present.

(b) The right to be a Christian

For Küng, on this presupposition a very simple formula follows, related to the person of Jesus and his own action. It is a formula which he was to repeat word for word eighteen years later in his exposition of the creed. It has already been discussed briefly above, and it sums up in an abiding way what Küng expects of Christian faith. He concludes not only *On Being a Christian* but also his later book *Credo* with this formula:

> *By following Jesus Christ*
> *people in the world of today*
> *can live, act, suffer and die in a truly human way;*
> *in happiness and unhappiness, life and death,*
> *sustained by God and helpful to fellow men and women* (OBC 602;
> Cr 190).

This formula is a prime example of Küng's quest for simple, comprehensible formulae which can also be repeated outside official church circles. It is obvious to him that such formulae are not everything, but need interpretation (cf. TTM 248–56); that different language can be used in the liturgy; and similarly that the unity of the churches can continue to be documented in the classical and traditional formulae – who could object to this? The hermeneutical simplification by comparison with the complexity of official christologies is obvious. But it is also possible to understand why there could be no agreement, and the questions could not be settled. Compared with a traditional creed, in this concluding formula at least eight perspectives have changed.

First, this concluding formula does not take the form of a direct confession, which is introduced, say, with the words 'I believe'. Instead of this, it states – in the form of an assertion, the formulation of a conviction – what human beings can do today, what they are given strength for. It is addressed not so much inwards (to the inner circle of a liturgical assembly) as outwards (for public communication). In traditional terms it is a soteriological formula, but without the traditional terminology of justification or grace. Its advantage lies in its performative force. It does not assert, say, something that it can hardly catch up with in reality. Rather, it is a call to rely on this possibility.

Secondly, this concluding formula defines the basic form of being a Christian not as faith, but as discipleship. It thus refers back to an elementary biblical description of being a Christian, which describes the praxis and process of being a Christian instead of the goal, and which activates the secular dimension of everyday life instead of the sacral dimension of the liturgy. It refers to a complex process which never comes to a end, instead of appealing to a final truth.

Thirdly, the significance of Jesus is not described with the help of biblical messianic titles or ontological formulae, but with reference to ideals, boundary experiences and hopes of men and women today. True humanity appears as the goal of present-day existence. Thus the formula creates an inner circularity which is not to be resolved ontologically or dialectically but hermeneutically. It will have to be reinterpreted and expounded anew time and again, and recalls the basic criterion of all human and Christian life and of all true religions, namely humanity.

Fourthly, God is not mentioned directly but indirectly. God is not mentioned at the beginning but at the end; not as Father of all human beings but as the Father of Jesus Christ; not as the creator or as an entity which is known above all else, but as the last support which transcends everyday experiences and which is in fact present in the experience of discipleship. Thus God does not become an abstract concept, but is perceived in the contexts of memory and life.

Fifthly, love of neighbour is introduced not as an invitation or a duty but similarly as a possibility of true humanity. Whereas classical creeds do not go into love of neighbour and solidarity, here they appear as a culmination and thus point to the last, decisive feature of Christian praxis.

Sixthly, the formula emphasizes the special character of Christian faith, and not its general validity. There is a statement of what distinguishes Christian faith from the faith of all other religions. What emerge from this are not so much its universally binding foundations (belief in one God, in creation and future), but the personal, relational and functional relationships between Jesus Christ and the men and women who follow him and thus give themselves a historical, rather than a generally binding, identity. Thus the danger of elitist or exclusive claims to truth and validity is avoided.

Seventhly, the formula – at least theoretically – presupposes belief in God and the need for solidarity between human beings, rather than formulating these in a distinct way. In practical terms, a specific way is opened up towards a belief in God that can be experienced and a fulfilment of the love of neighbour that can be lived out. So the formula does not begin with the question 'Who is God?' or 'Who is Christ?', but 'How is my life to be lived out in faith?'

Eighthly, the formula can only be convincing for those who try it out. It is therefore an invitation and not a defined truth. What is decisive is the speech-act, not detached and distancing information. The definitive truth of Christian faith is not located in particular statements, so its final formulation is not an aim. The definitive truth of Christian faith is sought in the open sphere between praxis and its interpretation of itself.

These eight aspects show the many layers and the complexity of the shifts in this understanding of faith. They cannot be analysed further here. But even so, they show that the current formulae about the end of classical metaphysics and the expansion or even displacement of a Hellenistic christology do not go far enough. Behind them stands yet another complex series of shifts. Among them should be mentioned:

- a new kind of public communication about binding values and norms,
- a new quest for a convincing way of life,
- new attention to questions about the boundaries and the meaning of living,
- a new grounding of the question of God in human experience,
- a rediscovery of love of neighbour and solidarity as a dimension of human life,
- a new sense of the plurality and peculiarity of different world views and religions,
- a new sense of morality and ethics which overcomes the former moralism, and
- a deliberate return to the reciprocal relationship between theory and praxis.

Against this background it may become clear that the deep-seated changes to our culture make new formulations of Christian faith indispensable. These new attempts can hardly be presented *a priori* as the only true new attempts. But no one who is far-sighted can simply see them as apostasy or a retreat behind traditional Christian faith. This is all the more the case since many of them, including Küng's scheme, can refer intensively and with impressively responsible scholarship to the beginnings, beginnings which were always recognized as a norm: holy scripture.

To sum up: it is striking that in the complex metaphor of a christology 'from below' the most different aspects fuse together almost seamlessly into a unity. That is no coincidence. The metaphor is an expression of a general attitude critical of society, the church and faith which at the same time includes a new solidarity with society, an affirmation of the church, and commitment in faith. Each of the aspects has two sides, and in each, personal styles of faith and life are interwoven. That may explain why the discussions between Küng and his opponents have been carried on with so much emotion and bitterness.

Does that resolve all the questions? Of course not. Of course new beginnings are also exposed to misunderstanding precisely because of their elemental force. Elemental beginnings are always also ambivalent and need gradual clarification. But Küng knew that better (or earlier) than some of his readers. *On Being a Christian* was therefore closely followed by a second project, without which the first would have remained a torso.

6

Believing Rationally: The Question
of God in Our Time

One can argue about whether this chapter about the question of God should have come before the chapter on the question of Christ, since this book is not a biography, which would have had to follow Küng's works in order of appearance. Its task is rather the reconstruction of a theological development which is determined by the connection between issues. However, for Küng the connection between the question of God and the question of Christ has not been linear, but circular. Walter Kasper, in his argument with Küng, at one point observed that in asking about Jesus of Nazareth a Christian theology could not bracket off the question of God. In other words, he gave the impression that something of this kind had happened with Küng. That is not the case. As we shall see, the question simply took a different shape for him. At the same time, as we saw, Küng could not have given another twist to the question of Christ had he not – previously or at the same time, who knows? – found another approach to the question of God. For a theologian who takes the connection between classical christology and the doctrine of the Trinity seriously, it cannot be otherwise.

1. The history of thought brought up to date

(a) A clear position

Küng had already demonstrated this at two points. The first was in his Hegel monograph, in the chapter on a 'future christology'. There the sections on the historicity of Jesus precede a chapter on the historicity of God. In it the suffering of God, God's becoming and the dialectic in God prove to be a decisive problem. Today we must discover more resolutely than before that God is present and active *in* our world. Küng already devotes himself intensively to the question in *On Being a Christian* (OBC 57–88). There he begins in the opposite direction. He does not ask 'from above' about God's nearness to the world and a historical understanding of God. We human beings are here 'below' and seek, wish, perhaps expect our access to God. God's transcendence is attainable only through our capacity for transcendence. Instead of God's will for forgiveness, there first appears the question of our guilt, and instead of God's revelation the human quest for orientation and meaning. So from below the question is put:

> 'In view of this human situation, therefore, must we not conclude – perhaps with a pious assurance of our horror of all "metaphysics" – that the really other dimension cannot be found at the level of the linear, the horizontal, the finite, the purely human? Does not genuine transcending presuppose transcendence? Are we not now perhaps more open about this question?' (OBC 58).

Thus Küng asks about the future of religion and follows a middle prognosis, which now has more supporters than it did twenty years ago: secularization continues in a modified form. 'It splits up the religious spectrum into ever new, hitherto unknown, social forms of religion, within the churches or outside them' (OBC 62). Religion is not replaced, but differentiated because of a shift in its function in society.

Thus Küng does not think that the question of God has been answered, but raises the question of the basis for God's existence. There now follows a very intensive and concentrated passage, taken up with theses and summaries. It shows that here no provisional draft is being presented, but a summary of a text which is clearly already more comprehensive and differentiated, and which is reproduced to the degree that in Küng's judgment it is indispensable in this context. In fact Küng took some time over deciding to devote a separate book to the question of God. The degree to which he also sees a connection between *Does God Exist?* – the book to be discussed here, which appeared in 1978 – and *On Being a Christian* in respect of disputed questions is evident in his arguments with bishops and colleagues in previous years.

Now of course our main question cannot be whether the new book gives an appropriate explanation of or resolution to the questions of the magisterium on christology. The bishops were not content with *Does God Exist?* either. But we may look forward expectantly to the way in which Küng's (new) theological scheme works out in the question of God. At all events, two separate themes are not being discussed here. The books 'are mutually complementary and – we hope – merge smoothly one into the other. When repetitions seemed appropriate, particularly of course towards the end of these books, no attempt has been made to avoid them. It should be possible to read and fully understand each book for its own sake. In the present work, the important thing for me was to set out as lucidly and consistently as possible the meaning of belief in God in its totality, even if in some particular questions this meant pointing to different ways of thinking, rather than producing ready-made solutions' (DGE xxiii).

However, already in the preface Küng can give a clear answer at one point:

'Does God exist? We are putting our cards on the table here. The answer will be: "Yes, God exists." And as human beings in the twentieth century we certainly can reasonably believe in God, even in the Christian God' (DGE xxiii).

'Believing reasonably': that is Küng's central question. In no way will he admit that 'believing' (shall we say decision and trust) is replaced by any kind of provable knowledge. Here he takes seriously not only the biblical but also the great church tradition and – above all – the present situation of humankind. But he insists (and he stakes everything on this in his argument) that one thing should become clear: this decision of faith is reasonable and responsible even today, even if it must be made in freedom. Here at the same time in outline an answer is developed to the question who God is, and then Küng finally builds the bridge to the Christian God. In this he is following up what he has already developed at length in *On Being a Christian*.

But how does one talk of God in an approach 'from below'? Of course for a theologian a book about God is the central book in which he gets to his subject-matter and keeps to it. Küng would not dispute this. However, in the specific way in which he deals with the topic, it is evident how much it is woven into an understanding of human beings, history and the present. In this book 'God' is more often an indirect than a direct theme, entangled in philosophy and the sciences, in sociology and the critique of religion, in cultural developments and theological discussions. Where the question is that of God, it is evidently about everything. So it is important even in such an lengthy book of around 850 pages how the mass of material is selected, organized, brought together. Küng's master stroke is that he gives the book a scenario in the history of philosophy and thought, and sometimes in the history of culture.

Probably a deep truth is hidden here, since it is present, and our thought about God is deeply shaped by this history. Our expectations and aversions, our doubts and our problems, are much more deeply connected with the history of this thought in our culture than we generally realize. So in referring back to this history of thought and following it, we are presumably descending into the well-springs of present-day awareness of God. This one universality is still alive today, in what is said publicly and what is not said; what is asserted and what is suppressed; what plays a part in philosophical and political, in cultural and socio-political, opinions and options; the offence taken at the church and the enthusiasm for its cause. Here at the same time we are probably assimilating the agreements and conflicts between philosophical and theological thought, and these in turn often represent the common interests of church and society or the conflicts between them. At important points the problem even relates to the conflicts between the confessions or the fact that the confessions tended to use belief in God more to prove that they were right, and in their authoritarian will for power. How could one, how can one, think ill of contemporaries for taking the behaviour of the confessions, including their lust for war, as valid currency? There is much that has to be worked through in our largely failed history of God.

I refer to this background for the following reason: a clear and distinctive position emerges from Küng's reflection on the question of God. The questions 'then' are still topical today. By means of Pascal or Feuerbach, Descartes or Hegel, he discusses present-day questions, not to mention the questions which were formulated by thinkers like Marx, Nietzsche and Freud. Problems which had not been worked out at that time need as far as possible to be settled today. Questions which were put to church and theology at that time have the right to an answer. And the church, which claims to represent belief in God, will also have to face its history of alienation, neglect and selfishness. In fact Küng, even when he does not say so, is practising a contextual history of thought about God which is related to the present. What we have here is a hermeneutic of relating to the present and of dangerous memories. It is because he brings the question of God so clearly into the present, even if indirectly, that this history is so exciting. It also becomes exciting for Christians, because this history of doubt and protest, with its calls for freedom and criticism of Christianity, is first and foremost a Christian history.

(b) The scenario of intellectual history

Küng begins with the primal heritage of modernity, which will later cause endless difficulties for the question of God: the way in which (instrumental) rationality has become independent from faith (Descartes and Pascal). We usually perceive this development not as a religious but as a general social problem (DGE 1–126). The following chapter gets closer to us. With Hegel, the question is raised whether and how God enters into the world and history and comes close to it. Is God really not an authoritarian and immovable God who is remote from the world (DGE 127–88)? Finally we touch on a present which begins with the atheism of the nineteenth century (Feuerbach, Marx and Freud, DGE 189–340) and which is then radicalized and summed up in Nietzsche's nihilism (DGE 341–424). As Nietzsche withdraws his trust not only from God but also from reality, he also compels us to develop the answer to the question of God in two stages. What is to be discussed is trust in reality and the Yes to God. Only now, after this long preparation, is the Christian image of God debated.

Each part works out the schemes of decisive thinkers, sums up what can still be taken over from them today, and each time draws the conclusions in the form of strictly formulated theses. The result is a model work not only in terms of content but also in didactic presentation. Of course the many analyses cannot be described here; some perspectives must be enough. First we shall concentrate on the core question of the book, that of the existence of God.

In the Western tradition down to the present day the discussion about God has been carried on with only a few patterns of argument. Mention should be made first of the aprioristic proof of Anselm of Canterbury, which infers the existence of an utterly perfect being, i.e. one which is also unconditionally necessary, from the idea of that being. Despite all the criticism which began at a very early stage, even later this argument gained convinced supporters. The same is true of the well-known 'five ways' of Thomas Aquinas. They too presuppose the readers' assent to God's existence. Therefore, strictly speaking, they do not seek to prove God's existence but to demonstrate to believers God's relationship to them. They seek to make clear the significance of belief in God for the meaningfulness of the world, for its order, and for thought. Küng presupposes this and at the same time is aware that with the beginning of modernity a new situation also begins for the question of God. I shall describe his train of thought briefly here.

As I remarked, Küng's report begins with Descartes (DGE 3–41). He attempts to reconstruct the notion of God in a methodologically precise way, i.e. to develop a sequence of precisely defined steps in thought. Therefore from an ontological perspective God's existence must precede the possibility of knowing the world, for God alone can guarantee the truth. But the beginning of all knowledge lies in human beings, and that makes it possible to dispute God's existence methodically. Yet here too much is asked for the capacity of reason, as though it could unconditionally also analyse its own presuppositions. Pascal (DGE 42–92) is a clear-sighted contemporary critic of this development. He refers to 'reasons of the heart', and in so doing guards himself against the dictates of a purely calculating reason. The later debate over rationalism, which is still topical (DGE 93–126; cf. LR 10–29), took its start here. Pascal's critical extension of the concept of reason plays an important role in Küng's later argument. Already at that time there was a split between distancing reason and involved understanding, a gulf between knowledge and trust. This observation plays an important role in Küng's answer to the question of God.

To continue: Kant then gave classic formulation to the question of reason in respect of 'God' (DGE 536–51). As the thought-processes and proofs of 'theoretical reason' cannot themselves penetrate to reality, he introduces a second process of offering proof. 'Practical reason' does not draw any compelling conclusions, but postulates God's existence as a theoretical principle in connection with virtue and happiness. God becomes the 'leading idea', and this indwells our understanding of the world and self as a condition of all practical knowing. Now it can be disputed whether with this 'leading idea God' Küng already envisages the dimension of an ultimate trust which is later so important for him. But it is certainly the case that Kant takes a way that avoids a course of argument involving rational proof which nevertheless cannot be called irrational. But what can there still be between rationality and irrationality? So Kant introduces an abiding unrest into the guild. Since then 'theoretical reason' has been fundamentally mistrusted. But how far does that practical reason without which none of us can live take us?

When Hegel, the last comprehensive thinker on this matter, wants to overcome the dualism which has come about in this way (DGE 129–61), he has to get beyond Kant's position, and thus reflect more radically on God. God must be attainable rationally, and at the same time be unattainable; must remain distinct from history, the world and humankind, and at the same time embrace them; it must be possible to experience God in a way which precedes all argumentation. God gives himself to the world; at the same time the world becomes God's interpretation of himself. The divine spirit 'appears' in history and society, in art, religion and philosophy. Therefore Hegel speaks of the 'phenomenology of the Spirit'. So does God legitimate himself, because he can be experienced by any thinker? Again Küng argues the point of a past thinker. God is not (just) an other-worldly being, but at the same time historical reality. God is before all time and at the same time human, present in humankind, not neutral towards human suffering; he does not lose his divinity through his mutability.

So Hegel makes a total claim which cannot be surpassed, as he is thinking the unthinkable – in the literal sense of the word. Thus Hegel also introduces the decisive shift in the critique of theology, which Küng analyses for the first time in *The Incarnation of God*. According to Küng, Hegel fails in his tremendous claim to understand the whole of reality and its history strictly from God. But this understanding has a dangerous effect. What would it mean for freedom, and thus love, decision, trust, to be taken up completely into this way of thinking? Doesn't Hegel force into thought something that fundamentally evades it? Hegel compels us to all or nothing. Now we can only 'think' of God totally or reject God in his totality; there is no third possibility. Therefore down to the present day Hegel continues to exert a theological fascination and a theological repulsion.

For this reason, Hegel's pupil Feuerbach (DGE 191–216) can open up an equally radical counter-movement, which at the same time reflects a general shift of cultural mood. Now begins the history of the public critique of religion which emerges in the name of scholarship. Theologically the critique of religion becomes a fruitful foundation, since it opens up more subject-matter for the contemporary question of God than the whole previous history of the proofs for God. What new positions are introduced which are important for Küng? Why can Küng now exclaim consistently that there is 'No going back behind Feuerbach, Marx, Freud'? His terse answer, which relates to all forms of the critique of religion, runs: 'Belief in God is proved in practice' (DGE 326). Thus the question is no longer one of abstract logical proofs for or against the existence of God. God is intrinsically inexpressible. The controversies in the critique of religion are always about God's relationship to us, about freedom and justice, about coming of age and walking upright, i.e. simultaneously about the human person, about society, about the relationship between materiality and intelligibility, about reality generally. Here finally Küng has reached his point.

Feuerbach, for example, develops his critique of religion as a dispute over the humanity of human beings. Looked at superficially, he dissolves theology into anthropology. On closer inspection, for the first time he raises the question whether in the meantime 'God' has not come to function as the one who fills the gaps in unfulfilled needs (DGE 208–16) instead of being the goal of true human longing (DGE 323–40). Karl Marx couples the critique of religion with the verification or the misuse of faith in social praxis (DGE 259–61). Sigmund Freud (DGE 262–340) raises the question of the repressions and dishonest sublimations to which Christian faith too fell victim in its everyday exegesis. According to Küng's interpretation, these critics have not only extended the chain of arguments within philosophy by some links, but also qualitatively extended the horizon of the argument.

So can our history get by without God? Küng does not strike sail so quickly, since the critique of religion convinces him that he should add the model of Habermas (Habermas 1, 43–74), with arguments about correctness (Feuerbach, Marx) and credibility (Freud). That does not decide anything about the truth itself. However much the question of God and the question of the church, the understanding of God and church reform, theology and ecclesiology, belong together, the criterion for the truth of belief in God is not simply practice (DGE 326). Küng urgently advises theology to take atheism seriously, but consistently keeps the question of truth open (DGE 323–40). Does the discussion necessarily remain in permanent dispute?

(c) The turning-point

Nietzsche gives the topic a new depth which is decisive for Küng. Küng characterizes his position as 'nihilism' (DGE 343–424). Nietzsche combines his critique of religion with a radical critique of religion and morality, culture and reality. This is the new element which is of interest to theology. For he also reflects with great seriousness not only on the 'death of God' (for Nietzsche a public event which is extremely significant for culture) but also on its consequences. He combines his plea for a consistent atheism with the 'overcoming of man by man' (DGE 375), and that requires everything of human beings. God's existence or non-existence at the same time entails a statement about human beings and the world, and also a statement about the meaning and reasonableness of an ultimate trust in reality. In nihilism Küng discovers the dispute over a fundamental certainty which began with Descartes and Pascal (DGE 380–4) and cannot be resolved consistently even now. Thus the circle has closed. It is as if Nietzsche were recalling God, the 'executioner' whom he once chased away ('My pain! My last . . . happiness!'). But this God who is never completely indispensable remains remote (DGE 395).

With Nietzsche, Küng can now finally formulate the appropriate opposition to belief in God. Here the 'most extreme opposite position to belief in God' (DGE 416) is presented. Its claim to truth also remains open. But the problem is accentuated, for the certainty of faith can now no longer be separated from the certainty of reason. What is being debated is the 'fundamental certainty of being' itself (DGE 417). Nietzsche refuses to place an ultimate 'fundamental trust' in reality itself. That is the new, the existential, dimension which Küng introduces into the debate about faith and from which he interprets the question of God. Is nihilism then in principle possible, irrefutable and unprovable, like the existence of God (DGE 423f.)? If that is the case, then faith is not the reflex of an irrational, more or less arbitrary, decision but is grounded in a last confrontation with reality itself.

Nevertheless Küng is concerned for nihilism and atheism to be distinguished. An atheist need not be a nihilist. But because Nietzsche shows up the refusal of all fundamental trust as the radicalizing of all unbelief, conversely Küng can relate fundamental trust in reality to belief in God. Thus the question of God is raised to a new level. More precisely, Küng now sets the question of belief in God against the comprehensive horizon of an ultimate trust in the world, human beings, reality. In so doing – so to speak from the negative side – he again manages to interlock God and the world, nearness and remoteness, in a way that he could learn from Hegel. Although, as I have remarked, reality and God, fundamental trust and faith, are to be distinguished, the question of God does not first emerge behind reality (as still in Descartes), but already in it.

With good reason, Küng speaks of a fundamental 'Yes to reality', a basic attitude and an 'inner' rationality, which so far has been mentioned remarkably little. He devotes a separate part to it (DGE 425–77). Of course 'faith' in the normative sense of the word, understood as a comprehensive and radical attitude of trust, always includes trust. But if I understand 'faith' in an everyday factual sense of the word, i.e. as the explicit presentation of the phenomenon of 'faith in God', which in some circumstances abstracts from the inner attitude, then things become more complicated. In that case there is not only a Yes to reality without religious faith but also a faith in God without fundamental trust; this is probably the more dangerous alternative, which is in no way convincing and is fundamentally a hypocritical and destructive one (DGE 475). Faith in the everyday sense of the word is not a simple system elevated above all criticism. It can also degenerate into cynicism, which Nietzsche had indicated in the mockers who are amused in the market place by 'foolish people'. In modern times, 'faith' can no more be objectified than trust, perhaps because human beings can never completely 'objectify' themselves. But Küng thinks that in cases of happiness we 'understand' ourselves from within.

Küng's asymmetrical argument can be understood against this background. On the one hand he distinguishes consistently between belief and unbelief, between fundamental trust and a fundamental mistrust; at the level of a reason that argues rationally (which he in no way rejects) he notes a stalemate between the two which hovers between affirmation and questionableness ('unproven – not refuted'). On the other hand he differentiates at a deeper level, which we can call 'inner understanding', without any equilibrium. Certainly the inner contradictions of reality and a religious faith cannot be discussed away, but the Yes to reality and the Yes to God each time represent the intellectually more conclusive and more comprehensive position. At least the way to this Yes is never completely blocked, but keeps emerging as the 'other dimension', as a more comprehensive, indispensable dimension, as a possibility which opens up the future (DGE 481–507). Seen from the outside, the grounding of truth remains hidden and only shows itself at the goal.

So must we provisionally (and thus arbitrarily) affirm something which can only be known later? This circular argument presupposes a clear separation and separability of an objective and a subjective part in the process of knowledge. But that is not the case in an act of trust, for trust in reality or God is not just reflection with a view to later action, but direct involvement in a committed process of knowledge. We cannot describe this in a neutral, detached way, but only report it affirmatively and attest it as a possibility. This interweaving of decision and understanding, this interlocking of knowledge and action, this priority of an inner understanding over rational knowledge, represents the decisive shift in Küng's argumentation.

2. Inner reason

That is the reason for the unusual form of Küng's decisive argument. Where proof should be offered, an *if* appears, which is unusual and provokes questions.

(a) The argument

Küng sums up his argument in two core texts which look like theses. The two texts, which supplement each other, run:

1. In respect of reality as a whole:
- *If God existed, then the grounding reality itself would no longer be ultimately groundless. Why? Because God would then be the primal ground of all reality.*
- *If God existed, then the supporting reality itself would no longer be ultimately unsupported. Why? Because God would then be the primal support of all reality.*
- *If God existed, then evolving reality itself would no longer be ultimately without aim. Why? Because God would then be the primal goal of all reality.*
- *If God existed, then reality suspended between being and non-being would no longer be ultimately under suspicion of being a void. Why? Because God would then be the being-itself of all reality* (DGE 566).

2. In respect of our human existence, and thus the particular personal reality of each of us, each with our own history:

If God existed,
- *then, despite all the menace of fate and death, I could with good reason confidently affirm the unity and identity of my human existence. Why? Because God would indeed also be the primal source of my life;*
- *then, despite all the menace of emptiness and meaninglessness, I could with good reason confidently affirm the truth and meaningfulness of my existence. Why? Because God would be the ultimate meaning of my life;*
- *then, despite all the menace of sin and damnation, I could with good reason confidently affirm the goodness and value of my existence. Why? Because God would then be the all-embracing hope of my life;*

- *then, against all the menace of non-being, I could with good reason confidently affirm the being of my human existence. Why? Because God would then also be the being itself of human life (DGE 567f.).*

On a first reading, the manner and mode of the argument might provoke astonishment and resistance. As he said at the beginning, Küng is putting his cards on the table: given his conception, he cannot do otherwise. He makes the logical structure of his (positive) argument clear and basically tests the reader without the reader noticing it. First of all he sustains a hypothesis, a great 'if-then' connection. He points out that these great formulae about ground, support and goal; unity, truth and goodness, merely summarize what has already been said. Anyone who stops at these abbreviating formulae and thinks that the answer can now be suggested and recommended has not understood much. No, the great formulae are the summaries of what has been thought about God in our history.

A second observation is more important: behind this conditional way of speaking lies not only encouragement but also a warning. The encouragement goes: possibly there is this solution, and it is very promising. The warning goes: this solution cannot be demonstrated; no one can take it home in black and white. So Küng also goes on to make it clear that 'the fact that God is . . . can be assumed only in a confidence rooted in reality itself' (DGE 569f.). Thus any compelling proof is repudiated. However, this dispensing with a compelling proof does not bring confusion, but makes room for shifting the perspective. Where is the perspective to be shifted to?

(b) Binding knowledge

Methodologically speaking, as has already been said, this is not a logical process of proof but a reference to an inner possibility of understanding, the discovery of concrete complexes of meaning. God's truth is not striven for through a screen of logically correct conclusions, but through a comprehensive interpretation of reality. 'God' does not prove himself from individual arguments but from the truth-content which arises only out of a comprehensive understanding of reality. Thus the apparently logical stringency of the statements which seem almost tautological and nevertheless are maintained in unreality become an invitation to decipher anew our experience of the reality of God's existence. 'God', in a way comparable to Pascal's wager (DGE 61–3), is offered as a working hypothesis in the best sense of the word for thought and life. But the proof, the appearance, the nearness of God can only convince those who follow this proof and this nearness by means of their own or shared experiences.

Küng gives the name 'trust' to a readiness to accept complexes of meaning even if they are not compelling or objectifiable. Now he states that God can be accepted only in an attitude of trust – thus he does not break through the neutrality of questioning reason but states that, given the questions which are pending, neutrality is impossible. In this case the neutrality of reason would become the withholding of assent, veiled repudiation. Trust here means a readiness for binding knowledge, the recognition of a reasonable commitment. With this trust Küng is not adding a new fundamentally irrational quality to knowledge; rather, he is pleading for 'trust' once again to be accepted in general discourse as a framework for understanding, and for understanding once again to be accepted as a genuine dimension of trust.

This trust is first of all directed to the reality which can be immediately experienced; therefore Küng must distinguish between 'fundamental trust' and 'faith'. Only at a second stage is this trust directed towards God. In this case Küng speaks of 'faith' as radical fundamental trust. He does not understand this faith either as a supplement to or a substitute for knowledge, but as its framework. Conversely, he understands the knowledge of God as a genuine dimension of faith in God. Thus it finally it becomes understandable why for him Yes and No to the meaning of reality and to God's existence do not stand side by side with equal rights. Only in the assenting thought of reality is such clear assent possible for him. Anyone who relies on reality by trusting it can also experience the meaning of this trust. However, in refusing this assenting thought, thought stops before the possibility of saying Yes.

By contrast, the Yes to God at the same time affirms an ultimate ground for trust in reality. Küng says: 'As radical fundamental trust, belief in God can suggest the condition of the possibility of uncertain reality. Those who affirm God know why they can trust reality' (DGE 576). However, this statement must not be understood as a compelling proof, since no grounds are given for fundamental trust. The experiences which justify trust and faith can be given as examples, but they cannot be universalized, verified, quantified or even repeated at will (DGE 465–77).

It is precisely this access to reality which has disclosed itself anew to a hermeneutical way of thinking in the nineteenth and twentieth centuries. It is an understanding which is related to concrete texts, experiences, images and hopes, and expounds these. It is a language which makes a claim to truth but relates this claim to a speaker or a text. It is finally an interpretation which knows very well that this speaking, this complex of problems and this exposition apply to the historical, cultural and social situation here and now.

That can also be made clear by means of the question who or what 'God' really is for Küng. Must not this concept be defined before one advances such far-reaching reflections with it and about it? For Küng things are different. Of course he can presuppose a general knowledge for his book, and of course with all the posing of problems, questions and corrections he establishes a particular picture of God. But he develops a profiled scenario of the image and significance of God rather than devoting himself to a definition, because God evades any definition. At the decisive point he then introduces metaphors like 'authority', 'ground', 'support', 'goal' and 'being', and each time radicalizes them with the prefix 'Ur-' (primal). But it cannot be his concern to decipher these metaphors as external information; rather, they are immanent signals for 'God'. God's 'causality' appears in Küng's context of understanding as the effect of the subject-matter itself, its goal and cause as a dynamic of human beings and the world, its order as the structure, life-principle or cultural process of the real in itself. The limitations of talking in analogies, in which God can never be grasped as God in himself and according to himself, at the same time makes it possible to name God from the dimensions of human experience as an authority which is concerned for us and which – if it exists at all – is close to us. So the claim 'God exists' does not have a conclusive meaning for Küng, but one which creates meaning. He does not want to stylize responsible discourse even indirectly as proofs of God; he simply wants to justify actual talk of God and actual trust in him.

(c) The God of Jesus Christ?

In *On Being A Christian* Küng had already anticipated core statements of *Does God Exist?* The question there was not primarily one about God's existence, but about who the God of Jesus Christ is. There is now a reference back to the earlier book in the last part of *Does God Exist?* Who, since the biblical tradition has been bracketed off for so long, is the God of the Christians?

As in *On Being a Christian*, Küng recalls a horizon which is important for him: anyone who speaks of the Christian God should not forget the non-Christian religions. Just as in *On Being a Christian* Küng relativized the church's claim to have the sole truth, so here he relativizes the claim of the Christian religion to absoluteness. 'Mutual challenge' (DGE 600) is the slogan which he will then present consistently in the 1980s and 1990s, against the background that God 'cannot be grasped in any concept, cannot be fully expressed in any statement, cannot be defined in any definition'. 'All talk emerges from listening silence and leads to speaking silence' (DGE 601f.)

Now some remarks need to be made about the transition from the general part about God's existence to the separate part about the Christian image of God. The question has to be answered: which God has been spoken of so far, and how is the tradition of the God of Jesus Christ to be fitted into what has been said? At all events, now the character of the account changes. Narratives, images, the story of Jesus are expounded. The link is not with boundary experiences and experiences of trust but with the everyday experiences which are related in scripture and which are comparable with the scriptures of other religions.

Nevertheless not everything is equally true. Küng does not *a priori* see a greater degree of truth in the biblical tradition, though he does see a greater degree of clarity. Here is a God who has a name, related to history and the world, not apersonal but at the same time more than a (human) person, one who is friendly to human beings and can be relied on unconditionally by them. Precisely this distinguishes him from the anonymous God of the philosophers (DGE 613–66). In the Christian image of God, Küng again sees a greater degree of clarity than in the other religions, at any rate the non-biblical traditions. The God of Jesus does not have any arbitrary demonic features and, as we see in the message and fate of Jesus, he is the Father of the lost. He showed his true face in Jesus of Nazareth, and at a very early stage the Christian community formulated its conviction: 'From eternity, there is no other God than the one who manifested himself in Jesus.' Furthermore, in the light of this universal God, Jesus himself has a universal significance (DGE 683), though the Father remains greater than he is (John 10.29; cf. Mark 13.32; DGE 684f.). In view of the controversy with the bishops, here Küng is particularly careful to be accurate. Here he defines and demarcates against misunderstandings, albeit within the framework of personal categories:

'For believers, the true man Jesus of Nazareth is the real revelation of the one true God and, in this sense, his Word, his Son' (DGE 686). A short summary of the christological message is thus: the God of the Christians has a name and a face. He has revealed himself not only in the history of Israel but at the same time 'in an individual human form in which God's Son, Word, will and love assumed flesh'. Or once again – as already in *On Being a Christian* – an even shorter summary: 'The Christian feature of the Christian God is this Christ himself' (DGE 690).

It is really enough to read the few but very dense pages on the christo-logical question, sometimes filled with emphatic formulae (DGE 667–91), to be clear that, as at the beginning of his theological career, Küng's understanding of God and faith is still stamped by a strong christo-centricity. Christ is the only figure in whom all that is specifically Christian can be summed up. There is really no other name for him than that of Jesus of Nazareth, in whom the truth of God was fulfilled. That makes all the more incomprehensible the again restrained, if not com-pletely negative, reaction by the church authorities. Once more people were not ready to follow Küng's thoughts with him and thus judge him on his own terms. Official church theology always believes that it can also impose its scheme of thought from outside.

3. The use of an understanding theology

As I have shown, Küng develops his argument about the existence of God against the background of a long history of the problem. This is significant for several reasons.

A first reason, which I have already mentioned earlier, lies in Küng's historical procedure. Historical research had already proved itself to be a critical instrument in the nineteenth century when applied to timeless, dogmatic and undialogical thought and had secured an indispensable place for itself, especially in historical criticism of the Bible. It is beyond question that the history of dogma did inestimable service for Küng's theology – as already for many of his predecessors, for example those of *nouvelle théologie*.

A second reason clearly emerges in *Does God Exist?*. Küng not only reports the result of historical research but takes up the basic act of historical investigation: reconstruction by report. By giving biographical accounts of the decisive thinkers whom he discusses, he produces multi-dimensional reports, the experiential content of which in principle goes beyond the analytical framework. By doing this he activates something which plays a very central role in his book: a sympathetic understand-ing, the rationale of which is concerned with both the issue as a whole and its details. Otherwise the task would be almost impossible: the focussing of the central argument on an unreality (a 'hypothesis', as

Küng calls it) has in fact shown the difficulty. But as long as the view and the background are given a narrative form, the dynamic of understanding, the use of words, and the appeal remain fluid.

What emerges in *On Being a Christian* from the history of Jesus could emerge in an analogous way from the history of modern thought: the concrete perception and growing awareness of messages, basic attitudes, invitations to deal with ultimately binding questions. For Küng it is of vital importance for theological contexts not only to be demarcated, analysed and worked through, but also to be understood as specifically and as comprehensively as possible, in the light of human existence. Küng practises an understanding theology. For him that is a theology which goes beyond traditional structures and limits.

On this basis Küng has crossed three frontiers of theological discussion so far. They are the frontiers between Protestant and Catholic tradition, between philosophy and theology, and between a reflective and a hermeneutical model of understanding. These frontiers grew up over history and are usually observed in order to protect logic and strict conceptuality, and also to protect confessional demarcations. Within their particular rules, apparently compelling proofs or refutations then arise. However, as we shall see, these rules are also always the result of prior decisions which were made in history. They have reduced the complexity of our experiences. The important thing now is to regain this complexity.

(a) Bringing Protestant and Catholic together

In the theology of the 1970s, ecumenical openness was no longer anything special, at any rate in Tübingen, where two theological faculties often thought, fought and trained alongside and often also with one another. There is no doubt that Küng – as an expert on Karl Barth, a representative of an ecumenically open ecclesiology, an undeterred critic of anxious church governments and a critical interpreter of christology, moreover as a colleague who was fond of dialogue – was generally accepted, even if his pros and cons were not formally discussed. Nevertheless, he in particular was the one who liked to point to frontiers which were still open and called for them too to be crossed. One example of this is his treatment of what the professionals called and still call 'natural theology' and to which he devotes around twenty pages (DGE 509–28). For him this is a 'theological discussion', the significance of which for our world is not to be overestimated, since theological decisions are no longer to be taken on the basis of confessional traditions but in the light of the contemporary question of an ultimate fundamental truth. I shall be returning to this later. Nevertheless, various confessional approaches have engraved themselves on our consciousness. What is the problem? Küng describes it like this:

> 'Does God exist at all? Must we simply believe it? We are constantly told to do so by all types of believers in God. But the response, that it is possible not to believe in God, comes not only from those who deny God but also from those who doubt his existence or who are still seeking him. Some Catholics suggest that we must first know God if we are to believe in him. But Protestants especially deny this and claim that we must first believe in God before we can know him. Belief in God is a matter of dispute between believers and unbelievers, between believers of one kind and believers of a different kind' (DGE 509).

The discussion over the priority of faith and knowledge is thus not just carried on between Christians and non-Christians, but is also reflected within Christianity, with its confessional stamp. Of course caution is needed here: both Catholic and Protestant theology are now displaying a variegated multiplicity. Nevertheless here a constantly recurring problem emerges, along with two lines towards a solution. Obviously they converge only if they can be related in some complex way. We shall have to discuss later how at the point at which Küng discusses them for the most part they have already been answered by the analyses of trust, certainty and knowledge.

Küng reports two histories which run almost in opposite directions. There is the history of Catholic theology, which since the Enlightenment increasingly parted company with culture, reacted in a markedly defensive way and at Vatican I – here too unfortunately – sought 'final' clarity. The result is at first sight balanced, since it does not damage either the rights of reason or those of faith. According to Romans 1.20, God can be known with the reason (though that does not mean that he is proved or necessarily known), but of course God's revelation is decisive. 'Natural theology' arises along the first way of knowledge (if it is thought possible). In principle, at that time Protestant theology could live with this solution. As always, the problems lay in the detail. In the tradition of Thomas Aquinas, wrongly understood, natural theology and a theology of revelation, a 'natural' person and one endowed with grace, fell apart in an increasingly disastrous way; 'nature' and grace became increasingly lifeless abstractions. In what was theologically not a very creative time, these solutions would perhaps have remained episodes had critics not been pursued with the Index, banned from teaching and discriminated against within the church. Here criticism of official doctrine as a rule simply argued that the two levels, reason and revelation, a longing for salvation and God's gift of grace, always refer to the same person. Does it make sense to separate the two? A concrete anthropology cannot separate them in the long run. Or does this piece-meal thinking simply serve to stabilize the inalienable rights of the Catholic Church and its exclusive claim to salvation?

Protestant theology had its own way of thinking about this unity. Here faith arose in history and culture. It would probably have done better to have more discernment, and Catholic theology more of a sense of the whole. Both sides lost detachment as a result of the political turmoil, the enthusiasm for the First World War and the Fascism which followed. It was Karl Barth who reacted decisively; his exciting history need not be related again here. He radically repudiated natural theo-logy, called the analogy of being an invention of the Antichrist (CD I/1, xiii), and in so doing took up an old Protestant tradition – albeit in radicalized form. A deep mistrust of reason led him to the priority of faith and an exclusivism of salvation and truth which are intolerable for us today – contrary to many observations on scripture and public life. But the later Karl Barth (CD IV/3) comes to Küng's aid. Now, while Christ remains the only light, not only the church but also the world is reconciled in him. The creation is conceded its own lights.

Küng sums up his balancing position, which seems more Catholic but overcomes the dualism (DGE 526–8). Belief in God must not be blind and devoid of reality, but responsible and related to reality:

'• Not a blind, but a justifiable, belief: people should not be mentally abused, but convinced by arguments, so that they can make a responsible decision of faith.
• Not a belief devoid of reality, but a belief related to reality. People should not simply have to believe without verification. But their statements should be verified and tested in contact with reality, against the background of the experience of the individual and of society, and should thus be covered by the concrete experience of reality' (DGE 528).

Against this background Küng can answer the question of the proofs of God in a sophisticated way.

With these initial rules, the question of the proofs of God can then be discussed with an eye to both the Catholic and the Protestant traditions. By comparison with the length of the book, this discussion is relatively brief and concise. Perhaps an ecumenist would have expected rather more than this and at an earlier point. It must also be clear that such statements make important decisions about the significance of the religions and other world-views. So this discussion is carried on at a relatively late stage. Perhaps the church Christian must or can begin *Does God Exist?* (which in the end is not a book to read but a study book and a work book) with Part F, and then go backwards. This comment also makes clear what questions govern the book's agenda. This is not the agenda of an everyday life integrated into the church, but the agenda of all those who ask the one important question here, regardless of their religious or confessional socialization: How do I become certain that I can trust human beings and the world in a way which (if things go well) is held fast by what we in our history call 'God'? To put this particular question at the centre is an ecumenical decision which gives a subordinate place to the traditionally confessional questions. This question of certainty leads directly to the crossing of the second frontier which must be discussed here.

(b) Philosophy and theology in dialogue

It may perhaps have been noted that 'faith' is a deeply biblical concept and at the same time one which is central to the Christian message, as central as the concept of all theological concepts. 'God'. Thus it was necessarily an advantage for theologians to develop both concepts from their own tradition. Who else had thought so existentially and so intensively about it as the theological tradition? One might suppose that philosophy has always merely been an accompaniment. It made attempts to break out and repeatedly had to be called to order. In *Justification* Küng had still spoken in biblical terms, and in *The Church* still in strongly New Testament terms. It was different in *On Being a Christian*. There the New Testament message appears in a pure form, though this is deliberately and consistently contemporary. Now, particularly now, when God and faith are no longer spoken of directly but indirectly, most energy is used in the discussion with philosophy. Is the dogmatic theologian returning to preliminary questions, to the business of fundamental theology, which consists in laying foundations? Does Küng merely want to do preliminary work, in order to make room for true talk of faith later?

Of course here too Küng could have gone other ways; his decision was not forced on him, but was a possibility grounded in the subject-matter. Nor does it represent a detour into theology, but rather a departure from the place where the dispute about God and faith is carried on. Küng is not the first to take this course, though he is more clearly concerned than others to engage with the great modern doubts about and attacks on God. I can discover three characteristics which distinguish his approach from most others. Küng intensifies the dialogue with the critique of religion, shifts the dialogue 'outwards', and concentrates on the question of certainty.

(i) Critique of religion

Theology had already encountered the critique of religion long before Küng, but for a long time it was intent on refuting unbelief. Theologians rescued what could be rescued, conceded abuse and misunderstandings, but essentially remained firm: the opposing arguments were said to be untenable, lacking credibility, and not particularly successful. Feuerbach's projection theory seemed to have been refuted, along with Marx's materialism, Freud's psychologism or even the nihilism of Nietzsche, in whose hands norms and values disintegrated. Küng does not practise such simplistic apologetics, but takes another course. He draws conclusions for the question of faith in which the critique of religion as a whole comes into play. In his programme of 'self-appraisal' (see 58f. above) he remains true to himself, and thus seeks a self-critical approach. At the same time he goes beyond this elementary aim. Already always interested in other, challenging conceptions, he does not limit the dialogue but intensifies it. Above all he gives the critique of religion a place in the overall development of philosophy. From Descartes to neo-rationalism he stands up for his dialogue partners as critics of religion: he does not assign them their topics but allows them to present these topics to him. Of course he does not do that naively. Küng would not be Küng did he not organize the masses of material, structure them and focus them on questions which seemed important to him. But he does this by first allowing his partners to speak, seeking to discover with analysis and intuition their real concern in arguing with faith and God in the present situation, which is in fact critical for religion and faith.

So he develops his own train of thought with philosophical material. By means of Descartes he analyses the broken unity of faith and reason, by means of Pascal the problem of an answer orientated on faith alone. With Hegel he shows the possibility and also the limitations of a great intellectual synthesis and the question of the historicity and nearness of God in our world. Only against this background can he analyse Feuerbach, Marx and Freud as real milestones in a critical idea of God: as a critique of ideology, society and culture, as a question of the possibly devastating effects of a badly-understood religion on men and women. Finally he sees Nietzsche as the great herald of an anti-Christianity in which the challenge is formulated. He does not go into the content of scripture in detail. So he avoids skirmishes which then lose sight of the real, comprehensive questions.

(ii) Open dialogue

Again it proves that this historical sketch serves a very present memory. By 'open dialogue' I do not mean a sympathetic degree of mobility, which in the end serves any dialogue, but the deliberate breaking through of boundaries within Christianity and within theology. As a rule theologians are accustomed to engaging in dialogue with those who share their Christian presuppositions. That is the concern of dogmatics in the classical sense. Now Küng takes the dialogue outside the walls of the churches, by not simply arguing about Christian subject-matter but going into its presuppositions. Among other things he attempts to be a philosopher to the philosophers.

From the controversy between Descartes and Pascal Küng goes over to the epistemological discussion of our century; one thinks of Wittgenstein, Carnap, Popper and Kuhn. Science and the question of God are set over against each other. Hegel too becomes the occasion for a completely modern question: how can God be all-embracing and at the same time present, eternal and at the same time changeable, superior and at the same time the one who is not indifferent to human suffering? And of course Feuerbach, Marx and Freud lead to highly topical questions which do not just concern religious people. What about truth and projection, praxis as the criterion of truth, the difficult relationship between religion and its psychological effects? Finally Nietzsche leads to the great chapters, which are theologically and anthropologically exciting, on trust and mistrust, certainty and nihilism.

What happens in them, and what is the inner logic of this train of thought? By means of the sketches and figures used as examples, Küng carries on a dialogue with our time. The frontiers of discussion within the church and within theology are crossed; links are made with the problems of those who question and search, with the accusations of those who are disappointed (over faith or the church), with the desperation of those with no guidelines and those who reject Christian belief. Here Küng makes a fundamental preliminary decision. His basic assumption is that human questions, regardless of belief and unbelief, are the theologically important questions, no matter whether they come from the church or secular humanity. At the same time he assumes that these fundamental questions are alive and in search of answers inside and outside the church. This crossing of boundaries is of elementary significance in defining tasks for contemporary theology:

> 'Many are at a loss between belief and unbelief; they are undecided, sceptical. They are doubtful about their belief, but they are also doubtful about their doubting. And there are many who are even proud of their doubting. Yet there remains a longing for certainty. Certainty? Whether Catholics, Protestants, Orthodox, whether Christians or Jews, believers in God or atheists – the discussion today runs right across old denominations and new ideologies' (DGE xxi).

The frontier between the church and the world still goes deep. The demarcation of philosophy from theology was necessary for reasons of self-respect. Here it is consistently broken through. Here is a theology which seeks advice from philosophy, since it has not only erected intellectual structures but given intellect and voice to the questions of modernity and has been a critical companion to theology. Now it is time for philosophy and theology to go along together again. Küng's firm conviction is that with his approach, dialogue with all men and women is possible, without complexes and a sense of superiority, pertinently and with a great degree of commitment. This secular dialogue in partnership can and must therefore be the test for Küng's enterprise.

(iii) Certainty and orientation

But what is the dialogue to be about? Certainly many interesting questions can be raised: current and archaic, on individual statements of faith and on the properties of God, on one's personal future, the experience of God and God's absence in our time. Guided by his philosophical course, Küng has concentrated the conversation on a single question. For him it is the most important question, on which all others turn and in the light of which they can be resolved. He concentrates on the question of certainty. At the beginning of Küng's career justification already turned on the 'certainty of faith', there formulated as the central religious question whether and how we can trust in God without our own merit. In a radicalized form and under the conditions of human autonomy we now face the same question: how can we be certain of the existence of God and our knowledge of God? This is a question which now coincides with two others: how can we be certain of reality and ourselves?

Now the analysis of fundamental trust has shown that these questions of certainty do not first seek an answer as philosophical or even as speculative questions, but are grounded in the living of our daily life. With the discovery of this dimension of life, Küng also restores vital dimensions to faith in God. In so doing he lays the foundation for the knowledge that God can govern our certainty in life.

But what is this certainty, the only thing which can resist nothingness (thus Häring), and what does it live by? As Küng shows, the problem arose at the beginning of modernity in the emergence of a new objectifying rationality which controlled and could be controlled methodically. But this overlooks the capacity for truth and the force of an intuitive reason which is always there, which sees through what it experiences and therefore also recognizes what it does as reasonable. Küng speaks of an inner rationality. This is there; it sees through itself and is the foundation of all rationality:

'The trustful Yes in principle to uncertain reality is distinguished by an intrinsic rationality. I can experience that my fundamentally positive attitude to reality has a real foundation. For reality manifests itself through all uncertainty and permits my fundamental trust in it (not blind confidence!) to be seen as justified. In other words, in my very trust in being – which is not mere credulity – in the midst of all the real menace of the nothingness of being, I experience being and with it the fact that my trust has a real foundation. In my trust in reason, which again is not credulity, and thus in the confident use of reason, despite all the real menace of unreason, I experience the fundamental reasonableness of reason. Like other basic experiences (for example, love and hope), the basic experience of trust is apparent only in its realization, through practice. It is only in saying it that I experience that my Yes to reality (which still remains questionable) has a foundation' (DGE 449).

If I see it rightly, here Küng's position is based on two statements. One is that in the basic experience of 'trust' reason is completely with the subject-matter before it speaks about it, reflects on it, and before it attempts to safeguard its cause from outside. Therefore Küng speaks of an 'inner' rationality, one which cannot be objectified. Only in the framework of this rationality can faith, i.e. 'belief in God as ultimately justified fundamental trust' (DGE 571), come into being and know that it is well-founded. This is the kind of reason that Schleiermacher rediscovered in his hermeneutical approach. It criticizes the reflective model, as though from the beginning reason could already stand alongside or even above itself and reflect itself. Such a model inevitably leads to insoluble epistemological problems (as Frank points out). By contrast, a hermeneutical understanding of reason begins from the assumption that reason is first of all there with the subject-matter. But such an understanding cannot be demonstrated from outside. Is that not expressing – in a different way – what was formerly called the gracious knowledge of God?

The other statement is that this fundamental trust creates a certainty which enlightens men and women in the process of what they are doing. So reason cannot anticipate its subject-matter. But this standpoint ensures that knowledge already comes about in action, and not first in the reflection which follows. The weakness of this certainty lies here: it communicates itself only to those who have already committed themselves in trust. That lays it open to misuse: anyone can refer to a knowledge or insight that others do not have because they do not trust. Discussion of this inner reason and argumentation will therefore function only where it allows mutual respect and freedom.

What is to be made of this concentration on the question of certainty? Quite certainly it is theologically legitimate, philosophically fruitful and of central significance for the analysis of our time. It continues to be of central importance in the face of all new discussions which are critical of modernity. Probably it is not the only way; one need think only of the approaches of political theology and liberation theology. But it cannot be denied that Küng has taken up a central point which is also extremely critical for our situation. Furthermore, the theology of Western Europe is fully behind this approach, because it takes up its most distinctive problem and does not over-hastily deviate into the fundamental problems of other continents or cultures. Thus Küng's trusting alliance with philosophy has certainly paid off here. He takes up the problem of faith from a point at which the almost irreparable religious violations of our culture become clear, and can perhaps also be discussed and healed.

(c) Understanding texts and actions

Where he is interpreting himself, Küng insists on precise, logically stringent argumentation which cannot be corrupted by the legitimations and interests of institutions. He has not unconditionally subscribed to 'hermeneutics' in the sense of a free-floating interpretation of the text (see above, 154ff.), or even 'hermeneutics' in the sense of an overall theological enterprise. I suspect that Küng underestimates himself at this point. Certainly he cannot want to make friends with a hermeneutical idealism with a traditionally Catholic structure, nor does he want to. But I see him constantly engaged in interpreting texts: in the interpretation of scripture, philosophical texts and the sacred texts of other religions. The reason for his restraint presumably lies in his reluctance to give up clear speaking, the laws of a logic which makes strict distinctions, and the expectations of an argumentation which is clear and capable of criticism. So, over against the positivists on the one hand and the hermeneuts on the other, I see him, rather, attempting to cross the boundaries which both have drawn. Unfortunately, Küng himself hardly talks about this at all. So far reference has already been made to two aspects of this process. They are on the one hand the great importance of the interpretation of scripture (above 81–8) and on the other the justification of belief in God (see above, 178–81).

Of course any arguing and therefore any scientific theology contains an element of reflection. It is also to be hoped that conscious processes of reflection take place in any theology which claims the name. The issue here is not the quality or the academic level of a theology. It is the question how trains of thought, arguments and discourses are built up in a theology and when an argument is held to be decisive and convincing.

I use the term 'objectifying' of a model of argument which – presupposing logical clarity and clear definition – leads to content, concepts and trains of thought which are valid independently of writer and reader. Subjective additions can at best serve as an illustration, facilitating an understanding. But they are disruptive and are to be excluded if they are taken as the truth itself and confused with it. So an objectifying argument strives for universality. Or, as Dilthey explains in the context of the humane and natural sciences: explanatory sciences always seek the universal law in the individual instance. It may be surprising that with this recollection of Dilthey theology takes the side of the natural sciences. It is decisive here that Catholic theology above all has always insisted on the objectivity of its divine truth. It has heartily agreed with Barth's criticism of Schleiermacher. Hegel was accepted because he too – albeit in a speculative way – promised the return of the one and universally valid truth. Many German-speaking renewers of Catholic theology in the first half of the twentieth century saw the Catholic Church as the advocate of the objective over against Protestant subjectivism. So we should not be surprised that this has had its effect on Catholic theology and the thought of the leaders of the Catholic Church down to the present day.

I apply the term 'hermeneutical' to a model of argument which – here too presupposing logical clarity and clear definition – does not stop at finished trains of thought but seeks to initiate understanding, and thus stimulates a dialogue between text and readers. The author does not want to stay out of the process of understanding, nor should readers. Only together do they bring the truth into being. Of course extremes are being formulated here; usually there are overlaps, but a development can clearly be noted in Küng's theological thought. I shall first clarify that by the way in which he deals with scripture.

Scripture already plays a fundamental role in *Justification*. How could it be otherwise in an interpreter of Barth? Of course Küng's scriptural interpretation at that time was still in the classical tradition of both Catholic and Protestant dogmatic theology. There can be no question of objectivism or even biblicism; statements of scripture are too constantly interpreted or reinterpreted in a Catholic or Protestant way. But a marked trend towards the objective becomes evident. With Barth, Küng argues in a markedly christocentric way, with a massive christology from above. That is what appears in scripture, whose statements Küng, very much in line with the later orthodox tradition, interprets with realistic immediacy. He refers to statements 'which too often are not taken literally enough' (thus Küng forty years ago). He refers to the 'faultless and spotless lamb Christ' who was 'chosen already before the foundation of the world' (I Peter 1.19f.) or 'the lamb which was slain before the beginning of the world' (Rev.13.8). Paul's way of talking about incarnation and pre-existence, too, 'is not to be construed as a primitive and undifferentiated type of speech' (J 281; Kuschel 1990).

As became clear, the argument in *The Church* was essentially more open. One might say that it was far more about questions of structure than about questions of faith. Now the statements about the church as the people of God, the body of Christ and the temple of the Spirit often have an immediate, direct impact. But their aim becomes clear: in no way is there a concern for the repristination of New Testament times: Küng does not look back lovingly to the charismatic circumstances in

Corinth. Now he is concerned for a return to the *spirit* of that church and therefore for keeping many possible forms open. In hermeneutical terms, the readers, or at any rate the decision-makers who read, should find solutions appropriate for today on the basis of this interpretation of scripture.

I have already described how the theoretically decisive breakthrough takes place in *Infallible?* (and in earlier preparatory texts). Thus it is also clear that Küng's shift towards a hermeneutical argument – unlike the approach of many imaginative hermeneuts in the theological guild – comes about above all in a practical, reforming, one can even say critical interest. In *Infallible?* Küng must in fact develop an argument for a critical purpose. Therefore he talks of what a statement cannot do: it never reaches reality itself and means different things depending on the context. It is a misfortune for German-speaking Catholic theology that Küng's opponents did not take this point and understood his advance as a betrayal of the truth – not because of a lack of hermeneutical understanding but for fear of dangerous consequences. Here a mediating or even open word should have been spoken gently on Küng's behalf; in that way damage to the Catholic Church would have been averted.

The issue here involves two hermeneutical principles which had hitherto been suppressed in dogmatic discussions. The first is: no understanding without experience, and no experience without understanding. We do not understand anything which does not in some way take up our questions, disappointments, surprises or hopes. That is precisely the danger that Küng sees in the 1970s. He thinks of those whose dogmatic formulae no longer mean anything because they cannot link up with people's experiences any longer. But we also experience little if we have not learned to understand. Schillebeeckx has pointed this out clearly (Schillebeeckx 1980, 30–64). That is the specific motive which makes Küng now work so hard in his coming books. He hopes once again to bring Christian faith nearer to people.

The second, equally important, principle is: any understanding leads to reinterpretation. Certainly we always want to understand earlier things (written or said) afresh; conservative hermeneutics (I am speaking of idealistic hermeneutics, see above, 125, 150) draws its strength from that. But those who allow only retrospective repetition are guilty of a reactionary misuse of hermeneutics. They overlook the other side, which has become vitally necessary in a time of cultural upheaval: as soon as people understand the Christian message afresh, they look forward, interpret it and abandon old ideas in order to introduce new ones.

As long as Christian faith lives, the act of interpretation does not cease. It is the miracle of the Spirit that the truth can always be restated. So statements are not only limits, but bear endless surpluses of meaning within themselves. Instead of simply noting the mistakes, errors and limitations of heretics – as is preferred by the infallibility model and the way in which it is implemented in Rome – Küng therefore now looks at the positive side. He reinterprets. He shows that the 'old' – even in old Europe! – can be restated in this way. So he makes it possible for the cause of Jesus to be understood anew as the cause of God. The narrative quality of the Gospels has led him to this. In *On Being a Christian* and the last part of *Does God Exist?* this process of interpretation, this interplay between what was said then and what is said now, this constantly new fluctuation between human experiences and accounts, conclusions, testimonies which take it further, becomes the exciting basic process of a Christian theology.

From *On Being a Christian* onwards Küng constantly builds bridges of understanding: from the texts to their motives, from the cause to people, from hearing to appropriation, from challenge to decision, from offer to realization. Küng has repeatedly emphasized that it is also possible to adopt other approaches. But what I have described here as hermeneutical argumentation is indispensable. As a rule the great importance attached to scriptural interpretation is interpreted as an influence of Protestant theology. That may be correct. But in long years of intensive dealing with scripture, the nature of Küng's scriptural interpretation shifts. Now it is no longer (merely) a description of the content of scripture. Rather, it becomes an exegesis which corresponds to the ideas, questions and longing for truth of present-day men and women.

Even more interesting are the lines of subject-matter which have developed on Küng's hermeneutical way. In biblical interpretation it was presumably the account of Jesus which led to the hermeneutical shift and thus to the inner concentration. In the question of belief in God the issue was how significant trust is in this development. Even more clearly, this element, which cannot be reduced to the dimension of objectifying arguments, was in play here from the beginning. The most important subsidiary questions in *Does God Exist?* were: what is 'God' really and how can belief in God be justified when God cannot be seen and cannot be understood, and the world has so many contradictions? Here too the principle that we have discussed applies: no understanding without interpretation. Thus Küng does not develop a complicated picture of God of the kind that can be read in dogmatic handbooks and catechisms, or in famous theologians down to Karl Barth. He limits himself to a few basic lines which are drawn towards human beings. In principle every woman and every man must know how to experience, understand and interpret for themselves, individually and collectively, the meaning of an ultimate ground, an ultimate goal, an ultimate support, unconditional reliability and goodness, concern for the lost, the meaning of God and the world. Nowhere is the basic feature of Küng's hermeneutics clearer than here.

Here too the other principle applies: no experience without understanding and no understanding without experience. So not only does Küng create for himself a critical framework of understanding which is resistant to ideology, which can be talked about in general and topical terms, but he also relates experience to this. How is that to happen? He cannot neatly separate understanding, experience and interpretation and put them in order as in an objectivistic model of truth. They can only be had together, because they are related to one another in a circle and govern one another. Reality and God's existence can no longer be demonstrated independently of our attitude, nor can trust and faith as legitimate modes of understanding or presuppositions of insight into reality and the existence of God. So with his call for trust Küng does not want to avoid the necessity of matter-of-fact argumentation, but in any argument he must take account of the practical dimension of his concern for truth. He must succeed in giving a description which readers can follow – at least as an acceptable interpretation. At the same time (and there is no alternative!) his personal conviction must come into play in the offer of an interpretation. So how can Küng argue responsibly without giving in to the pressures of rational argument? How can he speak of the element of freedom in this decision without including a moral condemnation of those who have made, or are making, a different decision? The full significance of three characteristics of his approach appears only against this background. They are: concentration on the phenomenon of trust, emphasis on the asymmetry of trust and mistrust, and the grounding of all analyses in a practical report.

4. As faith lives

(a) Concentration on the phenomenon of trust

In the Protestant and in the Catholic theological tradition the question of faith has been handled in characteristically different ways. As a rule

Protestant authors insisted on the element of freedom and one's own decision, and the paradoxes and inexplicable elements associated with it which bear witness to God's action. Thus human beings came to stand directly over against God. 'God's Word' became a hypostasis with an authoritarian effect. Anyone who did not believe, failed God; here dealing with the world played a secondary role. By contrast Catholic authors, in a way comparable to Catholic catechisms, put the emphasis on the content of faith and the possibility of realizing faith, its (almost compelling) reason. Anyone who did not believe rejected reason, which could be read off the world. In both traditions there was something immoral about unbelief, seen from the outside. It was no longer integrated into the innermost life of human beings.

Now Küng, as we saw, understands faith in principle as trust. That is an attitude which arises from the interplay of understanding and chosen behaviour, from the dialectic of choice and necessary correction, from the drama of human experience. Here the role of reality, good or evil, inviting or deterrent, remains open, and there is the involvement of the will, positively or negatively, in weary resignation or with a new energy, hidden yet always present. Trust cannot be reduced to good will. Nor can trust be explained from its preconditions. A happy childhood and youth, good experiences and successes, friendly people and love, do not in themselves guarantee a trusting attitude. There is the classical case in which nature, biography and faith coincide: the mistrustful villain, humiliated from childhood, standing beside the Sunday's child with a happy youth. But we also know the extremes: deeply humane people who develop from the worst misery, despite all prognoses and regardless of their psychological make-up, and egocentrics to whom any commitment to others and any faith in God remains alien all their life, although they have had a protected childhood and later good fortune. In the middle are all kinds of others whose lives can be fitted somewhere on the scale between fundamental mistrust and fundamental trust, unbelief and belief. In that case, the way to a clear attitude is probably the result of personal maturity.

The analyses of Erik Erikson (DGE 453–7) have become important for the anthropological analysis in Küng's theology, but he is interested in a psychological phenomenon only to a limited degree. He writes about an attitude which shows itself in all spheres of life, relationships, knowledge and culture. Therefore for human beings fundamental trust often becomes a lifelong gift, in any case a 'lifelong task' (DGE 457) and a lifelong necessity. For Küng, 'without trust a decent human life is impossible', as he says following F. Bollnow and others (DGE 458).

Indeed I must develop trust in myself if I do not want to fail. However, that does not mean that one day trust is achieved and remains an inalienable possession. Mistrust forms a lifelong counterpoint: there is enough occasion for it and temptation to it (DGE 468).

No life, no progress and no testing is conceivable without this vital tension. Mistrust and trust, unbelief and belief are not separate, internalized decisions, reflections directed upwards, but an everyday concern, grounded and earthed in the everyday and in expectation, in behaviour and fate. They do not just determine the small decisions, but also the social contexts, science and ethics, planning and communication, and the capacity to perceive the offers of transcendence and the world of the religious. There is a need for faith in reality and in life, in one's meaning and feelings, and according to Popper also for faith in reason. The Cartesian concept of a reason which grounds itself in reflection has failed (DGE 448).

Küng's analyses represent a fundamental change of paradigm and starting point for what we in our religious tradition call faith. They represent the return of the modern concept of faith, which is partly rationalized and which partly has drifted into the irrational, into the vital centre of human, cultural and social existence. Küng does not develop any psychological moral or religious concept of trust and mistrust, but a quite practical one (Tracy NHFT 88f.). If I am right, this concentration on the phenomenon of trust is one of the most important new approaches in theology in recent decades.

(b) Distinction and asymmetry

It is a bold enterprise to make a clear distinction between trust and mistrust. Certainly it is conceptually possible; they have a contradictory relationship like Yes and No. But in concrete, so to speak 'normal', life they are constantly mixed. Küng's concern is to set the two opposing attitudes over against each other. He achieves this by means of a twofold strategy: he radicalizes the attitudes so that they become what he calls fundamental mistrust and fundamental trust, and first of all he leaves aside the question of belief and unbelief. He is given this possibility not only by Nietzsche, whose level and radicalism he maintains, but also by the experience of many people, whether they live by existentialist, humanist, spiritual or mystical roots. In them fundamental trust and fundamental mistrust have become comprehensive alternatives in life. In essence they manifest something that is presumably latent in many men and women. Küng quotes Dag Hammarskjöld:

'I don't know Who – or what – put the question, I don't know when it was put. I don't even remember answering. But at some moment I did answer Yes to Someone – or Something – and from that hour I was certain that existence is meaningful and that therefore my life, in self-surrender, had a goal.

From that moment I have known what it means "not to look back", and "to take no thought for the morrow" . . .

After that, the word "courage" lost its meaning, since nothing could be taken from me' (DGE 442).

So there is the difference, and theologians may also think that it is there in its 'secularized' form. Here secularizing of language is part of Küng's method. It enables him to make distinctions without moralistic connotations or overtones. Here opposition and comparability seem to work perfectly. Trust stands over against mistrust, acceptance over against refusal, No over against Yes, as though these were two comparable actions or attitudes. Now in a formal analysis of action, which is about acts of decision, about the moral consideration of fulfilment and refusal, of obedience and stubbornness, that may be the case.

It is part of Küng's method to take the distinction seriously as a process, as an element of relationship, of making contact, of involvement. This indicates the opposition. But the asymmetry also appears. The two attitudes are opposed and irreconcilable (DGE 442–52). Over against the No to reality stands a Yes, over against the 'nihilistic fixation on the nothingness of reality' a fundamental Yes to 'questionable reality', the resultant 'abysmal uncertainty' of an 'antinihilistic fundamental certainty'. So there can and must be a point at which the ways of attitude and decision fundamentally part. Being human has to do with this parting of the ways. Here Küng has already repeatedly pointed out that reality itself can give occasion for both ways, and this has become clear in all the analyses from Pascal to Nietzsche. It is questionable, steeped in contradictions and the inexplicable. Experiences and careers can be cruel, not to mention the whole of history, which no less a thinker than Hegel failed to justify.

Küng puts up for debate the possibility of a stalemate (DGE 446), and perhaps would not get beyond a moral appeal were there not two significant objections. As we saw, they are connected with his practical concept of trust and mistrust.

From the perspective of the subject, from social and cultural action, Küng shows that trust and mistrust are always connected with a projection into the future, with the giving or refusal of backing – this is something that cannot be demonstrated or objectified. There is no advantage in rejecting this anticipation of the future in a positivistic way as nonsensical or irrational, since as a possibility it is a necessary part of human life. As Ernst Bloch has taught us, human life includes a reason directed towards the future, which in this sense is transcendent (DGE 483–91). So it is not a matter of subjecting this praxis to the dictate of an objectifying reason; rather, the nature of such an existential reason has to be understood more closely. It is always preceded by an attitude of trust; it always goes deeper than a mistrust which possibly follows it:

'• Human beings are restless, unfinished, not completely fulfilled. They are not who they could be.
  Human beings are defective.
• Human beings are therefore constantly on their way, longing for more, seeking to know more, reaching out for what is different, for what is new.
  Human beings constantly surpass themselves.
  Human beings are expectant, hoping, yearning' (DGE 488).

From the perspective of the reality which human beings encounter in their lives, Küng points out that reality is not an abstract entity, the complexity of which we perhaps do not grasp for lack of intelligence. So 'fundamental trust' and 'fundamental mistrust' do not mean working out a theory, positive or negative. Reality extends in history and time, and in principle is orientated on the future. I do not know what tomorrow will bring or the precise reason for what happened to me today; nevertheless I am moving towards the future. This problem therefore also includes the shaping of social and political conditions and the question when and how everything will end, perhaps become qualitatively different (DGE 489).

However, for Küng far more fundamental questions precede these aspects. To what do we human beings really tend, with what attitude can the argument pertinently begin, and how do we sustain it (DGE 442–6)? Reasonableness and an appropriate rationality are thus to be judged in the light of this fundamental structure. Now if we compare fundamental trust and fundamental mistrust in the light of these questions, for Küng the result is clear. The answer to the first question is that human beings intrinsically tend towards the Yes. They may see, strive, have success, be happy. There is a vital positive dynamic in which we free beings are grounded.

The answer to the second question is more decisive. Fundamental trust opens us towards reality, and fundamental mistrust shuts us off from it. It is here that the special feature of Küng's argument emerges: trust and mistrust are to be strictly distinguished, but they are not strictly comparable. Trust means openness, controversy, and also vulnerability and the possibility of ever new disappointment. A fundamental mistrust of reality as a whole is not involved in this process. It breaks it off. In principle, surprises and disappointment are impossible. Here two people are not thinking, attempting, fighting with different results, but the decision is made for fighting or resignation, weariness or unquenchable curiosity.

> 'Is the fundamental decision a choice between two possibilities? No. The choice here is not like that between red and green, or even between white and black, but as it were between light and non-light, brightness and complete darkness. Nor is it the famous choice of Hercules at the crossroads. For here a choice has to be made not between vice and virtue, inclination and duty, but between being and not-being. Not-being, however, is neither a reality nor a (real) possibility, but unreality and an impossibility (though it is certainly conceivable) . . . Hence the fundamental decision is not a choice between two equal possibilities, but – seen more closely – one between reality and a possible impossibility. So it is anything but a stalemate' (DGE 447).

That also explains the answer to the third question: whereas the Yes can be consistently maintained, the No cannot. I cannot live without constantly entering into controversy with this reality: 'Those who nihilistically choose nothingness must in practice be continually borrowing from being. Those who want to live as nihilists cannot live on nothing, either physically or mentally. Even the most mistrustful person must be trusting from time to time' (DGE 444). In short, a fundamental trust lives on a constant loan, a constant fundamental contradiction. There is no need to explain here how in itself that does not legitimate faith. But it goes without saying that the question of reason and rationality poses itself afresh in this context, that rationality is to be redefined in respect of trust and faith. We shall be returning to that.

(c) A practical report

Perhaps by now readers are feeling oppressed. Certainly Küng is not constructing an ideological position here, but taking over from

Nietzsche a dramatic scheme which he has outlined with great emphasis. But is it correct to tie down any adherent of nihilism to these consequences? Furthermore, may we take this massive, radical and in fact uncompromising and boundless nihilism seriously as a reality for today? Nowadays isn't our attitude much more unprincipled, pragmatic and fragmentary, 'postmodern'?

Küng takes nihilism seriously as a theoretical but also ideologically effective construct. It helps him to show the serious and now really radical background which even today underlies such radical consequences. Though some mistrustful attitudes can arise from discontent with an uncontemporary and egocentric church, and the repetition of unhistorical formulae of faith, unbelief can be the consequence of protest against a reality which we are increasingly unable to see through, understand and accept. Theories do not cover a whole life, because life precedes any theory. Therefore Küng resists any limitation to theological theories. He grounds theories in biographies. It is these and not the theories that have to be understood.

The abstract summary of a problem must not become a substitute for complex reality with its many levels. That is why it seems to me so important that Küng has not depicted the whole modern history of rationality and trust as a series of abstract notions, but as an argument between living persons. Biographies are always complex. They help us to understand ideas but they relativize them, have inexplicable features and unresolved issues. Ideas suddenly reflect weaknesses or strengths, unsuccessful relationships or social success.

The history of faith is also ultimately a history of concrete action, life with all its incalculable consequences. Suppose we take Pascal, whom Küng depicts as a brilliant mathematician, physicist and engineer, a man of the world who moved in the best Parisian circles, finally as a brilliant man of letters and the first journalist in France, a person of method and solemnity. His critique of the (exclusive validity) of analytic reason becomes vivid and perhaps also understandable if at the same time we see his personal coolness towards Descartes. Specifically because of Descartes, Pascal, the expert on the human soul, came to see clearly that there is also intuitive knowledge and reason alongside this analytical reason. It became clear to Pascal that mathematicians also become people with a fine sensibility, and that the *esprit de géométrie* and the *esprit de finesse* must supplement each other. He recognized that all human history had a twofold foundation: human beings are both great and wretched. Finally he vacillated between dogmatism and scepticism, and existentially almost felt torn apart, until in an overwhelming inner experience he found the way to a faith which brought him as much conflict as comfort. In a quite modern way he discovered one of the fundamental principles of a society which was now becoming far more complex. Choices had to be made. Soon, having taken this discovery to heart, he became involved in the great dispute over Jansenism, which as a controversy with Port Royal at the same time became a highly political dispute. In it he finally became part of an authority which was quite merciless to the losers, so that he appealed against Rome to the judgment seat of Jesus (Congar, *Gegenentwürfe*). This man, who six months before his death organized the first omnibus company in Paris, was finally broken by the dispute with the church. At the same time, in this last phase he imposed the most severe penitential practices upon himself, sold everything and sought self-abasement. He not only renounced marriage, but wanted to forbid it to others; he called it the most dangerous and the lowliest of all forms of Christian life. So in the end this genius presents a fascinating but also a divided picture. He wanted to follow Jesus completely – but did not understand the decisive thing. Belief in God has never been solved by questions, like a mathematical task.

Only those who know Pascal's history will understand his words rightly. He was the first to champion the reasons of the heart and to reject Descartes' geometrical spirit. Against such a background any theory will have two bases. Biographies teach us to understand in a more concrete way, but they also create a remarkable freedom, since only the test of practice makes them binding. Any theory is more complex than its presenters, more susceptible than its critics, stronger than its defenders. The same is even true of the story of Jesus, who does not exhaust the freedom of his own life if it is understood as the 'criterion' of being a Christian, in other words a call to discipleship. Narrative theology first helps us to understand rightly the importance and liberating power of this theological argument.

5. God: the meaning of life and death

As we saw, Küng does not understand the statement 'God exists' as a descriptive statement about the existence of a super-being who competes with others and suppresses them. For him, 'God exists' is the summary of belief in God. For him as a Christian the statement is ultimately a confession of his faith in the God of Jesus Christ, the God of the godless, which nevertheless leaves rooms for other forms of confession of God. So he can end his book, full of reflections, questions and criticisms, objections and differentiations, with the recollection of a prayer:

> 'Does God exist? Despite all upheavals and doubts, even for men and women today, the only appropriate answer must be that with which believers of all generations from ancient times have again and again professed their faith. It begins with faith – *Te Deum, laudamus,* "You, God, we praise" – and ends in trust: *In te, Domine, speravi, non confundar in aeternum*! "In you, Lord, I have hoped, I shall never be put to shame"' (DGE 702).

In this book, together with *On Being a Christian*, Küng has done a great deal. He has made a first diagnosis of the religious situation of our culture and offers a synthesis for its twofold split. This is the split on the one hand between reality and God, and on the other between reason and faith. Thus in a way achieved by few theologians he has entered into the current 'world language' of our cultural sphere:

> 'The positions on the question of fundamental certainty, as we have come to understand them from the beginning of modern times onwards – fundamental certainty being based either on the *cogito* or the *credo* – appear to have been eliminated in our answer about fundamental trust. But the same positions have been taken up again and maintained even more strongly in regard to the question of the certainty of God and must be studied in greater depth here. Does certainty of God arise from reason or from faith?' (DGE 507).

Together with *On Being a Christian, Does God Exist?* offers an overall scheme for questions of Christian faith. In it, central questions, answers and perspectives are discussed, interpreted and presented for further interpretation in such a way that they can stand up to the current dialogue inside and outside the church. This overall scheme is clearly governed by the inspiration and normativity of scripture; it gains its profile in a controversy with history, fights for renewal and a contemporary form of church and faith, and takes up the most profound human questions of present-day men and women. Thus Küng functions as a mediator for a dialogue between the message of faith and a society which is remote from the church.

Küng has incorporated his earlier works, especially the programmatic works and those which are critical of the church, into his overall scheme and thus protected them from misinterpretations and misunderstanding. With *On Being a Christian* and *Does God Exist?* he definitively avoids the great danger of wearing himself out in a dispute with the church leaders and the theologians who criticize him. Both books show how Küng's criticism of the church is rooted in an understanding of God, church and Christian faith which is worked out thoroughly and expressed in a differentiated way.

How did the way continue? As I have already said, anyone who takes seriously the tremendous number of levels of reality and faith which Küng often emphasizes will not expect a compelling plan, given the range of the questions which are still open. In 1982, four years after *Does God Exist?*, a book appeared which was very important to Küng. He regards it as the conclusion of the project which began with *On Being a Christian,* and along with *Does God Exist?* it can be taken to form a trilogy. It has the title *Eternal Life?,* and considers the questions of dying and death. It asks what hope, according to Christians, comes 'after' death: resurrection and eternal life. These will not be discussed separately here. Here too Küng takes up the secular questions in all their hardness and once again in decisive matters joins Karl Barth's school (EL 138f.): we will all live on in God's thought as what we were. A brief quotation may show how much the book lives by that power of hope and that fundamental trust which is analysed and developed in *Does God Exist?* Here too Küng takes seriously human questions and cares, the state of scholarship and the critique of religion. Finally ('summing up'), his answer is:

'What does it mean to believe in a consummation in eternal life by God as he showed himself in Jesus Christ?

To believe in an eternal life means – in reasonable trust, in enlightened faith, in tried and tested hope – to rely on the fact that I shall one day be fully understood, freed from guilt and definitively accepted and can be myself without fear; that my impenetrable and ambivalent existence, like the profoundly discordant history of humanity as a whole, will one day become finally transparent, and that the question of the meaning of history will one day be finally answered . . .

If I believe in an eternal life, then, in all modesty and all realism and without yielding to the terror of violent benefactors of the people, I can work for a better future, a better society, even a better church, in peace, freedom and justice – while knowing that all this can only be striven for and never be fully realized by human beings' (EL 231f.).

Other topics had already been largely prepared within the framework of Küng's teaching activity: a publication on the doctrine of grace and one on the sacraments. But as I shall now show, his situation was to change drastically in 1980. Only now would it emerge that there were two further quite different concerns in Küng's thought: the world religions and the responsibility of the religions for the world. First, at any rate from perspectives within the church, the 'classical' period of his creative work, focussed on the church, was complete. The official church response to this will be discussed in the next chapter.

7

A Case for Rome? The Difficulties of a Theology Focussed on Reform

'We reform-minded Catholic theologians find that nowadays, in contrast to the time of the Council, the wind from the official church often blows sharply. But is that a reason to slacken in commitment to church reform? Is that a reason to give up work for the church? No, this is just the hour to keep hope alive, the hope that reform of the church in head and members can and must go on . . . There is reason to keep hope alive' (RCT 1).

Küng did not always speak with such hope and joy in the previous years, above all in the days and weeks which followed 18 December 1979, certainly one of the most decisive days of his life. 'I am ashamed for my church,' he said that evening before the cameras, 'that secret Inquisition processes are still being carried out in the twentieth century. For many people it is a scandal that in a church which appeals to Jesus Christ and which recently has wanted to defend human rights, its own theologians are defamed and discredited with such methods.' What had happened? Three days previously the pope, who had by then been just a year in office, had confirmed the decision of the Congregation of the Doctrine of Faith to withdraw Hans Küng's official permission to teach.

The action had been well prepared and was discussed thoroughly in Brussels the day before. Rome had a lengthy statement ready. Cardinal Höffner, Chairman of the German Conference of Bishops, had prepared a declaration and taken responsibility for publicity in Germany. Küng's local bishop in Rottenburg, Georg Moser, was brought into the picture, and he informed the priests of his diocese the same day. In view of the unexpected public reaction Moser complained once again to Rome on 22 December, and on 24 December attempted to secure further concessions from Hans Küng in writing. Discussions and arguments went on over Christmas. Then on 7 January 1980 all the German bishops met in Würzburg to defend Rome's decision once again, in a joint declaration signed by each of them. So Rome remained unyielding and the German episcopate concurred.

Over the coming weeks discussions and negotiations shifted to Küng's future situation in Tübingen. The Institute for Ecumenical Research was detached from the faculty and put directly under the president of the university. Now the faculty left Küng only with the right to a place on committees for doctorates and habilitations where he was supervising candidates. But he could continue to call himself professor of theology. That was very important for him. In April 1980 the new situation could be said to have been clarified – for the moment.

This book is not a biography of Küng, but a reconstruction and interpretation of his theology. Therefore we shall not be pursuing further the details of Küng's personal situation. Nevertheless, in the interest of this theology the actions described above cannot simply be overlooked, since they have still not been resolved satisfactorily even today; they still influence many people in their judgment of Küng's theology and they still reflect the current state of the church, which has been Küng's theological concern from the beginning. The Roman Congregation of Faith, the representatives of the German Conference of Bishops and a small group of Catholic theologians personalized the dispute over the form of the church with reference to him. So he became involuntarily a symbol of dispute. It was not a matter of whose approach or conclusions were right, though Küng never yielded on the decisive points and naturally fought for 'his' cause; the issue was the theological programme of a reform of head and members which accords with both scripture and the present.

We have to discuss this issue. So I shall briefly clarify some facts and perspectives. I begin with some observations on the legal situation, even if it is only of relative importance in judging the substance of the matter.

1. The legal situation

The Roman decision of December 1979 has a long and complex prehistory. In 1957 the 'Holy Office' was active for the first time against Küng, in connection with *Justification*, but nothing came of the matter; since then his file has borne the number 399/57/i. This was to be the beginning of a controversy which has still not been resolved.

The opening of the file meant that from that point on everything that could be discovered about Küng, especially all the communications, complaints and denunciations about him, were registered and collected. The letter 'i' stands for the index section, which had long had to decide about prohibitions relating to reading, printing and circulating written material. The appearance of *The Church* sparked off new proceedings. According to a decision of Rome communicated in the week of Christmas 1967 Küng might not disseminate the book further or have it translated. In May 1968 Küng received a direct invitation to a 'colloquium' in Rome. An extensive correspondence followed: negotiations over fair procedures (inspection of the minutes, specification of the charges, confidentiality), later about dates, appropriate support and defence, a correct and transparent distinction between the activities of the German and the Roman authorities. The appearance of *Infallible?* prompted yet more proceedings – this time predictable; these proceedings in fact came to be combined with the earlier ones. Rome publicized the matter from the start and co-ordinated it with other Roman and German legal, publicity and quasi-academic activities (a hearing, press statements, the organization of a composite volume against *Infallible?*).

In 1971 the Roman Inquisition authorities (now the Congregation of the Doctrine of Faith) received an order for proceedings, but this had no influence on subsequent proceedings, nor did it work. The proceedings came to an unexpected climax in July 1973 (Küng had not yet been invited to a single hearing). The investigating authority composed and published a general 'Declaration on Catholic Teaching about the Church, which is to be defended against some present-day errors', entitled *Mysterium Ecclesiae* (indisputably a *Lex Küng*), and told Küng that he could now carry on a dialogue with representatives of the Roman authorities or 'immediately accept [sic!] the teaching contained in the declaration, in which case the current proceedings over your two books would be ended'. Rome was convinced that the situation had now changed. No longer were the disputed points up for debate, but Küng had to prove that he was not offending against *Mysterium Ecclesiae*. Küng's protest against this illegitimate procedure and the extremely critical reaction of other individuals and groups (including the Tübingen Catholic Theological Faculty) continued to be fruitless. In 1974 the proceedings were resumed; they ended in February 1975 with an admonition to Küng, who had not indicated his acceptance of *Mysterium Ecclesiae*, not to put forward again the doctrinal views to which objection had been made. Rome was convinced that its reaction had been mild. Cardinal Döpfner called the proceedings 'fair' and spoke of a 'new style'. The presupposition here, that the views expressed by Küng were 'incompatible with church teaching', really needed clarification. The state attorneys set themselves up as judges. So Küng's readiness not to go on insisting on correct legal proceedings worked to his disadvantage.

No formal proceedings were opened against *On Being a Christian*, but from the moment it appeared official dissuasives were issued against the book. Thus in February 1977 the German Conference of Bishops already mentioned *On Being a Christian* in the same breath as the earlier books to which objection had been made; in January 1977 a colloquium was held with representatives of the faith commission of the German Conference of Bishops which avowedly was not part of any proceedings (see above, 151ff.). In March and September 1977 the German Conference of Bishops again made a public statement against *On Being a Christian*, in September even in an extended, dense and closely worked out text. Its personal and somewhat sweeping view was that justice was not done to the divinity of Jesus and the reality of redemption. After that the situation seemed to quieten down. Within the framework of Küng's intensive and varied writing activities, in March 1978 *Does God Exist?* was published, a year later a preface to A. B. Hasler's book *How the Pope Became Infallible,* and at the same time a theological meditation, *The Church Maintained in Truth?.* Rome took this – without any further procedural steps in accordance with its own procedural order – as the occasion to resolve to withdraw Küng's licence to teach. Procedural lawyers may form their own verdict on such proceedings.

It is laborious to pursue in detail the course of events outlined in brief here. The complex legal situation is difficult to assess, even for experts. Here some central problems connected with the current structure and form of the Catholic Church play a role. I shall mention seven points:

- The transition from the 'informal' phase, with no order of proceedings, to a phase in which the Roman authorities adopted a procedure which was observed only approximately, if at all (1971): in the transition there was no clarification of the situation, the rules to be observed, the open questions or the aim of the proceedings. The Congregation of Faith dictated the whole proceedings unconditionally.
- The fact that two authorities and levels, each with its own functions (the Roman Congregation of Faith and the Faith Commission of the German Conference of Bishops), co-operated, each with its own procedures, in a way which was inscrutable to outsiders: the lower authority presumably always acted by agreement with the

higher; the higher authority did not function as a court of appeal but as an initiating authority.

- The fact that the texts to which objection was made were already being branded officially and publicly as unacceptable while the outcome of the proceedings was still open: here there can no longer be any question of an unprejudiced examination.

- In connection with this, the claim of the Roman Congregation of Faith not only to examine publications to see whether they corresponded to the 'faith of the church', but also to interpret this faith itself in a legally effective way (each time confirmed by the pope); to be specific, during the proceedings the Congregation of Faith composed a text by which it then measured what had been published previously. Here we have the impact of a church structure into which (despite the first beginnings of an administrative jurisdiction) the current division of 'authorities' – or analogous structures for more effective mutual control – has found no entry in either letter or spirit.

- The utilization of public opinion (the condemnation of Küng) inside and outside the church: the attempt to launch manifestly misleading and prejudiced information about the opposing party, during proceedings which had not come to a conclusion and with the aim of influencing them.

- The fact that current distinctions within theology were not taken account of at any stage: I need mention only the distinction between dogmas and universally binding doctrinal statements (which Küng never denied) on the one hand and their time-conditioned interpretation (on the right to which Küng insisted) on the other, and also the distinction between Christian doctrine and theological research, between official doctrinal statements and discussion within the church.

- The fundamental question whether and how matters of faith and the interpretation of faith can be subject to judicial proceedings at all in a highly institutionalized monolithic church structure. Connected with this is the question whether the synodical structures of the early church, or of the Reformation and later churches, are not adopting or have not adopted more effective and credible procedures.

Thus from a legal and theological perspective, the course and development of the conflict produced more questions than answers. But two statements are significant. First the charge of the Congregation of Faith that Küng had broken rules was untenable. The presupposition here is that one does not confuse the rules with the demands of church authorities. That applies, for example, to collaboration in proceedings without formal agreements; the demand to see the record and to be given legal support in a dialogue; and to the failure to observe a vague request to stop disseminating a book. Nor could objections really be made to a press release which reacted to the world-wide publicity by the Congregation of Faith or the German bishops.

It also applies to the last phase of the controversy, which began with the 'conclusion' of the proceedings in February 1977. The repeated charge of undue delays (the laying down of conditions, reference to pressures of time, the call for deeper study, the invitation to study conferences and symposia, answers at the last possible moment) was inappropriate, since all the demands put forward by Küng were the minimum requirement for fair treatment according to the rules of the law then current in Western Europe; they were supported by 1,360 theologians. So Rome's procedure at the end of 1979 cannot be justified by agreements which were not kept.

Küng's letter to the Congregation of Faith dated 4 September 1974 (FK 124–32) gives an impressive account of his position, including a conciliatory statement which at the same time leaves no room for misunderstanding:

'And of course I also by no means exclude the possibility that in the course of time I shall come to know the revealed truth better and more clearly. On the contrary, that is my daily concern, and I am always ready to make any correction which is reasonably required of me. And to that degree I also gladly claim the "time for reflection" to "examine my doctrinal views" which the Congregation has graciously granted me. This is the responsibility and task of any serious scholar and especially of any serious theologian. So I certainly do not want to exclude the possibility that in the course of time my doctrinal views "could conform" to those of the magisterium, since the Congregation will certainly also hold itself open for new developments and insights. In particular a fundamental reflection on the self-understanding and methods of the Congregation might suggest itself, as was indicated at the beginning with reference to important voices' (FK 131f.).

Quite clearly Küng is not allowing himself to be forced into the role of someone who has been condemned in advance, who may not describe his position appropriately or bring it to bear. Once again, here the argument is strictly legalistic. Anyone can follow it who puts himself or herself in the perspective of the person concerned and considers the possibility that perhaps the accused should be acquitted. Then such a person will want a good and open answer to this question.

Secondly, before 1971 the Roman authorities did not see themselves tied to any rules, and afterwards they did not keep either to the letter or the spirit of a rule book which many people will regard as defective. There are impressive examples of this, as is shown by Küng's letter mentioned above. He writes:

'I could have mentioned many important individual questions relating to the legal basis of the proceedings, for example, about the two-phase theory which hitherto has been unknown to me, and especially the secret phase "within the Congregation";

about the character of the proceedings, which while not criminal can have criminal consequences;

about the *"relator pro auctore"* [legal support] who assists the Congregation "in a dialectical way" and whose identity the author himself may not know;

about the "documentary investigation" produced by the Congregation ("letters and opinions of individual specialists, consultors or members of the Congregation"), which the person is not allowed to see, for reasons which are not clear to me;

about inspection of the minutes generally, which has again been denied to me, and the incomprehensible background to this;

about my exclusion from the first phase of the proceedings which decides on the "accusation" and similarly from the final phase which is decisive for the judgment or condemnation;

about the "possible further steps" which are not discussed in the procedural order but mentioned in your letter;

about the possibility of an appeal on the basis of the Apostolic Constitution *Regimini Ecclesiae,* which is still unclear to me;

about the colloquium which is carried on "at a scholarly level" yet is not to be "free academic discussion", and which clearly does not envisage that the Congregation might even once be theologically in the wrong;

about the prejudicing of the whole proceedings by the declaration *Mysterium Ecclesiae,* which in various respects goes beyond Vatican I and II.

But all these questions merely show how justified is the demand for a general revision of the procedure of the Congregation . . .' (FK 127f.).

Even in March 1974 (FK 99–108) the Congregation does not seem to have had any understanding of the significance of an order of proceedings. Its interpretation seems pedantic. The request for such an order is still interpreted as delaying tactics; there is an insistence on observing the law about the *imprimatur*, and the request for legal support is answered with a remark which sounds cynical. 'The author has the right to defend himself; he is invited to explain himself in writing' (FK 103); rather, believers should have a right to the protection of their faith.

How is that to be explained? Rome's starting point is evidently never that a suspicion has still to be substantiated, or a difficult conflict situation has to be resolved. The starting point is always that the charge of an error over questions of faith is correct, to be substantiated in the proceedings, and followed up if the person concerned does not retract anything. Therefore the requests, say, to see the record, to be given legal support and firm dates, are never taken seriously. My own view is that anyone who does not dismiss the requests mentioned as the monstrous product of a bourgeois individualism but thinks that a fair and proper hearing is indispensable may perhaps find the Roman proceedings very understandable for historical reasons, but will not think them convincing.

Küng's letter of 4 September 1974, mentioned above, shows how the starting points and expectations converged to the end. As a further interpretation of his action we might add that Küng did not put these requests *ad hoc* and to save his own skin, but, as we saw, developed them in extensive theological publications as an outcome of his understanding of the Christian message and a renewed Christian church. So Küng's criticism of the proceedings has a theological quality; for him this criticism is virtually the test of whether the church is being renewed in the spirit of Jesus and therefore a theological obligation. Anyone to whom that has become clear will no longer be very interested in the psychological components and the references so often made to Küng's personality, to his concern to be in the right, his persistence and his publicity work. The reduction of the problem to such questions is of no interest in this context, which is concerned with the understanding of Küng's theology.

The most serious and unforgivable error in procedure was the multiplication of charges in the decisive decision of December 1979. There a lack of restraint in the disputed books *The Church, Why Priests?* 'The

Reform and Recognition of Church Offices', and *Infallible?* is given as justification for the Roman intervention. The measure should only have related to them – if the Roman argument was taken seriously for a moment. But the declaration states:

> 'The conclusions which follow from such a view, above all the contempt (!) for the church's magisterium, also appear in other works which he has published, very much to the detriment of some of the main points of the Catholic faith (e.g. in connection with the consubstantiality of Christ with the Father or the Virgin Mary). Another sense is given to these statements of faith from the one which the church has understood and still understands' (FK 90).

In his statement, Cardinal Höffner devotes a good deal of space to precisely this point. In his view the centre not only of the Catholic faith but of Christian faith generally is threatened (FK 94). The same sort of thing is said in the commentary by Rome (FK 108). According to the statement made by the German bishops on 7 January 1980, to be read from the pulpit, Küng's christology endangers 'the faith which supports our living and dying' (FK 160). Such monstrous statements about Küng were certainly important to secure the assent of the German public (in Germany the question of infallibility is of relatively little interest). But they should not have been part of the grounds for removing his licence to teach – which is a legal judgment. So a suspicion which is more devastating for a legal process than other high-handed actions can hardly be avoided, namely that the final verdict had already been arrived at before the proceedings started, and now reasons were being produced which were thought to go down best with the public. Küng was experiencing personally what he suspected in his ecclesiological criticism: the myth of infallibility offers decisive protection against the implementation of a programme of church reform which understands being a Christian as shared discipleship of Jesus Christ. So was Küng hastening towards the fate of Cassandra, who has to pay for the realization of her warning?

Nevertheless the discussion of the law and the procedure is only part of the issue. The developments were also the outcome of the political situation in the German and Roman churches and of their theology. Investigation of the reasons and the judgment must go deeper. Why could this catastrophic development come about? A further reason for the disaster lies in the way in which Küng understands theology, as compared to many of his colleagues.

2. The theologian who knows the facts

From a theological perspective there was a strange helplessness about the arguments between Küng and those officials named the 'magisterium'. One side argued, compared, reported and concluded, and the other side wanted finished results. One side made sure that formulae became flexible, were relativized and again understood in their original sense or in a biblical sense, and the other was afraid that a formula was being handed over to 'theological discussion'. One side was enthused by the idea that his church could renew itself in the discipleship of Jesus, could understand the world afresh and discover a new responsibility; the other knew only the ideal of a unified church which had never changed in essentials from the beginning and never should. Here was the interplay of two worlds which clashed and basically remained speechless. Bishops had nothing better to do than to investigate a complex, 650-page text in terms of the two abstracts 'pre-existence' and 'divinity' (see above, 151f.). Küng was seized by a passion to translate precisely these concepts into action and event, into the experiences of concrete life. The concern of one side was that the faith of the church would be torn from its firm anchorage in the centuries; the other saw that only a voyage across to new shores could bring salvation.

What kinds of worlds are these, and why are they like that? Of course one could give an answer here by means of a broad historical survey and show how 'magisterium' and theology were once much closer to each other. In antiquity there was the time of the bishops who were also great theologians: Basil and Chrysostom, Ambrose and Augustine. The great doctrinal decisions were made after argument and dispute at ecumenical synods. There was also the time when theologians made the decisive statements in matters of faith; one might think of the University of Paris – a dangerous development, since gradually Christian doctrine got entangled in the specialist questions of theology. Later the rudder swung over: it was now popes and bishops (of the Western church) who were concerned for a theology which was legitimated, moulded and from the time of the Counter-Reformation spoon-fed by the magisterium. Vatican I and the opposition to modernism brought the climax of a forced submissiveness, an end to which was hoped for in Vatican II, though in many places it still seemed to have a psychological effect. From the nineteenth century onwards a third force came to have unexpected influence: church public opinion, which was first claimed by the bishops but later became independent.

The process of emancipation was vigorous and long. In 1950 it suffered its last serious setback before Vatican II with the disciplining of the *nouvelle théologie* (DGE 572). Soon people were convinced that such a thing must never happen again; from 1962 people then thought that they knew that it never could. Küng had studied in Rome from 1950 on and experienced at close quarters the oppressive events of the time (the disciplining first of the Jesuits and then of the Dominicans). For him, reinforced by his ecumenical studies, this emancipation became a theological programme. Theology can only perform its service to church and world as a free discipline, engaged in responsibly and with a rational backing. But soon reaction regained strength. It raised its head under Paul VI; under John Paul II it was ready to strike. In the course of what is now twenty years it has struck repeated blows.

Now in the 1970s there was no theologian who embodied this new self-confidence and sense of obligation more intensely and uncompromisingly than Hans Küng. Not only was this the way in which he acted, but such action was his programme, supported by intensive biblical, historical and ecumenical studies, reinforced by the question of the church and on being a Christian, intensified by strong currents within the church and made unshakeable as a living conviction. Nowhere did he embody this programme more strongly than in communication with the outside world: in the lecture room and in publications, in the media and in public appearances, in public calls for a renewed and ecumenically open church, in criticism of an authoritarian pope with a leaning towards centralism, and finally as a voice of the many who felt misunderstood or betrayed in their understanding of the church and being a Christian. Küng put forward this programme with brilliant arguments; nowhere more resolutely than where his own theological freedom was being disputed. That encouraged or irritated – depending on one's standpoint.

Nevertheless, in writings, letter and conversations it is striking that while Küng insists on his rights, on rules for fair procedures and correct behaviour, he presupposes theological reasons rather than repeating them. He goes into individual statements only when he is misunderstood. Often he emphasizes that the questions are difficult, that he has to study and wants to study; often he announces new studies and books. But precisely that is said to be an evasion on his part.

Why does this remarkable lack of clarity develop? Why does a more restrained Küng then suddenly appear, a Küng who defends himself resolutely but is almost insecure? Why does he not also go more on the offensive in arguments, get involved in the dispute, compel it to grapple, say, with statements and lines of argument from scripture or the patristic tradition? Of course there is a good deal of shrewdness here. Küng knows all too well how quickly statements can be understood wrongly, interpreted over-hastily, how far he would have to to link up with aspects critical of the tradition or the hierarchy: no conclusions without opening up two new battlefields! Hermeneutical arguments are not linear but circular; they do not end with a compelling 'therefore', with univocal or perhaps dialectical statements, but with the discovery of new connections. Those who make hermeneutical statements leave their flanks open because they do not appeal for an enforceable agreement.

I think that the decisive reason lies in the character of Küng's theology. Of course Küng has clear ideas and visions, shining beacons by which he organizes his arguments. But what is characteristic of him is the detail in which he argues. For example, the question of church reform directs him to an intensive study of exegesis and the history of the church and theology. He never expresses satisfaction with general and necessarily abstract theories. As a result a process of multi-level and differentiated verification develops which his opponents then do not follow. Questions of church structure must not only – still – be compatible with exegetical data which are then extrapolated; their whole dynamic must be capable of being incorporated into what is taking place at that time – as concretely as possible.

One example is the assertion often made that the later hierarchical structure is already making itself felt in the Pastoral Epistles – including the conferring of ordination and sacramental authority. No Catholic dogmatic theologian, however, has summarized and analysed the state of research more intensively than Küng. This shows the arbitrariness of the assertion. But who can be convinced of this if they do not have as much knowledge as Küng? For a long time he could still disturb his opponents by asking who read the mass in Corinth when Paul was away travelling. Another example is provided by the assertions about the historical setting and development of early christology which scholars are fond of making and repeating intensively. However, only detailed investigations indicate the fractures which open up between the New Testament witnesses and early Hellenistic patristics. Comprehensive statements can be substantiated only with historically precise verification, and for systematic theology that means only if the results of specialist research are worked out in detail, synthesized and taken note of.

For Küng, critical theses have never followed from abstract surveys

but always (only) from specific totalities, detailed and put together carefully. In the long term, that of course is the strength of his work, but in
the short term this effort makes him vulnerable. He has always kept in
touch with exegetes, historians, philosophers and scholars in the
humanities; he has never been disowned by them because he has scorned
their results, smoothed over their problems or distorted their perspectives. How then can Küng defend the statements in the dispute – which
usually sound simple and far too understandable? Certainly he could
make corrections from his perspective. But it was this very perspective
which was being criticized for disloyalty to the church, for confusing
believers or scorning the magisterium. The only possibility would be to
reconstruct his results, step by step. But the overall perspective (let us
call it the spirit) was the problem, and not brief statements (let us call
them the letter). So when Höffner asked Küng for a formula about
Christ's pre-existence which he could not find, Küng was forced on to a
level on which he could no longer make his concern visible. But did that
depend on the one formula which leads into the sea of general knowledge? We shall have to discuss later why Küng nevertheless did not add
this formula which was being sought.

Küng's theology lives within the difficult span between overall interpretation and detail. A theologian of his kind really needs to be both a
synthesist and a polymath historian. Those who do not want to follow
him cannot devote themselves to working out the individual details. In
fact, over the course of the decades this approach has given Küng a
tremendous advantage in knowledge and argument. His judges in the
magisterium neglected to make this advance in knowledge or to catch
up with it: they did not once discuss with him, did not even take the
trouble to evaluate just a few stages in the overall argument, perhaps
bring in experts. Had they done so, they would perhaps have had to
differentiate or even correct their own positions. Even worse, it seems as
if they were already suspicious of this work in exegesis, history, the
humanities or philosophy. Too much exegesis smacks of a Protestantism
critical of the church and historical study smacks of relativism; the
humanities level down all revelation; philosophy is arbitrary and subjective. This was not the way to reach what Cardinal Volk called the
'level' of faith. People did not see that the faith and doctrine of the
church are not an item of knowledge which can be isolated and brought
in to correct individual disciplines, but a new understanding which
takes seriously and can make use of all that can be known. People did
not see that only as a counterpart to this process of opening up does
an integration begin which is appropriate to God and the matter in

question. Küng was to become the victim of his theology, orientated on the tension between knowledge and understanding; Rome evidently felt it to be threatening.

3. The critical interpreter

The controversy shows a further problem which gives rise to questions. At the high points of the conflict not only representatives of the church government but also colleagues were intensely active. In the composite volumes which have often been mentioned there are emphatic arguments from a variety of sub-disciplines; apart from one unmistakably dismissive contribution, the criticism put forward there remains within the framework of scholarly discussion and discussion within Catholicism. The situation is different with the representatives of dogmatic theology, in terms of task, competence and self-understanding the guardians of the holy grail of Catholic doctrine. They must be assumed to have specialist knowledge – at any rate in part and in their specific areas. How is their largely critical understanding to be understood? Of course we need not be surprised that bishops (usually former professors of theology) and systematic theologians (later often bishops) often advocated substantially the same positions, but Küng's expert knowledge should have been worth the effort of grappling with; given their daily work, they should have to read books not just cursorily, in quest of formulae, but right through.

But here too we make amazing discoveries. Hardly one of them goes into facts, events which are against the grain, contradictory evidence from scripture or tradition. All kinds of questions seemed to be kept out of the substantive discussion and swept away. To mention only a few examples: the idea of an authority to consecrate or transform emerged only at a comparatively late stage, and the New Testament knows no ontological equality of Christ with God (Kuschel 1990); Rome's theory of infallibility was initially rejected as an invention of the devil (Tierney); the freedom of Vatican I was highly questionable (Hasler) and the theory of infallibility was characterized by an extraordinary hostility to any idea of hermeneutics; from an ecumenical perspective certain Catholic positions seem unacceptable, if not absurd; the sheer failure of other well-meaning contemporaries to understand particular Catholic views could not be without significance; the inflexibility of the Catholic Church after the Council could be connected with particular marked structures in it; conflicts in the discussion broke out in particular over the privileges of the pope, hierarchy or clergy and over the demands for reform. This amazing lack of a capacity to react must also be connected with the attitude of theologians who deliberately and in awareness of the threats of the magisterium kept Küng at a distance or opposed him.

It is striking that all of them practised another theology, usually shaped by philosophical positions. They were indebted to the philosophical legacy from Hegel to Heidegger, to the hermeneutical legacy from Schleiermacher to Gadamer, or simply to neo-Thomist positions. Thus there is hardly any discussion among them of refractory knowledge, or at most of its domestication. On the contrary: they knew the facts, so where were Küng's new ideas? Or there were remarkably apologetic reactions to Küng's own information, with references to Adorno: 'If one repeats the complete catalogue of arguments . . . one is exposed to the charge of being eclectic; one is said to be basing oneself on what has long been known and in which no one is interested any longer.' But if one refers to the earlier success of the arguments, 'one is exposing oneself to the suspicion of being old-fashioned' (Adorno 20). Moreover, according to Karl Lehmann, wisely and with a reference to Nietzsche (!), the 'really revolutionary ideas came . . . on the feet of doves' (Lehmann, PU 349).

Karl Rahner was most open in the dispute and had the most catastrophic effect for Küng. His argument concentrated on the unsubstantiated assumption that Küng was contradicting a defined doctrine. Others wanted to overcome the fixation on individual statements and at the same time preserve the dogma of infallibility. In so doing they do not get beyond vague formulae supported by gestures of superiority, stating that such an infallibly defined doctrine is true in so far as it 'swims in' the stream of the history of faith. That gives it its 'direction' (F 86). Küng is said to have no view of either the depth or the whole. Here too there can hardly be any question of mutual understanding or discussion on a common level; here too the discussion tends rather to be helpless. Reasons have been sought for this: Küng exaggerates, is aggressive, no longer argues within the sphere of the church. As we saw, this last is nonsense, although the assertion made an impression.

But if we leave aside anxiety and a desire to please the hierarchy, what was the theological problem? Anyone who has understood the development of Küng's theology, his gradually maturing programme of reform, his questions about the reasons for the lack of flexibility after the Council; anyone who, like him, has seen the problems of the Reformation break out again and is not content with developments after the

Council, can rapidly discover the reason. As a rule Küng's opponents are not reactionary hard-liners; their arguments are speculative and interpretative. 'Transcendental theology', 'historicity' and 'hermeneutics' are the great key words of a theology with which church, tradition and the mutability of Christian doctrine disclose themselves harmoniously. The church becomes the hermeneutical context of Christian truth (see above, 150).

What is more natural than to interpret the doctrine of infallibility in this incomprehensible sense? But in the theology of Küng's opponents the 'interpretation' takes priority over the substance. The substance retreats into the background. What becomes decisive is the intuition, sometimes certainly brilliant, indeed the result of genius, which gives a new splendour to the old cause. The Assumption of Mary now becomes the symbol of fulfilled humanity; the definition of the indissolubility of marriage at Trent an action against the arrogance of the Reformation; 'original sin' becomes the cipher for our disastrous situation; creation the expression of our origin from God; eschatology the reflection on our 'futurity'. In their beauty the new interpretations are neutral towards the images which are interpreted.

I call this a naive and conservative hermeneutic which is prone to becoming an ideology. It is naive because it intuitively develops interpretations and does not reflect on their possible misuse, but brings the original statement and its interpretation into an uncritical relationship. It is conservative because it gives priority to the authority of a valid interpretation and supports it. It is prone to become an ideology because the influence of preunderstandings and interests is confirmed instead of being investigated critically. The characteristic of such a hermeneutic is its lack of interest in facts, conflicts and situations which go against the grain. Those who practise it are happy about the act of interpretation as such and the amazement that it provokes. Space is gained by understanding much as interpretation of much and discovering extraordinary depths in the everyday. There are delusions about the banality of power, riches and the quest for domination, above vengeance and disapproval, because the 'true' meaning always lies below the surface. People forget that the work begins only with the discovery of a pre-understanding, namely getting wise to it.

Against this background of intuitive theologizing, the difficulties with Küng become understandable. Küng, the theologian with the encyclopaedic orientation, time and again referring to facts and conflicts, learns the meaning of a critical hermeneutic precisely through this. He does not work it out theoretically (unfortunately), but practises it. This

critical hermeneutic becomes his indispensable instrument for a programme of church reform. In his criticism of infallibility he not only
criticizes possible abuses, but also subjects the naive hermeneutic –
which its representatives called 'ecclesial' – to criticism. He forces his
opponents also to reflect on the framework of their understanding of the
church, but they will not engage in any dialogue about this. That is
consistent with their conservative hermeneutic, and it shows the dead
end to which their argument leads. Küng was left with only one way
out, which amounted to refusing to engage in dialogue. Sometimes
implicitly, and sometimes explicitly, his loyalty to the church was being
denied; this simply showed up the provinciality of the opposition's
understanding of the church. It was said that Küng is a liberal
Protestant. So no one dared to take Karl Rahner to task for his negli-
gence, and no one noticed that the great theologian was thus catapulting
himself out of the orbit of the dialogue. He went, showing others the
door.

This labelling has its effect: all later criticism of *On Being a Christian*
and *Does God Exist?* was projected on to it. Instead of criticism of
infallibility, people talked of 'contempt for the magisterium', and the
reconstruction of belief in Christ became its destruction. Such discrimination brought polarization and prevented creativity. The damage done
to German-speaking Catholic theology in terms of a church which was
to be renewed is evident: there is good reason for the helpless silence of
the years that were to follow. Reforms can obviously neither be implemented with Heidegger and a transcendental theology nor justified
cleanly and if need be in conflict. That is an oppressive result.

4. Magisterium and theology

I have depicted Küng over against the magisterium as a theologian
focussed on research, and over against his fellow theologians as the
representative of a critical hermeneutic. In the controversy of the 1970s,
as a result of *Infallible?*, *On Being a Christian* and *Does God Exist?*,
Küng involuntarily assumed a key role. Why did the controversy
suddenly become so significant? We should remain matter-of-fact. Küng
was a very eloquent champion of renewal and critic, undeterred and full
of insight, but certainly not the only one. Emancipatory theologies were
beginning to become established: non-European trends announced
themselves, critical of ideology, feminist and contextual. They too
caused friction. But why was the confrontation with Küng in particular

so harsh, carried on with so much effort and so much theological commitment? In my view the reason lies in the particularly close relationship between magisterium and theology in Germany, which has not been clarified.

Despite all the criticism of the concept and actions of the 'magisterium', Küng never denied the special responsibility of the bishops for the church as a whole; they had to ensure that it was in accord with its apostolic origins. He insisted that questions should be asked about scripture and always saw this as an act which united him with the whole church. For Küng the episcopate – in the framework of the fundamental charismatic structure – was one ministry alongside others, albeit exalted and with the right to represent the church both to its members and to outsiders, and also bearing ultimate responsibility for its apostolicity, i.e. for its discipleship in the original faith. Now this apostolicity embraces more than faithfulness in teaching. It is faithfulness in the whole of praxis, which includes action, celebration, diakonia and community. Küng did not expect less of the bishops than is involved in the task of the magisterium, but more. So a lofty claim, not contempt, seems to have been the starting point of a permanent misunderstanding between Küng and the bishops. However, the starting point of this high expectation was that first of all the church as a whole is engaged in this apostolic service and that the New Testament knows 'teachers' and 'prophets' alongside the responsibility of the apostles (Ref).

The misunderstanding was continued in the dispute over the grounds for episcopal responsibility. It was Küng's main aim that the episcopal office, and especially the magisterium, should be freed from its centralistic form, which is isolated and focussed on Rome. Secondly, he saw the 'magisterium' of the bishop and the pope in a broader perspective. The first task of these ministries is a concern for a Christian church: for it to live by contemporary discipleship, to confess its faith in understandable forms, and to be able to have exchanges over questions and problems in freedom, in brotherhood and sisterhood. The bishops are both arbiters and teachers. Similarly, their task is both to protect minorities and to ensure order, to guarantee communication and to introduce linguistic rules, to further creativity and to present binding doctrine. Though it was discussed widely at academies, in lecture rooms and in communities, this conception was never studied, let alone seriously discussed, by bishops or by many fellow theologians. What Küng intended as an increase in function and authority is still understood today as an undermining of church order.

In concrete terms the question focussed on the relationship between magisterium and theology, or more precisely on the question of the rights and responsibilities of theologians over against the episcopal 'magisterium'. Here there was full readiness for concessions, as long as the right to settle conflicts, which meant the right to have the last word, remained in the hand of the bishops. During the Council, theologians performed indispensable services; why should that not have continued to be possible? But that was no reason for the revaluation of theological ministries in principle. Other bishops and Rome had different views here. The strictly authoritarian and sometimes humiliating way in which Rome has treated theologians as disloyal dissidents is to be seen against this background: after the unruly years of the Council the old order had to be restored. Many theologians learned this lesson. They were happy to assume their new functions (and status) if asked. They were ready to be at the service of the bishops and understood this rule just as pragmatically. That meant that the service of the theologians remained strictly subordinated to the rights of the bishops. But it was shaped more by personal commitment, shared thinking and the strictest loyalty, and not by separate functions and possible criticism. In Germany the mutual relationships tended to be particularly close, since the way to the episcopate is marked out for many dogmatic theologians at a very early stage. That is not without significance for the self-understanding of those concerned.

On this presupposition a conflict over church teaching becomes particularly explosive: it escalates into a history of misunderstandings. At the latest after Trent, concern for the truth of faith is regarded as the prime task of the episcopal ministry; here we have a 'theologizing' of this function. Extreme loyalty is required of theologians precisely here. So Küng's conception proved particularly liable to cause conflict. First he saw theologians working on their own, underivable responsibility. The first task of theologians is not to work with the bishops but to come to their own conclusions – within the church community. In Rome people saw, and in Germany feared this as an attack on the genuine rights of the bishops. Thus it was thought important to resist Küng's action as such, in principle and independently of its intellectual content. The controversy over him assumed symbolic proportions.

Finally, the misunderstandings and fixations were transferred to the discussions of the content of *On Being a Christian*. After the memorandum on priesthood and after *Infallible?*, this christology from the perspective of discipleship was understood simply as an attack on episcopal rights and responsibilities. Here too something else was intended. The distinction between doctrine and theology, i.e. between binding basic statements and further critical interpretation of them, is important for Küng's theology. But what is doctrine and what theology? From an abstract perspective one can hardly deny that something which is supposedly part of doctrine can relativize itself with increasing distance. Once people believed that heaven was above the clouds and hell consisted in physical fire. Now the transitoriness of this world of ideas has been recognized.

Does that have consequences for christology? Küng's conviction – which is shared by many – was that Hellenistic thought led to the doctrine of the pre-existence of Christ and his divine nature and to the classical models of the Trinity. He did not deny the doctrine, but expounded it. He did not do away with it, but transferred it to another model. However, what he understood as an aid towards the bishop's task of preaching was interpreted as an attack on the truth. The magisterium had not yet grasped the distinction between doctrine and theology. Why did no help come from theologians? That was amazing, since the thesis of the Hellenization of Christian doctrine and of the limits of Hellenistic ontology is standard teaching. It can hardly be proved that categories of action ('God speaks, acts, reveals himself in Jesus') convey less than categories of being ('Jesus is God'), and it is difficult to understand why biblical phrases (to which Küng refers) should be discriminated against, as compared with phrases which breathe the spirit of Athens and Alexandria. There was no substantive basis for interpreting Küng's new attempt almost of necessity as a repudiation of the centre of Christian faith, but this projection of the problem made things easier. Here was a scapegoat who in his Swiss stubbornness (thus the German perception) even matched the projection. A William Tell was not wanted – and this thought struck deep emotional chords (Baumann, NHGD 724). There was little understanding of the democratic self-confidence of the Swiss citizen, his honest and sometimes blunt talk. Given the knotty problems being discussed, the theologians were incapable of being detached mediators. An uncritical concept of the function of theology, a strong identification with the bishops, the pressures of 'church circles' and the anxious fantasy that faith would be ruined robbed them of any impulse to act on their own.

Their theological self-confidence and *esprit de corps* had already crumbled previously. No adviser dared any longer to object to such monstrous episcopal assertions as that Küng fell short of the statements of the creed. Just as little objection was made to Höffner's cynical observation (a quotation from Rahner) that one may in some circumstances leave 'the early church, which is no longer one's own, but one may not attempt to undermine it in a modernist tactic' (FK 143). The statement shows the lack of detachment and the hardening of which the magisterium had meanwhile become the victim and which was no longer tempered by any of the theologians. Moreover the call for a christological confession which Küng – if one follows his express statements – never denied but wanted to reinterpret was prejudiced and out of context: 'In the central christological question, whether Jesus Christ is *really* God, i.e. occupies the status and level of being of God undiminished, he has evaded a resolute confession expressed in binding words despite all attempts at clarification' (FK 94). One notes that the formulation simply accentuates the 'really . . . is' and agrees with an explanation of God's 'level of being' , which has no analytical content. This merely emphasizes that the language of metaphysics and not that of the Bible is the really normative language.

Only now may we recall that earlier what Küng had proposed as a linguistic rule of language had been torn apart by the theologians so that it became an alternative: 'Who is Jesus Christ? Is he a human person in whom God reveals himself in speech and action, or is he the eternal Son of God who becomes a human being in history?' (GfC 182). Such disjunctions are highly regrettable and signs of resignation, since with his capacity for reflection, this theologian could also have shown how the two statements are indeed different, but for reasons of hermeneutics and inculturation need not be mutually exclusive. So even after eighteen years one cannot rid oneself of the suspicion that in the end the issue was not the formula but the whole programme; the controversy was over Küng as a symbol, over order in the 'church'. Thus in retrospect the Küng affair becomes a justification of his own criticism: the magisterium and theology should finally give up their mutual embrace and grant each other some independent functions. Only in this way, in the course of time, can they win back their freedom, contemporaneity and appropriate Christian nature.

5. The church as myth – on what does Küng ultimately stand firm?

It is time to sum up the problems of the withdrawal of Küng's licence to teach. I have attempted to describe the legal situation and to show why there was no dialogue between the magisterium and Küng. This was probably because the bishops did not take note of Küng's issue-related theology. The dialogue with important fellow-theologians who thought historically foundered on their misunderstanding of a critical hermeneutic. To make things worse, the unclarified relationship between magisterium and theology, also the subject of Küng's reform proposals, made it impossible to overcome the misunderstandings and resistance to mediation by third parties. In the end the affair was a battle over the renewed form of the church.

Küng's final statement addressed to his local bishop was dated 20 December 1979. In it Küng attempted – on the basis of the most recent reactions, a conversation with his local bishop and long telephone calls with colleagues in the know – to go as far as possible towards meeting Rome. Could he have hoped that Rome would give way at the last moment? The reactions of many observers at that time were clear:

- Anyone who has not forgotten the extent of Küng's argument in those hectic days, worked out in terms of the Bible, church history and dogmatics;
- anyone who reflects that Küng professedly and out of conviction did not deny the office of the pope, the bishop, or the leadership of the community;
- anyone who takes into account that in his view, statements of Christian faith call for an unmistakable yes or no;
- anyone who has not forgotten that Küng is convinced that
  – the church has the responsibility and task of clear proclamation, and the bishops have the responsibility and task to make binding statements in particular situations and distinguish what is Christian from what is not;
  – and that here the bishops have a special authority;
- anyone who investigates Küng's statement that
  – 'also and specifically' in questions of christology he stands 'in principle' on the ground of the councils of the early church and is trying to make them understandable to men and women of today;
  – he wants to raise real and not spurious questions about the basis of the Vatican I definition of infallibility;
- anyone who notes all this can hardly see why his commitment to an *ecclesia reformanda* was answered in such a petty way. It becomes all the more difficult for those responsible and those involved to justify this, the longer they abide by the decision that was made, now eighteen years ago.

But didn't Küng refuse to answer a further letter from Bishop Moser on 26 December 1979? Indeed Bishop Moser asked for further precisions, which probably indicated more mistrust than a desire to reach an agreement. Küng was confronted with astonishing, now pettifogging charges, to the effect that:

- He was avoiding the world 'infallibility' in his answer;
- he spoke only of 'binding character' and not of 'ultimate' binding character;
- he did not see an ecumenical council as a representation of the episcopate as a whole but (only?) of the whole church;
- he only stood 'in principle' on the ground of the old councils, whatever that might mean in specific terms;
- he granted the magisterium only a 'special authority' of the kind that ultimately any teacher has;
- it remained completely open whether Küng recognized a binding magisterium for himself (!);
- his remarks on infallibility were disappointing (here only some quotations which in Moser's view were contradictory were cited 'merely by way of example' [!]).

This Christmas brought Küng his most bitter hour. He had to realize that this letter had not built any bridges but had gone back to the initial questions and was intent on setting the mills grinding all over again. Moreover it was not a personal statement by the mediating bishop. Evidently the bishop was making himself – one gradually gets to know the style – the mouthpiece of a particular theological script. Now doubt was suddenly being cast on Küng's personal credibility and readiness to be corrected ('whether you yourself recognize a binding church magisterium'). So the necessary basis for trust in this last attempt at mediation was lacking in Rome. Perhaps Moser had overestimated his personal possibilities; he still wanted to mediate, but the die had been cast. Küng was not even spared having to play for the last time the role of the spoilsport in this unworthy game. So he did not accede to Moser's request for further precision; for the last time he asked Moser for a personal conversation with the pope (FK 135–8), but since he was neither a statesman nor a sporting star, of course this was not granted him.

Emotionally and obviously also intellectually, Küng had reached rock bottom. Cardinal Höffner was no longer speaking frankly, although his last decisive conversation in Rome had not yet taken place. When journalists addressed the problem of 'rigid formulae' he was not embarrassed to draw National Socialist parallels to Küng's demands (the passages in Rosenberg et al. had been carefully chosen and precise references were given); he cynically presented modern theology as a junk shop of random contradictory views (he mentioned six examples, from the devil to the indissolubility of marriage), and finally put forward an argument for a biological understanding of the virginity of Mary which was meant to make it clear to the believer that 'Jesus cannot owe himself to two fathers' (FK 138–44). In his pastoral message for Lent 1980 he said: 'Were Jesus Christ not the eternal Son of God, of the same substance as the Father . . . then something would have happened on Mount Calvary similar to what happened on Mount Moriah, where a ram was sacrificed instead of the son' (Höffner 9). At such a level of argument it is almost an honour to come off worst.

These remarks should not be taken wrongly. This is not a matter of good will or bad will, of openness or spiritual immobility, of understanding or hardening of the heart. In the last phase, none of those involved was any longer unemotional, and they had reached the limits of their strength. Moreover the days after 17 December showed how many committed Catholics throughout the world were on Küng's side: Küng received mountains of letters. Quite evidently this was not the case of a sectarian individualist, but rather, of an image and understanding of the church which appealed to the spirit of Vatican II with widespread assent. Now in this theological analysis objectifiable reasons were being sought. More than ever there were two fundamentally different conceptions of the church in the Catholic Church – not only in Western Europe but all over the world – but Rome and the hierarchs did not recognize that. On the basis of their own monolithic picture of the church they came to the conclusion that Küng's thought was no longer Catholic.

Rahner had produced the slogan 'liberal Protestant', and in so doing was saying what many people basically thought. Granted, Walter Kasper later supposed that Rahner had fundamentally strengthened Küng's position. He said that Rahner's proximity to Küng was so great that it could possibly even be understood as a 'combined operation' with Küng (F 87). This dialectic is not very clear, since a 'combined operation' is possible with many children of God. Nor does Ratzinger's remark, quoted by Kasper, that Küng remained 'remarkably undecided', help. Ratzinger had not meant this in a friendly way but was insinuating that Küng was not putting all his cards on the table. Nor did Kasper help Küng when he quoted Luther, of all people, against him and thought that otherwise (i.e. according to Küng's scheme) in the last instance Christianity would become myth. These were all intrinsically fine thoughts, but they had and have very little to do with Küng.

Kasper simply did not understand his colleague when he accused him of a 'functional and pragmatic view of the truth and language, related to the situation' and called for 'a union of propositional truth and essential truth' (F 82). The charges accumulated, partly indirect, implicit and hidden and partly formulated by Küng's accuser. On his premises a dogma was said to be only (!) a temporary measure; a final yes or no was no longer possible; basically there was a threat of totalitarian compulsion, 'cruelly arbitrary, absolutistic and violent' (thus Karl Lehmann). On his presuppositions, according to Kasper, dogma was 'not a form of the gospel that makes us free, but the deepest slavery to the law of the particular hour. Here in fact everything is at stake' (F 82). These gentlemen produced a cabinet of horrors which corresponded only to their own projections. Kasper came to the absurd conclusion that at least latently, Küng posed 'the danger that the absolutely binding seriousness of the claim of the gospel is being relativized in favour of provisional pragmatic solutions and an abiding in the truth which in some circumstances is completely shapeless'. At least that was the logical consequence of some (?) of his approaches (F 83).

So where was the problem? Why could Küng be misunderstood in such an absurd way? How could one oppose a colleague with so much factual (I do not mean personal) arrogance? The problem lay in the different understandings of the church. Küng's question in fact begins where Kasper still believes that there are simple solutions, namely with the need for clear statements and the notion that every statement is bound up with every other. Küng is not in fact concerned with an ecclesiastical process of truth, testimony and tradition as such (when had he ever put these in doubt?), but with the question of the specific course of this process and what it can and must be in the future. What is its concrete form, since there is no dispute that binding statements have a deeper meaning? How does one cross the bridge from profound theology to practical form? Can it be – on the assumption that all dogma is interconnected – that in the end one individual in the church not only establishes what is to be said but also claims the right to pass judgment on its interpretation?

The direction had of course been set long before the dispute over the question of infallibility. Where Kasper and others later (latently or explicitly) came to the conclusion that Küng's loyalty to the church left much to be desired, they might at least have asserted that their own picture of the church was not identical with Küng's. That was understandable, since their whole understanding of faith belonged within the 'transcendental' framework of the 'church'. So might they exclude Küng's scheme from the range of possible schemes? To put the question another way, would Kasper's harmonious scheme of the communication of faith have been recognized as ecclesial at the time of modernism? How would his colleagues from the great times at Tübingen, to which he now refers, have fared then? One involuntarily thinks of the grace of late birth.

I know that that is not the whole story. Kasper not only had another understanding of being a Christian; for him the church was a turning-point and a cornerstone. He imagined a church which understood itself as a living tradition and played a key role for itself. 'Self-realization' was the giveaway term taken over from Karl Rahner, and it has been going the rounds ever since. He could not give up this self-reference; the circle was closed. Therefore it became difficult for him to allow other schemes. In its self-reference this picture of the church was still strongly indebted to the one who sought to go beyond it. In good metaphysical fashion, 'church' was treated as a myth, as an entity in itself and not as an open process seeking fulfilment and discovery. So one possibility remained barred to Kasper: the discovery that Küng's enquiry, his concern for an appropriate interpretation of binding discourse which gave it concrete form, and his whole programme of church reform, was a thoroughly ecclesial activity. Therefore precisely for that reason, when it was completed, Küng's scheme could not be objectified and examined to see whether it was in keeping with the nature of the church. At this point his statements needed to be understood not only as communicating content but at the same time as speech-acts. The church cannot be reduced to an agency of interpretation and historicity in itself. The church is a living community, a comprehensive practical entity. So its nature is not to be understood as a profound, purely informative speech-event but in comprehensively pragmatic terms. Nor is the question whether Küng's theology too is in keeping with the nature of the church to be answered in terms of the great criteria which always have an undisputed validity: responsibility to scripture (which Kasper sees only as a kind of biblicism), and a readiness to engage in discussion with those who make up the church. Kasper would vigorously affirm both these, but he does not display a lively sense of either. He sees reference back to scripture merely as archaizing, and confuses faith in the present with its Hellenistic or Western form.

By contrast, the idealistic hermeneutic of Küng's theological critics was imprisoned in an idealistic construct of self-explication, which they called 'church', and which they *de facto* identified with the Roman Catholic Church. It was their focal point and at the same time their blind spot. Presumably it never became clear to these critics how they forged this matter of loyalty to the church into a deadly weapon against him.

Theologically, as we saw, the weapon was in any case blunt. In Germany (where the work of thinking and legitimation was done, rather than in Rome), it was too much the tool of apologetic pressures, particular parties and anxieties. The painful and highly unattractive judgment must be passed that in disciplining Küng, Rome was merely defending its own privilege. In the discussion with Küng, against the background of what church sociologists saw as the 'Catholic milieu' of a declining Catholicism (though it was and still is very much present in episcopal circles), that meant, 'He can expect nothing from us', since he has offended against the basic rules of good behaviour. The argument was thought of as one necessarily relating to the church, though no further reasons could be given. So from the beginning the debate had its emotions and personal hurts. It may be that the Swiss citizen did not understand its character sufficiently.

To conclude: the programmatic cry 'loyalty to the church' became a deadly weapon. Kasper, who was 'very close' to Küng, piled on the arguments (DisC 19–34): he said that Küng was making the priority of scripture over tradition a priority over the church, that he was detaching the apostolic tradition from the apostolic succession, and finally that the church set itself above the subjective interpretation of scripture by the individual. For Küng, he remarked, the criterion was not simply scripture, but scripture interpreted by historical criticism; the magisterium of the bishops was being replaced by the professors of theology. Finally, Küng was arguing from the standpoint of modern subjectivity: in scripture the gospel could be experienced only (?) 'in faith'. Such simplifications were then gathered up in an absurd but dangerous way: Küng was said to be overlooking the fact that the dogmatic content of statements of faith necessitated a dogmatic form. So in the end the hypostasis 'church' was once again overplayed and led to ecclesiocentricity, because it was narrowed: 'for without the church we have no Christ and no holy scripture' (Möhler). In that case all that was left was rationalism and, according to Käsemann, 'the Enlightenment as a modification of the *solus Christus*'. Was Kasper really accusing his colleague Küng with this arsenal of apologetic clichés?

Kasper makes a shrewd distinction. He says that of course Küng did not want that. 'But between the subjective intention and some objective statements in the book there is a tension which is hard to resolve.' Was this a colleague who understood Küng better than Küng understood himself? Why did Kasper not re-examine his own concept of the church? We should not underestimate the influence of the theological guild. German theologians denied Küng the quality of 'Catholic' before Rome adopted this verdict. If there was still a degree of restraint in Kasper's remarks and conclusions, this was completely lacking in P. Hünermann, Küng's successor to the substitute chair. For him Küng was simply disloyal to the church. Theological verdicts are forged as simply as that.

Has this chapter been in black and white, offering one-sided partisan support of Küng? Has too much polemic found its way into the analysis? It may be clear where the sympathies of the author lie, but the issue here is not the quality of the theological concepts discussed nor even a general defence of Küng. The one and only question under discussion is when and with what right theologians may deny that a colleague is loyal to the church, when and with what right a theologian may discuss the question whether his colleagues Leonardo Boff and Hans Küng are still Christians (thus in October 1985 in *Avvenire*, cf. Balthasar 1985). Only when such questions have been resolved, and an exclusivist mentality and a refusal to engage in dialogue have been remedied, is there room for the discussion of real theological questions. Criticism and counter-criticism can then be expressed. And then questions will also have to be put to Küng's approach.

But first there still remains the question: what is loyalty to the church? Who has finally removed himself from the centre of the church? This question, the answer to which was so fateful for Küng, ultimately remains open. It certainly proved fateful. The Küng affair also became the Tübingen affair, the affair of a polarized faculty. Küng's pupils have also had to pay. Every doctorate and every habilitation has been involved in a painful and often time-consuming investigation of its acceptability and Catholicity. German chairs remain taboo. That is bitter, unjust, and certainly not for the good of theology. It is understandable, however, that this should have come about. If a decision is made with so much effort, with such polarization and with such publicity, then it has to be maintained through thick and thin. So the question simply remains whether in the eyes of Catholics the problems are settled. Presumably one day people will again remember Küng's proposed interpretations.

But was that Küng's fate? Certainly not. It was a development with which he first of all had to cope personally. He did so not only in a negative but also (indeed even more) in a very positive sense, as we shall see when we go on to investigate the further development of his theological activity.

8

The Inter-Religious Horizon:
World Religions as Enrichment

1. How do I begin a dialogue?

Quite apart from the problematical reasons behind it, the withdrawal of Hans Küng's licence to teach took place in legally questionable circumstances. The implementation of the decision was left to state officials and the university. After difficult negotiations at various levels, Küng finally agreed to a provisional solution: he left the Catholic theological faculty, but was not incorporated into any non-theological faculty. Rather, the Institute for Ecumenical Research was given an independent status, which it was to retain until his retirement. Küng and others were very well aware that judicial arguments could lead to fundamental discussions about the Concordat and thus to very much more unacceptable measures, with incalculable consequences.

As the Swiss citizen told the president of the university, he did not want this. His minimal condition for a solution was: 'I am a theologian and want to remain a theologian' (FK 535). He was granted this, but the basis of his work changed. He no longer lectured on the great dogmatic treatises, nor did he take part in examining and in the administration of the faculty. Nor did it make a great deal of sense, in view of the momentary hardening, to go on promoting the disputed themes. In any case, those who wanted to see had had their eyes opened: 'If in my case the church authorities have attempted to impose the truth by force, as a Christian I trust that in the course of time the truth will impose itself automatically' (FK 535f.).

(a) Reorientation: the religions

There remained the Institute with its team of collaborators to whom reference has already been made; there were enough topics which in any case needed to be dealt with. Why not intensify these questions, and why not show within the framework of general studies the degree to which religious questions today still interest a wide public? In 1981 Küng gave a series of lectures on questions about eternal life (see above, 206f.). But in the meantime one of the great topics of the coming creative period had emerged, a discussion with the world religions.

The topic was not new for Küng. He had already provided critical commentaries on Karl Barth's approach, and at the time of the Council he was intensely interested in the arguments over religious freedom and the evaluation of the non-Christian religions. After a stay in India he wrote a meditation ('Christianity as a Minority') on the world religions, and in *The Church* he discussed intensively the Jewish roots of the church (C 107–25; 132–49); he also wrote extremely (self-)critically about the claim that 'outside the church there is no salvation' (C 313–18). In 1978 he spoke programmatically of the new 'external ecumene' as a 'global ecumene with all its different regions and religions, ideologies and disciplines' (Kuschel 1978). Later these statements became more powerful. In *On Being a Christian* Küng attempted a first systematization of the great world religions, though this was still very general in content and evaluation: the key words are India (Hinduism and Buddhism), China (Confucianism and Taoism) and Islam. Their great challenge must be taken seriously (OBC 89–116). So this book is to 'make a modest contribution also to the dialogue with the world religions' (OBC 116). Soon afterwards an intensive dialogue with Jewish theology developed (BoL). The topic returns in *Does God Exist?* (DGE 585–612), focussed on the image of God and the question of God, and as already in *The Church*. the inner relationship of Jewish and Christian tradition takes on a profile of its own (DGE 613–702).

Now the discussion with the world religions becomes the great topic. But how to begin? How is the vast amount of information, the reading of the great religious texts, the over-rich and complex histories of the religions ('world religions' too are already an evaluation and a selection) to be integrated, brought together into problems and results, linked into lasting threads of dialogue, so that a theology with a future can arise out of them, understood and organized as an inter-religious dialogue appropriate for both the Christian tradition and the other religious traditions?

Küng chose an effective way which called for all his energy and watchfulness, but which promised topical and flexible results that could lead to dialogue. Four evening dialogue lectures each on Islam, Hinduism and Buddhism were announced for the summer of 1982. Each time a specialist presented a theme from the ideas and reality of 'his' religion and Küng had to respond to this from a Christian perspective. The manuscripts were exchanged at short notice, but the attraction of immediacy and sometimes also of provisionality was preserved in the subsequent publication (CWR). Here was attention and intensive study; the framework of positions became clear and was at the same time open to correction. And above all here the first steps were taken which – in the long term – were not limited to the presentation and analysis of individual religions.

From the beginning Küng replies not only as an admirer but as a Christian theologian: *On Being a Christian* and *Does God Exist?* were now being put to the test. So this exciting publication is still a treasure-trove of expert and unfalsified information, self-critical and at the same time questioning reaction, from perspectives which lead further towards the development of future profiles for ecumenical dialogue. The project was later supplemented by a series of dialogue lectures on *Christianity and Chinese Religions*; this also became a book (CCR). In this way the foundation, as it were the first phase, of a comprehensive religious and theological programme was sketched out. As will emerge later, further stages would follow. The material produced here (two books amounting around 950 pages, and shorter publications, not including hermeneutical and methodological studies) is immense. I shall attempt to sketch these out in a systematic summary.

(b) What is religion?

I have already mentioned Küng's discussion of Karl Barth's radical critique of religion, which was later toned down. Küng's counter-proposal was that the traditional Catholic exclusivism ('outside the church no salvation') is untenable and therefore must be superseded. Instead of abstract norms, historically responsible assessments are to be sought. When for example it is said in *On Being a Christian,* 'not exclusiveness, but uniqueness' (a level of analysis which is again taken up in Jesus Christ as the 'normative one', OBC 110, 326), judgments are shifted to the level of historical judgments. No judgment is to be passed on the religions in themselves (how could that be done?) but on their power to shape culture, their humanity, the intensity of their experience of God, the clarity of their truth, the critical competence of their prophecy. This leads not only to the passages in *On Being a Christian,* but also to the many later individual reactions to persons, programmes, ethical approaches, to dealing with the disadvantaged, with women and with the social outcasts.

Otherwise the concept of religion was not at the centre of interest in Küng's previous work. He was concerned with the Christian message and proclamation as the normative content, with discipleship of Jesus as the great model for Christian life, with faith as unconditional trust in God. In the discussion within Christianity, the church as the advance post of Christian religion stood at the centre of the reflection and the programme. Thus the concept of religion was not the focal point of the formation of theological theories. Küng can now introduce it in phenomenological openness, so that he embraces a manifold spectrum of subjects, practices and options, contradictory pictures and non-pictures of the divine.

'Religion is a social and individual relationship, vitally realized in a tradition and community (through doctrine, ethic, and generally ritual as well), with something that transcends or encompasses human beings and their world: with something always to be under-stood as the utterly final, true reality (the Absolute, God, nirvana). In contrast to philosophy, religion is concerned at once with a message of salvation and the way to salvation' (CWR xvi).

Küng continues the practical approach of his theology in this way. In criticism and confirmation, theory is always to be related to practice:

'Religion is more than a purely theoretical affair, a simple matter of the past, a problem for researchers in archives and specialists in ancient texts. No, religion, as sketched out here, is always far more than this, a lived life, inscribed in the hearts of men and women, and hence for all religious persons something that is supremely contemporary, pulsing through every fibre of their everyday exis-tence. Religion can be lived traditionally, superficially, passively, or in a profoundly sensitive, committed, dynamic way. Religion is a believing view of life, approach to life, way of life, and therefore a fundamental pattern embracing the individual and society, human beings and the world, through which a person (though only partially conscious of this) sees and experiences, thinks and feels, acts and suffers, everything. It is a transcendentally grounded and immanently operative system of co-ordinates, by which human beings orientate themselves intellectually, emotionally and existentially. Religion pro-vides a comprehensive meaning for life, guarantees supreme values and unconditional norms, creates a spiritual community and home' (CWR xvi).

Moreover such a phenomenologically open description of religion corresponds to an open definition of the relationship between the religions aimed at their co-existence. The relationship between the world religions and world history is as important a subject of exploration as the reciprocal relations between the religions. Therefore alongside information and comparison there must be discussion, with the possibility of reciprocal transformation.

> 'Thus we can slowly arrive not at an uncritical mishmash, but at a mutual critical enlightenment, stimulation, penetration, and enrichment of the various religious traditions, of the kind that has already been seen, in theory and practice, for some time now, between the various confessional traditions in Christianity itself. Indeed this should be the way leading to the sort of understanding between religions that does not give rise to a unified world religion but, after so many hot and cold wars, with their countless casualties, seeks to bring about a genuine state of peace' (CWR xx).

From the beginning Küng leaves no doubt that he is engaged in research into religion with a practical intent. The reformer cannot tame his global perspective. How could that be possible? Must not the religions begin with themselves, individually? Certainly. So do not those who already speak of permeation, enrichment, transformation, understanding and true liberation take on too much? We shall see later that Küng advances this vision to an amazing degree. Having so far engaged in critical discussion with a world church and having been able to visit all the continents, the Swiss citizen who had chosen to live in Tübingen would say no to calls overseas, but gradually be at home in the world.

The atmosphere has changed. First, dialogues lead to more concrete results. Action and reaction clarify problems and show better how far the answers extend. And a burden is taken from the individual speakers. I shall not be discussing here the contributions of the dialogue partners – the Islamist J. van Ess, the Hinduist H. von Stietencron, the Buddhist specialist H. Bechert and the expert in Chinese religion, J. Ching – who engaged in this adventure with Küng. But indisputably their presentations set the tone, formulate the problems and govern the discussion. They have put the bar at the right height for Küng. So they are to be thanked for what Küng subsequently achieves at the second or third attempt: concrete dialogue at the end of which the contributions can no longer be divided. However, this is a dialogue with scholars of religions, and not yet with the religions themselves. To begin with, this limitation can be useful.

(c) River systems

In *On Being a Christian* Küng sought to achieve a first structuring of the world religions. He then introduces the dialogue book on Chinese religions (CCR) with a first systematization: this he does not understand as a static geography of religion but rather as a dynamic typology. Here too, having intensively studied the academic literature, he does not want to add any new content, but to organize what is known in a theologically appropriate way as a basis for further discussion. So he speaks vividly of three great religious river systems. All have their history extending over millennia, and all emerged as reforms from controversy with former religions: they thus have archaic roots and are open to further developments.

The first river system, which is best known and closest to us, is of Semitic origin. It embraces the three Abrahamic religions which have developed in succession in their origins and later side by side: Judaism, Christianity and Islam. Their distinctive feature is their 'prophetic' character (they look towards the future and to a world shaped by justice), their belief in one God and their bond in Abraham as their ancestor. The basic feature of these religions is 'faith' understood as unconditional trust (CCR xiii; Cr 28–30).

The second river system is of Indian origin, with a mystical orientation and focussed on an ultimate unity into which all is taken up. This includes the high religions of India: Jainism and Buddhism up to the more recent Hindu religions.

Finally, the third river system for the evaluation of which Küng argues most resolutely has its origin in China; it has the character of wisdom. Its leading figure is not the prophet or the mystic but the wise man. This system includes Chinese antiquity, Confucianism, Taoism and (once again) Buddhism, as it further developed this sphere of wisdom.

Once again Küng avoids one-sided stylizations. The different forms of religion have influenced one another; they can have exchanges and enrich one another. This is to be presupposed, but then they have to be discussed separately. Rich and varied perspectives emerge. They overlap and, as will emerge later, time and again central perspectives can be gained. In general, against this world-wide horizon the perspectives now become wide and free. The horizon of Christian history, indeed of the Hellenistic sphere, is now transcended almost as a matter of course. The normativeness of the religious currents must be measured against other horizons. The institutional word, indeed the authoritarian and centralistic leader of the community, becomes almost unknown. So we may watch eagerly how a dialogue takes shape which is not between feuding theologians but between the great traditions. Of course it is inappropriate to depict this in black and white. To begin with, everything is friendly and the harsh oppositions perhaps still remain in the shade. Moreover what is beginning here is a dialogue of words, not of everyday practice. But no one will deny that here – at least for European theology – a new beginning is being ventured, the end of which still cannot be seen. In this chapter I shall discuss Küng's dialogue with the Far Eastern religions. I shall go into his discussion with Islam, the first part of the book (CWR 3–132), in the next chapter.

2. Hinduism: the power of the religious

Together with Judaism, Islam belongs to the 'religions of the book' which recognize Abraham as their tribal ancestor. That creates not only common memories and an appeal to the same God, but also comparable mental and perhaps cultural structures: challenges and dangers can be precisely located in common features and differences, compared and discussed in cases of dispute as a dialogue among brothers and sisters. I shall be reporting on this later (see below, 319–25).

It is different in dialogue with remote religions, i.e. in a discussion with the religions of India, which are rich, manifold, historically deep-rooted and stamped by another way of thinking. How is a Christian to respond to them appropriately? Of course here already much depends on the depiction and selection of the religious currents. According to von Stietencron, the Hindu religions are about cosmic order and time, about the world and the self, the one and the many, questions of redemption, of breaking free of actions and their consequences. He discusses questions of rite, myth and meditation. So quite different questions are up for discussion from those in the monotheistic religions, and Küng must immerse himself in another world. This dialogue creates – at first – far less a world of Yes and No, doctrinal assertions and refutations, than a world of philosophical sensitivity and imagination.

(a) The divine and the world

The decisive question for the Western understanding of Hinduism is: what is the relationship between the divine and the world, God and human beings, what we see every day and that invisible which is obviously the heart of all things? Much space is given in the culture of India to talking about human beings, the divine and reality. This is the sphere of myth, stories about the gods and a rich religious practice. Nevertheless, definitions of the relationship between the divine primal ground (Brahman) and the world are indispensable. We touch on a fundamental structure of religious thought generally. The monistic solution of Shankara (Brahman and the world are one) and the dualistic solution of Madhva (Brahman and the world are quite separate) have a home here. Küng inclines towards the 'middle way' of Ramanuja (Brahman and the world are one in distinction), which corresponds to our Western way. In Brahman he recognizes the 'personal' God of the West. For Küng that is no abstract speculation but comparable with the Western discussions of dualism, monism and intermediate solutions, which are important for one who has been to school with Hegel.

Christian theology attributes to 'God a fundamental relationship with the world, and to the world a fundamental participation in the divine being, in the dynamic Being that is God. God is immanent in the world precisely because he transcends the world. The reality of the world is not autonomous, nor is it only apparent, but relative. This is identity in duality (as Ramanuja would have it)' (CWR 206).

At the same time the creation can be seen as an unfolding of God and God himself as the ineffable mystery of this world. So Küng has found a positive starting point which makes a dialogue with this remote religion possible: God as a reality which penetrates and gives life to everything, as pure being, and the world throughout as God's game: 'The world, though it does not play games with God, is to be maintained and governed by him; its own game of chance and necessity may proceed. Human beings, however, are not to be God's toys, but his free partners in the game' (CWR 211). Against this broad cosmic-philosophical background the question now arises of human redemption with reincarnation at the centre. Are we human beings subject to a cycle of ever new birth? That is already an important and very serious question for Küng, because countless millions assent to this answer. For Küng it is a question how, with what principles and with what model the tremendously multi-level nature of human beings can and may be grasped. So he attempts to weigh up arguments and counter-arguments both forward-looking and backward-looking and, without decreeing the truth, formulates the preference that he gives to the Christian answer: whereas the Hindu will attach no importance to uniqueness, the Jewish-Christian view of history will 'emphasize that God has given human beings this portion of time and history as a task for which they must in the end give an "account". In this way, and only in this way, unrepeatable history gets its seriousness, as the place where individuals are put to the test in the presence of God, their merciful judge. Even if Hindus, with their basic concept of the world, can experience both the uniqueness and the continuity of history, we can scarcely exaggerate how far removed their view is from the biblical tradition' (CWR 234).

A comparable caution applies to the circularity or directedness of history and questions of suffering. Even more clearly than with other questions, Küng refers very simply to the fact that another experience has found expression in the Christian message. It is the experience of Jesus' death and acceptance into eternal life.

(b) A fluctuating relationship

Thus in the dialogue with Hindus there is always a fluctuating indecisiveness, a reciprocal report about the different solutions and conceptions. However, this is no longer the case in practice: there the parallels again pile up. Popular Hinduism is matched by popular Catholicism with saints, pious souvenirs and the worship of Mary; the polytheism in Hinduism is clearly orientated on a monotheism, just as Christian monotheism often enough assumes a polytheistic form (CWR 258f.). In both spheres of religion help is provided only by an appeal to a reasonable trust and to an understanding of human needs which are obviously ineradicable. Therefore Küng does not see the fundamental question of his position here either. More reflection is needed on the processes of secularization, which will hopefully lead to a transformation of these religions. It has already been introduced in the neo-Hindu reform movements to which in particular the educated, students and youth are attracted. Gandhi, Ramakrishna, Vivekananda, Aurobindo, Radhakrishna and Tagore are names worthy of our attention.

Küng constructs his answer on a basic tone of broad assent. It is a readiness to understand which at any rate does not exclude other conceptions, but meets them with respect. Thus Küng (and in my view this is a new development in his thought) shows a high respect for 'mythological thought'. The connection between mythical talk and talk about God on the one hand, and between mythical talk and social structures on the other, is indisputable.

'Regardless of whether these "sacred stories" tell about the genesis of the gods or the world, about the salvation of human beings or the world, or about its end – i.e., whether we are dealing with theological or cosmogonic, soteriological or eschatological myths – myth does not try to entertain, as a fairy tale does. It does not try to inform, as a historical report does. The gods of the Hindu pantheon, therefore, should not be made light of, as if they were fantastic figures out of the Grimm brothers; nor should they be objectified as historical personalities. Myth aims to express more original, greater, more important reality, which determines the entire life, work, and destiny of the human race . . . Myth tries . . . to open up this greater reality existentially, and so impart a direction in life, and – through ritual performance – to offer a share in the reality's saving power' (CWR 200).

There is a truth of images and stories; precisely in the age of science and industry there is the 'need for communication by narrative images', and just as according to Küng there are 'different levels and tiers and modes of reality', so he recognizes 'different levels and strata and modes of truth' (CWR 269). Precisely for that reason myths are to be interpreted in a differentiated way. Only now, after this has been sufficiently clarified and the power of Hinduism can be understood, does Küng introduce the dimension of history. That is in fact the difference between Christ and the 'incarnate god' Krishna (CWR 278–91). For Hindus, too, the one God has revealed himself at a particular time. But Jesus is a historical figure, while Krishna is the fusion of different mythical traditions. Jesus is the one in whom God received a human face; by contrast Krishna is one revelation or incarnation of God among many. Thus the figure of Krishna becomes the sign of precisely that cyclical understanding of history which governs Eastern religion (see also Cr 47–9). At this point Western theologians raise questions about history, relationship to reality and the basis of action. For Küng, it is the Sermon on the Mount by this historical figure which should also become significant in the Hindu sphere (CWR 280–2).

This is probably the point at which the agreement becomes a dispute with clear positions. For despite and because of all the need for inculturation and a theology critical of the context, here fundamental questions remain open. This complex system, which commands respect, also has another side. It has infanticide and the burning of widows, early marriage and temple prostitution, ritual mass slaughters and open superstition and magic. What is to be said about that and why do we have the right to criticize such practices? For the first time Küng raises here the question of the criteria of true religion (CWR 272). We shall go into that later.

3. Buddhism: the mystery of the Enlightened One

Here there is a clearer situation than with the fluctuating and always ambiguous comparison with Hinduism. Christians can probably feel more at home in Buddhism than in the Hindu religions. Here there is a reform movement and a founder figure. Certainly Buddha points away from himself to his teaching, but the teaching of Buddha is reliable. Certainly legends and titles have accumulated around Buddha, but much of his history can be reconstructed. Certainly Buddha himself already indicates that his person is extremely unimportant, and his teaching at most has the significance of a current. Nevertheless, time and again the question of precisely who he was and precisely what his teaching was has played and still plays a role. Certainly Buddhism has developed into many currents, but it is time and again worth asking about its beginnings. The doctrine of this Buddha was the occasion for many modifications: from an elite to a mass religion, from the small vehicle to the large vehicle, from a monastic piety to a lay piety. How can an ascetic ideal, with the highest claims, be fulfilled by normal people (working hard, socially weak, married)? What is the significance of sexuality on the way to salvation?

(a) Buddha and Jesus

Question upon question arise which are comparable to those of Christian theology. So we should also note Küng's answers, the degree of intensity with which he goes to work, the extent to which he recognizes the problems of Christian theology and how much this material attracts him. It is as if he too could fall under the spell which the Buddha has exercised since the nineteenth century on many European philosophers and theologians, as if Buddha were the Eastern figure who can challenge Western Christianity in an incomparable way. Küng clarifies this by first of all outlining a 'sketch of the history of the encounter between Christianity and Buddhism' (CWR 306–12) and then raising the question of the historical Buddha – which is fascinating for Christians and comparing this with the figure of Jesus (CWR 311–26).

So who was Buddha? Who is Buddha? These pages read like a

reflection of his works on the figure of Jesus. They begin with some hermeneutical statements.

First of all Küng defines the relationship between experience and interpretation. Of course the inexpressible experience of the mystery itself stands at the centre; nevertheless all experience is already interpreted and therefore can be discussed, with a quite concrete interest which is vital. Dialogue, too, is not without a purpose and may not be without purpose, as will later emerge much more clearly. He explains:

'In the meantime, my experience has been that even members of Buddhist elites – precisely in the interests of world peace – increasingly understand how important it is to exchange not just religious experiences, but the religious teachings implied in them, to have a sense for the theory underlying the practice. Terribly difficult as this is, only through such interweaving of theory and practice, experience and reflection, will we be able to put the dialogue between Buddhists and Christians about the message of the Buddha and the message of Christ – a dialogue that is indispensable for humanity and peace – on a solid foundation. Otherwise, the points of agreement will be obscured by all the differences, or the differences will be obscured by all the points of agreement' (CWR 312f.).

The next issue is the definition of the relationship between cause and person and the need to investigate the 'Buddha of history' (which is infinitely more difficult in the case of Buddha than it is in the case of Jesus). Then at last comes the decisive question which can gain decisive significance for any further dialogue: 'What unites Jesus and Gautama and how do Jesus and Gautama differ?' (CWR 321–6). This is important: in all his conduct Jesus shows more similarity to Gautama than to Muhammad. Both appear as teachers, proclaim good news, want to liberate human beings from their desires and their self-centredness and point out a middle way, of selflessness, of concern for fellow men and women.

That makes the differences all the more significant. Jesus was not a solitary, but a master in an alternative community; no break can be established in his life. The differences can be clarified most plainly by means of the distinction between a prophetic and a mystical spirit.

'The Buddha Gautama is a harmoniously self-contained, peaceful, enlightened guide, inspired by the mystical spirit.
    Sent by no one, he demands renunciation of the will to life for the

sake of redemption from suffering in nirvana. He calls for turning inwards, away from the world inwards, for methodical meditation through the stages of absorption, and so finally to enlightenment.

Thus he shows calm fellow feeling, with no personal involvement, for every sentient creature, man or animal; a universal sympathy and peaceful benevolence.

Jesus Christ, however, is a passionately involved emissary and guide, inspired by the prophetic spirit and, for many, even in his own lifetime, the Anointed One ("Messiah", "Christ").

He calls men and women to conversion for the sake of redemption from guilt and all evil in the kingdom of God. Instead of demanding a renunciation of the will, he appeals directly to the human will, which he bids orientate itself on God's will, itself aimed entirely at the comprehensive welfare, the salvation, of humankind.

Thus he proclaims a personally concerned love, which includes all the suffering, the oppressed, the sick, the guilty and even opponents and enemies: a universal love and active charity' (CWR 324).

This is a key text for Küng and his understanding of both Christianity and Buddhism. It is given prominence at the point indicated and is repeated, with only a little expansion, in Küng's exegesis of the creed (Cr 49-56). But the decisive thing for Küng has not yet been said. It does not lie in the comparison of action and preaching but in the fate which distinguishes the two. On the one hand is the Enlightened One, who at the great age of eighty finally enters Nirvana as a respected teacher peacefully and in the circle of his disciples. Over against him stands the highly tense story which ends prematurely because of a fatal conflict. 'It remained a fragment, a torso. There was, in any event, not a trace of success in his lifetime . . . Jesus was the image of the sufferer pure and simple.' Jesus does not enter history as a calm man but as one who has failed, and who is then taken up into a true life (CWR 325).

(b) Religion without God?

So from the beginning this Christian-Buddhist dialogue has found a marked basis of mutual comparability. It has yet to emerge whether this corresponds only to a Western perspective or also to an Eastern one. Certainly after reading the subsequent reactions one cannot claim that this approach is not fruitful, for now begins an extremely sophisticated argument in which the questions, alternatives and evaluations keep being reflected in the figure of Buddha and in which Christian theology recognizes its own problems, the criticism of inappropriate developments, resistance to reform programmes and the breaks of contextual and cultural transformations. For here too there is a discrepancy between ideal religion and religion as it really lived. There is first of all the question of monasticism and the monastery, an occasion for positive comparisons between the two religions which nevertheless remembers that Jesus did not found any monasticism nor even strive for it as an ideal. That is the great 'paradigm shift from elite religion to mass religion' (CWR 346–60), which finds a striking parallel in the Christian shift in the direction of becoming a popular church. There is the enviable discovery that Buddhism developed a great capacity for toleration.

'There is no room in Buddhism for religious persecutions, crusades, or an Inquisition. Throughout Asia, Buddhism has had a humanizing impact, and the Buddhist centuries in India, China, Japan and Sri Lanka belong to the most brilliant in the history of those nations. On the whole, mystical religions seem to have an easier time with tolerance than do religions in which God's prophetic word demands a decision, provokes a "crisis", and so virtually creates a division between those who listen and those who do not, between the chosen and the not–chosen, and finally between the saved and the damned' (CWR 353).

Here Küng is fond of recalling the history of toleration which is also part of our history and which established itself in an epoch-making way in the religious freedom of the Enlightenment. Küng sees parallels, yet he thinks that the life-style of Jesus can solve the problem of elite and mass better: 'Jesus' radical message (the Sermon on the Mount) can in principle – because it was not designed for monks – be lived out by anyone in everyday life and, for all the visibly un-Christian behaviour going on in Christian countries, it is being so lived out, unobtrusively, by innumerable men and women in the West and the East: people who strive day after day to love and sympathize with their neighbours, to serve others regardless of their status, to forgive without limits, to renounce power or rights without getting anything in return, to put love into practice, indeed to love their enemies. The ideal Christian is simply not the monk' (CWR 357f.).

Finally, for Küng the theologically decisive question is whether Buddhism really is a religion without God or – better – what the foundation for the constant misunderstandings in this question is (CWR

389–98). These pages become a treasure trove of aspects which show how difficult the dialogue can become at precisely this point. For all, or almost all, the words that can be exchanged about 'God' provoke counter-reactions. But at any rate the one solution remains: God as the 'all in all', thus as *the* mystery of reality, towards whom silence is the only appropriate attitude: 'a silence which comes from the negation, on which the East so urgently insists and that is not continually being drowned out by the affirmations, to which the West is undoubtedly inclined.' That would perhaps be a formula about which people could agree (CWR 395).

Precisely because the starting point made comparisons practicable – or seemed to make them practicable – in the past the analysis has shown a bewildering complexity. Objectifying, over-hasty comparisons clearly do not get us very far. Küng therefore argues historically and systematically at the same time, deriving each of the great Buddhist forms of religion, 'from early Buddhism, through the three vehicles, all the way to Zen and Shin' (CWR 413), and warns that one may not play the most important forms of Buddhist religion off against one another.

Thus here too, over broad areas, Küng depicts the exciting history of Buddhism. This emerged as a multiplicity of religious currents, which all nevertheless find their unity in a few starting points. We are imperfect beings, cannot redeem ourselves, and whether man or woman, priest or lay, educated or uneducated, can attain redemption only through another power, indeed – thus the form of Buddhist teaching in the true school of the Pure Land – only by faith. The Pure Land is realized where human beings believe, renounce their own power and recognize that they are not capable of anything by their own efforts. But this too is only one form alongside others. The dialogue is open, its horizons have been sketched, but no results have been achieved; nor has it come to an end.

4. Chinese religions: the integration of human experience

An unexpected dynamic sometimes comes into play in *Christianity and the World Religions*. This dynamic is governed by the growing complexity of the questions to be discussed. As has already been said, a relatively simple, albeit argumentative dialogue can be carried on with Islam, although it, too, already bears witness to a complex internal history and complex forms which make things difficult for us outsiders. Hinduism, with its unimaginably long history and its extreme multiplicity, hardly directed but uncontrolled in its growth, is in any case only a collective term, which is justified only as an outsider's characterization, from a world-wide, macrocontinental perspective. The discussion with Buddhism has shown this intrinsic multiplicity and complexity. Certainly here is a beginning with more clarity and historical profile, but precisely for that reason the breaks, the paradigm changes, seem to have been so far-reaching.

It seems as if this complexity becomes even clearer in the discussion with the river system of Chinese religions. Now the investigation takes up a whole book (CCR, of more than 300 pages), and here Küng's developed methodological awareness becomes evident.

(a) Archaic religion: belief and superstition

Now Küng already reacts in a more fundamental way. He universalizes more quickly, discovers the general problem and attempts general answers, frameworks which indicate the general background to the question. The first part discusses the varied and comprehensive history of the religion of Chinese antiquity. This involves divination and sacrifice, shamanism and monarchy, the ecstatic character of the old religion. Küng reacts: 'religions are grounded in an experiential unity of knowing, willing, and feeling', and religion always understands itself as a response to encounters with and experiences of 'the holy, Heaven, the divine, God, or whatever one calls it' (CCR 33). And he adds: 'archaic religions do not disappear but live on in what today is called folk religion'. Therefore it is not a matter of rejecting but of understanding and transformation, possibly of the inculturation of old customs (ancestor worship), the processes of interiorization and spiritualization (sacrifice). There is also the knowledge that the question of the other dimension of life has to be sought and discovered in often unaccustomed forms of religion. One might think of 'divination', the present-day misunderstanding of which is an indication of a religious and spiritual alienation of our society.

Religion is not just to be understood from above, but also from below; it is always about the well-known primal human needs: protection and help, encouragement and consolation. Küng shows consistently that comparable distinctions were constantly made in the Bible and how this came about, and as a result of a first answer arrives at a fundamental distinction between faith and superstition. Religion does not recognize anything 'as absolute authority that is relative, conditioned, or human, but only the absolute itself, which in our tradition we have called God since time immemorial'. By that Küng means 'that hidden first and last reality that not only Jews and Christians but also Muslims worship – and that Hindus seek in Brahman, Buddhists in the Absolute, and of course traditional Chinese in Heaven or the Tao' (CCR 56f.). Superstition, to put it briefly, makes the relative absolute.

(b) Confucianism: Jesus and K'ung

Confucianism is the second theme. For Küng it becomes the occasion to investigate the image of the historical master K'ung and compare him with Jesus of Nazareth. The two are comparable in origin, way of life and failure. Their message is a response to a social crisis. They gather disciples and live a 'highly individual and personal ethic'. Neither of them can be described as an ascetic, a mystic or a metaphysician. But whereas K'ung's orientation is backwards, Jesus's is forwards. Whereas for K'ung human beings are the centre of interest, for Jesus this is God. A radical anthropocentricity thus stands over against an equally radical theocentricity (CCR 105–10).

The differences come into view even more clearly when a distinction is made between the three great basic types of religion: the prophetic, the mystical and the wisdom form. Thus Jesus, Buddha Gautama and K'ung can be compared with one another: the Enlightened One and the prophet with the teacher who does not proclaim the kingdom of God and does not call for redemption from suffering. K'ung requires a social order and harmony in family and state. His supreme commandment is not love or benevolence, but justice. His love of human beings remains orientated on natural feeling and on the ties of family and nation. It is precisely here that Küng's question begins, namely whether the philanthropy of Confucianism is accompanied by as strong a love of God which if need be also transcends the bonds of family and nation. This would be all the more important, as Confucianism in the present displays a large degree of flexibility.

(c) Taoism: the great corrective

There remains the third stream of Chinese wisdom, which is often presented as an opposite to Confucianism. Whereas Confucianism is regarded as a religion of the successful, Taoism is regarded as a religion of the unsuccessful. Küng prefers another fundamental definition: Taoism is a religion of salvation, 'concerned with redemption from guilt and sin, with prayer and consolation, with long life, indeed with immortality. It is a kind of mystery religion, at first for the initiated, but then also for the masses' (CCR 160). It has retained several levels of Chinese religion: archaic elements from shamanism to sacrificial rites, a religious spirituality, a manifold mysticism and elements of a later folk religion with priests, monks, hermits and a Taoist pope, the 'heavenly master'. As a religion of healing Taoism has developed its own healing art, which sees human beings holistically; in other words, it starts from an indissoluble connection between healing and salvation.

But Küng is most interested in the question of the Tao, the way, or, as one can also call it, last and first reality: history, fate and event in one, time and again explained as a unity and summary of oppositions, in which Yin and Yang, i.e. even good and evil, are united, an intrinsically contradictory God. Really? For Küng it is important to look closely here and note that Tao ('God', if you like) precedes these polar primal forces. It is the origin of the world before all worlds, thus not intrinsically ambivalent, but hidden in its nature from us human beings, with no evident property and in this respect an abyss. Küng sees deep parallels to this in the picture of God in Meister Eckhart or Nicolas of Cusa. So in this thought he discovers a decisive corrective to the Western picture of God which also has its history here, as far as Hegel, in whom the Last Reality dialectically opposes itself and embraces the whole world process.

However, even Taoism cannot do justice to evil in its harshness and the horror in which the twentieth century has experienced it. In the end there remains submission to nature. But because this nature is so transitory and offers so little support, Taoism teaches people not to be tied to it. The solution is anarchy. 'Only not-ruling keeps order in the world' (CCR 189). But precisely at this point Jesus has another solution. For the last time the death of Jesus becomes the great distinguishing mark for Küng (CCR 190) – for Küng himself the great decisive reason for remaining a Christian.

(d) The opportunity for inculturation

It may seem surprising that Julia Ching, Küng's informant on Chinese religion, devotes a quarter of her contribution to Buddhism as an 'alien religion in China'. At the beginning she makes a clear distinction between religions which came to China as the legacy of ethnic minorities (Islam, Judaism, Nestorian Christianity) and those which came with missionary intent (Buddhism and Christianity). But Buddhism had decisive advantages over missionary Christianity: over a long time-span it succeeded in adapting itself. For Küng this approach is an occasion for sketching out in principle some models of encounter which clarify the problem of cultural bridge-building. He mentions (with examples): outward assimilation (Nestorianism), syncretistic mixture (Manichaeism), complementary levels (Matteo Ricci's mission 'from above'), missionary confrontation (the rites dispute in the seventeenth century), cultural imperialism (nineteenth-century mission), the anti-missionary reaction (the twentieth-century rebellions) and contextual inculturation (CCR 233–56). According to Küng, even now religion is still capable of assimilation. So he thinks an inculturated Christianity possible, if it is orientated on biblical faith, adopts authentic present-day China and is understood in the light of practical discipleship.

Küng thinks it possible that such a Christianity can also help towards the renewal of culture in China and ensure that with growing industrialization and secularization the East does not repeat the notorious mistakes of the West. He sees four problem areas which Chinese theology has to face: people and land, religion and ideology, technology and ecology, militarization and power. In the end he is convinced that the figure of Jesus as the crucified can stand at the centre of such faith:

'The Korean theologian Ahn Byung-Mu has presented an impressive version in his exegesis of the Gospel of Mark. Here, Jesus Christ is the man of the *minjung*, of the alienated "people" without power or possessions. He is one of these people; he speaks their language. All his life, he identified with them right up to his violent end. And in his announcement of the coming kingdom of heaven, he ushered in the end of the old world and the creation of a new world. This is a Jesus therefore, who, "together with the suffering *minjung*", fights "at the front of this advent". It is from him that God's will is revealed "in the event of the love of Jesus for the *minjung* and in the identification of Jesus with the *minjung*" ' (Byung-Mu, quoted in CCR 264).

Just as Küng on the one hand hopes for a Chinese theology for post-modernity (CCR 256), so for him a time of change has been reached in which the West, too, can learn from Eastern thought: criticism of a one-sided anthropocentricity and the exploitation of nature, a new sense of a balance between nature, human beings and animals. Of course it is largely 'a matter of the human person and his or her dignity; not the person in isolation but rather the person in his or her being-in-itself and in his or her being-with. At this point the process should be reversed and Eastern thought should be challenged by Western, especially Christian, thought. As everywhere, learning, cross-fertilization and enrichment go hand in hand' (CCR 272).

5. Ways of inter-religious theology

Küng pursued a rapid course in the 1980s: he began to engage in critical dialogue with not just one but at least six great religious systems: Judaism and Islam, Hinduism and Buddhism, Confucianism and Taoism. He not only occupied himself with mountains of literature but made contact with expert colleagues, familiarized himself with English and American research, and repeatedly visited Asian, African and other countries to investigate the religions on the spot. He spoke with theologians, spiritual heads and religious leaders to get a sense of what religions and religion mean in their societies and cultures. He occupied himself with the political and economic situation of different cultural spheres in order to get a sense of the interaction between religion and society.

The books discussed amount to a first round. But despite all the intensity, this can be no more than a first encounter to gain information and, as Küng says, self-confidence. Still, it already penetrates deep into the discussion, makes exemplary advances and develops first profiles of dialogue. This is new ground. At one point Küng continues his theological style. He is not engaged in detailed research into religion but in developing theological syntheses. Here is the beginning of work on a comprehensive history of the religions, which involves two things: a comprehensive stocktaking of the world religions from an explicitly Christian theological perspective and at the same time a test for Küng's own theological scheme at the beginning of this dialogue. It will soon emerge that Küng is not beginning with a clean sheet. On the contrary, he is in fact continuing his previous work. His methods and results so far have proved themselves. His scheme for a theology which is historically responsible and therefore capable of dialogue is now paying off. Moreover he is not entering the discussion as a novice, but as a theologian who has already set down criteria in the dialogue within Catholicism and within Christianity in difficult circumstances. He has great experience in the art of firmly outlining his own position and at the same time keeping it open for dialogue. Küng's dialogues have always taken place on the foundation of a clarity which makes openness possible.

At the end of this survey, six characteristics have emerged which can be regarded as ways for an inter-religious theology. They are enumerated here without any claim to completeness and illustrated by examples from both dialogue books. Here I shall also refer to the part of *Christianity and the World Religions* which deals with Islam (CWR 1–132) and which I shall only be describing later.

(a) Research and noting facts

Küng never reacts directly and naively to his dialogue partners or simply to their accounts. He has more stamina. He studies research and orientates himself on it. He knows standard works and research trends, the critical points of dispute, sometimes specialist investigations. He also knows the history of relations between the church (Christianity, Europe) and the religions. So he keeps inserting information into his answers, making it more precise and interpreting it in terms of his questions. As already in *The Church,* he mentions the history of Christian guilt over against other religions and cultures. He shows the cultural or power-political background to failed encounters: they are systematized as an instructive warning (CCR 233–55). This knowledge may sometimes hold up the argument, but it gives it more depth and stability.

This is a formal perspective, but in view of the multiplicity and mass of material and also in view of the tendency to pass sweeping judgments on highly complex questions it should not be forgotten. It may be mentioned just briefly here that Küng often succeeds in giving lessons on history. Often the lines point into the open, to undisclosed sources or suppressed memories, to possible interpretations or a gap in research. Thus the dialogue does not become an edifying and finished treatise but the beginning of an exciting voyage of discovery which can be shared, through worlds of discourse about God and dealing with God.

(b) Standing up for the religions

Where he can, Küng stands up for the central concern of religions. That presupposes self-confidence and certainty in judgments. Such passages are among the high points of the internal drama and challenge the verdict of Christian theology. That is the case, for example, with the prophetic legitimacy of Muhammad and the Jewish-Christian memories which are taken up and surpassed in Islam. It is the case with the defini-tion of the relationship between Brahman and the world in Hinduism and the retrieval of the honour of mythical language in the religions, and also with the notion of reincarnation. One is spellbound by Küng's evaluation of the figure of Buddha Gautama, and theologians wake up when mention is made of the tensions with which Buddhism sees itself confronted: between history and interpretation, the ideal and its realization, between elite and mass religion, between original memories and later contextualization, in the face of the paradigm shifts which take place in this great system.

When Küng discusses the elements of archaic religion in China and compares them with their fate in Jewish religion, one understands and sympathizes: an attempt is made to overcome ancestor worship, divination and sacrificial practices, yet they remain present, however spiritualized and hidden. One would have expected a more thorough evaluation only in the case of shamanism and ecstasy. By contrast, one can hardly avoid the definition of superstition and the obvious fact that it simply cannot be exterminated. We hear only a little of the radical humanism of Master K'ung, with its focus on justice, but the lines of Küng's analysis are razor-sharp because of his urgent interest in such questions. At the same time Küng considers the fascination which Tao, the holistic picture of human beings in Taoism and its polar thinking exercises on us, not to mention the anarchism of Lao-tse and his refusal to be seduced by the charm of the world.

So Küng is never tempted to become a Muslim, Hindu, Buddhist, Confucian or Taoist, but he makes Christianity a strong partner in the field of force of a multiple truth. Christians must be curious and ready to learn if they consider the drift of these sections. Only against such a background can they give themselves an appropriate profile and at the same time become aware of their own limitations. But whether these are limitations or advantages, any absolute Yes or categorical No loses its point; what is left is the invitation to a mutual respect nurtured by the cause. Here an atmosphere of dialogue is achieved which elsewhere is only called for morally and practised as a matter of duty.

(c) Understanding the religions in context

Küng attempts to understand the religions in terms of their inner connections. This point is closely connected with the previous one. I already explained at an early stage that over the years Küng had accustomed himself to a style of thought which was hermeneutical, i.e. understanding and harmonious; which affirmed and at the same time differentiated. It was above all his exegetical and historical efforts, the questions of the significance and role of Jesus of Nazareth, which brought him to that. Only the dogmatic questions of the 1970s indicate how alien an unhistorical dogmatism had meanwhile become to him. What was by now a natural way of thinking also proved itself. Isolated facts and actions mean as little as sweeping verdicts or comprehensive descriptions. Küng goes into the deep interconnections; one does justice to the multiplicity, perhaps also the contradictoriness of a religion, only by a holistic approach. But that calls for an effort to appropriate it.

Given his criticism of Christianity, it may be easiest for him to achieve success in his dialogue with Islam. It is much more difficult to deal, say, with the doctrine of rebirth in Hinduism, with the nirvana of Buddhism or the question how meditation leads to the experience of the ineffable. Küng prompts question after question, on which he dwells and reflects. Often he shows a hypothetical, as it were transitory, involvement in other notions, when for example he describes the religious achievement of Muhammad in his world or the criticism of the law within Islam or the problem of the success of Islam. Here – one of the high points of that dialogue – there is a great agreement between the partners in dialogue. Thus van Ess says almost as though he were Küng: 'It seems to me that Islam's weakness lies just where its strength lies: in its success. For that reason the awareness Muslims have of their own orthodoxy is tied in with expectations of worldly glory. "The church beneath the cross" is barely conceivable in Muslim categories.' Is that still sharing in the other's complex of meaning? Yes, it seems to me, because a last sentence follows with a gentle way out: 'To balance things, we should discuss the weakness of Christianity. But I leave that to Christian readers. Perhaps Islam can be of help in recognizing the weak point(s) of their faith. In that sense it may be a real alternative' (CWR 107f.). That ends the lecture by the Islamicist, and Küng picks up what has been said without correcting it, now to arrive at an opposite self-critical result, namely that Islam has preserved an important phenomenon about Jesus (see below, 321f.) The fronts have imperceptibly changed. Thus understanding grows. Küng's statement about the truth of the other and one's own error (see above, 58f., SC 352f.) becomes concrete.

It is incomparably more important in the case of the Far Eastern religions to immerse oneself to their complexes of meaning and first of all – quite simply – surrender to their attraction. As Küng says of the world of Hindu religions: 'No one would deny the fascination of the infinite variety, complexity, colour and vitality of Indian religions, which appeal simultaneously to our intellect, imagination and senses' (CWR 160). Küng later asks what mystical experience is. He attempts to describe it, independently of Hinduism, and devotes a good ten pages to the question, after which he goes into the difference between mystical and prophetic religion (CWR 174–8), resolving it in such a way that the two forms of religion get their due. Here too he takes up a complex of meaning which must be clarified before individual questions are debated.

The examples can be continued: what can redemption mean in Christianity and in India (CW 225f.), what is worldly piety (CWR 227f.)? How do a circular and a linear picture of history interact (CWR 237f.)? How can the phenomenon of polytheism be understood properly and what lies behind popular piety (CWR 258ff.)? How is monasticism to be understood as a universal religious phenomenon (CWR 343f.) and what happens in the transition from a mass religion to an elite religion (CWR 346f.)?

What Küng here breaks up into countless individual questions is not meant to serve as a definition. He hammers home no firm answers, but blurs them, indicates connections. Here it becomes evident that there are two kind types of connection. Some connections are related and limited to a particular culture; others – and Küng is intensely interested in these – create inter-religious lines of understanding. Thus a dialogue profile gradually develops, a network of comparisons and references. There are structures and tendencies which are comparable here and there, sometimes more and sometimes less. Küng does not need to keep stressing this, because it is constantly evident that however different religions are, they are all in the same boat, whether we call that the world, cosmos or human nature, hope or trust, the longing for a comprehensive understanding or a relativization of all that passes away. It would be attractive and probably not difficult to extract a phenomenology of religion from these books, which have not come into being as an abstract construction but from concrete grappling with the questions indicated above.

(d) Detecting structural similarities

There is probably no religion which does not have current problems, dangerous developments and internal contradictions. As a rule they are played down by insiders and exaggerated by outsiders. Küng does not play them down either way. Precisely in these problems all religions are similar. So he has developed a sense for discovering structural similarities between Christianity and the church and other religions; reference is repeatedly made to this. It is to Küng's enormous advantage that he has already expressed his criticism of the church and Christianity often, laid the foundation for it in many studies, and has not given way even in difficult situations, but tested it in a dispute with those concerned. After 1980 he can speak with great credibility and also in a relaxed way without short-term concerns, to the advantage of all the religions discussed.

(i) No compulsion to self-defence (Islam)

This has interesting consequences for the dialogue about and with other religions: Küng is above the compulsion to defend his own church or religion, therefore his loyalty to Christianity seems more credible than ever. It does not exclude loyalty to other religions, to faith and religious practice, in whatever form. At no point, regardless of his Christian conviction, does he need to reserve a moral, institutional or even divine claim to truth for the institutions and practices of his own religion.

> 'The boundary between true and false today, even as Christians see it, no longer runs simply between Christianity and the other religions, but at least in part within each of the religions. The principle here is that nothing of value in the other religions is to be denied, nor is anything of no value to be uncritically accepted . . . We need a dialogue with give and take, into which the deepest intentions of the religions must be introduced' (CWR xix).

This is an important step towards the 'presentation of Christianity in the light of the world religions' which Küng plans (CWR xx). Thus many analyses of the other religions become a reflection of Küng's own religion.

Here are some examples. There are the doctrines of inspiration which sought to get the Bible or the Qur'an out of any crisis, and the vigorous reactions against any beginnings of historical criticism of the Bible or the Qur'an (CWR 33–6). In both instances a mediaeval paradigm which resists processes of secularization by every means is still at work (CWR 54–7). The programme of re-Islamicization is compared with a possible campaign of re-Christianization (CWR 61). Finally the virulent problem of legalism emerges in all religions (CWR 62). Like the 'outside the church no salvation', so too the 'outside the Umma no salvation' needs to be corrected (CWR 89). Finally, criticism of the Islamic picture of women is immediately followed by critical questions about Christian practice: 'Christianity has scarcely any reason for pride in its historical record in liberating women.' 'For Christians, this means that they ought not to boast too much of their moral superiority here' (CWR 84f.).

The same is true in discussions with the Eastern religions. There contradictions and abiding questions are discovered at still deeper levels. Mystical experiences which are not contradictory cannot be discovered in cultural areas stamped either by Hinduism or by Christianity:

> 'One can and must reflect on them, but they cannot be simply removed, like some superimposed screen or railing, so that a "pure" mystical experience is left. There is no method for extracting "pure" mysticism from all explanatory structures, just as no "pure" crystal can be extracted which has no crystal structures. Even if we appeal to an individual experience to justify such a claim, it is a dogmatic, illegitimately generalizing line of argument to assume the existence of a pure, uniform, universal mystical experience, monistic or otherwise. Those who do, forget that they make this sort of assertion on the strength of their own monistic (or non-monistic) predisposition' (CWR 173).

In such a consistent strategy of interdependence and quest for a common basis for dialogue it is no longer surprising that even in the most fundamental questions, which seemed to us Christians to have been resolved clearly, Küng compares the answers and leaves them in the air. Just as in India one cannot just speak of a monism, as if the world and the divine fell apart, so too Christian thought cannot simply be reduced to the formula of a dual relationship. No, the positions are more interlocked. As we saw, in India Küng discovers at least three solutions. In the West a complicated interplay of forces has developed. There are clear and strong monistic tendencies, and a climate of mystical religion which has constantly found expression. At the same time the prophetic character of biblical religion has had a dualistic effect:

> '. . . trends towards placing an extraordinary stress on opposition between God and Satan, God and the world. Along with this usually went the conflict between spirit and matter, soul and body, good and evil, light and darkness' (CWR 204).

Greek philosophy tended towards a similar dualism, but one could not claim that for Christianity as a whole. From the beginning Christian theology reacted against the dualism of classical Greek metaphysics. So the notion of the creation of the world by God does not just have a dualistic but a contrary tendency. This very idea 'did not allow the world, matter, the body to be devalued *a priori*'. 'According to the biblical account of creation, the world in general and in particular, including matter, the human body and sexuality – is fundamentally good' (CWR 205). In this question, too, which often enough is discussed as the decisive difference between West and East, there are therefore comparisons, permeations, open questions. Küng even attempts to mediate over the question whether God is personal or not, though this had already been prepared for at length at an earlier stage (DGE 631–5).

(ii) Religions of redemption (Hinduism)

This is also the context of the decisiveness with which Küng calls Christianity and the Hindu religions religions of redemption and recognizes three ways of salvation for each of them: the ways of action, knowledge and surrender (Karma margha, Jnana margha and Bhakti margha); these can be compared to the basic Catholic, Protestant and Greek Orthodox forms of Christianity. But as soon as he states this comparison, of course he also knows what the reaction must be. It is all far more complicated!

In fact, according to Küng,

'Just as, in India, these three ways are bound up with each other in a complex system, so we find a similar pattern in Christianity, where in each of these Christian confessions the believer can (though with different emphases) draw upon a complex combination of knowledge, activity and devotion. And so the intellectual, practical, and emotional factors are in continual interplay.'

And that is not to mention the well-known way of the monkey and the way of the cat, the basic activities of passiveness and activity, which does not let religion – as in Buddhism – become monkish (CWR 227).

Küng insists very stubbornly on the comparability of religions, even over the question of incarnation, where he at least holds firm to a binding presupposition: 'Just because Christianity and Hinduism start from different anthropological presuppositions, there need not be conflict between them' (CWR 231). Hinduism and Christianity begin from a spiritual element in human beings, from two or even three principles in all. Only when that has been made clear can the discussion begin, though Küng makes his own (Christian) decision in it.

Of course the Catholic Küng is in his element when the multiplicity of the rites and customs of 'popular Hinduism' are discussed: the echo of this is 'popular Catholicism', which he treats sympathetically.

> 'In Hindu-Christian dialogue, therefore, it would be silly to play the purist, theoretically ignoring and denying practices that have been accumulating for centuries, that have blended into the fabric of Christianity, have been lived by millions of Christians and so in any event – whether one deplores it or not – now belong to the phenotype of Christianity. In a phenomenology of religion equally applicable to Hinduism and Christianity, all this would have to be critically analysed' (CWR 260).

> 'Consider medieval-Baroque popular Catholicism, which has survived to the present day, often on something like religious reservations, with its many churches and chapels, roadside shrines and ways of the cross, all its countless pictures and statues (sometimes decorated), all its candles, flowers, aromatic incense, holy water and music. Christian Europe, too, has its patron saints, votive tablets, dashboard amulets, and every sort of religious sign. In the West also there are sacred seasons and holy days; great popular festivals celebrated at home, in church, and on the streets; processions, parades, etc., day and night, all year long. Christianity has its great pilgrimages, with millions of pilgrims, many of them old and sick, with countless priests and beggars, brightly painted plaster statues, amulets, religious objets d'art and souvenirs, art and kitsch in every shape and size. Everyone can be caught up in the joy of the feast and feel part of the great community of the faithful when the saint, in the form of a picture or statue, is received and greeted like a god, carried through the streets, and accompanied back home. Not to mention the myriad patterns of devotion to Mary' (CWR 258f.)

Just as in Hinduism myths are not to be taken literally, so too they must not be eliminated from Christianity.

> 'Should that happen, the religious community would be depopulated, and the spiritual vacuum it had itself created would become suscep- tible to remythicization. If the mythical element is simply eliminated, it will be at the expense of religious content, which thus reduces faith to a sort of pious rationalism' (CWR 270f.).

I suggest that without the systematic discussion with other religions and the associated question of what religion and religious feeling really is and means, Küng could never have found his way to this open, relaxed and understanding discussion. The former programme of reform, the constant call towards the centre, the constant misuse of popular religion for populist aims, did not allow this openness. So Küng himself practises in advance what is one of his goals in this exercise: insight into the relationship with the context and what can be said within it. It is with good reason that in this question Küng singles out the question of inculturation and critical contextual theology as a topic (CWR 283f.).

(iii) Renouncing the world (Buddhism)

Buddhism calls for confrontation at another, perhaps more intellectual, level. This has already been discussed. A burning question for Christians, to which Küng has deeply committed himself, recurs in the encounter with Buddhism: how do we relate later development and change in cultural and social contexts, in the shift of paradigms, to a normative origin? Later, in a way comparable to his analyses of Christianity (see below, 308–19), in Buddhism, alongside an origin Küng will establish six paradigms in all, 'turnings of the wheel' (Brück 18), which keep relating to their beginning. It seems to me that Christian theology could also study the 'Buddha of history' here in order to rediscover the quest for the 'Jesus of history'. For that very reason a 'Christian' study of Buddhism is worthwhile:

'In principle, the parallel holds: just as for Christianity as it is actually lived out, a radical critique must always mean a confrontation with the concrete Jesus of Nazareth, with his life and teaching, so the confrontation of Buddhism in the Theravada countries as it is actually lived out with the Gautama of history, his teachings and practices, would have to be nothing less than a radical critique that could be an occasion for self-appraisal and a radical change in one's life' (CWR 357).

But that is not the only aspect which interests us. Küng goes into the 'tension between monastic and lay existence' (CWR 356) and the far more urgent question how a religion creates the transition from a form which is critical of the world to a form which affirms the world. In other words, he asks what can be said from the Buddhist side about the 'Constantinian shift'. Here too new tones emerge, more understandable and more conciliatory than have been found hitherto in Küng. The decisive mediation then takes place from an unexpected standpoint, a climax of the comparative and interlocking discussion. This happens in those very dense passages, differentiated and at the same time showing respect in the argument, in which the anthropology of Theravada Buddhism is discussed. Küng begins from the doctrine of 'selflessness', the human 'not-I', and attempts mediations by the rediscovery of a relational understanding of the person. So the reality of the human person does not consist in being an individual. Rather, it is radically, essentially and firmly related to the other self and to all reality (P.F. Knitter, quoted in CWR 381).

The statements clearly cannot be understood precisely without taking precise note of their contexts. A self (thus Luis Gomez) that does not change, that has things, ideas, feelings, clearly does not exist. But a self that is in flux, accessible to constant guidance and transformation, does (CWR 382). Along with contributions from experts, Küng shows how little this conviction – whether analysed in Western or Eastern terms – can be reduced to a literal and clear definition of existence and non-existence, of self and not-self, of I and not-I. Only then (in company with Kant, the critic of metaphysics), does he resort to an ethical argument.

> 'Should not Buddhist thinkers, as they critically assess their own and alien traditions, attempt more clearly than before to establish an anthropology centred upon human dignity (which the Buddha himself deeply respected)? Buddhists are fully aware that human beings can be adequately understood only as conditioned in every way, as relational beings within the totality of life and the cosmos. But should they not reflect more earnestly, especially in an ethical vein, on the problems of the unique, inviolable, non-interchangeable human self, with its roots in the past and its future destiny?' (CWR 384).

This seems to me a prime example of the way in which Küng takes up a problem as a problem of his own tradition, learns to understand it from within, and precisely for that reason may add a proposal without immediately emerging as someone who knows best: the prime example of a dialogue which is open and at the same time decisive, which presupposes not only empathy but also analysis and thought.

(iv) A comparable religious ethos (Chinese religions)

In the dialogue with Chinese religions, the later of the two books, the appropriation is methodologically tauter. Küng consistently compares historical process with developments in the history of Israel, Jesus and the early church: in the spiritualization of sacrifice (CCR 39–41), in divination (CCR 43f.), the protest against wisdom (CCR 168–71) and the fusion of the names of God (CCR 99f.). He brings to a more profound level what has already been discussed in *Christianity and the World Religions*: the origin and significance of folk religion (CCR 46–53), the problem of rites, salvation and mysticism (CCR 159–67), the manifold ways of inter-religious encounter (CCR 252–68); and finally he points to a striking parallel in intellectual history which is clearly typical. This is the neo-Confucianism in tenth-century China and Catholic scholasticism, both evidently 'mediaeval' phenomena (CCR 181–4).

In other respects, it seems to me that Küng goes a step further here. This is a step towards a phenomenology with an inter-religious motivation. It is a response which not only shares in thought, relates and attempts to appropriate hermeneutically, but also itself develops the framework of reference in which we can then order, think and analyse. That happens with the phenomena of folk religion (CCR 46–53) and superstition (CCR 55–7), the ambivalence of the world (CCR 201–6) and a radical humanity (CCR 114–16), of a holistic anthropology (CCR 163–7) and the provocation of the negative (CCR 184–7), indeed ultimately of the great programme of an inculturation within the framework of a contextual theology (CC 252–68). Thus at the end of the development not only are comparable statements made and criticism is seen as self-criticism, but a framework has been created in which this exchange in dialogue is possible and can be realized.

6. Relational fields of inter-religious theology

Ways or strategies have resulted from the analysis of Küng's texts on which an inter-religious way of thinking develops. He takes note of research and facts, stands up for the non-Christian religions, understands them as comprehensive collections of meaning, and traces binding structures of similarity. This enumeration makes no claim to completeness, nor has Küng himself made this claim. The same can be said of the question what he sees as the decisive fields of inter-religious

theology. Here too I am stating my own views, and not Küng's programme. Three key words emerge: God, origin and present. The logic
can easily be seen. Every religion lives from a relationship to 'God' or
an 'ultimate reality'; every religion relates to an origin or at least to
texts which were regarded as original; and every religion is constantly
related to a present which keeps changing and therefore makes the
religion change.

(a) The question of God

Küng would not be a flesh-and-blood theologian, and he would deny his
own past, did he not always and emphatically focus on the central
question: in a religion, who or what is God, the divine, or what is it in
this religion which is comparable to our talk of 'God'? So on the
question of God his concern is for a differentiated and differentiating
clarity. This is matched by the question of a trusting faith, which also
embraces suffering and failure. Each time the core concern of each
religion emerges for him from here.

Again proximity and remoteness make themselves felt. The dialogue
with Islam is intrinsically easy, but a well-known and clearly defined
problem gets in the way of clarifying it:

> 'In confronting pagan polytheism, Judaism, Christianity and Islam
> are just as united as they are against modern gods of every sort that
> threaten to enslave humanity. Long before Islam, in fact, Judaism and
> then Christianity overthrew the old gods of the pantheon.'

It is the common faith in one historical, merciful and gracious God, a
God who can be addressed (CWR 86).

Küng has already engaged in the specific discussion of God's Son and
a threefold God which is to be supported on the basis of the Bible. He
makes a longer approach to the Hindu religions. Strictly speaking,
the question is talk of God: this – in a way similar to Greece in the
threshold period – is mythical and philosophical at the same time, in
both instances fluctuating between the unity and the difference between
the divine and the world (see above, 243f.). At this point earlier
thoughts crystallize more clearly as a basis for dialogue. Küng discovers
a God who is beyond in the midst of our life (Bonhoeffer), a God who
while immanent in the world is over the world (CWR 207).

God is,

'as the bearer, maintainer and companion of the world, simultaneously the depth, the centre and the height – all images! – of the world and humankind. Precisely because God is like this, he can justly be called the creator, sustainer and completer of the world. That is why Christian thinkers have understood God's creative nature as his vitality and the power of his being, as the fullness of his self-giving to the other, the world. Christians see this process, in the deepest sense, as love' (CWR 207).

Thus the world can be understood as the creation and at the same time as the development of God, as the 'omnipresent, ineffable, mystery of this world' (CWR 207).

The dialogue with Buddhism – which is often said to be theistic – is more difficult to shape, since in fact the term 'God' is so to speak prohibited in Buddhism: it is thought to be manifestly a projection and an illusion, and taboo in the face of flourishing Hinduism with its unbounded fantasy (Abe, NHFT 306–25). Küng recognizes the problem, but contradicts his Buddhist colleague when he interprets the 'kenosis' of Christ in the light of the same impulse (ibid.). Küng asks whether 'God' is not to be found under other names. Now in 'emptiness' the deepest reality of the Absolute is recognized at the highest mystical level. The same is true (according to the way in which it is understood in Mahayana Buddhism) of the supremely filled concept of nirvana and finally of dharma, the eternal truth of salvation which can save people in this transitory world (CWR 391f.; cf. GE 62f., see below, 335f.). Küng's suggested interpretation, which later he will only extend in insignificant ways, runs:

'If God is truly the Absolute, then he is all these things in one:
nirvana, in so far as he is the goal of the way of salvation;
dharma, in so far as he is the law that shapes the cosmos and humanity;
emptiness, in so far as he for ever eludes all affirmative determinations;
and the primal Buddha, in so far as he is the origin of everything that exists' (CWR 392f.).

Of course this calls for intensive reflection. Küng by no means regards the question as answered, let alone solved. He points out that many modern individual interpretations must also be taken into account. Above all he wants to avoid Buddhism thus being commandeered for a

Christian understanding of God. No, he recalls the contrary: Christian theology has no right simply to deny such an interpretation. Therefore he adds that (this) God may not in any event be understood anthropomorphically as a person. But here the problems of thinking begin which force all discourse to a limit.

Küng follows the dialectical steps of Nagarjuna and disputes 1. that the Absolute is personal, 2. that it is simply apersonal, 3. that it is both in one, and 4. that it is neither. Compelling arguments can be advanced for any step in thought. Anyone who takes all four steps seriously must keep silent. God is quite simply the mystery of this reality (CWR 399). If Küng then decides for the 'limit concept' of 'transpersonal', this is so as not to have to remain in sheer silence but at least to mention the reason for our silence.

Is that a solution for Küng? It is not meant to be more than a bridge, and as far as he is concerned an appeal that in the West, at least, respect for the ineffable should be taken more seriously and the limits of our thought be perceived. However, he also maintains the experience of the prophetic religions. It is not as if they could say more about God, but:

'Where others only heard an infinite silence, the Jewish, Christian and Islamic scriptures tell of a people being addressed and claimed by its God. Where others experienced unechoing space and the void, this people was allowed to discover for itself and others that the Absolute can be heard and spoken to, that it is a mysteriously communicative and responsive Thou' (CWR 398).

Here possibilities and limits of understanding are sounded out, but the dialogue is opened up to sharing thought and following it through.

Once again – after the extreme challenge of Buddhism – the theme is taken up in connection with Chinese religions. Popular belief knows myths and practices, magic and often enough superstition. Here it is important for unconditional trust to be given only to the real Absolute. Thus 'God', understood anthropologically (and with biblical legitimation), would be that authority and person which deserves unconditional trust. The specific question which arises in China is that of the opposites (the different names in Confucianism, CCR 99f.) and their possible unity. 'Tao' is the way, an unfathomable reality, from which the world and human beings arise and to which they return (CCR 173f.), but at the same time a reality which quite manifestly is thought of in opposites or on the basis of opposites. Küng also attempts to reflect on this approach in comparison with Western traditions, with Hegel,

Goethe, Böhme and Jung. Is it all up with the old saying which calls for ultimate trust? Can it really be said that no one can be against God but God himself (CCR 175)? No, for Küng it is also clear from Taoist texts that 'God' precedes the opposing fundamental forces, so that Taoism, which thinks in opposites, no longer has any category for this. Küng also agrees with Chinese thinkers in interpreting this finding as the hidden being of God. However, in contrast to Confucianism, which tends towards harmony in the world, he makes sure that the negative element of this world is not forgotten. This problem is no longer resolved in the image of God. I shall be returning to this later.

So here questions remain open. But what holds for all the religions discussed also holds here: Christians do not have the right to deny any religion the utmost seriousness and profoundest experience in the question of God (Brahman, the emptiness, heaven or Tao). What Christians have to learn from such dialogue is that they speak too quickly and too easily of 'God' the inexpressible, and that they are not aware of the limits of thought and language.

(b) The origin – in Jesus?

Küng develops a theology of the religions, but he develops it as a Christian theologian. That may sound astonishing and has led to discussions (I shall be coming back to them later). Thus, as he expects every religion to understand itself in terms of its origins, dialogue with other religions resolutely leads him back to the Christian starting point. This is not the place to discuss the problems which arise in all religions in connection with the question of their origin. But the world religions have canonical texts. However, it has already become clear how important the canonical, i.e. normative, texts are for Küng's criteriology. In contrast to other religions, for us they bear witness to a person, Jesus of Nazareth, who constantly becomes the criterion in Christian discipleship. In this, too, Küng takes the dialogue of religions seriously.

Therefore for Küng, the cornerstone of a critical discussion is the question of the Jesus of history, as he has interpreted and understood him – above all in *On Being a Christian*. We cannot go into this more deeply in theoretical terms. Rather, I would point to an amazing phenomenon. The appeal to the Jesus of history in particular does not narrow Küng's argument to a narrow pedantry or a sense that Christians are in the right. On the contrary, wherever the figure of Jesus appears in the texts, it gives surprising and refreshing turns to the discussions. The question arises: how does it come about that Küng the systematic theologian, with his very clear and well-defined views about Jesus – though these have developed over the years in intensive studies – can deal so openly with the many world religions to the point of forgetting himself, follow their thoughts and derive these positive aspects from them? How can he not only accept these religions but endorse them from within, even present them as a challenge to Christian religion without denying his own positions?

My guess is that the secret lies precisely in the key function which he gives to Jesus of Nazareth in the understanding of Christian faith. We should remember that in defining what is Christian Küng breaks out of doctrinal definitions. The specific element of Christian faith is this Jesus himself, and the specific element of Christian action is becoming his disciple. Küng does not concentrate on an 'essence' of Christianity which would have to be understood as a static and self-contained definition. He looks for the 'specific', i.e. historical and relational, definition which does not exclude other things but relates to them. Now if this special feature is a (historical) person, the definition draws all that is to be said about God, faith, goodness and the world, creation and religion into historical, personal, practical relations. If the specific feature of Christianity is a person, then all texts, doctrines and practices have to be relativized in terms of this person.

So it is not surprising that Küng is particularly successful in those definitions of relationship in which he can compare persons. He can also depict most coherently the internal problems of those religions which in whatever way relate most closely to the doctrine and life of a person. This comparison may be most difficult to achieve in the case of Jesus and Muhammad. There for internal reasons Küng sees the question more as being one of how Muslims regard Jesus and how Christians regard Muhammad. Muhammad does not seek any position in Islam comparable to the position of Jesus in Christianity, nor should he have it. Here a specific problem of monotheism is worked on. But according to Küng another specific feature of the figure of Jesus, also against Islam, is his failure, his involvement with suffering and death, to which Islam is remarkably closed (CWR 122–7).

The comparison in Hinduism does not produce much, since no historical event is taken up and surpassed in Krishna, the incarnation of the divine. Thus this figure cannot serve as the illustration of an action, as the symbol of a practice, as the report of a concrete event. Only indirectly does it become clear what are the different axes on which these religions turn and how asymmetrical is the relationship between them (CWR 225–8).

The comparison between Jesus and Gautama is the best and most successful. It is so illuminating for Küng that he takes it over in his explanation of the creed (Buddha in a book on the Christian creed!). It is in his passion, his prophetic will, his active love and his failure – taken up by God – that Jesus differs from the great Enlightened One (CWR 321–5, see 247f. above).

There remain two figures from the Chinese sphere who can be compared with Jesus. These are Confucius (Master K'ung [!]) and Lao-Tzu. As we saw, in Confucius the perspective is backward-looking rather than forward-looking, and an anthropocentricity (with a religious direction) stands over against a radical theocentricity (with a human orientation)(CCR 110–16). One could also say that here a prophetic and a wisdom religion are realized in an overpowering way. The great educator stands over against the great proclaimer of the kingdom of God. Finally, the comparison with Lao-Tzu, the drop-out and man of the poor people, who can only laugh at what the world has to offer (CCR 189f.), is fascinating. Küng quotes Bloch: 'If instead of the three wise men, Confucius, Lao-tzu and the Buddha had come out of the East to the manger, then only Lao-tzu would have noticed the insignificance of the mightiest, although he would not have prayed to him' (CCR 192).

So is one practice being compared with another? For Küng another aspect which has become deeper as a result of his dialogue with the religions plays a role. Precisely where the comparison of practices is symmetrical, it is not questions of message and action which become relevant, but Jesus' suffering and death. This fate in particular shapes Christian origins. This premature and violent death is a price which only one of these 'greats' had to pay and which decisively determines not only the piety and action but also the image of God in Christian religion:

If Islam took the message of Jesus seriously, it could learn to relativize the law and to see 'that Jesus' life, death, and new life gives us a new and deeper understanding of God as one who loves and has compassion for humanity. That Jesus' death offers us a fresh source of meaning, in the name of this God, however meaningless our suffering and failure may appear to be' (CWR 128).

This example makes it clear that this Christian contribution to the religious world dialogue is not suitable for controversy but for being an offer and a recognition which Christians contribute from their own tradition and can convey to others.

The same is true of the dialogue with Hinduism. There Küng sees the real offer of Christianity not in all kinds of speculations or new theories of salvation but – here too – in reference to the Jesus of the Sermon on the Mount and the way of the cross. Salvation is offered particularly to the poor and outcast. Here the one who interceded for the poor and the despised in practice was consistently non-violent. Gandhi was not the only one to be impressed by him (CWR 280–2). This dialogue, too, is not about corrections to content but about unexpected aspects of action, and according to Küng finally again about a love which 'goes all the way into the negativity of suffering, abandonment, dying, the cross' (CWR 282). Thus Christianity does not offer a new and better teaching but an experience confirmed by God which is also possible elsewhere, but which does not shine out more clearly anywhere than in Jesus of Nazareth.

The same is true of the Enlightened One who departed laughing into nirvana and to whose religion the practice of an elite religion is always attached. Jesus also stands in a remarkable contrast to Buddha as 'the one who suffered, was killed, was crucified', but was taken up into eternal life (CWR 326).

Over against Confucianism, the words and practice of Jesus can clarify how much this ideal of human love is orientated on 'natural feeling and family and national ties' (CWR 118). Jesus breaks apart these very limitations. For him 'every human being – as in the parable of the Good Samaritan – can become the neighbour, can become my neighbour', even my rival, adversary, enemy. Here according to Küng, is 'the decisive point of theological controversy between Christianity and Confucianism. It is the understanding of God to which corresponds an understanding of the human person. This love makes it possible for people to feel that they are the sons and daughters of God, not only within the confines of the family, the clan, or the nation, but in the world in general. Enemies can become brothers and sisters!' (CCR 120).

Lao-tzu, Bloch said, would have been the only one to recognize Jesus' greatness in the manger. He continued: 'But even he would not have noticed the stumbling block that Christian love represents for the world with its old associations and hierarchies of power. Jesus is the very symbol that contradicts the power of domination. It is precisely this symbol that the world contradicted on Calvary' (CCR 192).

At the end of his survey of Taoism Küng also touches on what he has learned from the memory of Jesus' life and fate. The wisdom of Taoism, which is defined by the opposites in the world and therefore deeply mistrusts the world, can still learn from this experience of Jesus. Only in trust in the God of Jesus will it be possible to endure in ultimate failure.

The goal of Christian wisdom is neither to fit into the curse of the world nor to depart from it in anarchy. The goal is the capacity to let go of 'surrendering to the one God', the one Tao, the one 'heaven' which makes the rain fall on the good and the evil. Today there must be further discussion between Confucians, Taoists and Christians about this wisdom, which at the same time is God's foolishness. Here, too, the figure of Jesus stands clearly in the background as an inspiring memory.

(c) Getting to know the present situation

Just as the question of God is closely related to the future, so the question of the origin of a religion has a conservative tendency directed towards the past. Despite his orientation on the figure of Jesus, Küng does not succumb to an archaic or historical nostalgia. For him the task and function of the religions clearly lie within their present-day society; they lie together in the present-day world. This orientation is very important for inter-religious dialogue.

Ecumenical dialogues are often painful. One community tells others about itself and its identity, its ideal, perhaps its disappointment, the good and heroic things that people have done. Strikingly, faith communities are often preoccupied with themselves. According to Küng this egocentricity must be broken through. Therefore the question why dialogues are carried on is extremely important. What does each community hope for, and what do we hope for together for ourselves? What are our concerns and what do we want to achieve together? Küng will give a clear answer to this question later. Now already implicitly and sporadically there is no longer any doubt about the question of what must be the concern of religions. Of course he too is concerned, but not just and not primarily about the interests and future of (the Christian) religion. The perspective is clear from the first line of his book. His concern is a new knowledge of the world, a renewed responsibility, 'global ecumenical consciousness'.

This aspect returns in all the individual dialogues. Today the dilemma of identity and relevance occupies Islam in many countries: now Küng has been right for more than fourteen years. He does not fear the end of religions, but he calls for watchfulness: all religions must face the new times. His plea applies to a new ecumenical paradigm of secularity against a religious background (CWR 56). Thus he discusses the beginnings of a reform within Islam. From this standpoint he raises the question of Islamic fundamentalism and from there the question of a legalistic religion. Only from this perspective does he see in Jesus' criticism of the Law an offer which could also help Islam.

In India, too, concern for the future also plays a role that must be taken seriously. 'Progress' is the watchword which is regarded as a consequence of Western religion. Here Küng sees Hinduism as a help – for all his caution in an overall judgment.

> 'Today we realize that everything depends not on negating progress, but on relativizing it, controlling it, taming it for the sake of humanity, so that human beings may remain human and the world inhabitable. And might not this be done in a new way . . . on the basis of that true faith which worships not the false god of progress, but the one true God? And might not such a faith be common to Jews, Christians, Muslims and Hindus? Because all these religions share the same fundamental experience: only the people whose faith in the true God has swept away their illusions about themselves and their world will be truly free from this world and from themselves and will also be able to transform this world into a more humane one. All these religions are convinced that without God the human being remains a torso, a fragment, a *homo in se curvatus*, a creature warped in upon itself, as Augustine and Luther keep stressing' (CWR 240).

If Küng finally offers to Indian culture Jesus' Sermon on the Mount, the picture of the poor man who is in solidarity with the poor, he does not do so out of personal preference but in view of the social situation there. With good reason it was Gandhi and other people with a wide political view who saw this social and deeply human connection (CWR 280–2). Finally, Küng is interested in the transition from the elite religion of Buddhism to the religion of the masses, from the question of how the ascetic finds the way of renunciation to the question of how ordinary people live here and now and learn to cope with life. Renunciation of the world and shaping the world, the quest for salvation and economy, must discover one another (CWR 346–59). Where there is reflection in differentiated anthropological analyses on the relativity of the self, Küng finally introduces a political and ethical argument as a plea for a reinforcement of the self:

> 'Should not Buddhist thinkers, as they critically assess their own and alien traditions, make a more direct effort to establish an anthropology centred upon human dignity (which the Buddha himself

deeply respected)? Buddhists are fully aware than human beings can be adequately understood only as conditioned in every way, as relational beings within the totality of life and the cosmos. But should not they reflect more earnestly, especially in an ethical vein, on the problems of the unique, inviolable, non-interchangeable human self, with its roots in the past and its future destiny?' (CWR 384).

Finally, traces of this concern for the social function of the religions can be discovered in the discussion of the Chinese religions. There is repeated reference to the influence of Confucianism (the state religion) and Taoism on society. Küng thinks that Confucianism has a future; it is not at an end,

'certainly not if now, free from all unnecessary premodern, ideological and institutional ballast, it emerges from its impotence to concentrate on its original essence. This presupposes a reorientation on the original and central impulses of Confucius himself. Not on his hierarchical and static world-view, on patriarchalism and immobility, but rather on his great ethos of true humanity and of moderation between the extremes. This is an ethos of the mean between a Buddhist-Taoist emigration out of the world and an unbridled absorption in this world (in the spirit of Mo-tzu and the Legalists) – all according to the Golden Rule . . . Confucianism has a future not as an ideology of human domination, but as a philanthropic truth' (CCR 122).

Küng wants strong religions which are capable of taking up the challenges of the present so that they cope with the present-day world. This impulse is shown most strongly in the closing remarks in *Christianity and the World Religions*, in which the great slogan of the coming years appears for the first time: 'No world peace without peace between the religions.' Küng sees a significant connection between ecumenism and world peace. Can the religions achieve this?

'This is not demanding the impossible of religions and the churches, it is merely asking them to live up to their own programmes and basic intentions, asking them to direct their appeals for peace not only outwards (important as that is), but also inwards, and thus to perform acts of reconciliation and set up signs of peace at their heart. We can be sure that these acts of reconciliation, these signs of peace, will not

fail to radiate powerful signals onto the fields of conflict "out there"'
(CWR 442).

That is the basic tenor which makes the whole intensive, sympathetic
and yet self-confident discussion so credible. Küng wants no less than a
religion of unity: he wants the religions to move towards one another as
dialogue partners of equal worth and with equal rights – n.b. from
below – but to keep their character. Küng wants to stand up for the
religions, and wants them to stand up together, so that they shape the
world at a time of epoch-making change. Precisely this aim ensures that
at no point in the texts do even stubborn discussions over the truth
become self-opinionatedness.

To conclude: Küng has succeeded in making a large-scale and rich
beginning. In these dialogues we do not have a disappointed theologian
active in a marginal sphere, an esoteric subsidiary job. For Küng, the
world ecumene is now at the centre of his Christian theology, and
world-wide recognition has not been long in coming.

But what is the next step to be? Here and there an important question
has already made itself felt in *Christianity and the World Religions*:
what are the criteria which allow an appropriate assessment of the
religions, religious phenomena and religious action? A further question
is: is it possible to improve the dialogue between the religions and the
comparison between them; can a canon of questions and points of comparison be found, and how can we deal with the uncontemporaneity
which occurs among them world-wide? The question is that of the
method of an inter-religious dialogue which is related to the present and
theologically responsible. We shall be discussing it in the following
chapters.

9

The Religious Situation of Our Time

In the 1980s, Küng, as I remarked, succeeded in making a rapid new start, based on intensive work at his desk and worldwide theological and inter-religious communication. As always, he was not so much concerned with the internal academic discussion as with concrete questions and solutions:

> 'Reflecting in a "faith-free" environment . . . has never appealed to me. I found myself directly challenged by the task of rethinking my way through the Christian message – against the constantly changing experiential horizon of our time. In other words, I have never felt compelled as a theologian to write a learned methodological and epistemological theory (hermeneutics) before proceeding to deal with the substance of theology. "My" hermeneutics – in the final analysis, despite all the controversies, it has always been seeking internal Catholic and ecumenical consensus – was rather woven into the process of theological work, and it always had to prove itself, theologically and practically, in the "stuff" of theology' (TTM xiii).

Küng's account is probably correct, but he has also overlooked the fact that time and again he provided his work with indications of method and hermeneutics, and above all presented a way of working which was methodologically clean and open to checking. Work and analysis, study and discussion of research, reasons for divergent standpoints had always been announced. That already became clear in his first book in the reference to scripture and tradition, in *The Church* in the working out of exegesis, in *On Being a Christian* in the realization of his basic decision for the Jesus of history, and in *Does God Exist?* in the consistency with which he works out in European intellectual history on the one hand the diastasis of faith and knowledge and on the other the central significance of a reasonable trust. Nor should the short but highly effective book *Infallibility?* be forgotten: it discusses the modern criteriology of Catholic theologians, including its sore point. Here Küng repeatedly goes into questions of method and the discussion of criteria.

They also played a key role in the books just discussed – in keeping with their content.

1. Clarifications and breakthroughs

But it was a rough ride. Readers (and certainly previously also listeners) probably found it difficult to sort out and put in order the wealth of information, research reports, case studies, judgments and conclusions. Küng himself, confronted in the shortest possible time with material which was at the same time being coped with by several professorial chairs and currents of research, made his way through the jungle of possibilities, strategies and goals at the gallop. That inevitably prompted calls for clarification. The coming years had to be planned and deliberately shaped; an account had to be given to the theological public and to a Christian public, and also to a wider public of interested people. At this time Küng raised four questions and answered them. Not all of them were new, so he could refer back to what he had written; others emerged now. It was to emerge that they had already been prepared for by earlier works. Only now did they receive a definitive answer in a book called *Theology for the Third Millennium*. The four questions are: (a) How does a Christian theologian committed to ecumenism work? (b) How are the epoch-making revolutions in theology and religions to be explained? (c) Is there a true religion? (d) In what period are we living?

(a) Theology in an unruly time (Erasmus of Rotterdam)

How does a Christian theologian commited to ecumenism work? This first question had largely been answered: Küng could refer to earlier remarks. Over against Protestant theories, at a very early stage he defended the unity and the authority of the whole New Testament canon (see above, 94ff.: TTM 64–84). In a new contribution he incorporates orthodoxy into the criteriological triangle of scripture, tradition and church. He opposes biblicism, traditionalism and authoritarianism – again finding the appropriate key words. Christians believe neither in the Bible nor in the tradition nor in the church, but exclusively in God, who has spoken for believers through Jesus Christ and whose faithfulness alone we seek in scripture, tradition and church (TTM 47–63). He summons Catholic theology once again to treat its dogmatics in a responsible historical-critical way (TTM 85–100) and demonstrates by means of Erasmus where the renewal of the church foundered at the beginning of the Reformation period (TTM 15–46).

Erasmus is another historical figure who clarifies the heart of a problem better than abstract reflections. An emergency had unexpectedly arisen in his time: over-hasty insistence on the gospel in Wittenberg and inexorable restoration in Rome. In between them there was a third force (as F.Heer has pointed out), but it was too weak. It could have rescued the renewal had Erasmus, who was unpopular on all sides, come out of his reserve to adopt a clear position. Küng recognizes the topicality and the indication for action: in such moments neither aggression nor flight is any help, but only the kind of unyielding resistance which Paul offered to Peter, 'opposing him to his face': 'Neither attacking nor avoiding but resisting . . . Holding one's ground, in loyalty to the Christian cause, incorruptible, and without fear of reprisals' (TTM 41). There is no question that this was at the same time a kind of commentary on his own case. This particular personal note is part of the success of a balanced criteriology. There is the truthfulness about which Küng has already spoken and the insistence on the 'authentic' of which he speaks later (TTM 246), and which is the structural component by which the virtue of truthfulness is measured.

However, theology does not advance without personal commitment. For this reason, the consensus between himself and Schillebeeckx is also important for Küng; it is dealt with under the core question, 'How does one do Christian theology' (TTM 103–22: see above, 157ff.). The consensus relates to the bipolarity of God's revelation and the world of personal experience, of 'norm' and 'horizon', which are correlated and if necessary come into a confrontation, which should not be feared. As I have remarked, it was a stroke of luck that in the 1970s two theologians at the same time made scripture the starting point for their christology and their analysis of being a Christian in such a new and comprehensive way. With good reason both were called to order by Rome at the same time. In the meantime, with his inter-religious research Küng had gone a step further; here his previous methodological approaches have proved themselves. But increasingly clearly a new question forced itself to the fore which Küng now answers in principle: how are the epoch-making changes in theology and religions to be explained?

(b) Changing paradigms (five theses)

This question leads to the centre of the problem of the religions. Every religion already displays a tremendous variety of developments, new forms and inner revolutions.

(i) Starting point

That became particularly clear in the analysis of Buddhism. Küng gives it as an example: this 'powerful and many-branched two-and-a-half-thousand-year-old structure' in which even the experts can find virtually no unity.

> 'Thus, for example, the Tantric Buddhism of Tibet is viewed by some as a "re-Hinduization" and a backsliding from pure Buddhism, while others discredit the Japanese "Pure Land Buddhism" as basically un-Buddhist "Amidism". Both these criticisms, of course, run contrary to the believers in question, who despite the many differences from other Buddhists feel themselves to be thoroughly authentic Buddhists' (TTM 224).

Now this problem also emerges between the Christians of different traditions, although the Orthodox and the Protestants both call themselves Christians. Finally, it has a further aspect of which Küng had personal experience. How is it that his theological proposals about doctrine and christology came up against such bitter and irreconcilable resistance? Why was an open conversation suddenly no longer possible? Why did people react emotionionally, discredit him and impose church sanctions? What was the source of these abysses of misunderstanding between people who were committed to the same goals and to mutual understanding?

Küng was already on the track of an answer in *Does God Exist?*. It was developed by the American scientist Thomas S.Kuhn with his analyses of the structure of scientific revolutions. The key term is 'paradigm change'. Not only individual statements or convictions but comprehensive models of explanation can suddenly change (DGE 106–15). According to Küng, the fact and structure of such paradigm changes can also apply to the development of the religions (and their theology). In this way they can explain some things which otherwise we can only be amazed at and note helplessly.

Küng took a great deal of trouble to study this theory and apply it. In

1983 a congress took place on this question in Tübingen with colleagues from Tübingen, from Chicago and from the journal *Concilium*. Some months later a congress at the University of Hawaii was devoted to paradigm change in Christianity and Buddhism. So Küng spoke on the issue several times (TTM 123–226). I shall refer to decisive points here.

Paradigm, initially a phenomenon in the natural sciences, denotes 'an entire constellation of convictions, values, techniques, and so on shared by the members of a given community' (quoted e.g. in TTM 132). So it is an open and descriptive concept, the application of which is not always clear. Küng knows this and does not go deeper either into more precise definitions of the concept or into further epistemological discussion (e.g. that between T. Kuhn, I. Latakos and S. Toulmin); he is also less interested in the question what evolutionary and what revolutionary elements are concealed in a paradigm shift. But he thinks that the concept can be applied to theology. More precisely, he also recognizes the sequence of paradigms in theological revolutions, following the rules which Kuhn describes for the natural sciences. Such religious changes are deeply embedded in cultural changes, far more clearly than the natural sciences (which represent a very recent and narrow sector of a culture). The deep-seated revolutions, for example, in Christian theology are to be put in this context. So there is paradigm change in religions, even in the Christian religion, and in an interchange of macromodels, say from patristic to mediaeval theology, theology certainly performs a representative function for epoch-making revolutions of a general kind. In later analyses it emerges that in a reciprocal comparison the religions can also be understood and analysed as paradigms.

What Kuhn now discovers and describes for the natural sciences shows a striking similarity to what goes on in theology. Küng sums up its application to theology in five theses (TTM 137–53).

1. First of all there is the rise of a 'normal science' with its classics, text-books and teaching traditions. It accumulates knowledge, solves increasingly difficult 'puzzles', and blocks off the significance of knowledge which could put this model of understanding in question. One might think of neo-scholasticism with its stable, reflected and broad state of knowledge, a structure of imposing dimensions.

2. Where existing rules and methods fail, they lead to a quest for the new: a sense of crisis emerges, which leads to the breakthrough to new models of understanding. One might think of the crises of anti-modernism, the 1960s and the rising new theologies.

3. As soon as a new model of understanding is ready, and only then,

it replaces the old. One might think of the stubbornness with which the theological dispute has been carried on since then.

4. The next perspective, which is difficult for the sciences and theology, is the occasion for some discussion: when a new paradigm is accepted or rejected, extra-scientific factors (the behaviour of scholarly communities, political relationships and ideological needs) play a strong part. It is immediately evident and also understandable that the proportion of such extra-scientific factors is extremely high in the interplay of theology, the churches and religion.

5. Therefore the interplay between two paradigms can never be predicted either. The new model of understanding can be filed away, absorbed, or replace the old model. In this case innovation is consolidated as tradition until it faces the fate of the past model. The victory of new models thus never falls into our laps.

(ii) Conclusions

Thus far the abstract context. Over the years four concrete conclusions have crystallized for Küng. The first relates to the present situation of theology, in which he sees himself playing an active part. In *Does God Exist?* this aspect is still markedly in the foreground (DGE 111–19): a correction of course, a consistent rethinking of theology, is called for. The new model solutions, the questions from the side of exegesis, history, the humane sciences and the natural sciences, have broken in on theology. The consequence is 'as if the ground had been pulled out from under one, with no firm foundation to be seen anywhere, upon which one could have built' (thus not a theologian, but Einstein, DGE 112). Rome's great mistaken decisions of the 1960s and 1970s are listed and the pseudo-adaptations are castigated. The discussion with a new paradigm is overdue: *Infallible?* served as a signal here, as is now evident.

But things do not just stop at an oration for home consumption. In the 1980s the tone becomes more relaxed, combined with the reinforcement of a second conclusion supported by an interest in historical description: such overall constellations, whether in a particular religion, a particular understanding of faith or the particular formation of a theology, cannot be measured by isolated convictions or individual statements. To persist in old paradigms does not simply show foolishness and a concern to preserve power, since functioning paradigms have always developed their own, perhaps abiding, rationality (otherwise they would not have carried any conviction). Paradigms are comprehensive complexes of meaning, convictions, practices, ideals which are related to one another. What at first sight may seem absurd becomes understandable in wider contexts (see above, 258f.). Thus the quest for comprehensive paradigms helps us to understand overall complexes more precisely, better, more appropriately from within. When applied to religion and theology, paradigm analysis is a project with hermeneutical dimensions.

A third conclusion which extends beyond Kuhn's analyses establishes itself quite clearly in the 1980s: paradigm analysis not only helps towards a systematization of the history of Christianity but also clarifies the fact that obsolete paradigms can remain as permanently powerful complexes. Paradigms assert themselves not only in succession but manifestly also side by side.

So for Küng, certainly since 1983 there has been a church-historical and at the same time confessional scheme which has persisted right down to the most recent publications (described in Küng–Tracy 1989, 21–3; TTM 128, and further differentiated in the preface and epilogue of *Christianity*). Here five paradigms, i.e. forms of Christianity, which have become historical have been distinguished, which have led to five comprehensive models of understanding.

In this structuring it becomes clear that apart from the first 'primitive Christian – apocalyptic paradigm', which disappeared with Jewish Christianity, all the other 'paradigms' have existed side by side to the present day, three of them in distinct churches or confessions: 'paradigm' sometimes becomes a synonym for 'confession'. Paradigms have an extraordinarily high capacity for survival (something similar can be observed in other religions, TTM 217). There are the early church, the mediaeval, the Reformation and the modern Enlightenment paradigm. Once up to date with their time – summed up in brief headings which are at the same time critical of ideology – they have turned into 1. Orthodox traditionalism, 2. Roman Catholic authoritarianism, 3. Protestant fundamentalism and 4. liberal modernism. Each in its own way has become 'backward, anachronistic'. Küng speaks vividly of them being 'doctrinaire and authoritarian, their condition marked by narrowing, fixation, intimidation and repression' (TTM 221).

On the other hand, the criticism of old paradigms and the legitimation of a new paradigm has only limited justification – precisely because it is new. Küng rejects the idea of progress and the notion that all continuity with the origin has now been broken off. So differences in paradigms do not justify excommunication, as has happened in the past (TTM 222). It must be possible to relate each of the forms of being a Christian that have been mentioned to its age, at the same time to relate it to earlier and later developments, and finally to illuminate it more sharply from the new ecumenical situation. A new paradigm is arising which Küng calls ecumenical and postmodern, and to which a contemporary theology should devote itself completely for the sake of the future.

Finally, in a fourth conclusion it can be discovered that paradigm changes also take place in other religions and that in an age of globalization (worldwide politics, economics, technology and communication) all of them together are moving towards a new paradigm. If they want to have a share in shaping their cultures in the present day, a new – perhaps a shared – 'conversion' is needed (TTM 151).

But we must understand Küng correctly on this point. He does not explain religions by particular models of understanding, nor does he strive for a unified religion (CWR xx). The interpretations of the world by the religions cannot be derived from one another, nor does the new world situation necessarily call for a uniform answer. What is making itself felt globally today cannot replace the present paradigms of religion, but compels them to a new controversy. Here we have paradigmatic structures which run straight through existing religions. As in Christianity, so too in other religions the one original fundamental testimony does not disappear in a paradigm shift. On the contrary, if things go well, this fundamental testimony is brought to bear again each time, so that – as also in the natural sciences – a continuity is preserved despite all the breaks.

Thus Küng remains loyal to his earliest theological approaches, but an interesting shift of emphasis has taken place. Alongside the 'norm', the 'source', 'the centre', in 1979 our world of 'human' experience appeared as the 'second pole' (see above, 158); now the 'present' world of experience appears as the 'first pole', characterized as the 'world of experience in all its ambivalence, contingency and mutability' (CWR 88, 127). Both times it is called 'horizon'. Nevertheless it is the horizon of a Christian theology, which is now a 'critical ecumenical theology'. At that time it stood over against a source; now – in a more appropriate metaphor – it stands over against a 'centre' which is later described in a more technical sense as 'indispensable constants' (Ju 457), 'formative elements and key concepts' (Ju 47), 'the central structural elements and leading ideas' (Ju 459). For all the continuity, that is a new emphasis. It shows that the centre of Küng's theology is no longer, as still in the 1970s, self-confidence about what is Christian, but appropriate life in the present and an appropriate way of dealing with it.

(iii) Discovery of the present

This shift of accent is understandable, since within Christianity and in controversy with the inflexibility of his own church Küng had to insist strongly on the normative origin. Now, in the dialogue between Christianity and other religions, the question of contemporaneity takes on new weight, for only it can open up and advance the dialogue with the world. We are bound together by the fact that we are living today. Now Küng can also give a clear theoretical formulation to his new aim:

> 'Only a theology that does its work against the background of today's horizon of experience, only a strictly scholarly and, precisely because of this, a cosmopolitan and up-to-date theology; only this sort of theology, it seems to me, deserves a place today in the university amid all the other sciences and disciplines. Only this sort of theology is a truly ecumenical theology, which has laid aside the still widespread denominational ghetto mentality and can combine the greatest possible tolerance of extra-ecclesiastical and generally religious phenomena, of the simply human, with the task of elaborating what is specifically Christian. Which brings us to the second pole of a present-day paradigm of modern theology which has, so to speak, moved elliptically from one pole to another and back again. Hence there is not only tension between both poles, but constant movement in "critical correlation" (Paul Tillich). If we want no "world-less" theology, we also want no "god-less" theology' (TTM 166).

With this new perspective for his theology Küng has created an important instrument with which he can analyse both Christianity and the other religions more strongly as a unity in the light of their 'essence' and at the same time can describe their historical dynamic. Here too his material theology again goes beyond reflection on method. These questions are sketched out, and in the course of time are made yet more precise. What is the foundation and chronologically changing horizon of a religion (how is a horizon to be taken over and when is it to be resisted?)? How can a theology react within this comprehensive process (does theology advance such processes, does it accompany them critically, or does it simply have to follow them?)? What is the sequence of paradigms (how are the 'thresholds of epochs' to be discovered and distributed?, TTM 213–15), say, within a confession (how far has the Catholic Church remained in the Middle Ages and how far has it

entered into modern rationality?)? Who heralded and possibly established the postmodern paradigm (what is the role, say, of Karl Barth or
European theology?)?. Küng approaches his project in such a fundamental way that it cannot be coped with in just a few years.

Factual answers are given to many of these questions, thus in *Great
Christian Thinkers* in the argument with Erasmus (see above, 280f.),
and in the big books on the religious situation of our time (see below,
296f.). Küng can happily leave other questions to the reflection of
others. It is clear that he has yet again gone a step further in dealing with
a theology which has an inter-religious orientation. Now it is no longer
merely a matter of describing Christianity, Judaism or Islam in the
mirror of the world religions (CWR xx), but of working out the actual
religious situation of the time. There is also consistency in this development, since the ultimate issue is not Christianity and religions but
human beings themselves.

Really human beings themselves? That can be rapidly said by
Christians. But can members of other religions assent to it without
further ado? Küng sees himself confronted increasingly acutely with a
problem which no dialogue can avoid in the longer term. This is the
quest for a minimal, perhaps a fundamental, agreement in assessing
what is true and good in a religion and the question what makes a true
religion. For Küng it is the fundamental question of an ecumenical
criteriology.

(c) Is there a true religion?

It is neither healthy nor fruitful to want to pose or to resolve the
question of the 'true religion' (or better, the truth in religions) in the
abstract, as a speculative exercise. It is a hermeneutical question, not
devised in order to obtain recipes but only soluble by dealing with existing experiences and texts, as a help in bringing to birth insights which
were already there in embryo, in testing out a practice, discovering ultimate connections so that the background comes into view. Since 1957
Küng has posed questions about the true religion with increasing
emphasis. The positions that he compressed into around thirty pages for
the first time in a 1986 publication can hardly be understood without
this prehistory. Here he works out and sums up what he has already discovered; he is not presenting theses.

Küng surveys one-sided positions and sums up refutations of them.
There is the claim that no religion is true. One might recapitulate all
that Küng has said previously on the question of atheism and the

reasonableness of trust. There is the claim that only one religion, the Christian religion, is true. One might recall Küng's repeated arguments with Karl Barth and his constant reference to the declarations of Vatican II. For Christianity, the other religions today represent not just a quantitative but at the same time a qualitative challenge: 'It is no longer just the fate of the world religions that stands in doubt as it did in the "Christian" colonialist epoch. The fate of Christianity itself is at stake' (TTM 233). So is every religion true? No, for religions come only in particular forms and experiences. If every religion as such were true, everything in it (and in the others) would at the same time be relative. Finally, there is the well-known thesis that all religions have a share in the one true religion. Just as Küng earlier already rejected such inclusivism for Christianity in arguments with Karl Rahner, so too he cannot accept it for the religions of India with their inclusivist statements (cf. also CWR 179–81).

Küng's answer to the question is given on more than one level and consists in the correlation of a general ethical criterion, a general religious criterion and a specifically Christian criterion, and he sees the answers arranged like a narrowing spiral. Of course this is the spiral that Christians depict; here too Küng is speaking as a resolute Christian theologian.

(i) Universal: humanity

Küng starts from general ethical reflections which increasingly become more significant in the face of a world which is growing together and a common future:

> 'Are charlatanism and bogus miracles, every possible kind of lying and deception allowed, because they are done for a supposedly "holy" purpose? Is magic, whch aims to compel the deity, the same as religion, which implores the deity? Are imperialism, racism, or male chauvinism to be affirmed where they appear with religious underpinnings? Can one even have nothing to object against a mass suicide like the one in Guyana because it was religiously motivated?' (TTM 240).

Here Küng is not engaging in discussions about ethical foundations but appealing to minimal basic consensuses which he is presupposing in readers. He points out that Christianity in particular must relearn the criterion of humanity from currents which are critical of religion. He can point out that there is also new thinking about being human and humanity in other religions. So his arguments do not drop out of thin air. A religion is true and good in so far as it serves humanity, human beings in their identity, their senses of meaning and their values, and allows them to gain a meaningful and fruitful existence. It is false and bad to the degree that it disseminates inhumanity, gets in the way of people's senses of meaning and helps them to go wrong in their existence.

It is clear that such general descriptions have to be interpreted in concrete terms. Küng is very brief. But as he already shows in his dialogues, he also knows in concrete terms that such references will be understood by all great religions, e.g. by Islam (CWR 63–9), by Hinduism (CWR 225–34, 267), by Buddhism (CWR 460, 414–19) and finally by the Chinese religions: by Taoism, which understands itself as a religion of salvation and healing (CCR 159–67, 185–7), and of course by Confucianism, that religion of social humanity which formulates this criterion in explicit terms (CCR 114–18). So Küng is not speaking like a sighted man among the blind. In none of these religions is humanity set over against the religious, but it is called for and interpreted and grounded in the practices specific to each of the religions. Küng must concede that the interpretation of the *humanum* offers many possibilities, but he has learned that a minimal basic experience of the *humanum* can be named in all religions.

(ii) General: authentic religion

The same is true of the second criterion, which Küng calls 'general religious' (TTM 245–7): now attention is turned away from human beings towards the religious system. Every religion has developed its own normative foundations. Therefore – in accordance with its own intentions – it is to be measured by its own canonical criteria. It is true in so far as it is 'authentic', i.e. in so far as it corresponds to its own claim or the form which is normative for it. In a long theological career, Küng has developed and differentiated, worked out and fought through this criterion for the Christian religion. He has experienced the purifying and liberating effect of such a reference. He imposes the same obligation on other religions, but also the same right, because they all – despite great differences (TTM 246) – correspond to the same structure of a normative starting point and later realizations.

Of course the scope and points of reference of the two criteria are different. The first stands with a universal claim 'over' the religions, so it was necessary to point out that they in fact recognize themselves in it.

The second relates the different religions to itself. The issue is not a universal religious truth in itself but a 'true' (i.e. authentic) Christianity or Judaism, an 'authentic' (i.e. true) Hinduism, Buddhism, Confucianism or Taoism. Therefore a further point needs to be made here in connection with Küng's hermeneutics. It is one of the strengths of Küng's analyses of the religions that he in fact (!) recognizes in all of them – even in Buddhism and Confucianism – not only their humanity but also the nucleus of a reference to 'God' or the 'divine', to an 'emptiness' or the 'way'. So in all religions there is true religious feeling which relativizes all secular reality and is orientated on an ultimate reality. Thus he can call on all of them to seek themselves, to come to themselves and keep to themselves. Only in this way can they exhaust their potentials. I see this religious criterion as an advance of trust in principle which Küng grants to each and every one of the individual religions which he discusses on the basis of his studies.

(iii) Specific: discipleship of Jesus Christ

The last, the 'specifically Christian' criterion (TTM 248–53) seems to break out of the series. Diverging from my own terminology, Küng calls the first two 'general' and this one 'specific'. In the case of the first two he speaks as someone who is committed in religious and ethical terms, in the third as a Christian.

Perhaps any terminology which puts the three criteria side by side and adds them is deceptive and thus misrepresents an overall universal claim. Certainly, on close inspection Küng is existentially involved in all three criteria, and above all these criteria serve first of all and without any curtailment for the assessment of his own, Christian, religion. But the positions become differentiated in inter-religious dialogue. One takes part in this from a universal perspective as a human being, from a general perspective as a believer, and with one's specific identity as a member only of one's own religion. As will become abundantly clear in the next chapter, in the first criterion Küng speaks as a world citizen who is in the same boat as the whole of humankind and whose survival depends on a minimal standard of ethical reflection. So he does not require any abstract criterion of humanity from others, but joins all concerned in seeking ways to a liveable future. The criterion for this quest is that it is a search for the well-being of humankind. As emerges in the previous chapter and the following parts of this chapter, in the second criterion he is speaking as a researcher and a human being who with unquenchable religious curiosity is investigating the ways and possibilities in world cultures of speaking about and experiencing God and the divine, and on the basis of this appeal practising a humanity which can be sustained without contradiction. At the same time he is speaking as a citizen of the religions in so far as they express the all-embracing and the absolute. So here too he does not simply attest an outsider's perspective but defends the fundamental concerns of the religions together with the other religions. He himself gains in his search for truth if the other religions find a way to themselves and communicate it to him.

Now Küng's position in the third criterion differs from his attitude in the other criteria not by his involvement and commitment, nor by the degree of his identification, but by the particularity of 'his religion', Christianity. That is understandable. But can and will Küng require the criteria of discipleship of Jesus Christ from other religions as well? Here a problem of religious plurality emerges which in the view of many people must not be resolved by reference to one's own Christianity but in a pluralistic way. In dialogue I can and must *a priori* relativize my own view. Küng does not let himself be forced into this alternative of a monological Christian or a dialogical pluralist solution. He reacts with a distinction: 'I apply this theory directly only to Christianity, in posing the self-critical question whether and to what degree the Christian religion is at all Christian' (TTM 248).

As a Christian he does not activate this criterion from outside, in the sense of a purely intellectual examination, but from inside. Here he is affected not only by an intellectual challenge but by a religious provocation which challenges his whole personal standpoint, his discipleship – in the sense of inner rationality which is mentioned in *Does God Exist?* Only in this way does the dialogue about the truth attain a gripping depth, and only in this way do his own life and experience enter the judgment. There is only one religion with which he (like others) can identify in practice; thus in the sense of this intellectual identification, Christianity is the only true religion for him. Therefore he has the right (and the duty) to judge the whole reality of the world from this perspective (TTM 250f.).

So does this specific criterion have nothing to do with the other religions? 'Indirectly,' says Küng, 'the same criterion can certainly also be applied to the other religions: for critical clarification of the question whether and to what degree one also finds in other religions (especially Judaism and Islam) something that we would label as Christian' (TTM 248). So he maintains the second criterion, that every religion has to examine its own authenticity. This autonomy of the religions must not be interrupted by the third criterion. No one can come to the conclusion that another religion is untrue or false because and in so far as it does not accord with the Christian spirit. But Christians may (and should) tell their non-Christian fellow believers where their own religion is different, what they are missing and where they find a supplementation or correction to what they as Christians regard as true. Here again, what Küng means by this in concrete terms can be illustrated in his dialogue with the world religions.

Küng never says that another religion must change in this or that respect or that it is unacceptable. He does not think in alternatives, but in extensions and by relating specific experiences. He finds addiitonal elements: another or a more intensive experience of God, another language, more consistent humanity or humanity developed in another way, more encouragement of peace and tolerance, more respect for life and nature etc. than in the Christian religion. That is already an application of the third criterion. But he also indicates where the Christian religion has to offer important additional elements: for example in the relativization of the Law, in the radicalization of the Sermon on the Mount or in dealing with suffering and pain. But this last point in particular introduces a decisive modification. Küng does not argue, criticize or demand. Jesus' suffering, for example, is not a demand but something that happened to him. Küng simply reports a radical experience which is not specifically Christian but took on a central role in Christian religions. It is the injustice, the suffering, the death (in short, the cross) which Jesus experienced. So there is no criticism of ethical principles – Küng sees a profound correspondence in these – or of official doctrine but the report of an experience with which he identifies as a Christian. Thus in my view it becomes clear that this 'indirect' third criterion (comparable to the first two criteria) represents an existential offer, an authentic narrative and a question from personal experience. Only in this way will inter-religious dialogue become what it can be or must be. In other words, in inter-religious dialogue, too, things are carried on 'normally', questioning and enriching, doubting and assenting, listening and reporting.

Given the complexity of the problem, Küng's article is short, perhaps too short. Questions of detail still have to be clarified. Certainly a tension remains between the criteria, and this could be the occasion for a far-reaching and quite modern discovery. Modern theories of truth and science are deceived if they presuppose the possibility and reality of a truth without tension. There is no such thing. Habermas, for example, as we saw, distinguishes between right, true and truthful. Possibly Küng is on the track of these three levels of truth with the three criteria: a religion is 'right' in so far as it serves the ideal of humanity, i.e. the survival and future of humankind – individually and socially. A religion is 'truthful' (or 'authentic') which fully stands by its own revelations, sources of truth and experiences of the divine. A religion is 'true' which . . .? Here generalizing talk gets stuck, because in concrete terms I can speak only from my particular religious experience, so I continue: . . . which also takes into itself those specific exercise of suffering and death and the overcoming of both, of which the story of Jesus tells.

No one need be anxious because the last truth of God is still hidden, for all religions guard this secret, each in its own way. Habermas too solves the problem in the medium of communication. But the fact that we correspond with one another in those elements of truth to which we here apply the abstract terms 'rightness' and 'authenticity', i.e. which we call humanity and a competence for religious community, contradicts all theories of an irresolvable pluralism. The great hope is that the three great aspects are increasingly corresponding. That this correspondence (in union leading to a true religion) will become an undiminished reality here and now is improbable and perhaps not even desirable.

Küng has already mentioned both these points at least indirectly. Following on from his great thesis from *On Being a Christian*, he remarks that the great specifically Christian criterion is a 'new, true, humanity' (TTM 252). That is none other than the ethical criterion with which the criteriology begins. The particularism of an existential Christian identification calls for the most general openness. At the same time the quest for the true religion must be relativized. However rightly, truly and authentically a religion may be practised in reality, it does not become the truth itself. Christians believe in God and not in Christianity. But though Christianity may be the true religion for a Christian (and this does not exclude other true religions), it is not absolute: 'No religion has the whole truth, only God alone has the whole truth . . . Only God himself – as I have always said – is the truth' (TTM 255). Küng has stirred things up with this statement. It is for present-day theology of religion to create more clarity about itself on this point.

(d) 'No world peace without peace between the religions'

Küng has always sought the challenge of the present, but this present, understood as the present-day world which determines us, is expanding more and more. Initially it was the contemporary internal Christian ecumene; then it was the upheavals in the Christian world. Each time Küng sought counsel and provocation in the Christian message, but he always formulated an advancing horizon as the goal of the reforms. Finally, with the study of the world religions he expanded it to the question of the world situation: what other horizon could they still be given? In 1985 Küng described the development of his theology as the way to a new paradigm (TTM 182–206). Precisely what was this horizon?

(i) A postmodern age

Until well into the 1960s the horizon was the form and limits of an ecumenically reconciled church. The discussion was about the tradition and the present structure of the church, the church's present. In the 1970s (*On Being a Christian* and *Does God Exist?*) the analyses of modern intellectual history and the secular present occupied the centre of interest. Description of these was limited to questions of detail (though these were important). In the 1980s the extension became completion – how else could it be? Anyone who considers the world religions is confronted with the normative cultures, with all the continents and their central problems. Therefore the urgent question became, 'What age are we really living in?' (TTM 1–12, 257–77; GR 2–24; Ju 443–63; Chr 773–89).

Of course the European Küng initially put the question from a European, Western perspective and he attached it to three developments: Karl Barth's theology of crisis (TTM 257–33), the inner problems of modern rationality (DGE), and the crisis of the modern ideal of progress, which has now become obvious (GR 12f.). This crisis has brought us more misery than salvation. More and more resolutely Küng also formulates as a failure of the current paradigm (which in any case is still mediaeval) the internal problems of the Catholic Church and theology, with its attempts to overcome modernity by a conservative approach, i.e. with an authoritarian anti-modernism which has been catastrophic for the church and from which even so great a theologian as Karl Rahner did not dissociate himself with sufficient determination (TTM 186–8).

It is not surprising that while Küng takes up the concept of post-modernity, he does not use any of the classical descriptions or current definitions. For Küng 'postmodern' can be no more than a heuristic concept; it has a heuristic function. The term, which is devoid of any indication of time, in any case has no intrinsic meaning, and is to be replaced as soon as the contours of the new age become to some degree clear. He prefers to refer to the symptoms of crisis which have shaken our culture since the beginning of the twentieth century and which do not manifest themselves simultaneously in the different sectors of our culture (social order, art, politics). This has been happening with increasing clarity: still in a restrained way in 1987; with all the directness one could desire in 1990. There is the collapse of civil society and the Eurocentric world around the time of the First World War, then there are the subsequent catastrophic false developments of Fascism and National Socialism, which brought Europe the Holocaust and a terrible war, the militarism of Japan and the great ideology of Communism. There is the demystification of all modern ideologies of progress associated with this, a crisis of the modern understanding of reason generally (GR 6–15).

> 'The major modern ideologies which in the past two centuries functioned as "scientific" total explanations and attractive quasi-religions are on their last legs. And this is not just true of the revolutionary ideology of progress in the Soviet East. There is also a crisis for the evolutionary-technological ideology of progress in the West, which developed in modern times on the basis of a new kind of confidence in reason and a consciousness of freedom, and which beyond question could point to enormous success. Is everything always going to go on like this? Unlimited growth? Endless progress?
>
> In fact eternal, omnipotent, all-gracious progress, that great god of the modern ideologies, with its strict commandments, "Thou shalt do more and more, better and better, faster and faster", has disclosed that it is fatally two-faced, and belief in progress has lost its credibility' (GR 12f.).

So for Küng, the failure and the crisis are clear. But even more important for him are the new beginnings: a rising world-wide polycentrism, the peace movement, the criticism of civilization, the women's movement, the ecumenical movement (GR 4), attempts at an eco-social market economy, the rise of a mixed system, to the point of a post-capitalist and post-socialist constellation.

(ii) The religious situation of our time

I shall break off here and raise the question what all this has to do with theology. Küng sticks to his last by putting all these observations (which he does not claim as his own) in the perspective of a single point of criticism: these crisis symptoms of our culture are decidedly governed by the religious crisis, which is constantly suppressed. The dying-off of religion which the critique of religion expected has not taken place, but it has accentuated the intrinsic contradictions of an unconditional confidence in reason and a purely secular ethic.

> 'Unless all the indications are misleading, religion, which in the modern period (for thoroughly understandable reasons) has been ignored, tolerated, repressed and persecuted, should once again play an important, though more diffuse, role in the postmodern paradigm. After all, the new religious sensibility has to a large extent set off on its own, outside the bounds of the institutional religions and churches, or at least against the grain of their official teaching. And after every epoch-making paradigm change the same religion turns into a different one' (TTM 10).

So religion and theology will change; in no case will it be possible to isolate them from the new world situation; the rediscovery of religion throughout the world is extremely significant. Küng develops the problem by means of the twin concepts of trust and reason, and thus shows that *On Being a Christian* and *Does God Exist?* provide central answers to the new problems (TTM 201–6). Later he will go a step further and formulate the role of the religions in the political play of the world. The co-operation of the religions is indispensable for the future of the world: 'no peace among the religions without dialogue among the religions' (GR 138), or, as the mature formulation on the religious situation of the world puts it (cf. Ju 624–33):

> 'No peace among the nations
> without peace among the religions.
> No peace among the religions
> without dialogue between the religions.
> No dialogue between the religions
> without investigation of the foundations of the religions.'

(iii) A new approach: critical ecumenical theology

For that, a new theology is needed. Küng speaks of its ethos and its style, and above all of the way in which it integrates the great branches of knowledge – inside and outside theology: exegesis, history, the humane sciences, knowledge of religion and knowledge of the present world (TTM 195–203). Küng calls the goal a 'critical ecumenical theology' which is already still in the making.

What does this mean? Imperceptibly a qualitative shift has taken place. Küng, who has investigated the foundations of Christian faith for so long and so intensively and has issued so many admonitions about them, has worked them out sufficiently for himself. At the same time it has emerged that the present day with its epoch-making upheaval needs extended analysis. By 'critical ecumenical theology' Küng means a theology which is guided by the three criteria which have been discussed: discipleship, authenticity and humanity. It works (in fact and deliberately) from a Christian perspective, is developed in inter-religious dialogue, and is at the service of the present-day world. So strictly speaking the world religions are not in debate for their own sakes. They are, rather, the material object of the whole enterprise. The formal object is the present day (men and women, society and the world), which – as we shall be seeing in more detail – is characterized by processes of increasing globalization and increasing destruction. The catalogue of questions which it raises must include the quality of the life of coming generations, and its provisional or underlying structures are described by Küng in the scheme of a postmodern paradigm.

Such a critical ecumenical theology, understood as an overall theological scheme, runs in three stages, which can easily be read off Küng's theological development. The first is investigation of one's own religion, or better, one's own faith (lived out and formulated in the light of Jesus Christ). Küng worked on this in the 1960s and 1970s. Afterwards this work was set against a wider horizon. The task of this second stage was first of all investigation of the (world) religions. Küng has devoted himself intensively to it since the 1980s. As we saw in Chapter 8, it builds on the first stage and initially understands itself as a discovery of the world religions – driven by curiosity, open to dialogue, and with a theological interest. But an unexpected dynamic quickly establishes itself within this stage. There is only one theme, only one horizon, which is irrefutably a common one, which holds together this inter-religious interest and makes it interesting and compelling. That is the fact that all the religions together have a share in shaping the present state of the world and at the same time are shaped by it. Religions are cultural, political and sometimes even economic factors of enormous significance. At the same time all religions experience the development of the present-day world as a great question, as a challenge, possibly as a threat. This perspective gives a clear direction to curiosity between the religions (as Chapter 9 shows). All research is ultimately related to one question, 'the religious situation of the time'. In the third stage the situation of the time itself then becomes the theme (see Chapter 10).

We shall keep to the second stage. Because the goal is so comprehensive, much comprehensive work has to be done, namely deepening and integrating the inter-religious work done so far, engaging in comprehensive research into foundations, and systematizing work with the aim of comparing and co-ordinating results and discovering how the religions have an effect on one another culturally and politically, how they become factors of conflict or reconciliation, what reactions to world-wide developments are possible among them and are to be expected from them, and how their inner structure changes on the basis of their own foundations, stages of development and possibilities of learning and transformation. Theology can (and must) make its contribution to this not only by investigating the contribution of the religions to the world situation, describing it and evaluating it, but also by introducing it actively – in keeping with the time – into the present world situation, the present world dialogue. The issue is the activity and the message of the religions in our time. So the programme is a secular theology which does not get bogged down in the secular age, and does not become unworldly, precisely because it does not want to be ungodly.

That is a new field of work which hitherto had not been considered by theology. It marks out what at first is a breathtaking range of questions and areas of subject-matter. But Küng would not have been true to himself had he not followed up this insight with case studies. So he developed a research project, and was able to describe its social relevance, with the result that he got financial support for it. The project began in 1989 under the title 'No World Peace without Peace between the Religions'. The three monotheistic religions – Judaism, Christianity and Islam – were to be investigated as certainly important factors in the present world situation. Three publications were originally planned (*Judaism, Christianity* and *Islam*). Since 1989, all in all ten titles have appeared within the project, amounting to almost 4,000 pages of text. With the programmatic work *Global Responsibility*, the internal dimension of the overall project expanded yet again. Chapter 10 is about that. Here in the chronological sequence of Küng's work we shall be discussing the three great themes: Judaism, Christianity and – albeit fragmentarily – Islam.

2. Judaism: a God of all

'There can be no analysis of the religious situation of our time without an analysis of living Judaism. What will be the future of Judaism,
with a new millennium just round the corner and the whole world
puzzling over it? Judaism, the oldest of the three great prophetic
religions, reflects as in a burning glass all the religious problems of
our time, on the threshold of the new millennium. Few though its
adherents may be numerically, Judaism is still a spiritual world
power' (Ju xv).

Küng's *Judaism* was published in German 1991 (in English in 1992). It
is of impressive length (more than 750 pages) and, as I have remarked,
pursues a twofold aim: analyses and perspectives, i.e. a diagnosis and
approaches to a solution, communicated in the three classic steps of
past, present and possibilities for the future. Its starting point is that no
religion any longer lives in splendid isolation and that therefore an
'ecumenical, global responsibility of all for all' must develop' (Ju xvi).
This presents Judaism, like all great religions, with new challenges. The
work is stamped by Küng's new methodological concepts. For the first
time it makes use of paradigm analysis on a large scale; it attempts a
comprehensive and integrating account of Judaism, i.e. one which is not
limited to individual branches of scholarship, and it presents this
religion against the background of the present time. Küng speaks of an
'integrated multi-dimensional approach which combines literary,
historical, sociological and theological methods' (Ju 26). We shall return
briefly to the more precise form of the new method at the end of this
chapter.

(a) Paradigms of Judaism

There would be no point in giving an account of the whole study here.
The historical part (the first of three, Ju 1–216) begins with an analysis
of the 'origins' (Ju 3–35); what is meant by this is the beginning which
constantly gives new inspiration to the later development and to which
later generations continually refer self-critically. These origins are
summed up in the figure of Abraham, who is rightly called 'father of the
faith' and is father of the three great religions of faith. Faith as unconditional trust is fundamental for him. The Jewish religion owes its
marked effect to the establishment of monotheism, i.e. faith in 'this one
invisible God Yahweh who is at work in history' (Ju 27); this excludes

all subsidiary deities, a rival evil God and a female partner deity. This is the universal God who has entered into a covenant not only with Christianity and Islam, but in Noah with the whole of humankind. In keeping with his polarity of the abiding centre and changing horizons, Küng then discusses the question of the 'centre' of Judaism (Ju 36–56): what has persisted as permanently valid despite all the changes, and what has established a perpetual binding character? Küng mentions as central structural elements God, people and land, i.e. the idea of the exodus, the covenant on Sinai and Canaan as the land promised by God. But even more important is Moses, the great central leading figure, who became the prototype of the prophet.

Against this background the discovery and analysis of the five great paradigms of Jewish faith, each so different, begins (see endpapers of *Judaism*). The key words of these paradigms are: tribes (the period before the state), kingdom (the period of the monarchy), theocracy (post-exilic Judaism), the synagogues and the rabbis (Middle Ages) and assimilation (modernity).

The tribes of Israel have only a loose federation and charismatic saviour figures in critical periods. They are held together by faith in Yahweh, in which they find a common self-understanding. The decisive stage was the transition to the kingdom, a state with Saul as its first king and David as the formative figure (at the same time a leading prophetic figure for the three Abrahamic religions), with Jerusalem as the capital, which still has a sacral character today, and with an empire which still serves as a paradigmatic ideal. Here the role of the prophets is of particular interest. The era of theocracy begins with the experience of exile and Diaspora, is consolidated with concentration on the 'Law' (Torah), and is completed by the formation of a theocratic community which no longer finds its identity in the monarchy, but in the temple and the Holy Scriptures. Prophecy was quenched, and the Hellenistic alienation gradually caused a serious crisis.

After the conquest of Jerusalem, moderate Pharisaism became the normative authority. People gathered round scripture and synagogue, and the scribes were the group which determined the character of Judaism. The Mishnah and the Talmud were composed; the great centres of Judaism were scattered over Europe and Asia Minor as far as Babylon. This long phase of a good 1600 years (a history of success but also a history of subordination, persecution and suffering) led to a great internal multiplicity and to processes of cultural assimilation. However, the sense of unity was not lost. Finally, in modernity, the late and dramatic epoch of assimilation followed.

This epoch led to the most serious internal changes and burdens. The Kabbala, a kind of Jewish secret teaching to be understood as Gnosis, was refuted by the unrealistic messianism of Sabbati Zvi. The anti-Judaism of the reformers of the Counter-Reformation already imposed severe burdens. In the framework of the social, economic and state changes in Europe the roles and situation of Judaism changed. Benedict Spinoza (1632–1677) is an example of a changed religious thought, and Moses Mendelssohn (1729–1786) is an example of the 'modern' Jew. The new paradigm is characterized by the integration of individuals and 'cult communities' into the modern nation state, and modern universal education instead of rabbinic-talmudic training. The rabbis became academically trained preachers, pastors, liturgists and pedagogues; the liturgy was reformed and put in the vernacular, and the Jewish way of life modernized. The new paradigm was also opposed by strong counter-forces within Judaism, namely Orthodox and secularized Judaism.

At one point Küng quotes Hegel's remark, 'The things in my books that come from myself are false' (TTM 182). In the wealth of historical information which he offers Küng hardly ever appears under his own name; that is his strength. As a rule his contribution is not detailed research but synthesis and an overall view, a summary and unitary perspective on complex connections which extend beyond disciplines. Thus he produces a general survey of the history of Judaism and works out its formative characteristics and problems – divided into paradigms – in order not to get bogged down in incidentals in his understanding of Judaism. He consistently relates the results to Christianity and Islam, so that at the end of the book the readers (who are above all Christian) are at the same time provided with a rich catalogue of questions for their own faith community.

Provided? The Küng of the 1990s in particular pursues intensively the goal of teaching and education in the best sense of the word. He wants to communicate knowledge, perspectives and questions in as universal a way as possible. He wants to create an awareness and have a long-term effect. His goal is to provide background knowledge and the out-lines of problems for education and research in theology. Thus in the course of time the big monographs on Judaism, Christianity and Islam will prove themselves not only as books to study but as reference works which provide information, interconnections and the solutions to problems – for the expert on the paradigm theory the best way to help his own paradigm to break through. As the bibliography and the preface to the book show (above all Ju xxf.), Küng therefore does not limit himself to personal hobby-horses or private interpretations. He seeks to change attitudes and to intensify the reciprocal network of the three prophetic religions. The signs of menorah, cross and crescent keep appearing. They point to common roots, attitudes and aims, to common 'Questions for the Future' which arise for Judaism, often in an agonizing way.

(b) Questions for the future

Küng understands himself as a theologian, albeit as the representative of a secular and inter-religious theology, and not as a political theorist or church politician. Anyone reading the book should not forget that, for the reading now becomes interesting even for people who are not specialist theologians. In Part Two (Ju 217–440) he poses three different yet interconnected questions. These are the questions 1. of the state of Israel, 2. of Jewish-Christian relations, and 3. of the overcoming of modernity. Here it is necessary to work out the past with its terrifying questions of guilt and suppression, the present situation of the state of Israel, and also the history of alienation between Jews and Christians (the Jewishness of Jesus, the question of guilt over his death and of course the self-criticism which Christians still have to make in the face of Judaism). Only then, in the light of the Sermon on the Mount and in full awareness of the risk, is the question of Jewish self-criticism raised (Ju 390–9).

How are the questions answered? First of all, in this part it becomes abundantly clear how closely the history of Judaism is interwoven with that of Christianity, and how closely the self-awareness of Christianity is interwoven with that of Judaism; how closely the net of Christian guilt towards Judaism is woven, and how impenetrable therefore the history of the suffering, disappointments and unsuccessful expedients of Judaism towards Christianity is. Here Küng, who still recalls his Jewish fellow schoolboys and his easy relations with them, is not sparing in critical reactions towards Jewish behaviour, in a way which is possible only among friends. Indeed Küng has supported the Jewish cause from his early years on and has constantly referred to it (C 132–49, OBC passim, BoL). Are all Küng's judgments to be accepted? From the beginning he has expected to be contradicted; he wants to make a contribution to a constructive dialogue. He answers as a Christian and he reacts as a Christian precisely where the death of Jesus and the 'ambivalence of the Law' (Ju 464–74) are being debated. Jewish authors have reacted very positively, but also with critical remarks. Here it can be reported with pleasure that models of critical discussion have come about which have not destroyed the dialogue but have made it a living matter. Some conversations between Küng and Jewish personalities are documented in the workbook *Neue Horizonte* (NHGD 519–86, there is a briefer selection in the English translation, NHFT 258–79).

The third part progresses almost automatically to an internal analysis of Judaism. Now we consider the great perspectives on the future which stand over against land and religion. Küng attempts to give his answer – so to speak from outside, but in a committed way of thinking. First of all he remains loyal to his paradigm theory of religion. Judaism, too, is confronted with the origin of a new paradigm, and almost automatically Küng assumes that the constants of Jewish faith can prove permanently to be its centre: God, people and land (see above: Exodus, Sinai and Canaan, Ju 37–46; cf. Chr 32f.). In terms of the theology of religions these are probably among the most important remarks in the book:

'The centre of the original Jewish religion as attested by the Hebrew Bible is indubitable even after all historical criticism, and it persists through all the changes of epoch and paradigm shifts: the one God and the one people Israel. The whole as it were elliptical testimony of the Hebrew Bible and finally also that of the Mishnah and the Talmud, of mediaeval Judaism, swings round these two focal points. The central structural elements and leading ideas of Israelite faith are therefore the people chosen by God, and with them the land promised by God' (Ju 457f.)

According to Küng, these elements can not only persist but once again come more clearly into view in a postmodern paradigm. After the fascination of the secular, the striving for universality and the legitimation of the Diaspora, now God, the particularity of the people and the significance of the homeland again come into the centre.

'Where in modernity people saw above all the demands of the new secular time (*vox temporis*), now in postmodernity they are recognizing anew the central significance of the biblical belief in God (*vox Dei*).

Where in modernity there was all too one-sided a stress on the universal human significance of the Jewish belief in God ("universality"), now in postmodernity there is again a recognition of its roots in the Jewish people ("particularity").

Where in modernity there was primarily a stress on the dimension of Jewish belief in God in human history ("Diaspora"), in post-modernity there is again a relationship to the Jewish land ("home-land")' (Ju 459f.).

Küng envisages a Judaism which in the light of these presuppositions can relive the universal horizon of the Hebrew Bible and thus a recon-ciled plurality, and also carry it outside, since if this people takes itself seriously it cannot isolate itself. To give only a few examples: God is the creator of all human beings, races and nations; Adam is not a Jew but 'the human being'; the covenant with Noah was concluded with all of humankind; and not only the Israelis but all peoples will be blessed in Abraham (Ju 460). According to Küng, in view of the *de facto* multi-plicity of Judaism there can also be an internal pluralism: of course it must remain open to the emphasis on tradition, but also to influences from the non-Jewish world (as Rabbi Dov Marmour calls for, Ju 461). This general definition of position is now worked out in three direc-tions: the future way of dealing with the 'Law', the Jewish-Muslim problem of the state of Israel and the Holocaust, and the future of speaking about God.

In the question of the Law (Ju 464–518), Küng – who had already been sufficiently been confronted with Catholic fulfilment of the Law and Protestant criticism of the Law, with Jesus' relativization of the Law and Paul's reflection on the Law (both were pious Jews, cf. BoL) – presents a clear standpoint, to which not all Jews assent equally (see above, 133). Human well-being must be the goal of all fulfilment of the Law; men and women are to be judged in that light. God's will must not become a 'theonomous' burden, but can serve towards emancipation – in the best sense of the world. In Küng's view, thinkers like Rosenzweig and Buber have offered helpful reflections. However, the critical questions have to be addressed not only to Jews but equally to Christians, for the problem of the 'Law' (thus the Christian termino-logy) is a universal religious problem. As already in the dialogue with the Eastern religions, structural analogies offer themselves for a critical and at the same time a self-critical discussion.

(c) The 'Anti-Sinai'

Küng's position on the religious political problem of the state of Israel and the city of Jerusalem is also clear and critical of Israel (Ju 519–83). Of course Israel is a political entity, but the political problem stems from its religion, the lack of insight in what Küng regards as serious mistakes made at the time of the foundation of the state, and the dangers for human rights and peace which have lasted to the present day. Küng's 'real-utopian vision of peace' (Ju 566–83) formulates ways which look forward. Given reconciliation and a pragmatic balance of interests, Israel could become a bridge state and a peaceful people, a multi-cultural land, the guardian of a universalist ethical and religious heritage, and Jerusalem, which is holy to all three Abrahamic religions, the sign of understanding and reconciliation. Why not two flags over Jerusalem (as two flags also wave over Rome)? Why not make the Dome of the Rock (or a place on Sinai) the sign of unity for the Abrahamic ecumene? And why not pray together in the Dome of the Rock? Küng knows that this chapter is provocative, but he is also aware of the great assent which he will find to it in all three religions. And even those who do not agree with the proposed solutions will end their reading of these pages thoughtfully. At least they will have learned one thing: a contemporary Christian theology can no longer discreetly put these questions on one side.

Political theology in concrete terms? However, it is a political theology which immediately leads to the question of God. Küng's last question, which brings the book to a conclusion, is about God, and takes a form raised by the Holocaust (Ju 584–609). Historically the Holocaust has been treated earlier, in two impressive chapters: the reasons for it, its course and the complicity of the Christian churches and nations have been analysed (Ju 219–81). There is no question that this unprecedented, unique crime, unimaginable in its cruelty and its monstrous evil, sparked off a theological crisis in Israel of such a depth that in the end the question remained whether the Holocaust did not destroy the faith God which runs through Jewish history. Doesn't this event mean a break in continuity of epoch-making dimensions for Israel? Küng passionately opposes such a fixation:

'In historical terms I have set out in detail how neither moral levelling out and historical relativization nor mystifying over-heightening and unhistorical absolutizing will do justice to this truly singular catastrophe. While the Holocaust does not mark the end of Judaism, it does mark the end of a whole Jewish paradigm, that of assimilation. The Holocaust is and remains for Judaism a break in continuity of epoch-making extent. It remains an event far surpassing all previous history of suffering, an event of an unspeakable suffering of the people of the Jews which cannot be "understood" theoretically. It has a fundamental significance for our era, but one which is by no means exclusive for the future. Truly, one does the mass murderers too much credit if one stylizes "Auschwitz" as virtually a new revelation event, if one elevates it to what Richard Rubenstein has termed a "new Jewish Sinai". As if what was "revealed" here were not so much God's decree as human disintegration. No, this is no revelation of values and criteria, but a complete perversion and obsfucation of them. So a counter-thesis would seem in place . . . Auschwitz is not a place of revelation but the modern anti-Sinai. It is not a new beginning, but radically the end of that past era which produced it: European modernity' (Ju 587f.)

Here the change from an idealistic modernity into its nihilistic opposite took place. Modern belief in human greatness finally shattered. Küng sees his analyses of belief and unbelief, of the tribulation of the one and the self-contradiction of the other, confirmed in this apt culmination. From a theological perspective, the only consequence lies in the attempt to overcome this nihilism, which has become practical.

So who is God, if Auschwitz could happen? Küng is mistrustful of all solutions in which God appears as one who shares the suffering or is powerless, is to be pitied or hated. In his view, Jews and Christians largely agree that God, secretly present, truly taking part in history, is a merciful and compassionate God.

Küng looks closely and notes the difference between his solutions and those of other Christian theologians. Presumably he marks it too strongly, but he does not want to offer any theoretical solution. Rather, he insists that there is unanimity on the aporia, the theoretical insolubility, of the question. Here he is to be agreed with. Certainly God was also in Auschwitz, if God exists. But 'there is no answer to the question, "How could God have been in Auschwitz without preventing Auschwitz?" ' (Ju 603). At this extreme point Küng pleads for a theology of silence. For Jews he sees the figure of Job, and for Christians the figure of the man of grief from Nazareth. Here only helpless and painful memory is of any help:

'His betrayal, his being handed over, flogged and scorned, his slow dying on the cross, has anticipated what Susan Shapiro has described as the fearful threefold experience of the victims of the Holocaust; namely that all-pervasive experience of being abandoned by all human beings, even robbed of one's humanity, indeed of being abandoned by God himself' (Ju 606).

Again it becomes evident how one's own particular standpoint does not block the dialogue but makes it possible. Job on the one hand and the one who was senselessly liquidated on the other! In the suffering Jesus, Küng does not recognize that primarily Christians are redeemed, but rather that God remains present in hiding even where the suffering is apparently meaningless. So at the end of the book, as it were as the result of this detailed and comprehensive discussion with history, the present situation and the future perspectives of Jewish faith, Küng appeals to

> 'the way of unshakeable (not irrational, but completely reasonable) trust in God despite everything: of faith in a God who remains the light despite and in abysmal darkness. Because there is Auschwitz, say the godless, the idea of God is intolerable. And those who believe in God, whether Jews or Christians, may answer, "Only because there is God is the thought of Auschwitz tolerable to me at all"' (Ju 608f.).

Küng's long course through history, politics, exegetical and internal theological analyses ends with a notion which from the beginning has been quite central to his theology: the question of an unshakeable, constantly threatened trust in a God whose ways always remain a mystery to human beings.

3. Christianity: disintegrating into paradigms?

The analysis of Christianity is a special task for Küng. As a Western European scholar he is speaking here from particularly intensive knowledge. Can it be brought within the two covers of a book? As a Christian theologian he is speaking for his own cause. Will a way be possible between his partisan confession and a distanced report? Can Küng introduce his rich historical, systematic knowledge, supported by study of religion and the humanities, into the project in such a way that it will further the goal of a religious analysis of the time? Of course this is not just a question about Küng's personal capacities; it is a question whether the project can be achieved at all.

The mass of material has in fact led to a (provisional) problem. This monograph on Christianity, the second of the planned trilogy on the prophetic religions, is constructed like the book on Judaism. It begins with the questions of the essence and centre of Christianity and then goes on to an extensive analysis of the paradigms in its history. But by the time that the questions about the present and the future begin, Küng has already filled more than 900 pages with text and notes. So at the end of the book he writes 'Not an Epilogue' (Chr 792–8), in which he presents the continuation of the investigation – as though he were at the beginning of a life of scholarship. Thus the book has not become a historical work; the references to the present structure of Christianity and the internal Christian ecumene are worked out consistently; the open questions of a political, cultural and theological nature are continued intensively and tenaciously up to the present. The questions of which constants have failed, which have remained and which are new, what is possible and what has been left unresolved, serve as a constant foil to the present.

So Küng is aware of the problems; therefore already in the preface he mentions the focal point on which all the analyses will be orientated. It is the future of a Christianity which is identical with itself and thus is capable of a present, and which is aware of its world-wide role in the future.

'Christianity should become more Christian – that is the only possible perspective for the third millennium. The Roman system, Orthodox traditionalism and Protestant fundamentalism are all historical manifestations of Christianity . . . But if Christianity is again to become more Christian, conversion will be necessary: a radical reform' (Chr xxii).

In form the book is comparable to its predecessor: an explanation of the paradigms in the end-papers, tables and maps, questions and programmes, models and short classical texts make the book easier to read. It is not just a survey of the history of the Catholic Church, but as an analysis of paradigms it is a way through the great forms taken by Christianity: through the Eastern Orthodox Church, the Catholic Church and the churches of the Reformation. All these churches are grappling with modernity and ultimately with the developments which present themselves as a postmodern paradigm.

(a) The origin (Jewish-Christian paradigm)

An account of the book which does not succumb to mere repetition is even more difficult than in the case of Judaism. So we must keep to key statements which prompt further thought. The fundamental constants already make us think; they are taken over from Judaism (Exodus, Sinai, Canaan) but are differentiated, 'appropriated only in a complex spiritualized form: a people of God understood in spiritual terms and a land of promise' (Chr 33). As in Judaism, the issue is belief in the one God. The reason for this shift is the new centre, which persists clearly and in a form which is never disputed: Christianity always understands itself as discipleship of Christ, and thus relates to the central leading figure of Jesus of Nazareth. Again there is a brief summary of the memories of this historical figure which have survived (Chr 33–6), compared in diagrams with the other great figures of Moses, Buddha, Muhammad and Confucius; the description focusses on the one aspect which had already been crystallized out as the real distinction in the controversy with the world religions: the scandal of the cross (Chr 36–9).

Nevertheless, precisely in this experience of the cross it emerges that Jesus stands for a radical humanism. Here too Küng uses a succinct formula from the 1970s: 'What is distinctively Christian is this Christ himself, who was crucified and yet is alive' (Chr 39). Belief in the abiding power and presence of God and Christ is already articulated in Judaism, now more clearly as belief in the Spirit who is none other than God himself. However, with the insertion and increasing independence of the 'second article of faith', belief in Jesus Christ, difficulties of understanding develop with Judaism and Islam. The Decalogue and the Sermon on the Mount offer quite a different challenge to Christianity, the religions and humankind. Here Küng sees Christian bedrock which is highly relevant for the present. Here he formulates questions for the future which illustrate his inter-religious thought:

'What challenge would be posed to politics, economics, culture and private life if it were the rule:
- not only to have no other gods than the one God, but to love God "with all one's heart" and one's neighbour, even one's enemy, as oneself;
- not only not to speak the name of God casually but not to swear by God at all;
- not only to hallow the Sabbath by rest, but to do active good on the Sabbath;
- not only to honour father and mother in order to live long on earth, but to turn one's back on natural human relationships, if that was necessary for authentic life;

- not only not to kill, but even to dispense with killing thoughts and words;
- not only not to commit adultery, but even to avoid adulterous intent;
- not only not to steal, but even to renounce the right to retribution for injustice suffered; not only not to bear false witness, but in unconditional truthfulness to let one's Yes be Yes and No be No;
- not only not to covet one's neighbour's house, but even to endure evil;
- not only not to covet one's neighbour's wife, but to avoid intrinsically legal divorce?' (Chr 56)

Thanks to the clear history of the origins, the question of the normative centre can be answered briefly. Like Judaism, Christianity knows a paradigm which with its specifically apocalyptic expectation of the end did not last. But it led to forms of community which are still significant today. That applies to the provisional structures of the community, the significance of the prophets and the norms of diakonia which were already worked out in *The Church*.

The significance of women, who were later suppressed, is important and the result of later research. Incorporating this factor, Küng sums up: 'The church of the Jewish Christian paradigm could have called itself democratic in the best sense of the word (at any rate not aristocratic or monarchical): a community in freedom, equality and brotherhood and sisterhood' (Chr 79). The consistency with which Paul opened the church up to Gentile Christianity (free of the Law), so that the community developed into a fellowship of Jews and 'pagans', is of paradigmatic significance – a presupposition for early Christianity being able to develop into a world religion. The results above all of more recent research into the inner structure of early Christianity as it gradually differentiates itself make exciting reading: the reciprocal exclusion from church and synagogue (Chr 87f.) and the gradual suppression and vilification of Jewish Christianity which – east of the Jordan, on the Euphrates, the Arabian peninsula and elsewhere – evidently hung on for a long time and influenced Manichaeism and above all the Qur'an (Chr 98–109). To take it seriously is a great opportunity for inter-religious dialogue.

(b) The early church and Orthodoxy

The early church-Hellenistic ('ecumenical Hellenistic' or 'Hellenistic') paradigm begins with the transition to Hellenism, i.e. fundamentally with Paul, the Gentile-Christian community, say of Corinth (c.55), the loss of the Jewish community, the gradual rise of an episcopal-presbyteral church structure, Greek as the dominant language, the shift of the centre of the church from Jerusalem to Rome; all this in the framework of a comprehensive inculturation into Hellenistic-Roman culture (Chr 129). It is initially the time of the external persecutions by the Roman empire and the inner controversy with Gnostic tendencies. Following Peter Brown, Küng presents the gradual success of the church as a 'gentle revolution'. It must have been due to the everyday morality: regular solidarity with the poor and suffering, the social cohesion and humanizing influence, born of the striving for a juster society (Chr 149–51) – however, the women were the losers (Chr 155–60). The paradigm shift had the strongest effect on christology, which took on central significance in orthodoxy (Chr 162–83).

Then the span of this early church paradigm begins to extend beyond its time. Decisive phases of further development are the shift of the focal point to Byzantium, to the Eastern empire, which hands the paradigm on up to 1453 and continues it in Moscow as the 'Third Rome'. This high point of Greek Orthodoxy is described at a great pace: the state political situation, the church structure with monastic rule and the cult of images as its special hallmarks, and then of course the catastrophic history of the West–East split (Chr 196–257). Time and again the results are summed up in decisive points, for example in those which would make a reconciliation possible today (Chr 254f.). Around 1453 there then takes place the self-confident shift of the claim to leadership to Moscow, though its patriarchate could not break out of the old structures, and failed definitively when confronted with the Russian Revolution (Chr 257–81).

(c) The Middle Ages and the Catholic Church

Küng has time and again grappled with the 'mediaeval Roman Catholic paradigm', which has its roots in Augustine and his time (in the Western Roman Empire) and has continued in the Catholic Church down to the present day. Here, however, he puts it in a new perspective (Chr 283–523). What is new is the brevity of the account and the precision with which the most different dimensions (from theology and geopolitics to the legal and the spiritual dimensions, from constitutional issues to very individualistic matters) are related. As a result the whole model appears to be self-contained and unusually effective, but at the end also inflexible and self-glorifying. Of course succinctness also means abbreviation by definition, neglect of details, playing down contradictory perspectives. The reader hardly finds this to be a disadvantage. Polemic and personalizing of the problems, which has often appeared in Küng's work, are no longer necessary here. It is enough to understand the role of institutions and persons within this paradigm. The objectifying effect of this approach is enormous.

So here we are given an overall picture from Augustine through Thomas Aquinas to neo-Thomism; from Constantine and Leo the Great through the 'great' mediaeval popes to John Paul II; and from the constant controversy with Islam through the Crusades to the baneful Inquisition; from the political pre-eminence of Rome through the dualism of emperor and pope to the consistent Romanizing of a world church; from the mediaeval papal councils through Constance and Trent to the most recent assemblies of the church in the Vatican; from the grandiose cultural achievements in monasteries, schools (universities) and architecture, through the problems of a world which is becoming autonomous, to a Catholicism which reacted only defensively and refused to engage in creative controversy. Centralization, legalization, politicization, militarization and clericalization are the characteristics of the 'Roman system' (Chr 390–403).

But there are also the counter-movements which help the message of Jesus of Nazareth to be given its due. The history of the Roman church is not a history of decay but a history of vital controversy, and also of internal growth and spiritual maturity. One has only to read the chapter about Francis of Assisi (Chr 409–14). Reality and its real image are complex, and at least two dialectical poles constantly cross: the evaluating dialectic of essence and perversion (which Küng already established earlier, Chr 7–11; C 24–9), and the 'neutral' dialectic of essence and form that in turn is crossed by the question of the 'centre' – which is similarly new. The dialectic of essence and form can only be measured by the question whether and how the social and cultural reality of its time can adopt and use it. Küng's criticism also begins with this aspect. The Roman Catholic paradigm has been in crisis since as early as the thirteenth century; the Council of Constance (see above, 100f.) could not establish its claim in the longer term; the response to the Reformation – which over large areas was defensive – was a backward-looking 'Counter-Reformation'; and anti-Protestantism later became anti-Modernism. Küng ends the analyses by once again discussing the question of infallibility (Chr 522f.).

(d) Modernity and Protestantism

The Protestant ('Reformation Protestant') paradigm – like the Roman Catholic church – has had an eventful history down to the present. Many cultural, social, church-political and theological preconditions governed the new beginning, which proved to be the beginning of a new paradigm. At the same time a new person was needed to bring about a breakthrough. This person was Martin Luther (1483–1546). With his rediscovery of scripture and the question of salvation in the light of the Pauline message of justification, Luther set in motion a process which finally led to a new form of the church and unfortunately to a split in it.

For Küng, the advent of the Reformation is a prime example of a paradigm change (Chr 539–49). However, the results of the rising movement were problematical. The mediating 'third force' did not establish itself, above all because Erasmus hesitated (see above, 280f.). Luther marshalled all forces against left-wing non-conformity (called the 'enthusiasts'). Thus from the right wing there developed a Reformation by princes and magistrates; finally the local ruler became the pope of his territory; instead of the papal church a church of the authorities came into being (Chr 549–58). By contrast Calvin presents the most consistent Reformation programme. After Thomas Aquinas and before Schleiermacher he wrote the most significant Christian dogmatics and a viable church constitution. Through him Protestantism became a world power.

Anglicanism is of especial interest in the rising interplay of two paradigms within the Western church. Its merit is that it has combined the two paradigms in a *via media*, between Rome and Geneva (Chr 589–604). Tradition is treasured, but not played off against scripture. That is also true of the traditional liturgical order, which has been reformed in a flexible way. The episcopal ministry is combined with a broad toleration. Of course problems remain here. All in all, however, the Church of England has questions to put to the Catholic Church, above all because of its greater independence (in the appointment of bishops, questions of doctrine and education, liturgy, its own discipline).

So now two Western paradigms exist side by side. Can it be claimed that one is superseded and the other is contemporary? The calculation is not as easy as that. Advantages and disadvantages can hardly be compared directly. But all in all, Protestantism seems better prepared for modernity, especially as it allows internal renewals better than the Catholic Church. There was Pietism, which renewed the rigid paradigm in the nineteenth century; and the revival movements, which have given North American Christianity an unmistakable stamp. And there is also fundamentalism, which arose at the beginning of the twentieth century, first in the ranks of Protestantism, and which owes its success to a simple fact: men and women who feel threatened by modernity and its relativizations find consistent, simple and clear answers – developed from scripture. Fundamentalism always thinks in exclusive terms: there can be no answer but its own. But it is food for thought that all the prophetic religions are more prone to fundamentalism than other religions. Immovability seems to be the sister of a resolute trust.

This can be broken through only

'if one does not suppress the universal horizon of the great documents of revelation, the Hebrew Bible, the New Testament and the Qur'an, which is always the history of humankind as a whole, the history of all people. And if we understand these great documents of faith at the same time spiritually in terms of their spiritual centre and not in a naively literal way, we will arrive at another basic attitude to the other religions as well' (Chr 642).

What view is to be taken of the Protestant paradigm? At the end of this part Küng makes a surprising shift which then dissolves the schematic way of thinking in a scheme of paradigms (methodologically necessary though that may be). What we now hear is that despite all the difficulties, in the Second Vatican Council the Catholic Church made a shift towards the Protestant paradigm. The Catholic Church recognized its share of blame in the division of the churches, recognized the other churches as churches, and committed itself to an ecumenical attitude. It has a high esteem for the Bible and an authentic popular liturgy; it has revalued the laity, adapted the church to the wider world and reformed popular piety. Questions arise from this which the Catholic theologian puts clearly to Protestantism: in them he once more sums up his earlier ecumenical desiderata and sees them resulting in the rise of a shared form of a future church – presupposing a Catholic counter-movement:

• There is certainly more Catholic appreciation of the Bible. But in

Protestantism isn't there often a neglect of the common tradition of
the early church and the Middle Ages?

- The Catholic liturgy of the word and the people of God is
certainly more lively. But in some Protestant churches, isn't the
celebration of the eucharist still marginalized or neglected?

- Beyond doubt the Catholic laity, above all women, have been
rehabilitated. But what about the significance of ordination and
church ministry in the local, regional and universal sphere?

- Heightened decentralization and inculturation in the various
nations is urgently necessary. But what about the international
character and universality of the church, which is often put in
question by Protestant provincialism and nationalism?

- There has been yet further reform of popular piety, particularly in
certain countries. But aren't church and liturgy often kept remote
from the people by Protestant intellectualism (Chr 647)?

Given the complicated form and history of the Reformation paradigm
and the still more complicated relations of the Catholic Church to the
mediaeval paradigm, these are certainly simple questions. But they also
show what 'simple' structural characteristics can govern the form of a
church and how 'simply' they can be corrected in the light of the structural constants of Christianity. However, in the long term such simple
changes would have far-reaching consequences for structure, mentality
and practice. Therefore a simplicity would be required which would
require much effort of those concerned, even a conversion. 'What a
great new entire constellation of Christianity, newly shaped by the
gospel, this paradigm of the Reformers is!' (Chr 647). It would be even
greater if it managed to overcome the Catholic-Protestant split. Küng
the church critic knows the goal of his criticism only too well: it is a
reconciled community of equals, in keeping with the paradigm of the
new time.

(e) The church in modernity

Up to now the impression could arise that every new paradigm produces
a new type of church. That is not the case in the Enlightenment modern
paradigm ('the paradigm of modernity orientated on reason and
progress'). However, this paradigm has influenced the Catholic and
Protestant churches to a high degree, in an intensive exchange. So
Küng's perspective is above all forward-looking (Chr 650–709). New
political constellations in Europe since the sixteenth century, the change

of eras in the seventeenth century with the Thirty Years' War as a disastrous break, the shift of the centre of the power to the Atlantic, the new principles of European politics (with Bodin, Hobbes and Machiavelli as their ideologues) and then the revolutions in science and philosophy with Francis Bacon and the new world system of astronomy – revolutions of the most far-reaching kind – gave culture and society a new and totally unexpected face. The new motto was 'reason' and no longer 'papal church' or 'word of God'. The church initially reacted with the Inquisition. Küng shows how the Enlightenment then slowly established itself in theology and how above all a historical biblical criticism could establish itself with the great question of the Jesus of history.

Schleiermacher stands at the centre of Küng's discussion (Chr 694–717; cf. GCT 155–84), which culminates in the still controversial question whether or not he countered the spirit of modernity appropriately or whether he gave in to it. Küng does not pass judgment, but he raises questions. The revolutions in state and society were even more far-reaching for the church. The nation became sovereign, and democracy replaced mediaeval theocracy and Protestant authority as the new watchword. But the French Revolution combined this new ideal with an unprecedented (and hitherto unexplained) break with tradition; the idea of the nation accordingly became nationalism.

This is the point at which the tragedy of modern Christianity begins; now it finds itself in a cultural ghetto of its own choosing. Its reaction towards the fourth of the revolutions mentioned by Küng is no better. This revolution, in technology and industry, is achieving a tremendous step forward for the masses, but at the same time is causing misery for the proletariat. However, the awareness in liberalism and above all socialism is now changing, so that 'social justice' and a 'juster social order' are becoming the great watchwords. The churches are reacting only sluggishly to this, while the whole of church life and piety is changing almost imperceptibly.

(f) Present and future

What is the situation today? The ideological controversies are no longer at the centre. The central problem with which the churches must grapple is the change in religion itself: individualization and pluralization, which can have both productive and destructive effects. Here, in the part of the discussion which is still descriptive and analytical, the theologian's answers remain open. They have to remain open, since Christianity has manifestly not developed a clear attitude to modernity, and modernity itself is in crisis (Chr 765–73): faith in reason has been shattered at the very moment when large parts of the churches were beginning to become reconciled to it. But the watchword 'nation' and the great ideologies of liberalism and socialism have also gone downhill. The question is what way out can be found, or whether ways out will offer themselves of their own accord.

In a sense Küng seems to give a positive answer. Eurocentricity is being replaced by a polycentric paradigm, and ecology, the women's question, distributive justice and religion are becoming central problem areas (Chr 775–8). However, the latter appears, not as a problem to be solved but as a factor of immediate world political importance, since the way to world peace begins with peace between the religions. Therefore this question cannot simply be left aside. Peace is possible only if among other things it again becomes clear that Western and Eastern Christianity are two paradigms of one of the same religion, that Christianity and Islam have many far-reaching common features of faith and ethics, and that each religion knows other options than fundamentalism.

(g) World-wide responsibility

It would also have to become clear that a political ethic of responsibility, i.e. an ethically responsible human rights policy, can be quite realistic and be developed world-wide. But in the face of a world-wide vacuum of orientation, commitment to a binding and uniting world ethic is urgently called for (Chr 780–89, see below 328ff.). At the end of the book the perspectives have changed. The religions are no longer analysed in respect of their action and failure, but challenged to act. There is no longer an explanation of how they must be, but rather of what they have to contribute. What Küng said at a very early stage about the church evidently also applies to the religions. They are not there for themselves but for the well-being of the world. This already prepares for the next chapter.

As I have already indicated, the strength of this monograph is the wealth of material and information with which it deals, the synopses of the different Christian churches, and the rediscovery that paradigms in the framework of theology and cultural analysis are not just to be understood as a series of different solutions to problems but as contemporaneous overall conceptions. They have their own cultures, their own geography and their own technique for survival. Moreover some categories can no longer be applied in such macro-religious paradigm analyses without problems. For example, which paradigms are contemporaneous and which superseded? According to Küng, it is certain that none of the current Christian paradigms simply corresponds to the needs of the era which is beginning. But it is also certain that he would like to lead the Catholic and Protestant, and preferably also the Orthodox churches, into a new paradigm in which they would be reconciled with one another.

Now it is striking that the modern paradigm has no longer led simply to the formation of a new church. This is still less probable for the future, and in the face of a world-wide future of the churches evokes yet other dimensions of the problem. Küng takes these up in his closing words (Chr 792–3). They lead from the opportunities for a 'more Christian Christianity' to the vision of a religion which embraces humankind; Küng sums this up in the key words cosmic, holistic, liberating and ecumenical. They are directed towards the manifold relationship between Christianity and its prophetic sister religions, burdened with provinciality, failure and a sense of being in the right. Thus many questions remain open which will have to be answered in the second volume of this monograph on Christianity. There too some material will not be unknown. But there too Küng's art in integrating it, systematizing it and offering conclusions for a better future will be of interest.

4. Islam: dangerous memory

Perhaps this section on Islam is in the wrong place here. Küng already grappled with Islam in his first dialogue lectures in 1982 (Chapter 8; CWR 3–132). Comments on that must take the place of the third volume of the trilogy, which has been announced but which is still to come. By comparison, this series of lectures has more of a preparatory character. They are the first five-finger exercises for what will probably later prove to be a concerto.

(a) Comparable to Christianity?

At that time Küng's commitment and first attempt was in the direction of a knowledgeable and pertinent dialogue with Islam. His reactions, which have already been discussed, need not be repeated here (see above, 256); I shall refer – of course fragmentarily – to some central aspects which have not yet been treated. For example, Küng is concerned with secularization and the importance of Islam in our time. Taking up Parsons, he speaks of the changing function of religion, which – as in antiquity – is given a new task: 'faith in the one true God' must take the place of 'faith in the false gods of modernity'. Küng's strategy, which is grounded in the subject-matter, is clear: from the beginning he sees Christianity and Islam (together with Judaism) faced with a common task, the solution of which he evidently entrusts to the prophetic religions. At that time a 'new ecumenical paradigm of secularity against a religious horizon' is already coming into view: there is no God but God, you shall have no other God but me (CWR 63).

As in his discussion with Judaism, Küng also comes to speak of the many earlier and contemporary efforts at reform within Islam, which again make Islam – which also has a history of changes – a religion in transition, not only in Europe but also in the Middle East, as far as India and Pakistan. He offers many reasons for giving fundamentalism no chance of long-term survival, understandable and virulent though it is. However, Küng (who once learned the significance of ecumenical theology from the problem of justification) sees a serious problem posed by the Shariah, the Islamic 'law'. Here too there is the threat of a literalistic faith, evidently a universal phenomenon, whether it refers to the 613 precepts of the Torah, the 1752 (until 1983, 2414) canons of church law or the 7300 hadiths (a collection of religious precepts from the eighth century). Unconditional obedience to God must also be central in Islam, and there too criticism of the law for the sake of human beings must be possible. This is a criticism which has its forerunners in the critique of the Law within Judaism and by Paul, and which would have to begin theologically with a historical understanding of the Qur'an (CWR 62–9), just as historical criticism has brought modern Christianity out of its rigidity.

Küng has no doubts about how deep and fundamental the common features between Jews, Christians and Muslims are, but they are grounded in belief in the one and only God who is a historical and merciful God, in an Other who can be addressed. This trusting faith finds its parallel in a conviction that goes beyond religion, that we human beings are free and responsible, even if according to Küng the radical nature of Christian love is expressed more clearly and more radically in Jesus (CWR 90–6).

In all his remarks it becomes clear from where Küng often draws the power of his argumentation. Short summaries of his views are in fact usually deceptive, since they lead us to overlook the depth of his factual knowledge, his acquaintance with relevant literature. So here too it would have to be shown how much he has occupied himself with the discussion within Islam, with the earlier and the most recent results of historical research. He does not present any intuitions, but sums up discussions and proposed interpretations. That makes all the more credible the degree to which he endorses Islam, declares it to be a partner on an equal footing with Christianity, and depicts Muhammad above all as a prophet who – recognized as a true prophet – must also be taken seriously by Christians.

It also makes credible the perspectives (challenges and dangers) which in Küng's view are common to Christianity and Islam: confrontation with secularization, the danger of legalism, an unhistorical way of dealing with canonical writings, the sometimes unresolved tension between interiorization and outwardness. His clear points of criticism also need to be thought about: the status of women as compared to men, the way in which Islam deals with suffering and the question of non-violence, and the amazing reluctance of Islam to accept Jesus' death (on which meanwhile Islamic theology, too, is now reflecting, CWR 111).

(b) Jesus in the Qur'an

This brings us to the most interesting and also the most exciting question – as far as relations between Christianity and Islam are concerned. It is the question of the picture of Jesus in the Qur'an and the Qur'an's criticism of the Christian picture of God, in other words the charge that Christians destroy the unity of God by their belief in three divine persons. This theme is not unknown to Küng, and on the basis of his concern with the process of Hellenization in Christianity he has the necessary tools of historical criticism to hand for engaging positively with the Qur'an's criticism. It is obvious that here he can also mark the points at which Christian and Islamic tradition diverge.

The boundary lies where Jesus, according to the Christian interpretation, in fact goes beyond the claims of a prophet and claims God's authority for himself (CWR 95f.). It does not lie where a christology influenced by Hellenism begins to define Jesus as divine in essence. However, these reflections too take a surprising turn in Küng: historically, there is some support for believing that Muhammad adopted the traditions of Jewish Christianity beyond the Jordan, separated and largely forgotten within the realm of the empire, and branded as heretical. No exalted divine picture of Jesus ruled there, but the picture of the sufferer as attested by the speeches in the Acts of the Apostles:

'These passages plainly speak of Jesus as *God's* servant, *God's* Christ, *God's* chosen one: God acts through him, God was with him; he was killed in accordance with God's plan, but God raised him from the dead, made him Lord and Christ and . . . appointed him the Son of God. Don't all these statements . . . still very much fit into the framework of a strict Jewish or Islamic monotheism? And yet this was the faith of Christians – of Jewish Christians. And perhaps, of Muslims, too?' (CWR 122, with reference to Räisänen).

As we already saw, in *Christianity* Küng returned to this situation (see above, 311), and we may eagerly await the way in which it will finally be depicted in an analysis of the history of the origins of Islam. These connections are theologically exciting, because the memories of these Transjordanian Christians, separated from the mainstream church and despised by it – having been transformed by Muhammad's religious genius – became a dangerous challenge to the Christian church from outside. There is no historical proof of any dependence, but the analogies are perplexing for Küng. Islam reminds Christianity in a dangerous way of its past, of the repression and loss of its Jewish roots, which did not yield to the interests of the empire and the universalist ontological thought structures of its culture (CWR 122–6). Even those who regard Hellenistic christology as unsurpassable must be content with a more modest profile in the ecumenical dialogue between the monotheistic religions.

(c) An unexplored field

The great monograph on Islam, the last part of the trilogy on the religious situation of the world, is still to come. Around 500 pages have been written on the origin, centre and history of Islam (modernity apart). Obviously this topic has been much more demanding than work on Judaism and Christianity. As Küng remarks in an internal report, there were 'of course countless detailed studies by specialists of all disciplines on all the individual topics'. But there were only 'a few satisfactory systematic and analytical overall accounts which were capable of describing the wealth of Muslim tradition in its historical development and its intellectual context'. Moreover, the difficulty of describing the relationship of Islam to Judaism and Christianity is obvious.

Finally, there is Arabic, which is strange not only for Küng but also for many professionals in his circles. That means that he first has to make himself familiar with the basic Arabic concepts of Muslim philosophy, theology and history. In addition there are his contacts with various Arab countries and personal exchanges with experts in Islam. So it is also becoming clear that this monograph is claiming yet more energy.

Nevertheless, its appearance in particular will be of great significance for the construction of an inter-religious theology. In the meantime a historical and at the same time self-critical awareness has developed among many Christians. Knowledge of the history and faith of the Jews has increased considerably. Knowledge about the origin, history and internal divisions within Islam is growing only laboriously (Falaturi, NHFT 326–34). The arguments over the award of the Peace Prize of the German Book Trade to Annemarie Schimmel in the autumn of 1995 spoke volumes. The displacement of a differentiated picture of Islam by the political situation in Iraq and Iran, in Algeria or Libya, and the narrowing of all reflections to the slogan 'fundamentalism', are having devastating effects not only on politics but also on the religious encounter (E. Elsahed, NHGD 663–71). Three world religions of tremendous potential are clashing with one another, when they could once more be taking up and shaping questions for the future in the faith in the one God which they share. The average theology in Europe can hardly keep up with the development. So we may wait eagerly not only for analysis of Islam in itself but also for an analysis of the growing alienation between Islam and Christianity (Kuschel 1997).

5. 'Paradigm' as a category in religion and theology

What has been the result of this chapter? The world of an integrating, almost encyclopaedic theology which goes beyond the disciplines has been opened up to readers. Here no dimension has been spared; everything becomes theology. Or does theology here become a comprehensive horizon for the question of the future? I see a new invitation in the shift of perspectives from the past to the present; from the synagogues or churches to their context and vice versa; from the criticism of Judaism, Christianity or Islam to the tremendous hope in them; from the question of the centre of faith to the illustration of its incredible fullness; from the verdicts on abuse and distortion to the challenge of new possibilities. It is an invitation for the contribution that can be made to education by a global theology.

At the end of this chapter we must extrapolate the result of the overall project on the religious situation of our time. In addition to the analysis of Judaism and Christianity there will be the analysis of Islam. This too will in itself represent an extension of perspective for theology – especially in the face of contemporary problems. Questions of belief in the one God and belief in Jesus Christ, and questions about the unity of the three Abrahamic religions, will pose themselves more urgently. But the third monograph will also expand the overall view of Christian theology in another way. The consistent questions and cross-references, the tracing of structural analogies, the increasing comparability of intrinsically uncontemporaneous phenomena – all this will qualitatively determine the level of a future theology of religions – especially in the Abrahamic trialogue.

However, it has already also been said that Küng does not research either Christianity or the other religions for their own sakes. The goal of his work is a peaceful world which discovers itself from the power of the religions. That is what the next chapter is about.

We may leave to later discussion whether the paradigm theory has been exhausted and is always applied without contradiction, and how the constant change between three levels of paradigm (culture, religion and theology) takes place; whether the chronological extension of the paradigms which came into being in Judaism, or which became the church, can be fully justified. The decisive thing is that here the paradigm theory has helped to tie the material together tightly, and will do the same in the case of Islam.

If I am right, Küng's method of analysing paradigms of religion has meanwhile taken the following form. The paradigm analysis of a religion begins from the basic distinction between 'essence' and 'history'. The 'essence' of a religion means its original form, in which an abiding norm is later recognized. This includes a particular originating event, and particular basic convictions and dispositions, which are often set down in normative texts. The 'history' of a religion can be divided into epochs, which are to be investigated as 'paradigms' in accordance with what has been said (see above, 282ff.). Each viable paradigm develops its own rationality, can exist alongside other paradigms and will continually relate to its originally 'essence'. So terminologically – if I understand Küng correctly – it must be maintained that:

- Each paradigm within a religion maintains its affinity to other paradigms of the same religion and is to be regarded as a sister. It is the task of an inner-religious (e.g. Christian, Jewish or Muslim) ecumenical theology to ensure this.

- Each paradigm of a religion is to be understood from the circular connection with a cultural (political, social, economic) paradigm change, but can continue to exist if the cultural paradigm shifts. It is the task of paradigm analysis within the individual religions to illuminate these connections.
- All the existing paradigms of all religions are confronted with a new common challenge in the present. This is the coming paradigm of a world – called postmodern from a Western persepctive – which is growing together and as a result is yielding unsuspected possibilities, which can lead either to global security or global destruction in the future. The consequences of the religions and their paradigms will be :
  - a new (specific) reference back to their own values,
  - a mutual (general) approach and recognition as religions, i.e. peace between them,
  - a shared (universal) reflection on the common values of a future world which is globalized and increasingly interdependent.

A paradigm analysis has the advantage over a purely historical reconstruction that the depth structure of a religion, i.e. the interaction between origin and later form, is clearly worked out. Explicit attention is paid to the relationship between particular forms and their cultural horizon, and as a result it is possible to discuss the cultural, political and other relationships between a religion and its environment. Individual and chance phenomena are related to a dynamic connection between 'essence' and paradigmatic form and thus objectified. The enormous amount of knowledge about religious and historical memories is reduced and becomes available for systematic analyses. Religions can be compared in essence or in paradigmatic form. Finally, the method helps the aim of investigating the possibilities of all religions in a new world, which is growing towards a hitherto unprecedented unity.

10

A Global Ethic and Responsibility for Humankind

Are Küng's books the books of a theologian, the books of a specialist on questions of church structure, of faith, of the world religions? Are they the books of a utopian who writes his fantasies from the soul? Perhaps another verdict is also possible: after the great works on Judaism and Christianity has come a book of new immediacy. In recent years there has hardly been a book in which Küng speaks so directly to the point, hurls himself so directly into the discussion, and discloses so many of his original intentions. He is concerned with the spiritual foundations of humankind. Here truly is the essence of Küng, concrete, with real questions and aims. 'Wanted – A Vision' runs the heading to the preface of this latest, exciting book on *A Global Ethics for Global Politics and Economics* (GEGP):

'In this epoch-making paradigm shift in which the world, its politics, economy and culture are caught up, do we not need urgently to strive for at least basic orientation for the present in the light of the future, referring to the spiritual and cultural foundations of humankind? But who is in a position to offer such orientation? It is no small undertaking for an individual; a team could offer more specialist knowledge, but usually at the expense of the internal unity of the conception. It is a great undertaking if one is not on the one hand to give enigmatic oracles or prophecies, and to speak in dark suggestions and hints, yet on the other hand does not want simply to extrapolate particular data and statistical trends in order to give a supposedly certain prognosis of the future. Perhaps it is too great an undertaking, unless one simply wants to extol a "utopia" (a "nowhere") of the kind that in past centuries has so often led people astray and with its promises of a "whole world" has robbed them of the power to make decisions. What I shall attempt here will be quite the opposite: no noble ideas without any earthing, no cleverly devised plans which are impossible to realize, no enthusiastic notions of the future with no real reference to the present, no programmes for the doctrinaire and the dreamers, saviours of the world and moral preachers who are so prone to indignation' (GEGP xiv).

This comprehensive and demanding book has a prehistory: it has grown from two roots. One is the discovery of the world religions, the other the discovery of the world situation. The two hang together. The intensive discovery of the world religions has led to a global religious horizon, to a sense of what the religions really contribute and can contribute to the shaping of the world. An intensive and lifelong interest in the world situation (the key date for the ten-year-old Küng is 12 March 1938, the invasion of Austria by German troops, GEGP xvi) has finally led to a global political horizon, to a sense of what the world needs if it is to survive. But a specific occasion was still needed as a catalyst. In 1989 Küng gave a keynote lecture at a UNESCO symposium on the topic 'No world peace without peace between the religions'; it was as a result of this that the research programme of the same title on the religious situation of the time appeared in the same year (see Chapter 9).

The project is guided by three questions:

1. What are the paradigms of the past which are still active in these religions?

2. What are the challenges for the religions in the present?

3. What are the perspectives for the future and the possibilities for an understanding between the religions?

Küng understands his project as comprehensive research into foundations which is to help towards an understanding of the religious situation of our time. The analysis is to be carried through by means of the three religions of Near Eastern provenance: Judaism, Christianity and Islam. The results on Judaism and Christianity were already reported in Chapter 9. There already it became clear that these religions have not been discussed on the basis of immanent questions, but in their significance for the present time. So 'The Religious Situation of our Time' becomes the central theme under which Küng increasingly clearly brings these researches. This relationship to the world is reinforced in the course of further developments.

In 1990, at the World Economic Forum in Davos, there followed a report on the question 'Why do we need global ethical standards?' Now that the 'domestic policy' has been thoroughly discussed, the question is one of 'foreign policy' (GR xviii), which Küng has never lost sight of. Here I have to introduce three publications: *Global Responsibility* (GR), *A Global Ethic* (GE), and *A Global Ethic for Global Politics and*

Economics (which I have already mentioned, GEGP). They belong together and form – provisionally, who knows? – the conclusion and climax to his theological development. However, anyone who has not understood that these themes too are thoroughly theological, however secular they may seem, has failed to understand Küng's intentions. As Küng indicated as early as 1984, after his first great journey through the world religions, the issue is the situation of the world:

> 'Ecumenical dialogue is today anything but the speciality of a few starry-eyed religious peaceniks. For the first time in history, it has now taken on the character of an urgent desideratum for world politics. It can help to make our earth more habitable, by making it more peaceful and more reconciled.
>
> There will be no peace among the peoples of this world without peace among the world religions.
>
> There will be no peace among the world religions without peace among the Christian churches.
>
> The community of the church is an integral part of the world community.
>
> Ecumenism *ad intra*, concentrated on the Christian world, and ecumenism *ad extra*, orientated on the whole inhabited earth, are interdependent.
>
> Peace is indivisible: it begins within us' (CWR 443).

1. A project

Global Responsibility, a short programmatic book, came into being during the great project on the religious situation of our time; however, it is not simply a subsidiary offshoot, but the programmatic summary of the enterprise. It formulates the horizon, the great discovery and purpose which have gradually crystallized in Küng over previous years. It begins with the questions: What is happening in our time? What is the issue? What can we work towards? And here 'we' means all of us, not only we Christians but all who believe in God; not only believers but all men and women of good will. As I indicated, the question about our time was the second motive for the paradigm analyses, and Küng takes up the concept of postmodernity not with the intention of making a theoretical analysis but with a purpose which can be identified in concrete terms. He sees not only how since the First World War one bastion of our culture after another has collapsed, but also how the global developments of our time are increasingly losing direction and taking an arbitrary course. The achievements of science and technology present a second face which is becoming increasingly threatening; progress leads to disillusionment; the great ideologies of communism and capitalism have played themselves out. But at the same time, despite all the cries of gloom, a new breakthrough is making itself felt. The world is becoming polycentric, producing new holistic and ecological models and developing a partnership between men and women; a change of values is taking place in science and towards technology. Küng sees a new epoch which is taking up the humane content of modernity into itself and going beyond it.

(a) Human survival

The first part is about human survival, truly a vital theme. The conclusion from this first diagnostic step runs: 'At least on negative grounds, the catastrophic economic, social, political and ecological developments of both the first and the second halves of the century necessitate a world ethic if humankind is to survive on this earth' (GR 25). So there can be no future without ethical action which has a global orientation. Furthermore since ethics are not sufficient as a remedial technique, the question of a global ethic (by 'ethic' Küng does not mean ethics, but ethical norms, 'global standards', which are in fact binding) is to be responded to positively. So in many different and specific ways Küng asks why human beings (individuals and collectives) should unconditionally observe certain basic obligations, why particularly in democracies with a neutral world-view a basic ethical orientation with a minimal basic consensus is called for: the non-violent resolution of conflicts, self-obligation to a particular order and the acceptance of institutions which support this order. There must be an ethic of responsibility for the world around, the environment and the world of generations to come, aiming at the most humane society possible and an intact environment (GR 25–35). Here a coalition between believers and non-believers is necessary and possible (36–40).

In a second stage it then has to be demonstrated that religions can provide the unconditional foundation to which ethical obligations must ultimately appeal. Küng understands this with the reservation and claim of theological statements; this validity can be given an intrinsic basis, but is not exclusive: 'At least for the prophetic religions – Judaism, Christianity and Islam – it is the one unconditional in all that is conditioned that can provide a basis of the absoluteness and universality of ethical demands', that can provide a reason and a direction for our responsibility (GR 53). At the same time the religions agree in some fundamental ethical perspectives.

Now for Küng this is an extremely important statement. It follows at least provisionally from his knowledge of the world religions: they are concerned with human well-being, and this well-being is formulated in some basic maxims of elementary humanity. The religions seek reasonable ways between libertinism and legalism. In all of them the Golden Rule appears as an unconditional norm. They create moral motivations and order the obligations into an ultimate purpose (GR 55–60); or, put more cautiously, religions intrinsically have every possibility of doing this: 'Religions could do this if they wanted to. That reality often mocks such a programme in all the great world religions is, of course, well-known' (GR 62). Conversely, the contributions by individuals and groups which can be found in all religions are not to be overlooked. So Küng does not doubt the fundamental potential of the religions. His question is how this potential can be activated, reinforced and focussed as a shared global potential. The fact that this new consciousness has already made some progress in the Christian churches is important capital for him (GR 65–9).

So the project of a global ethic outlined in *Global Responsibility* first of all means commitment to the survival of humankind: an awareness that a new global responsibility for the world is indispensable; that this responsibility can be developed and adopted by believers and non-believers together; and that the world religions can be prominent supporters of such a global responsibility. Despite all the concrete examples and all the references to reality, the statements in this first part could sound abstract and demanding. Doesn't the theologian want to bring the world religions into dialogue, at whatever cost? Isn't there wishful thinking and a great deal of idealism here?

(b) Peace between the religions

No, Küng remains realistic, and precisely for that reason he emphasizes the positive possibilities. Secondly, the 'global ethic' project means a search for a peace between the religions. Are the religions capable of peace, and how can this capacity for peace be made fruitful, be activated? Here too the thinking begins from the negative side. Certainly religions are two-faced, but that is no excuse, since without peace between the religions, no peace between the nations is possible. It is beyond dispute that the religions have caused and still cause a tremendous amount of aggression, hatred, massacres, war and destruction.

Indeed, many conflicts are

'so indescribably fanatical, bloody and inexorable because they have a religious foundation. And what is the logic? If God himself is "with us", with our religion, confession, nation, our party, then anything is allowed against the other party, which in that case must logically be of the devil. In that case even unrestrained violation, burning, destruction and murder is permissible in the name of God' (GR 74).

So Küng is anything but naive; religions do not simply spread sunshine. But as a realistic observer of the world he also knows examples to the contrary. He refers to the ethical and religious motives in politics, which led for example to the reconciliation between Germany and France after the Second World War or to the reconciliation between the Federal Republic of Germany and the states of the Warsaw Pact. He mentions the Civil Rights movement in the USA in the 1960s, the peace movement worldwide in the 1980s and 1990s. Küng is convinced of the tremendous political importance of religion and the religions; here he presupposes that what he calls for can be attained, and he adds questions:

'What would it mean for tomorrow's world if the religious leaders of all religions, great and indeed small, decided today to give resolute expression to their responsibility for peace, love of neighbour and non-violence, for reconciliation and forgiveness? If from Washington to Moscow, from Jerusalem to Mecca, from Belfast to Teheran, from Amritsar to Kuala Lumpur, instead of helping to foment conflicts they were to help in resolving them?' (GR 75).

That makes him attack all the more strongly the main problem which has led and still leads to the failure of the religions. It is their claim to unconditional and exclusive truth (GR 77–83), which they defend with various strategies and which makes them forget any self-critical approach. Here one would have to concede that the frontier of truth and goodness runs straight through any religion (including Christianity); that every world religion must allow every other religion to hold up a critical mirror to it; that alongside their immanent criteria (their holy scriptures) and figures, the world religions must agree on a common, i.e. ecumenical, criterion for truth and goodness. As I have already indicated, this is not only well prepared for in the global political and inter-religious dialogue between the religions (one might think of the preservation of human rights, the emancipation of women, the realization of social justice and contempt for war), but can also be discussed. The issue is human dignity as a basis, the truly human as a universal criterion, and the conviction that humanity can be understood as a presupposition of true religion and religion as the fulfilment of true humanity (GR 84–93).

But a last point has to be added. Such a criterion and its consequences for an ethic capable of peace cannot be decreed, but have to be worked out critically and self-critically in dialogue. That may seem obvious, but Küng nevertheless puts an amazing and very realistic emphasis on this point over against all concepts of dialogue, however harmonious and focussed on consensus; we already investigated it in the previous chapter. He highlights the (apparent?) discrepancy between universality and concreteness in religious criteriology, between the criterion of universal humanity and the specific normative sources. This discrepancy is repeated in the fact that specific human beings, i.e. members of particular religions, enter into dialogue with one another. Küng sees steadfastness, i.e. being rooted in one's own religion, as an unconditional presupposition of dialogue, and associates this with the classic virtue of boldness:

'Resistance to external powers and those in power.' Thus it has to do 'with self-assertion, not giving in, holding firm; with courage, resolution, executive ability – all this with the freedom and responsibility of the individual in view. So precisely in the light of the classical tradition steadfastness is not a rigid and static reality, but a dynamic reality which proves itself in the processes of life' (GR 95). For Küng, only this approach makes a real dialogue possible.

Such a dialogue rooted in faith would:

'• begin with what is given and leave completely to the process of conversation and understanding what will finally emerge as a result and what can finally be said, say, on the relationship of Jesus Christ to the prophet Muhammad (to take just Christian-Muslim dialogue as an example here). This is emphatically an *a posteriori* approach;
• see the different traditions, their foundation documents and bearers of salvation, in their context and with their own status (for example, it is well known that in Islam the equivalent position to Jesus the Christ in Christianity is not occupied by Muhammad,

who did not want to be a Christ, but by the Qur'an), so that a differentiated overall view of interwoven traditions becomes possible. This is a strictly historical approach, for all its anchoring in faith;

- *a priori* accept the standpoint in faith of their conversation partners and primarily expect of them unconditional readiness to listen and learn, and unlimited openness which includes a transformation of the two conversation partners in the course of a process of arriving at an understanding. This is a patiently realistic way;
- *a priori* acknowledge their own conviction of faith (Jesus is normatively and definitively the Christ) and at the same time take seriously the function, say, of Muhammad as an authentic (post-Christian) prophet – especially his "warning" against a deviation from belief in one God in christology. This is a self-critical Christian standpoint' (GR 102).

Manifestly – given the lack of a theory of dialogue – it is difficult to describe and define one's own presuppositions without misunderstandings (see above, 288ff.). Therefore the first of the points mentioned is decisive for an understanding of Küng's position. Küng does not see steadfastness and a readiness to listed as alternatives. So he does not confuse 'rootedness in faith' with holding firm to formulae, to particular propositions or codes. For him, self-criticism is compatible with a confession of faith, and relativization of formulae of faith is compatible with resolute faith. All his life he has always fought for this from within his own church, and it is quite clear that in an idealistic or unhistorical approach 'steadfastness' and 'a capacity for dialogue' can get in each other's way. Thus precisely at this sensitive point an understanding of Küng's intentions presupposes a knowledge of his theological career.

I shall break off the discussion of this short book here. Some things have already been mentioned, and I shall return to others. Once again, *Global Responsibility* is not a monograph but a programmatic work; its emphasis is not on extended explanation but on urgent presentation. What stands at the centre are not the internal analytical connections (which are reflected on at length elsewhere), but the urgency of the matter:

'The slogan of the hour is therefore, "We must begin on global religious understanding here and now!" We must advance inter-religious understanding energetically in the local, regional, national and international spheres. We must seek ecumenical understanding with all groups and at all levels. As we saw, the "postmodern" paradigm can be described in religious terms as an ecumenical paradigm' (GR 135).

2. A declaration

How is that to be done in practice? Küng, who in constructing theories always wanted to make a connection with praxis and to change things, and was never at a loss over concrete initiatives, can plainly demonstrate the possibilities and effects of such a dialogue on a global ethic. He does not need to begin from scratch. As early as 1970 the 'World Conference of the Religions for Peace' passed a declaration which mentions central points like the equality and dignity of all human beings, the unassailability of the human conscience, the significance of right over against might, the value of love, compassion, unselfishness and truthfulness, and an obligation towards the poor (GR 63). The importance of this issue was emphasized in 1989 at a UNESCO conference on 'Education to Human Rights'. There for the first time the formula occurs which was later to become so central: 'No peace among the nations without peace among the religions.' The positive reactions of the World Economic Forum at Davos in 1990 had already found their way into *Global Responsibility*, which we have just discussed.

(a) A global ethic

But now Küng himself faced a demand. It was up to him whether the Parliament of the World's Religions, the background to which Kuschel reports (GE 77–105), was to make a concrete declaration. The preliminary work required a great deal of energy, but finally proved successful. So it was a great triumph for inter-religious dialogue and for the cause of world peace when the 'Declaration towards a Global Ethic' was passed at the meeting of this Parliament from 28 August to 4 September 1993. Of course it is the Parliament's declaration, and many proposals and suggestions from the world-wide preparatory body found their way into the text. But the shape, the inspiration and the final form of the text wholly convey Küng's intentions.

As Küng often explains, a 'global ethic' does not denote a developed ethical scheme. It does not represent an ethical minimalism but a minimum of what can be said in common today. Even more importantly, it is not an ethic which representatives of different religions have, say, worked out with one another, but an indication of the existence of ethical convictions which are in fact common to the religions of today and can be derived from their own binding sources. This point is of decisive significance, since only on this basis would the declaration have a chance of really being accepted by the various religions. It is also the test case for Küng's requirement that the representatives of a religion should really put forward their own convictions in a dialogue. Indeed, Küng's requirement is confirmed and supported by the hope that consensus really can be worked out and aimed at.

Finally, the 'global ethic' described here is to be distinguished from comparable possible or real texts. The Declaration of Human Rights is not to be duplicated; the issue here is action and responsibility, not rights. A political statement, a philosophical treatise, a casuistic moral sermon, and even an enthusiastic religious proclamation are to be avoided. The declaration is to prescribe irrevocable criteria and attitudes; it must be capable of commanding a consensus, self-critical and generally understandable, and have a religious foundation. These are no decorative epithets, but tasks which involve a great deal of work. The history of the origin and discussion of the document shows something of the drama that it finally provoked, but also how much tolerance those involved in its production had to show to one another, up to the point of the Buddhist refusal to accept a mention of the name of God.

The opening sentences of the declaration are dramatic:

'The world is in agony. This agony is so pervasive and urgent that we are compelled to name its manifestations so that the depth of this pain may be made clear.

Peace eludes us . . . the planet is being destroyed . . . neighbours live in fear . . . women and men are estranged from each other . . . children die!

This is abhorrent' (GE 13).

This diagnosis sets the decisive accent: the religions do not speak of themselves but of the world; this time there is no introspection.

'We all have a responsibility for a better global order.' This key statement from the first section of the first part sets a decisive emphasis. It lays down the decisive framework for the whole enterprise. The religions acknowledge their shared responsibility for the future of the world. 'As religious and spiritual persons we base our lives on an

Ultimate Reality, and draw spiritual power and hope therefrom, in trust, in prayer or meditation, in word or silence. We have a special responsibility for the welfare of all humanity and care for the planet Earth.' The second section sums up the core of the shared ethic in the statement: 'Every human being must be treated humanely.' The issue here is the dignity of human beings and the obligation to do good and to shun evil. Is that a tradition which is common to all? Indeed, uncontroversially the declaration can refer to the Golden Rule, which has a place in all religions. As Küng says, this declaration is not a new invention but a new discovery (GE 71).

(b) Four directives

Finally, four 'irrevocable directives' are mentioned, which to Jewish or Christian eyes seem very biblical. So is this a Western product? In fact the four directives can be read as the interpretation of four commandments of the Decalogue:

> You shall not kill! Or in positive terms: Have respect for life!
> You shall not steal! Or in positive terms: Deal honestly and fairly!
> You shall not lie! Or in positive terms: Speak and act truthfully!
> You shall not commit sexual immorality! Or in positive terms: Respect and love one another!

But it may be a surprise that these demands are also found in the other traditions and in principle are affirmed by all of them. Even more astonishingly, the current interpretation of them is accepted by all present: respect for all life and the dignity of the person, a just social order, the repudiation of lies and manipulation, a relationship of partnership between children, adults and old people, men and women; or, as the headings say, a culture of non-violence, of solidarity, of tolerance and truthfulness and of equal rights. Included in this are the great sectors of human life which extend right over the world: politics, finance and economics; the media, science and art.

And what is the declaration to achieve? As the fourth paragraph says, it is about a change of consciousness. We know that the many disputed individual ethical questions have not been solved, that ethical codes in keeping with our time have to be worked out for many professional classes, that finally each community of faith has to formulate its specific ethic.

'What has each tradition of faith to say, for example about the mean-ing of life and death, about enduring suffering and forgiving guilt, about selfless devotion and the need for renunciation, about com-passion and joy? All this will deepen the global ethic which can already be recognized now, and make it more specific and concrete.'

The declaration was signed by fourteen religious communities (Christianity counting as one), and now positive and sometimes lengthy reactions can be read from thirty-five international personalities from public life and the great religions (GE 37–9; YGE).

For Küng, a good deal has already been achieved with this first public shaping of consciousness and the activities which have followed. A process of world-wide religious communication has finally focussed on a crucial world-wide theme: the situation of the world. Here he finds confirmation of his conviction that the inter-religious consensus on basic questions of the global situation and common action goes very much wider; in none of the great religions is there a need for new rules.

What is still to come is the real change of consciousness, i.e. the recog-nition that – regardless of many disputed individual questions – there can be recognition not only of the inviolable dignity and the inalienable rights of each individual, but also of individuals' unavoidable responsi-bility for their own actions and the common future of the world. Therefore the specifically religious forces need to be mobilized.

'We pledge to work for such transformation in individual and collec-tive consciousness, for the awakening of our spiritual powers through reflection, meditation, prayer, or positive thinking, for a conversion of the heart. Together we can move mountains. Without a willingness to take risks and a readiness to sacrifice there can be no fundamental change in our situation! Therefore we commit ourselves to a common global ethic, to better mutual understanding, as well as to socially-beneficial, peace-fostering and Earth friendly ways of life.

We invite all men and women, whether religious or not, to do the same.'

Programmes do not set out to analyse but to convince. They do not pose questions but seek to show ways. They appeal, challenge and carry on an implicit dialogue with readers. From this perspective *A Global Ethic* can be seen as a continuation or a concrete form of *Global Responsi-bility*. Both have the same aim. *Global Responsibility* is a programmatic work, which may not have achieved this aim but has come considerably closer to it. It is not the task of this introduction to investigate the reception of the book by readers. But it is already certain that this programmatic work (so far translated into eleven languages) – quite apart from the further books published since 1990 – has provoked an unexpectedly intense response worldwide. It has smoothed the way for many people to engage in a discussion with the religious and ethical traditions of this world which is both critical and constructive. The contribution it makes to understanding, tolerance and peace between the nations and religions is indisputable. But the programmatic work had yet a further unexpected result: the establishment of the Global Ethic Foundation, financed by one of its readers. This has made it possible for Küng to continue his work without a break after his retirement. The work has been continued in his latest book.

3. Global politics and global economics

In the case of *Global Responsibility* one can think of earlier programmatic writings: for example, *The Council and Reunion, Truthfulness,* and *Reforming the Church Today.* Here Küng's strength has always been that his programmatic visions were supported by detailed analyses or led to detailed conclusions. Now the extensive works on the world religions were already well advanced or, as we saw, there were already a large number of them. But what about the horizon of the 'world'? Can the analysis of postmodernity be taken further? Can the connection between ethics and the contemporary situation be described more subtly? Can the concept of responsibility, the significance of an ethic for the world situation, be described in more detail?

(a) Four steps

Küng takes an important step on this course in his latest book, *A Global Ethic for Global Politics and Economics* (1997). From the situation of our time he selects two formative, if not indeed the two central, sectors: politics and economics. In these two sectors he works through his theme in four parallel stages. These are: 1. analysis of the situation; 2. dealing with the situation; 3. responsibility; 4. ethic. In the political sector there is a further step towards the question of 5. peace.

Küng is not originally an ethicist, far less a specialist in political or business ethics, nor would he claim to be. Precisely this gives him the detachment he needs for his comprehensive approach. He argues from principles and heuristically, but sometimes also as someone who is taking the first steps at diagnosis, directing knowledge and research. Above all his argument is committed. He closely scrutinizes important developments and applied theories and never lets go of the one question which is decisive for him: What is the significance of ethics, responsibility and a global ethic with a religious foundation for global politics and economics?

Of course here Küng has to cope with the problem of any systematic theology which unconditionally and integrally accepts present-day reality as its horizon. Systematic theologians easily become generalists, since they want to say what is the case today. At the same time they remain specific, for ultimately they illuminate this reality from the particular standpoint of their own religion. Here their work continues to be exciting. They make connections between different positions: normative and factual, narrative and analytical, visions and hard reality, incompatible interpretations and a common background. Their approach is historical, developing the significance of the past for the present and making it fruitful. At the same time – at any rate if they follow Küng's global approach – they have to make connections between world histories which so far have taken separate courses. What is called for, at any rate in the postmodern situation, is the ability to integrate a dialogical or what Welsch calls a 'transversal reason', which can connect what is fragmented and isolated. The spirit of such a requirement and such an achievement can be detected in Küng's *A Global Ethic for Global Politics and Economics*: a comprehensive plan which at the same time requires to be worked out further. But what is Küng's specific achievement here? I see four answers.

First, Küng exposes himself to the tension between the two poles (religious origin and contemporary world, see above, 158f.) which I have already described in two areas which are unusual for theology. So far virtually no work relates questions of political and economic ethics so directly to a global ethic with a religious foundation.

Secondly, as we saw, he reverses the common sequence, described there, of the origin (the source, the first pole) and the horizon (the present, the second pole). He begins with an analysis of the present (which is of course very concentrated); faces the concrete questions it poses; and then shows what answers the religions have. Here the train of thought is of course jeopardized. Religions are really put to the test, since they could now be convicted of uselessness, alienation from the world or harmfulness. However, if the argument succeeds, it will not be constricted by religious tradition (which indeed always simplifies) but from the start will be able to offer the breadth which is needed for an appropriate analysis of reality. Religion remains an interpreter of reality and has not degenerated to a domestication of reality.

The arrangement described above (first the 'horizon', then the 'centre', see 286f. above) is prepared for in Küng's christology 'from below' (first information and historical report, then the confession as its interpretation in faith). On close inspection it is already put into practice in *Does God Exist?*: here the question is not ethic and responsibility but faith and truth. The stages are:

1. Increasing narrowing of modern rationality [analysis of the situation];

2. The problem of atheism and nihilism and a necessary decision [coping with the situation];

3. Fundamental trust [responsibility];

4. Belief in God [an ethic with the Golden Rule as a foundation);

5. Lived discipleship [a religious praxis of peace].

This comparison underlines the consistency of Küng's theological thought. The analogy is certainly of interest for fundamental individual questions. Couldn't one learn something about the question of responsibility (GEGP 59–90) from the analyses of fundamental trust (DGE 442–78) and about the relationship of rights and responsibilities (GEGP 99–105) from the analyses of inner rationality (DGE 571–5)?

Thirdly, Küng offers a heuristic interpretative framework. In a way comparable to Einstein's theory of relativity or to metaphysical conceptions, such an interpretation releases a twofold dynamic. On the one hand it opens up new connections: it can explain phenomena and help to understand them; it develops hermeneutical powers of discovery, and by that it will finally be measured. Outside science, such a process is intuitive and has much to do with the inner perspective of committed participation. On the other hand, such a theory calls for ever more detailed verification or falsification. The work of the professional ethicist, the political theorist and the economist are thus not replaced, but provided with questions and research tasks.

Fourthly, the formation of Küng's theory on politics and economics is subjected to the analysis of the postmodern paradigm and related to it. It constitutes a building block, the sectoral field of verification for a comprehensive perspective. This is an important step towards a further 'earthing' of Küng's attempt to understand the present (and the role of religions and Christianity in it) appropriately, and to get nearer to an understanding for peace. It is necessary to work through the whole paradigm if the whole idea is not to die for lack of air. Furthermore, the paradigm analysis serves a vision which embraces the world. It then it becomes clear how many hard individual questions the visionary programme is prepared for, and how it is finally subjected to this test.

These indications make clear what is meant by the third stage of a 'critical ecumenical theology' (above, 298f.), which presupposes the first two stages but now reverses the perspective. The perspective is no longer that of the religions on the world but that of the world situation on the religions. Here we have secular theology. A theologian who is well up in current affairs is not simply gettting his views on history and politics off his chest; rather, a scholar is continuing on the way that he began in the 1970s. His research areas at that time were already well worked and established on the basis of theological theories. Now for the theologian a wilderness of autonomous, theology-free sectors opens up, each of which follows its own rules. A wilderness? Not for Hans Küng. Some scraping always lays bare the golden veins which are of interest to his vision. A short survey of the two parts of the book will show that.

(i) What is the situation?

For Küng's analysis of politics the modern heritage is represented in three figures. Henry Kissinger in his publications practises and justifies a harsh geopolitics which is contemptuous of human beings, discriminates against 'moral feelings', and ultimately provokes the question: 'Can and should freedom, plurality and human rights simply be sacrificed to international stability and order in a global "grand design"?' But can order be the supreme moral principle (GEGP 13)? Following Machiavelli, Cardinal Richelieu subordinates all moral rules to reasons of state, and Otto von Bismarck, in his time the prototype of the real politician, elevates power (albeit in an intelligent way) to be the supreme criterion of politics. For many he remains an ideal; in the long term, the political map which he shaped became the breeding-ground of many catastrophic problems. This 'political paradigm of modernity' was taken to absurdity by the First World War and even more so by the Second (GEGP 27f.).

The argument about economics follows a similar course, though persons are not at the centre here. As Sweden shows, the model of the perfect welfare state is in crisis for various reasons, and this crisis cannot be surmounted without reference to ethical dimensions (self-limitation and solidarity) (GEGP 170-4). The neo-capitalist concept – with self-regulation of the market, free trade, export of jobs, slimming down for the sake of profit – does not help, as is shown by the policies of Ronald Reagan and George Bush in the United States (1981–1993) and of Margaret Thatcher in Great Britain. The social stocktaking was finally devastating: the quest for profit as the ultimately decisive principle is anti-social and illusory (GEGP 174–83). The new economic situation is summed up under the term 'globalization'. According to Küng and his informants, it is unavoidable, deeply ambivalent, incalculable in its effects and yet can be guided. Questions relating to the whole of society, which are highly political and ultimately also ethical, are under discussion. Küng's conclusion is that a globalized economic system must go hand in hand with a global ethical basic consensus (GEGP 217–30).

(ii) How is the situation being coped with?

Two important figures from the history of the USA are discussed in connection with the question of an appropriate political reaction. In 1918, in view of the experiences of the First World War, Woodrow Wilson developed an American peace programme which – backed by a lofty ethic – strove for freedom for all peoples, justice for friend and foe, and the safeguarding of peace through the League of Nations. His programme of foreign policy, often branded idealistic, was unsuccessful, but in the long term he was right. H.J.Morgenthau, the important political theorist, influenced by Nietzsche, saw the national interest, on which all power must be orientated, at the centre of all political action.

'In the system of sovereign states, the survival both of the states and of the whole system depends on the national interest being pursued intelligently, and the power of one's own nation and that of the others being assessed rightly' (GEGP 39).

So the question is one of the shrewd management of power. In the face of Hitler's success, however, before Morgenthau emigrated to America he found himself in two minds. Now he saw the need for higher values and those binding measures which, under Nietzsche's influence, he forbade himself to develop (GEGP 44f.). He did develop them, but in America again became the advocate of a rational power politics (GEGP 45). From this part of his argument on, Küng can now base himself completely on Morgenthau and other authors. The split between 'realism' and morality in Morgenthau is characteristic of the problem of a modern theory of foreign politics. From 1952 other tones could be heard from him. In 1960 he finally gave a major endorsement of the significance and necessity of ultimate values:

'Society has not created these standards and, hence, could not abolish them . . . The validity of these standards owed nothing to society; like the law of gravity, they were valid even if nobody recognized and abided by them' (GEGP 47).

Thus the traditional conflict between power and morality also emerges in other authors. In the meantime it has generally been recognized that power must be tamed within politics, and the classical ways of doing that are well known: constitution and laws, division of authorities, participation in power, unassailable basic laws, the principle of proportionality, the participation of all in power (e.g. the right to vote), reduction of differences in power. Theories of foreign policy have not as a rule reached this stage, since ethical aspects seem to elude a 'scientific' analysis. Certainly all neo-realist theories (like that of K.N. Waltz) take strict note of the economic aspects of global political conflicts, but they suppress their historical, ethnic and religious dimensions and thus show indirectly that they are fundamentally suppressing questions of universal ethical values. What remain are universal confessions (which are very much open to misuse) of individualism, freedom and human rights; alongside formal rights, the dimensions of responsibilities and criteria are overlooked (GEGP 56). Küng finally notes an immovable tension between politics and ethics. Politics cannot simply be subjected to an abstract ethic, nor can it simply be detached from ethics. For the important thing is to relate the (political) human reality to the great goals of humanity: 'The supreme criterion, even for political action, must not be reality, which can also mean bestiality in politics, but humanity' (GEGP 58).

The argument about the (theoretical) elaboration of postmodern economic problems takes a similar course. The starting point is classical liberalism and the socialist reactions to it in the nineteenth century, together with the qualifications of or extensions to these theories in the twentieth century. Its many representatives will not be discussed in more detail here. Among the 'ultra liberals' they are L von Mises, M. Friedman, F. A. von Hayek and the influential North Americans J. M. Keynes and J. K. Galbraith (GEGP 186–96). But as K. Polanyi and others showed, all of them forgot the presuppositions of their forefather Adam Smith (1723–1790), who had already developed these in his classic three-volume work (1776). A year previously, he had described the three indispensable virtues: prudence, justice and benevolence:

> 'To put it simply, the motivations (especially economic motivations) stemming from self-interest are to be controlled by prudence, and the interplay of economic actions is to be balanced out by justice. But the basis of all moral judgment and also of moral self-examination must be benevolence' (GEGP 195).

So there is nothing about a 'natural' harmony and the ideologizing of the metaphor of the 'invisible hand'; it is possible for the market to fail, so state intervention canot be ruled out *a priori*. Finally, there is a need for a new awareness that – despite its undisputed autonomy – the economy 'has to do not only with money and community but also with living people' (GEGP 196).

Among the champions of a social market economy (order liberals), and alongside the successful Ludwig Erhard, theorists like Eucken, Böhm-Bawerk, Müller-Armack, Rüstow and Röpke are discussed (GEGP 196–208). It is important for the market economy to be accompanied by a consistent state policy of order, for social justice to be noted as a formative factor alongside individual freedom, and for both Protestant and Catholic notions to be taken up. The problem of this theory and of the politics which it inspired was its success: the blind trust in unceasing prosperity, an inexhaustible social policy and a democratic tendency in which welfare would be completely taken over by the state to which it gave rise. The subsequent problem was finally the fact that the 1968 protest movement did not succeed in developing and establishing convincing alternative models (GEGP 117–26).

This deficiency, alongside the rising ecological movement (nature is not a commodity), led to what Küng calls the ethical challenge of the 1970s. By this he means the 'women's, peace and alternative movement', and 'countless very different civic initiatives and life-style groups', which in one way or another protested against existing social conditions and political structures, and which raised questions about 'the meaning of life, self-determination and emancipation, along with new criteria for action'. For Küng these are 'an expression of that paradigm shift from modernity to a postmodernity which is no longer prepared to have people themselves primarily branded and treated as a "work force" and in this way as commodities' (GEGP 206). But the alternative has hardly yet established itself in public awareness. Thus unbridled economistic behaviour is accompanied by ineffective moral appeals to moderation, and against selfishness, profit and pleasure. That provokes fundamental questions: 'Why not be an egotist? Why be moderate? What is moderation? What is the standard for human beings? And what is the standard for society?' (GEGP 208).

Thus here – especially in a global perspective – an aporia comparable to that in political theories emerges. K.E.Boulding has already warned of an 'economic imperialism'. Küng can add other names from the USA, from Germany and from Switzerland. It must again be made clear that even elementary exchange relationships can function well in the long term only if they are supported by an ethic of mutuality (GEGP 208–11). And above all it is important to ensure that politics is not dominated by economics; rather, the primacy of politics needs to be strengthened in every instance. As Hauchler argued, what is needed is an international competitive order, stronger control of the flow of international finance, security against structural shifts, a compensation for drastic economic and social movements between the (areas of the) world religions, the internationalization of rising social and ecological costs, and international regulations against the excessive consumption of non-renewable resources. These aims cannot be achieved without a prior global ethical consensus, which will remain unattainable, above all if no stop is put to the growing economizing of politics at a global level (GEGP 215–19).

(b) Acting responsibly

The concept of responsibility plays a central role for Küng. Rights formulate claims and responsibilities which can be stipulated. It is also clear that with his concentration on the need to rediscover responsibility, Küng does not set out to develop a theory of international relations. That is a matter for precise and detailed professional knowledge. Küng's purpose is more limited, though of far-reaching significance: he calls for the basic ethical structure without which no appropriate humane world order can be attained in postmodern politics and economics (which are characterized by a polycentric globality). The classical concept of perceiving interests in an increasingly interdependent world is under discussion and has not just been discovered by Küng. Thus he mentions e.g. R. Falk of Princeton, who lists ten dimensions which are indispensable for a humane regime:

'Restraining war, abolishing war, making individuals responsible, collective security, the rule of law, non-violent revolutionary politics,

human rights, the stewardship of nature, positive citizenship, cosmo-
politan democracy' (GEGP 64).

Apart from fundamental questions, Küng restricts himself to the
problem of human rights. Instead of the real politicians' ethic of success
and the ethics of conviction characteristic of the idealistic politicians, he
calls for an ethic of responsibility.

'It presupposes a conviction, but realistically seeks the predictable
consequences of a particular policy, especially those that can be
negative, and also takes responsibility for them. The art of politics in
the postmodern paradigm consists in combining political calculation
(of modern real politics) convincingly with ethical judgment (ideal
politics)' (GEGP 66).

This is very much in line with Max Weber, whose definition of the relationship between an ethic of conviction and an ethic of responsibility is
usually misunderstood. Hans Jonas (*The Imperative of Responsibility*),
C. F. von Weizsäcker and U. von Weizsäcker, together with Al Gore,
have done important work here.

However, in addition to the substantive problem there is a personal
problem. Politics is not an anonymous business but always involves
decisions which ultimately have to be taken and presented by persons.
Must they fail because – according to a current alternative – either their
clear goals are unattainable or their attainable effects are immoral?
Küng rejects this alternative. Already classical and especially mediaeval
ethics knew the doctrine of the double effect (actions can also result in
unwanted effects), the collision of duties and the balancing of goods. An
ethic of responsibility is orientated on results, i.e. what is right in concrete terms, what is appropriate in a particular situation:

'Only in a particular political situation does a moral obligation
become concrete (here the realists are right). But in a particular
political situation, which only those involved can judge, the obligation can be unconditional (and here the idealists are right)' (GEGP
73f.).

Here Küng has two basic demands for the politicians: unconditional
truthfulness and the instrumentality of power, which must never
become an end in itself. These are not moralistic perspectives but completely realistic ones, since a policy directed by morality can also be
effective, and elections can be won with it. In particular a consistent

policy of human rights can be called for at an international level and demand respect from those concerned. So 'ideals and realities can be quite compatible' (GEGP 79–90).

Now as Küng shows, it is precisely the global (especially economic) constellations of problems which advance the call for world-wide responsibility, for an ethically motivated policy of world order (GEGP 220–33). Despite all the disappointments, here declarations and proclamations can show an effect. One might think of the Geneva Convention, the founding of the League of Nations, the founding of the United Nations with all its sister and subordinate organizations, and the proclamation of the Universal Declaration of Human Rights.

Küng mentions three more recent declarations in which the demand for a global ethic is explicitly made. These are the report of the UN Commission on Global Government (GEGP 223–7), the report of the Commission on Culture and Development (GEGP 227–31), and finally the Declaration of the InterAction Council on the question of global ethical standards (GEGP 231–4). Each in its own way calls for global values as the core of a policy of world order, a global civic ethic, and a global civic culture, but with the exception of the last document they shy away from referring to the incomparable resources of the world religions. So Küng calls in outline for a new paradigm of an ethic for the economy. It is an ethic which centres on the demand for justice common to all religions and at the same time is aware of the variables of these constant basic demands, and with deep commitment overcomes the gulf between an ethic of conviction which has no economic dimension and an economism which has no convictions. In other words, it aims at ethically responsible ways of doing business (GEGP 234–42).

One last aspect brings the ethical dimensions more strongly into the centre than those previously mentioned. This is the call for a 'sustainable', a 'lasting' development (the World Summit for Social Development in Copenhagen), and thus for a development which does not destroy its own goals by a definitive exploitation of resources. But the need for such a 'permanent' development, for the well-being of coming generations, cannot be supported scientifically. Quite evidently it is an ethical decision. Such a decision depends utterly on our ethical motivation.

'It is in fact a deeply ethical basic decision whether I think at all about the fate not only of our children but of future generations generally, not to mention whether I work so that things go better for future generations than for mine, or at least no worse. So ethic is more than weighing up interests in the specific instance. Ethic aims at a commitment to others which is both unconditional and universal' (GEGP 244).

However, in the face of these demands religions, too, can fail, as was shown above all at the UN Conference on World Population in Cairo (1994), in questions of sexual morality, and especially birth control. So a warning must also be issued against an incompetent religious moralism.

Küng begins with the question of survival, the maintaining of a world with a future. The new responsibility begins with the image of a humankind with a place in the cosmic order. Küng joins Hans Jonas in calling as a first imperative for an ethic of survival, growing out of the virtues of serenity, level-headedness, gratitude and provision for the future (thus Hoffe). Here is the point at which the question of an ethic with religious support comes into play.

(c) Consequences for a new ethic

Now, in a fourth stage, the results of these considerations can be investigated. First of all it is has been demonstrated that the way in which the political and economic situation is coped with, both theoretically and practically, is unsuitable for the dawning age of a global society. Küng has worked out that the situation can be tackled only if the dimension of responsibility is recognized and achieved for the whole world, for its present and future. This world-wide responsibility, which is open to the future, needs a code of universal ethical standards (moral values, norms and attitudes) that can hope for a world-wide consensus. It must be a necessary minimum of shared human values, criteria and basic attitudes.

How are these to be discovered or achieved? Küng does not follow the abstract procedure of J. Rawls or the discursive ethics of K. Apel or J. Habermas. First of all he follows the concrete approach of M. Walzer, who discovers in protest actions which carry conviction all over the world (for example in Prague in 1989) two basic demands that form a 'core morality'; from them a whole clutch of elementary ethical standards follows. These two basic demands are truth and justice. Walzer speaks of a 'thin' (i.e. elementary) morality which, depending on the historical, cultural, religious and political situation, then appears as 'thick' (i.e. differentiated according to cultures), and is offered in many concrete forms. A global consensus on the elementary morality is possible. Such an elementary morality 'can also be expected and promoted world-wide by other nations, cultures and religions: truth and justice. Here we have the claim of a "pure morality" which may never be given up.' But a consensus is necessary where moralities differ. 'In specific disputed questions like abortion or euthanasia, no unifying demands should be made on other nations, cultures and religions to have the same moral praxis' (GEGP 96). Küng follows this scheme up to a point, but thinks that here Walzer could easily have referred to great non-biblical religious and ethical-philosophical tradition. He illustrates that by the Golden Rule, which can be found in many religious traditions.

At a second point the relationship between law and the concept of responsibility, which with good reason has become a key concept in modernity (even if it is often misused and misunderstood), is clarified. Duty exercises moral but not physical compulsion. Not all responsibilities follow from rights, as Küng demonstrates by means of different examples, but rights cannot function without underlying customs. So right needs a moral foundation (as M. Huber has pointed out). 'Law has no permanent existence without ethics, so there will be no new world order without a world ethic' (GEGP 104).

Now the ground has been prepared for introducing the content of the 'first formulation of a global ethic' – i.e. the central statements of the Declaration of the Parliament of the World's Religions (GEGP 105–13), Even more sharply than in other texts, here Küng works out the core of the declaration. 'Every human being must be treated humanely! What you wish done to yourself, do to others' (GEGP 110). And once again he makes clear how significant truthfulness is for him, particularly in the sphere of politics.

When it comes to a global economy, hardly any further statements of principle need to be added to this chapter (GEGP 234–49). In fact world politics is a sector which comprises all important planned economic activity that can claim to be global. The economy has to accommodate to it. In other words, as soon as economic activity seeks to escape this overall context, it claims a domination which it does not have. But there are the first concrete formulations of a global economic ethic, to Küng's delight in a decade in which the question of morality is returning to discussions about economic activity. He refers to two international declarations, the 'Interfaith Declaration' (1993) and the 'Caux Declaration' (1994). Both declarations describe the responsibilities of businesses towards six parties: employees, customers, suppliers, financiers, the community and owners. The responsibility towards employees is of great importance. Thus the Caux Declaration:

> 'We believe in the dignity of every employee and in taking employee interests seriously. We therefore have a responsibility to:
> * provide jobs and compensation that improve workers' living conditions;
> * engage in good faith negotiations when conflict arises;
> * promote in the business itself the employment of differently abled people in places of work where they can be genuinely useful;
> * and finally, in addition to all the obligations of employers to provide information and communication, health care and further training, in particular to be sensitive to the serious unemployment problems frequently associated with business decisions, and work with governments, employee groups, other agencies and each other in addressing these dislocations' (quoted from GEGP 252f.).

Virtues like justice, mutual respect, stewardship, honesty and a spirit of trust, honesty, boldness, truthfulness, keeping promises and transparency play a role in shaping the declarations (GEGP 254). Of course such declarations do not yet secure the breakthrough to a new paradigm, and Küng still has plenty of questions to put about an appropriate business culture and an appropriate personality culture of business executives (GEGP 261–9), but I will not go into them here.

However, finally once again we find the real interest of a management which is ultimately orientated on results and wants to be successful. Does ethics have a chance in business? Küng's answer is clearly positive:

> 'A moral way of doing business has more chances. Only those who themselves have an ethic can give clear orientation to others, which is what strong leadership requires. They can give this orientation by pointing to all the values to which there must be an obligation, presenting aims, observing standards consistently, and adopting a quite specific attitude in practice' (GEGP 271).

Or in negative terms: in the long term an immoral way of doing business will lose out.

(d) World peace and peace between the religions

In the introduction to the book Küng shows something of the motive force behind it. It is the vision of world peace, preparation for it and a guarantee of it by the world religions. Anyone who wants to understand his motives and driving force must not forget this great aim. It began in his youth as ecumenical reconciliation between the churches, later took on its contours in his commitment to a Catholic Church and a Christianity capable of reconciliation, and finally – after the concern with the world religions – was worked out as a direct and explicit theme. It is not Küng's prime concern to bring the role of the world religions into play positively or negatively, but to change the general trend towards forgetfulness of the religions. Their role in forming a global ethic is surveyed, as is their role in destroying peace and creating peace in the world. Only those who discover the role of the religions will be able to deal with them realistically and react to them appropriately. And only those who see through the complexity of this role can recognize the potential of the religions and perhaps influence their behaviour.

(i) A clash of civilizations?

Küng takes up the question of world peace in the middle of the book. The problems are concentrated there. He knows that he is asking his readers to join in a 'forced march': first a march through modern world politics, and then a march through the actual problems of world politics:

'From the strengths and weaknesses of a real politics orientated on power and interests we arrived at the strengths and weaknesses of an ideal politics orientated on moral principles and finally developed the perspective of a politics of responsibility, which tries to take seriously ideals and realities, principles and interests, rights and obligations at the same time – all in the framework of a world society which needs a global ethic as a basis' (GEGP 115).

Küng's first question is about the role of the religions in coming conflicts; the occasion for his question is the discussion of S. P. Huntington's book on *The Clash of Civilizations*, and its main thesis that coming wars will be wars between the civilizations, which are primarily determined by their religions. Küng regrets that this simplistic thesis encourages thinking in terms of blocks, suggests a simple system of co-ordinates and ignores common features. At the same time he derives satisfaction from the knowledge that now at last the fundamental role of the religions is being taken seriously, and points out that in the modern world, too, religion is 'a central, perhaps the central, force that motivates and mobilizes people . . . What ultimately counts for people is not political ideology or economic interest. Faith and family, blood and belief are what people identify with and what they will fight and die for' (quoted from GEGP 117).

Küng takes over this thesis with qualifications. In the postmodern period, too, conflicts are breaking out over economic, political and military power interests, but here the ethnic and religious differences form subterranean structures. Thus religions do not offer a carto-graphical surface, but a conscious-unconscious depth dimension which stands at the beginning of many conflicts. Therefore a warning needs to be issued against Huntington's simplistic thesis:

> 'The allegedly unavoidable global clash of civilizations is perhaps the new anxiety-provoking model which is needed by some military strategists. But the vision for humankind which points towards the future is global peace between the religions as a presupposition and motive force for a global peace between the nations' (GEGP 119).

This thesis is followed by concrete examples, clear discussions (backed up with scholarly investigations by Johnston and Samson, Luttwak and Burnett) of 'secularizing reductionism' (E. Luttwak), i.e. of a policy and a diplomacy (of the USA and other states) which does not recognize the dimensions of religious, ethnic and spiritual conflict, far less take them seriously. This has resulted in numerous wrong foreign policy decisions (Lebanon, Iran, Palestine); the many contributions of religions towards furthering peace (France/Germany, Nicaragua, Mozambique, the Philippines, South Africa) have not been noted. For Küng, Yugoslavia becomes the warning example of the catastrophic failure of a short-sighted policy, but also of the failure of the churches not to take seriously their opportunities over fifty years.

(ii) The resources of the religions

But what holds society together? According to a common judgment, pre-modern systems of meaning and obligation are worn out. But Küng sees possibilities for a new reinforcement of a sense of values. He does not make any claims to exclusiveness but emphasizes the significance of the religions. What is their role? As always, he puts his cards on the table. Religions (or particular religious currents) can act as catalysts. In addition to a 'post-modern random pluralism' (GEGP 136), Küng mentions religious fundamentalism above all of Islamic origin, but also the religious moralism which is put forward, for example in questions of sexual morality, by John Paul II (GEGP 133–6). So religions do not have an exclusive function for a renewed future. However, for Küng, beyond question our society needs a new moral foundation, a new basic consensus 'on common values, criteria and attitudes which combines autonomous self-realization and responsibility in solidarity' (GEGP 141). Beyond dispute it has a binding force. It is an ethic which 'for believers is rooted in belief in a first and last reality' and which precisely because it has religious roots is adopted against a comprehensive horizon of interpretation.

Peace is possible, and the resources of religion must be mobilized for it. They by no means make other elements of a culture of peace (e.g. D. Senghaas's hexagon) superfluous, nor do they relieve us of the obligation to reflect on a new state order for the world (a kind of world republic with an understanding of states on many levels, GEGP 144–5). But work must be done on the possibilities of reconciliation between the religions. Küng envisages a reconciliation between Jews, Christians and Muslims (GEGP 145–8), and he asks himself what religions could – indeed must – undertake in connection with regional, national and international conflicts (GEGP 148–52). What is most important is first of all to interpret and practise human rights as human responsibilities. It goes without saying that Küng, who has never ceased to think and write as a Christian, entrusts these tasks to Christianity and therefore requires Christianity to resolve them – as one light among others (GEGP 148–52).

'The conclusion to be drawn from all this is that today we all face the tremendous ecumenical challenges of the third millennium. In the present century we have been able to make decisive ecumenical progress within Christianity (unfortunately the lifting of excommunications has not yet been achieved, nor has it yet been possible to achieve eucharistic intercommunion, but it is to be hoped that both will be realized under a new pontificate). Once again we must face the challenges of the interreligious ecumene. In a global society Christians are invited to take shared responsibility with those of other faiths for peace, justice, the preservation of creation and a renewed ethic. The fate of the earth is the concern of all human beings, regardless of the religion or world-view to which they adhere' (GEGP 156).

With this book Küng has presented a draft framework which represents the start, and by no means the goal, of the enterprise. The question remains whether alongside politics and economics he will investigate more closely yet other sectors of our present world situation. The situation and the upheavals in the world, responsibility as a decisively new paradigmatic element, the indispensable influence of the religions as a criticism of culture and society, and the sober optimism which makes him speak as a Christian – all these are elements of a new theology which is appropriate for the coming paradigm.

4. Secular theology

As we saw, Küng's theology has gone through several stages. Each new topic, from *Justification* through *The Church*, *On Being a Christian* and *Does God Exist?* up to the world religions, represented new theological ground. Does the question of a global ethic also present new criteria? The discussion has only just begun, and in both affirmation and criticism it is taking a haphazard course. So the following remarks are offered with considerable reservations.

(a) The language of the world

I begin with a general observation which is significant for Küng's work. His secular language is striking in a theologian. That was already the case in *On Being a Christian* when he discussed the figure of Jesus. Küng made full use of generally understandable categories of political and social life, individual experience, interpersonal relations and the history of Judaism and the Jesus movement which arose from it. He spoke of a completely worldly history with God. Only when one looks at the footnotes does it become evident how intensively Küng has discussed the Hebrew Bible and the New Testament, the later history of dogma and theology and specifically theological questions. This stylistic characteristic of a modest and generally understandable language was the result of the new approach 'from below' (see above, 160f.).

Initiates found little of the language and organization of a classical doctrine of God, and presumably it was this secular language which opened up a new approach to the topic for many non-theologians and suggested to many theologians that in this book the divine was being basically abandoned and sold off. Something similar applies to the concern with the question of God, in which Küng reconstructs the modern secular history of thought and makes Nietzsche in particular the foil for his own suggested solution. This characteristic is concealed in his preoccupation with the world religions, because religious material must constantly be treated. There too, however, over wide areas Küng has also provoked the question whether he has not stopped at the level of phenomenological or religious analyses. It is characteristic that his question, 'But does a reasonable person *today* want to become God?' (OBC 442), inevitably shocked his colleague Karl Rahner (DisC 108). Here the issue was not a substantive theological one, but a language game which was natural in the present but unacceptable to Rahner.

It was the same in *Does God Exist?* There the question of God was no longer discussed within the intellectual framework of the classical doctrine of the Trinity with its definitions of relationships in terms of essence and person, of proceeding and relation, of difference and the *communicatio idiomatum,* of the intrinsic and the economic Trinity, but within the framework of hiddenness and accessibility to experience, transcendence and historical nearness, eternity and mutability, mistrust and an unconditional trust, fulfilment and irresolvable suffering, distancing rationality and an inner affirmation by reason, in the notional world of a God who is unsurpassably near, speaks and acts in Jesus. Manifestly there were no conceptual worlds with their theological or sacral oaks, and this disappointed those who knew the language of Canaan.

This shift towards secular language continues, the more universal the horizon of Küng's questions becomes. In *A Global Ethic for Global Politics and Economics*, Küng moves as it were on the most secular level of his discourse. He does not discuss any history of images of God, piety or morality, but the history of political and economic theories. In no way does he draw attention to faith in God here, but (only?) to the forgetfulness – lasting from Machiavelli through Bismarck to Kissinger – of a guild which believed that it could leave out ethical principles in shaping the world. What is conjured up is not God's help or the power of an implicit or explicit faith, but the potential of the religions for furthering peace and an ethic to which a universal appeal can be made.

Is this still theology? The answer can be given in four stages.

- In the face of the present state of the world (economic and political globalization and independence), *A Global Ethic for Global Politics and Global Economics* quite certainly has a theological motivation and legitimation. There is certainly no doubt of that against the background of the investigations into the world religions and Küng's programmatic work on a global ethic. His remarks on securing and reinforcing world peace are the focus. That is the central utopia of the monotheistic religions.

- Given the dramatic problems of the world, it is the task of theology to join in the world dialogue in an effective way. So speaking in partnership, i.e. joining in with arguments which can be generally understood and thus collaborating in shaping the world, is a theological responsibility.

- To achieve a basic theological discourse which can be understood all over the world, the fundamental dialectic of any theology is to be taken seriously. Whereas God ultimately evades any objectivizing discourse, God is ultimately present in any inability to name him as such. Secular theology takes this heavy burden upon itself. But it can appeal to biblical and other traditions, according to which God is present where human beings are helped for their own sakes (Matt.25.40; see above, 135ff.).

(b) Activating praxis

As I have already said, Küng's book moves largely on the stage of political, social and economic debates. There are hardly any discussions with theological ethics; only in a few notes can the earthquake of internal discussions be detected. Moreover the first theological discussions – above all of *Global Responsibility* – have indicated that there are still misunderstandings.

The misunderstandings are sparked off above all by the term 'global ethic'. Küng points out that he is not talking about ethics, about a well-thought-out and well-argued system, from which minimal duties world-wide can be derived. With good reason, the term 'morality', which refers to a totality of norms to be accepted, a system of norms (religious or humane), does not appear. An ethic (the German *Ethos* is clearer, but will not work in English) is usually understood to be a basic moral attitude and disposition, i.e. not a system of abstract duties which first are given a rational basis and then have to be enforced. In the end, the question is whether world-wide there is a minimum of global standards, i.e. universal basic moral attitudes, which can serve as a starting point. If I understand Küng's approach correctly, three lines of thought which run in parallel are used to support one another.

The first is material and is worked out in the various investigations of the world religions and formulated as a programme in *Global*

Responsibility. It runs: amazingly, there is an indisputable basic consensus in the world religions. It relates both to matters of principle and to a contemporary formulation of some basic attitudes and dispositions. As we saw, the central key words are reverence for life and human dignity (the Golden Rule). In addition there are the key terms solidarity and justice, tolerance and truthfulness, equal rights and partnership. These basic attitudes are developed in very different ways in the different religions and cultures when formulated positively, implemented and concentrated as cultural values. Therefore there is still a polycentric ethic. At the same time each of the attitudes mentioned calls for a minimal form of behaviour (respect, right ordering, honesty, concern), so that one can speak of a global ethic, of elementary standards or a core morality (see above, 349). Moreover all world religions inculcate the awareness that these elementary basic attitudes are important for any survival in a world which is growing together and interdependent.

The second line of thought is more formal and is verified in the Declaration Toward a Global Ethic with its many signatories. Küng's slogan 'No peace among the nations without peace among the religions' presupposes and insists with great emphasis that the religions of the world (including Christianity in secularized countries) are a great influence intellectually, culturally and politically and in the shaping of life, an influence which can hardly be over-estimated. From this it follows for Küng that the basic attitudes and dispositions which have been mentioned (and which are not to be understood in terms of the current interpretation of Max Weber's 'ethics of conviction', GEGP 67) are not latent demands or abstract duties, but a reality of life which shapes the adherents of many religions. Misunderstanding them as a catalogue of duties which makes religions degenerate into a moral system is presumably the consequence of a traditionally Western and typically Christian misunderstanding of the 'directives' of the Hebrew Bible (Decalogue). They are no longer understood as the expression of a well-tried praxis which is engaged in and accepted as a matter of course. Religion is always a praxis which embraces the different dimensions of human existence. So the standards mentioned are not to be conjured up out of nothing but exist in the religions (and beyond them). That is Küng's conviction, without which his theology of a global ethic cannot be understood.

Only now can the third line of thought be mentioned. This is worked out above all in *A Global Ethic for Global Politics and Economics*. It is the confirmation and verification of the first line of thought. What the religions have to offer, or what they lay claim to and what they can bring to awareness more clearly than ever, are precisely those basic demands which arise out if the critical analyses which Küng presents, and for which he can introduce an impressive host of witnesses. They are the ethical dispositions and basic attitudes by which – contrary to modern theories – all sectors of life, including those of global political and global economic activity, must (again) be pervaded.

Here we must not forget the second line of thought. For the ethical demands which arise with the utmost urgency for the global situation can be resolved, among other things, by the ethical potential of the world religions. The one condition for this seems to me to be that the religions not only engage in dialogue (as happened programmatically in the 1993 Declaration), but are recognized and taken seriously as having a function in world politics. In other words, the relationship between the religions and other social forces in the world must be accepted. It is from this perspective that Küng rightly reacts very critically to Huntington's thesis of the 'clash of civilizations', because Huntington

1. speaks too sweepingly of religions and civilizations (as though Orthodox and Western Christianity had nothing in common);

2. does not see their potential for peace and reconciliation alongside their potential for conflict (as if religions had only provoked wars); and

3. provokes what he is warning against with his negative scenario.

Küng's genuinely theological conclusion is that we do not need to doubt the lack of an ethical global potential. Therefore he works with the means at his disposal and spells out this idea in a global language (of the religions, the sciences and world-wide organizations). A praxis is announced which can prove itself the foundation of a democratic society.

(c) Neither unworldly nor godless

In an article which first appeared in 1984 (see above, 287), Küng made the programmatic demand: 'If we want no "world-less theology", we also want no "godless theology"' (TTM 166). Expressed positively, this slogan describes the formal principle of Küng's secular theology. It is unconditionally worldly, and therefore unconditionally related to God. Certainly, caution is needed with big formulae. And what Christian theologian does not see his or her work within the field of tension between these two poles? But too often there is toning down, compromise and anxiety about being too much on one side or the other, as if too much is taken from God if everything is given to human beings, or human beings fall short if all trust is put in God. It is already remarkable how this tension is virtually transcended and abolished in Küng's last works. In them the world is unreservedly present. It is not (just) a matter of church or believer, not (just) a matter of religions or piety. The issue is quite simply the future of humankind, in a comprehensive perspective. The European Küng is concerned with all continents, the older theologian with youth, the scholar who has a very successful past with an unendangered future. The man who has been disciplined by his own church expects a change of consciousness from the whole world and is not afraid to end his book with a very worldly saying of Victor Hugo about the future:

'For the weak it is the unattainable.
For the fearful it is the unknown.
For the bold it is the opportunity' (GEGP 277).

But with this saying Küng makes clear a specific theological connection which at a very early stage already governed the in-depth structure of his theology. I might recall:

- his image of universal salvation, which God offers to all men and women. In the end there is no difference between Christians and non-Christians;
- his image of Jesus, who is wholly human and as such becomes the place of divine action. The divine is wholly taken up in human beings;
- his understanding of a contemporary faith, in which an unconditional trust in God and a comprehensive trust in human beings belong indissolubly together. The practice of faith can be fully realized in this world and for the sake of men and women;
- his conviction of God's presence in all religions, even in those which reject the word 'God'. God is there wherever religions devote themselves wholly to their cause;
- his discovery that, despite all the individual questions, an attitude of the deepest humanity, of reverence for life, of a sense of justice, honesty and partnership has developed in these forms of faith, which are so different in cultural and religious terms. That has to do with God's will and truth.
- The depth-structure of his secular theology runs: God is always present in this world, in the questions of its future, in dealing with human action and human behaviour. We cannot speak in too

worldly a way if we are to take this reality seriously as God's creation. The most comprehensive task of theology is to work as concretely and as universally as possible on the future of this world. If fortune favours the brave, Küng is saying that his work on a global ethic is not a detached diagnosis, but a committed appeal, that he will not and cannot offer any rational proofs, but wants to show the inner rationality of the utopia to which he has subscribed as a Christian. For him, speaking and writing have become action for a better future with a Christian motivation.

5. From ethics to responsibility

Küng's goals can be illuminated with another key word. In summary he says that the issue in both the political and the economic sphere is a new sense of responsibility (GEGP 277). Küng is not the first to have recognized this, either, and he refers with gratitude to authors like H. Jonas or C. F. von Weizäcker. Not only are the rights of individuals and peoples to be protected, but their responsibility is to be called for, since in the face of scientific and technical possibilities, from gene technology to nuclear energy, it has become boundless (GEGP 68).

How, in Küng's view, do rights and responsibilities differ? Rights offer protection from the interference of third parties and in state constitutions have developed above all as the safeguarding of justice and protection against interference from the more powerful. But rights do not take into account that all human beings can also be asked about their action towards others and in particular situations. Whereas rights make individuals think about themselves, responsibilities direct their attention to others, to the common good and to the future of our children. Precisely this is the point on which the religious traditions need to be heard. Religions think holistically; they do not speak *ex cathedra* but from millennia of practice. And they make it clear that a catalogue of rights can only be meaningful and function if it is embedded in a functioning network of responsibility, of mutual respect, solidarity, fairness and partnership.

Responsibility has been a central notion for Küng since the beginning of this work. That was already the case in the first lecture, 'No World Peace without Religious Peace', which he gave to UNESCO in 1989. It was even more so in the question to which he responded in Davos in 1990: 'Why do we need global ethical standards in order to survive?' There the issue was in fact the responsibility which rests on politicians and economic leaders, indeed which they have to assume. There too it finally became clear that this issue calls for a powerful coalition not only between the religions but also between believers and non-believers. In other words: here men and women are not addressed on the basis of their faith or the religion to which they belong, but on the basis of their humanity and on the basis of a common future which binds us all. Is that a theological programme or a programme for world politics? Certainly it is the latter. But one would have to be blind to miss the affinity to the great biblical utopia of a kingdom of God which is at peace, reconciled, and is constantly to be discovered afresh. One would have to be blind to fail to see that here in a very sober and pragmatic way work is being done on the questions which were once treated in apocalyptic in a dramatic way, and with the help of fantasies of catastrophe.

Küng not only calls for a responsible humankind; he has also done work here on his own responsibility. The questions which have been put to him from the economic and political side are clear. His answers not only met with a powerful response, but have had an effect at a political level all over the world. October 1997 saw the publication of a Universal Declaration of Human Responsibilities (Helmut Schmidt), which was approved by the InterAction Council and presented to the General Assembly of the United Nations for discussion and for a decision. This declaration explicitly sets out to supplement the Universal Declaration of Human Rights and, if it is passed, will be significant for shaping the public world consciousness in the next century. The structure of the core text can be indicated quickly. It calls for:

- Fundamental principles for humanity,
- Non-violence and respect for life,
- Justice and solidarity,
- Truthfulness and tolerance,
- Mutual respect and partnership.

One need not puzzle over the manuscript of this document nor doubt the fact that here a theology which works in a scholarly way and is related to the world has been taken seriously in public and heard by those who hold positions of responsibility in the present. Thus Küng's work is also a warning to all theology which condemns itself to ineffectiveness by a self-chosen limitation.

Conclusion

A Voice of Hope

'Hope also radiates from Küng's *Credo*, indeed from all his books and from the whole programme of his life. The call for hope in Küng is incomparably stronger than the words of his sometimes harsh criticism. Hans Küng brings hope, also and particularly in his contribution to ecumenism within the church and beyond it, the opponent of the present-day prophets of disaster inside and outside Christianity and the church' (Fries, NHGD 323).

1. What had to be clarified

In both content and method Küng's theology has a wide span, which reflects the dramatic developments of the past forty years. He shared the verve of the new beginning in the 1950s, engaged powerfully in ecumenical discussion and gained the stature which marked him out during the Council. He strode out in the first rank of the church's reform movement and at the head of those who do not abandon the call for renewal. In the 1970s he was the champion of a renewed understanding of being a Christian and of faith. In 1970 he attacked the claim to infallibility as a symbol of the Roman inability to reform; ten years later – now chosen by Rome as a symbolic figure of insubordination in the church – he had to pay the price with the withdrawal of his *missio canonica*. But Rome has not achieved its aim; Küng remains rock-hard in his cause, and is ready at any time to make accusations even against an inexorable pope. Outside the church his reputation has increased, and within it his credibility. At the same time he is now entering the forum of the world religions and finally those international organizations which are seeking to strengthen the forces of peace, world-wide justice and the preservation of the planet. H. Fries is right to depict his colleague and ecumenical fellow-fighter as one who brings hope, who does not give up because he always thinks that success is still possible. Both Hans Küng's biography and his theological development have elements of the heroic saga about them.

But it would be foolish to repeat the mistake of an English author of twenty years ago who wrote a *roman à clef* about Hans Küng; to do so would neither make sense of his person nor be in the interest of his cause. Those who follow the history of the making of church heroes always suspect the worst anyway. Such a move is usually started by groups which kept clear of their hero in his lifetime. No Neoscholastic would have been a friend of Thomas Aquinas; no present-day admirer of the pope would have been a supporter of St Peter; and no defender of infallibility a fellow-fighter with Petrus Olivi. No, the cause is served only with a critical discussion. What greater honour could one do a scholar, a person of the church, a middle man between the religions, a champion of the dialogue between church and world?

Here only a preparatory step has been taken in this direction. My concern has been to offer a sympathetic introduction to Küng's life's work, from which an overall picture can gradually be constructed. At the same time there was a need to contradict a Rome which refuses to learn, which still believes that it can pronounce on the catholicity of its boldest and most committed spirits by an administrative decision. This contradiction is all the more important to note, since the obsession with measures of every kind (from penitential silence and a ban on preaching to expulsion from religious orders and a withdrawal of the *missio canonica*, to deposition and recently even excommunications) has grown and is again being practised quite publicly. Küng's local bishop, too, needs to be reminded once again of a letter signed by myself and Professor Kuschel in March 1993, five years ago. In this letter we asked for the rehabilitation of Hans Küng; an acknowledgment of its receipt has yet to arrive. The view of the Catholic Theological Faculty of Tübingen University on this matter has been sufficiently made known since February 1996.

2. What still has to be discussed

Such a correction was necessary in order to clear the way for an open involvement with one of the most important Catholic theologians of our time. However, that is not easy and efforts so far have been inadequate. There are various reasons for this.

(a) Personalization

A first reason may be Küng's person. He always states his positions with great personal commitment. On the one hand he engages in anything but an anonymous theology and has never felt easy within the rules of that game. So anyone who grapples with Küng's work, as a rule grapples with Küng himself. Thus quite a number of discussions have led to vigorous controversies. However, at this point Küng's defenders do not fail to mention that these controversies were usually tied up with conflicts over positions held by the church. The issues were church office and church reform, criticism of papal centralism and the claim to papal infallibility, the right to a christology from below and mariology, the position of women in the church or Küng's style, which was often castigated as being immoderate or 'too harsh', as disobedient or arrogant.

So it is time to write the history of Küng's controversies and Küng's reception, and in so doing to raise the question what a generation after him thinks about the questions he has touched on. Here I do not exclude the possibility that many of the positions which twenty years ago were still being hotly argued over have now tacitly been adopted. The difficulty discussed here can be surmounted by investigating the different stages of Küng's innovative theology. Precisely what new things were being said in his book about the church? What is his attitude to exegesis and Protestant theology? What perspectives were once again made the centre of interest by this publication? How does Küng select (by highlighting or being one-sided)? What aspects does he bring into the centre? For what motives? Does his great personal commitment tend to ideologize or refine what he writes?

However, it is not enough to raise these questions in a purely functional way, since behind them lies another question, whether Küng's theology is 'credible'. Reactions to this question tend to be split. On the one hand we expect theologians to put forward their convictions existentially and without reservations, but on the other hand we quickly and readily entertain suspicions of vanity and inappropriate posing, and usually do not distinguish between objective and psychological, personal components. Uncertainty is overcome by finding scapegoats. Or has Küng too quickly looked for and found scapegoats for objective difficulties? A clarification of these matters which are often left unclarified could free our theology from some unnecessary animosities.

(b) Comprehensive theology

A second reason is the nature of Küng's themes and the problems to which he draws attention. Chapter 10 spoke of the comprehensive perspectives and horizons which are already evident in many titles of his books: *The Church, On Being a Christian, Christianity and the World Religions, Christianity, Judaism*. I already indicated in Chapter 1 that Küng develops more limited themes (e.g. justification) in the light of their contexts. The first reviews, but also later more comprehensive discussions, often react unspecifically and very generally to such titles: with sweeping praise or censure, with qualifications which confirm or cast doubt on Küng's scholarly seriousness, with reference to his loyalty or disloyalty to the church, in other words by personalizing his achievement and the questions he asks. As a rule, little note is taken of methodological perspectives. Then people seize on a few controversial statements: what matters is not a renewed church but the apostolic succession; not being a Christian today but the pre-existence of Christ; not a faith which can be given an account of today but contempt for the magisterium. The filters immediately come into play and cut out the cosmos of the real questions; one can have a splendid dispute, but touch only on incidental issues and not see the whole picture.

Moreover Küng has developed his theology in a period which – as a result of the universal explosion of knowledge – expects less and less material knowledge, and which therefore measures its views more by intuitions, philosophical tendencies, (church-)political correctness or edifying perspectives. This raises a whole series of questions about Küng's theology. These questions relate to method, content and strategy. Method: how does the wealth of Küng's material relate to its integration? Precisely what does it mean for scripture to be the norm and source of theology, and how has this normative function changed? What guiding function does historical recollection play (to warn or to inspire, to legitimate or to sanction)? Content: what strands of exegetical development and what historical lines are significant for Küng? Can principles of selection be discovered, and how have they changed over the decades? Strategy: can specific goals be identified in the light of which historical recollection is used, instrumentalized or brought to light again? How is the relationship between history and systematic statement to be described in Küng's theology generally?

As well as these formal relationships, one perspective needs to be noted which is important for Küng but which lacks theoretical clarification. Already in *Justification* Küng speaks of 'self-appraisal', in other words a self-critical process which accompanies any assimilation of information. Now as a rule Küng's 'criticism' is perceived as criticism of others. He criticizes the bishops, the popes, a past era, colleagues, particular positions in Israel or Calcutta, in the Protestant churches or in liberation theology. We need to look closely here. It will quickly emerge that as a rule Küng's criticism has two sides. In any case he always criticizes a church, a Christianity or a belief in God with which he identifies himself in principle. Küng's often-announced refusal to leave the church does not simply arise – as opponents are fond of claiming – out of defiance of Rome ('I'm not going to give them the pleasure!'). It is rooted in his faith in the cause of this church, so that in his theology of religions he does not depart from the criterion of Christianity. I personally find this position legitimate, but many colleagues do not yet find its presentation convincing. So here too is a point for critical deepening and argument.

(c) Writing as interaction

A third reason is the intensive interaction which is bound up with Küng's theology. It is perhaps the decisive secret of the polarizing, and in any case vitalizing effects of his work. Of course any theological statement produces interactions between speaker and readers. The author has readers in view. Even in his most exalted mood of scholarship, without any ulterior motives, he wants to achieve something (knowledge, conviction, a following or further action). This interaction is most clearly activated in Küng's programmatic writings: in *The Church and Reunion*, in *Truthfulness*, in a sense in *Infallible?*, and then of course in *Global Responsibility*. Here Küng relies on a gesture which scholars often scorn. So we must ask: how does Küng argue in his programmatic writings? Does he presuppose? Does he insinuate? Does he make unproven assertions? Does he steer away from critical objections or does he incorporate them into his arguments? How far are statements in his great works provided with a basis and explained?

Those works of his which are full of material would need to be analysed in a similar way. Here the concern for interaction is evident in the often highly didactic presentation, in the frequent sharpening of concepts and thesis-like summaries, and finally in the frequent attempt to incorporate the reader's moods, disappointments or expectations into the discussion. Küng's often urgent and intense style was discussed in the very first chapter. Does it help or hinder a sober scholarly presentation? Is polarization sometimes intensified where Küng wants to do away with it? Does an atmosphere of strain develop where there should have been an effort to pacify? Is sometimes enthusiasm whipped up where readers should generate it for themselves? These are difficult questions. Perhaps they have little to do with the quality of his theology, but they have much to do with his style. At least they could lead to a location or a criticism of a theological style which is less accepted in Germany than in other countries. And why cannot on the one hand an understanding of different styles of communication, and on the other of sensitivity in cautious but also honest dealings, grow together?

However, yet another theologically difficult problem is connected with this character, which is not simple to resolve. It is striking that it is not always clear even to well-disposed critics what loyalty to the church means for Küng. Doesn't being a Christian also mean 'believing with the apostles' (Tracy, HKFT 85)? I think that this critical question rests on a misunderstanding, though Küng himself has not clarified it sufficiently. Küng believes *with* the church (and with the bishops) and carries on a dialogue *with* the community, specifically – or at any rate that is his intention – by drawing fellow-believers into his thought-world through his urgent, interactive, indeed often active language. Precisely for that reason, for him, theology *is* church action, in my view in such a direct, committed and immediate way that he has always been stunned by the charge of disloyalty to the church and often has been able to react to it only with indignation. And why should someone who feels himself to be so directly *in* the church community not be able – along with others! – to put directly the question of a scriptural basis without at the same time exposing himself to the suspicion of dispensing with tradition? To say more would take us too far afield here. But the complex of questions has been sketched out and could rescue the traditional criteriology of scripture, tradition and the present from its barren schematism.

(d) Dealing with the public

A fourth point is the way in which Küng deals with the public inside and outside the church. I have already indicated that the church authorities discovered the significance of public opinion as early as the nineteenth century. Only since the 1960s has it played an independent role in the Catholic Church and in an interplay with theology. Beyond question Küng is a master at this game. This has always caused his opponents annoyance and anxiety and given them a feeling of helplessness. That is understandable. But at the same time it must also be understood that Küng, too, has often taken refuge in publicity (i.e. the press and the media) in critical situations when he has been himself annoyed and anxious and has felt helpless. Of course that is not the whole story. Küng could in turn be accused of frequently resorting to the press not merely for sheer defence, but also to launch his own attack. Who is right?

Presumably this question is simplistic because church authorities and theology, communities and the interested public, workers in church education and the social sphere, are all in their own way familiar with the press and media, involved with them and dependent on them. It seems to me that any other position is provincial. Thus theologians learn how to work with the press legitimately on behalf of the church in the same way as bishops. Both want to inform, to urge, to give the community a voice. This too is a point in which actual practice is still far ahead of reflection. Küng's conflict has strengthened it enormously, and perhaps made it insoluble. So far most reactions have used moral rather than soberly analytical criteria.

In view of the experiences with Küng this deficiency needs to be compensated for; in the coming discussion questions need to be asked. Precisely what were and are Küng's dealings with the press? What effect has his information, action and reaction had on the public? What were and are his aims? And finally, how much has this led to polarization and how much to healthy clarification?

(e) Worldwide action

To the German public Küng is known above all as an ecumenist, as an honest critic of the church and as the author of *On Being a Christian*. The questions of interaction, belonging to the church and dealing with the public which we have discussed relate to this period. With the discovery of the world religions, as we saw, an extremely complex voyage of discovery began, which Küng has then extended in the 1990s to the great themes of comprehensive paradigm analyses and the global ethic. It is still too early to make a final scholarly assessment of these new perspectives, their strengths and weaknesses. The first reactions seem to be more supplementary questions than corrections. But questions are being discussed not only about the foundation of this programme, presented at the highest level, but also about how it is to be put into practice within individual cultures and religions. The question, therefore, is that of the relationship between global requirement and polycentric implementation.

Here too the discussion has a profile typical of Küng. It begins with great assent, but a clear distancing. Here too it is evident that Küng has addressed a question which many people find to be a great problem and is beginning to work it out with a comprehensive approach. Initially and necessarily this begins in a sweeping way; only at a later stage do further foundations and differentiations follow. Once again Küng proves to be a thinker who occupies himself with everyday practice and is inspired by it. That is precisely why he feels the need constantly to be quite concrete less than many abstract thinkers, who then break through to concrete practice in their heads. This is also evident in the formulation of the three criteria by which Küng sees his religious and theological thought directed, and which have not yet been sufficiently discussed. So here already there are sufficient questions for discussion and clarification.

3. How has theology changed?

In the individual chapters of this book, reference has often been made to the development of Küng's understanding of theology and the methodology which follows from it. The new or expanded approaches of his theology have been indicated with terms like 'ecumenical' (Chapter 2), 'catholic' (Chapter 3), 'metadogmatic' and 'responsible to history' (Chapter 5), 'inter-religious' and 'secular' (Chapters 1 and 10). The references here were not to approaches and methodologies which needed to be distinguished strictly, but rather to sometimes abrupt but usually smooth transitions, expansions or corrections of detail. They are always influenced by questions of content. Therefore we will hardly find that Küng announces changes of methodology or formulates them prematurely. Rather, the concerns and the acknowledged goals, the assimilation of new material and counter-positions, always precede a presentation of method. Küng never ties his readers to a desk, but professional colleagues – curious people who are often also curious to learn – would often like to see more closely what happens at Küng's desk.

Here a wide field of work lies open. Critics sometimes point out that by no means all the philosophical and epistemological questions have been clarified, and that his theology has not been protected sufficiently from misunderstandings. But the clarification of these questions and the uncovering of misunderstandings could be of enormous significance for the future of European theology (Catholic and ecumenical, inter-religious and secular), since with the intensity and concentration of his style, with his unwavering criticism of ideology and his wealth of material, and finally with the continuity of a very varied theology which constantly makes new starts, Küng has clearly established criteria. These still needs to be discussed in criticism and counter-criticism.

Here we must not forget one aspect which is central for Küng: theology for him is an open concern, a matter of supreme social and political relevance, a process of communication, interaction and exchange between the places at the frontiers at which crisis experiences and problems of orientation are noticeable, and at which the experiences of millennia in dealing with them are taken up and transcended. Only those who learn to discover the religions, especially Christian faith, in the light of this public frame of reference will understand Küng's theology. So too, only those who measure the churches by this public task have access to Küng's criticism of the church. Therefore the growing interest of a secular public in Küng's work represents not only a human but also a theological endorsement of his concern. The fact that for years he has been able to engage in research with the help of third parties and now has his own Institute symbolizes – after a period of unhappy privatization – this new opening up of a new potential which is important for both religion and politics.

Therefore the hope which continues to radiate from Küng's theology despite all the criticism is not just the result of a personally sympathetic basic attitude but also the result of convictions which Küng keeps gaining from everyday theology, from reflection on the religious traditions, from contact with questioning men and women, and from the challenges of our present world situation. His benevolent critics are fond of saying that self-confidence is a mark of the Swiss. It would be good for all theologians to learn something from this, and in particular to draw a new self-confidence from the great possibilities of their cause, for the benefit of a future shared world-wide, a future which can only be coped with by the great-hearted among responsible people. To put it in theological terms: the saving presence of God which can be experienced in this world and God's faithfulness to our future are among the most precious things that have ever been revealed to us human beings. We have to continue to hand them on to coming generations. Commitment to this task continues to be worth while. And for that, Küng, beyond the bounds of all the controversies, has earned gratitude and recognition.

Bibliography

This select bibliography contains basic details of works by Hans Küng in English, or works relevant to the discussion in this book. A complete bibliography up to 1992 is to be found in H. Häring and K.-J. Kuschel (ed.), *Hans Küng. Neue Horizonte des Glaubens und Denkens. Ein Arbeitsbuch*, Piper Verlag, Munich 1993, 831–914, and an abbreviated bibliography in the English translation, *Hans Küng, New Horizons for Faith and Thought*, SCM Press Ltd and Continuum Publishing Company, 1993. The date of the original German publication is given in brackets

A. Works by Hans Küng (alone or in collaboration)

Justification. The Doctrine of Karl Barth and a Catholic Reflection (1957), with an introduction by Karl Barth, Thomas Nelson, New York 1964 and Burns & Oates, London 1965

The Council and Reunion (1960), Sheed & Ward 1961 (US *The Council, Reform and Reunion*, Sheed & Ward, New York 1961)

That the World May Believe. Letters to Young People (1962), Sheed & Ward, London and New York 1963

Structures of the Church (1962), Thomas Nelson, New York 1964 and Burns & Oates, London 1965

The Living Church. Reflections on the Second Vatican Council (1963), Sheed & Ward, London 1963 (US *The Council in Action*, Sheed & Ward, New York 1963)

Freedom in the World, Sir Thomas More (1964), Theological Meditations 1, Sheed & Ward, London 1965

The Theologian and the Church (1964), Theological Meditations 3, Sheed & Ward, London 1965

The Church and Freedom (1964), Theological Meditations 6, Sheed & Ward, London 1965

'Christianity as a Minority' (1965), in *Christian Revelation and World Religions. The World's Religions in God's Plan of Salvation*, ed. J.

Neuner, Burns & Oates, London 1967

(the above four titles are collected in *Freedom Today*, Sheed & Ward, New York 1966)

Gott und das Leid, Theologische Meditationen 18, Einsiedeln 1967

The Church (1967), Burns & Oates, London and Sheed & Ward, New York 1967

Truthfulness. The Future of the Church (1968), Sheed & Ward, London and New York 1968

The Incarnation of God. An Introduction to Hegel's Theological Thought as Prolegomenon to a Future Christology (1970), T.&.T. Clark, Edinburgh 1987

Infallible? An Enquiry (1970), Collins, London 1971, reissued with additional material (including *The Church – Maintained in Truth?*), SCM Press, London 1994

Was ist Kirche?, Freiburg 1970

Why Priests? A Proposal for a New Church Ministry (1971), Collins, London and Doubleday, New York 1972

What Must Remain in the Church (1973), Collins, London 1977

Fehlbar? Eine Bilanz, 1973 (edited by Hans Küng)

On Being a Christian (1974), Collins, London and Doubleday, New York 1977

20 Thesen zum Christsein, Munich 1975 (English translation in *Signposts for the Future*)

Was ist Firmung?, Theologische Meditationen 49, Zurich 1976

Brother or Lord? A Jew and a Christian Talk Together about Jesus, Collins, London 1977 (US edition in *Signposts for the Future*)

Gottesdienst – warum?, Zurich 1976 (English translation in *Signposts for the Future*)

Why I am still a Christian (1976), T.&.T. Clark, Edinburgh and Abingdon Press, Nashville 1987

Signposts for the Future, Doubleday, New York 1978

Does God Exist? An Answer for Today (1978), Collins, London and Doubleday, New York 1980

The Church – Maintained in Truth? (1979), Seabury Press, New York and SCM Press Ltd, London 1980

24 Thesen zur Gottesfrage, Munich 1979

Wegzeichen in die Zukunft. Programmatisches für eine christlichere Kirche, Hamburg 1980 (this differs from the English *Signposts for the Future*)

Art and the Question of Meaning (1980), SCM Press Ltd, London and Crossroad Publishing Company, New York 1981

Glauben an Jesus Christus, Theologische Meditationen 59, Zurich 1982

Eternal Life? (1982), Collins, London and Doubleday, New York 1984

Christianity and the World Religions. Paths of Dialogue with Islam, Hinduism and Buddhism (1984, with Josef van Ess, Heinrich von Stietencron and Heinz Bechert), Doubleday, New York 1986 and Collins, London 1987

Literature and Religion. Pascal, Gryphius, Lessing, Hölderlin, Novalis, Kierkegaard, Dostojewski, Kafka (1985, with Walter Jens), Paragon House, New York 1991

Paradigm Change in Theology (1986), T.&T. Clark, Edinburgh and Crossroad Publishing Company, New York 1989 (edited by Hans Küng and David Tracy)

Theology for the Third Millennium. An Ecumenical View (1987), Doubleday, New York 1988 and HarperCollins, London 1991

Freud and the Problem of God (1987), Yale University Press 1990

Christianity and Chinese Religions (1988, with Julia Ching), Doubleday, New York 1989 and London, SCM Press 1993

Anwälte der Humanität. Thomas Mann, Hermann Hesse, Heinrich Böll (with Walter Jens), Munich 1989

Reforming the Church Today. Keeping Hope Alive (1990), T.&T. Clark, Edinburgh and Crossroad Publishing Company, New York 1990

Global Responsibility. In Search of a New World Ethic (1990), SCM Press, London and Crossroad Publishing Company, New York 1991

Judaism (1991), SCM Press Ltd, London and Crossroad Publishing Company, New York 1992

Mozart. Traces of Transcendence (1991), SCM Press, London and Eerdmans, Grand Rapids 1992

Credo. The Apostles' Creed Explained for Today (1992), SCM Press London and Doubleday, New York 1993

A Global Ethic. The Declaration of the Parliament of the World's Religions (1993, with Karl-Josef Kuschel), SCM Press, London and Continuum Publishing Company, New York 1993

Christianity. Its Essence and History (1994), SCM Press, London and Continuum Publishing Company, New York 1995

Great Christian Thinkers (1994), SCM Press, London and Continuum Publishing Company, New York 1995

A Dignified Dying (1995, with Walter Jens), SCM Press, London and Continuum Publishing Company, New York 1995

Yes to a Global Ethic (1995), SCM Press, London and Continuum

Publishing Company, New York 1966

A Global Ethic for Global Politics and Economics (1997), SCM Press, London and Oxford University Press, New York 1997

A Global Ethic and Global Responsibilities (1998, with Helmut Schmidt), SCM Press, London 1998

B. Composite volumes involving Hans Küng or about him

Das Neue Testament als Kanon. Dokumentation und kritische Analyse zur gegenwärtigen Diskussion, ed. E. Käsemann, Göttingen 1970 (this includes H. Küng, 'Der Frühkatholizismus im Neuen Testament als kontroverstheologisches Problem' (originally *Theologische Quartalschrift* 142, 1962, 385–424), 175–204

Zum Problem Unfehlbarkeit. Antworten auf die Anfrage von Hans Küng, ed. Karl Rahner, Freiburg 1971

Diskussion um Hans Küng, 'Die Kirche', ed. H. Häring und J. Nolte, KIeine ökumenische Schriften 5, Freiburg 1971

Reform und Anerkennung kirchlicher Ämter. Ein Memorandum der Arbeitsgemeinschaft ökumenischer Universitätsinstitute, Munich 1973

Grundfragen der Christologie heute, ed. L. Scheffczyk, Freiburg 1975

Diskussion über Hans Küngs 'Christ sein', with contributions by H. U. von Balthasar et al., Mainz 1976

C. Hempel, *Rechtfertigung als Wirklichkeit. Ein katholisches Gespräch: Karl Barth – Hans Küng – Rudolf Bultmann und seine Schule*, Frankfurt 1976

Um nichts als die Wahrheit. Deutsche Bischofskonferenz contra Hans Küng. Eine Dokumentation, ed. W.Jens, Munich 1978

Hans Küng. His Work and Way (1978), ed. H. Häring and K.-J. Kuschel, Collins, London 1979 and Doubleday, New York 1980

Der Fall Küng. Eine Dokumentation, ed. N. Greinacher und H. Haag, Munich 1980

Gegenentwürfe. 24 Lebensläufe für eine andere Theologie, ed. H. Häring und K.-J. KuscheI, Munich 1988

Neue Horizonte des Glaubens und Denkens. Ein Arbeitsbuch, ed. H. Häring und K.-J. Kuschel, Munich 1993 (abbreviated English translation, *Hans Küng. New Horizons for Faith and Thought*, SCM Press and Continuum Publishing Company 1993)

Walter Jens, Karl-Josef Kuschel and Hans Küng, *Dialogue with Hans Küng* (1996), SCM Press Ltd, London 1997

See also R. Nowell, *A Passion for Truth. Hans Küng. A Biography*, Collins, London and Crossroad Publishing Company, New York 1981

C. Further literature mentioned

T. W. Adorno, *Stichworte, Kritische Modelle* 2, Frankfurt 1969

H. U. von Balthasar, *The Theology of Karl Barth* (1951), Holt, Rinehart and Winston, New York 1971

M. von Brück and Whalen Lai, *Buddhismus und Christentum. Geschichte, Kunfrontation, Dialog*, with a preface by Hans Küng, Munich 1997

Y. Congar, *Vraie et fausse réforme dans l'Église*, Paris 1950

M. Frank, *Die Unhintergebbarkeit von Individualität*, Frankfurt 1986

J. Habermas, *Theory of Communicative Action*, 1, *Reason and the Rationalization of Society*, Polity Press 1986; 2, *Critique of Functionalist Reason*, Polity Press 1989

A. B. Hasler, *How the Pope Became Infallible. Pius IX and the Politics of Persuasion*, with an Introduction by Hans Küng (1979), Doubleday 1981

——, *Pius IX. (1848–1878), Päpstliche Unfehlbarkeit und 1. Vatikanisches Konzil. Dogmatisierung und Durchsetzung einer Ideologie* (2 vols), Stuttgart 1977

J. Höffner, Cardinal, *Jesus Christus, Hirtenwort zur Fastenzeit 1980, Presseamt des Erzbistums Köln*, Cologne 1980

T. S. Kuhn, *The Structure of Scientific Revolutions*, Chicago University Press ²1970

K.-J. Kuschel, *Jesus in der deutschsprachigen Gegenwartsliteratur*, Ökumenische Theologie 1, Zurich and Gutersloh 1978, with a preface by Hans Küng

E. Schillebeeckx, *Jesus* (1974), Collins, London and Crossroad Publishing Company 1979

E. Schillebeeckx, *Christ* (1977), SCM Press, London and Crossroad Publishing Company, New York 1980

O. H. Pesch, *Die Theologie der Rechtfertigung bei Martin Luther und Thomas von Aquin. Versuch eines systematisch-theologischen Dialogs*, Mainz 1967

Wils, J.P., 'Handeln und Sinnverstehen. Prolegomena zu einer hermeneutischen Ethik', in: T. van den Hoogen, H. Küng and J. P. Wils (ed.), *Die widerspenstige Religion. Orientierung für eine Kultur der Autonomie?*, Kampen 1997, 42–84

Translator's Note

Where English translations exist, I have given page references to them; full details are listed in the Bibliography. However readers may notice that the translations here do not always correspond to those in the versions referred to. In checking them against the original I have found, as others have before me, that particularly in the case of some of the early works, the English translations do not reproduce at all accurately what Hans Küng wrote; moreover in many cases the rendering is less than happy. Even where the published translation is accurate, I have not hesitated to replace 'man' (German *Mensch*, which is of course inclusive) with a more inclusive rendering. I am most grateful to Hans Küng's colleagues in Tübingen for their help in making available texts of translations which are difficult to locate in Britain.

John Bowden   July 1998